Married, Middlebrow, and Militant

This Alfred Praga painting was hung in the Guildhall of Bath and is currently owned by the Victoria Art Gallery. (Courtesy of the Victoria Art Gallery.)

MARRIED, MIDDLEBROW, AND MILITANT

Sarah Grand and the New Woman Novel

Teresa Mangum

Ann Arbor

THE UNIVERSITY OF MICHIGAN PRESS

Copyright © by the University of Michigan 1998
All rights reserved
Published in the United States of America by
The University of Michigan Press
Manufactured in the United States of America
⊗ Printed on acid-free paper

2001   2000   1999   1998   4   3   2   1

A CIP catalog record for this book is available from the British Library.

Library of Congress Cataloging-in-Publication Data

Mangum, Teresa, 1954–
    Married, middlebrow, and militant : Sarah Grand and the new
woman novel / Teresa Mangum.
        p.   cm.
    Includes bibliographical references (p.   ) and index.
    ISBN 0-472-10977-4 (acid-free paper)
    1. Grand, Sarah—Criticism and interpretation. 2. Feminism and
literature—England—History—20th century. 3. Feminism and
literature—England—History—19th century. 4. Women and
literature—England—History—20th century. 5. Women and
literature—England—History—19th century. 6. Women's rights in
literature. 7. Married women in literature. 8. Sex role in
literature. 9. Suffrage in literature. I. Title.
PR4728.G112   Z78   1998
823'.8—ddc21   98-40079
                                                              CIP

11489

Acknowledgments

I have been keeping company with Sarah Grand for some time, and our relationship has benefited from the kindness and intelligence of many friends and colleagues. For their encouragement and suggestions, I wholeheartedly thank Dale Kramer, Peter Garrett, Cheris Kramarae, Florence Boos, and Jeff Cox. I extend heartfelt thanks to Kathleen Diffley for rigorous readings and ebullient encouragement. I am also very grateful to two fine Grand scholars, Gillian Kersley and Marilyn Bonnell, for their unselfish sharing of sources. I was extremely fortunate to have well-informed, energetic readers, Ann Ardis and Sally Mitchell, who offered precise, insightful suggestions. I was equally blessed in a patient, encouraging editor, LeAnn Fields. I am indebted to Julie Schmid and Margaret Loose for their work as my graduate assistants. Both of my work groups—first Sally Kenney, Geeta Patel, and Susan Lawrence and later Judith Pascoe and Kim Marra—have been great sources of inspiration and amusement.

Various friends have been witty and wonderful companions along the way, especially Paulette Roberts, Susie Dupree, Sheri Hyatt, Amy Creekmur, Rebecca Stott, Barbara Eckstein, Jon Wilcox, and Hap Endler. My companions at the Annual Interdisciplinary Nineteenth Century Studies (INCS) meetings—Mary Jean Corbett, Susan Morgan, Deborah Morse, Ron Thomas, Anca Vlasopolos, in particular—remind me of the pleasures of this profession. Ellen Brown, Janet Eldred, Karen Ford, and Pamyla Yates, graduate school classmates, continue to teach me the power of narratives—in life as well as novels—to sustain and transform us.

Most important, my family has offered unstinting practical support as well as encouragement in this and other projects, and I thank with all my heart Fred, Joyce, and Lisa Mangum.

I am also grateful to institutions for their support, including the Graduate School and the English Department for fellowships at the University of Illinois and the Graduate School, Sponsored Programs, and the English

Department (with special thanks to John Raeburn, Ed Folsom, and Dee Morris) at the University of Iowa.

I am indebted to numerous libraries for making Grand's letters available to me. As indicated throughout my book, many of these libraries also generously agreed to allow me to include excerpts from letters that document the trajectory of Grand's career and her relationships with other writers and publishers. Many thanks to the Department of Special Collections of the Research Library of the University of California–Los Angeles, the Lilly Library at Indiana University, the Berg Collection of the New York Public Library, the Pattee Library at Pennsylvania State University, the Mortimer Rare Book Room of Smith College, the Harry Ransom Collection at the University of Texas at Austin, the Library of Congress, the Trustees of the National Library of Scotland, the National Library of Wales, the British Library, Bath Central Library, the Birmingham City Archives of the Central Library at Birmingham, Leeds University Library, and the Richmond Library. I am grateful, also, for the use of portions of "Style Wars of the 1890s" from *Transforming Genres,* edited by Meri-Jane Rochelson and Nikki Lee Manos, © M. Rochelson and N. Manos, reprinted with permission of St. Martin's Press and Macmillan Press, Ltd.; and to Bowling Green State University Popular Press for allowing me to use portions of "Sex, Siblings, and the Fin de Siècle" from *The Significance of Sibling Relationships in Literature,* edited by JoAnna Stephens Mink and Janet Doubler Ward. I also thank special collections at the University of Iowa, Indiana University Library, the Victoria Art Gallery, the Library of Congress, and the National Portrait Gallery for permitting me to reproduce visual images of Grand.

Finally, I dedicate this book to Corey Creekmur, my longtime intellectual companion, dear friend, and fellow protagonist in an unpredictable and entertaining marriage plot.

Contents

Introduction

Between 1880 and 1920 the British New Woman novel outraged "womenly women," inspired women's rights activists, and provided grist for both radical and reactionary reviewers. Loosely connected by their fascination with female characters who crossed the boundaries of late-Victorian feminine proprieties, New Women novels and short stories absorbed public attention as readers, writers, and critics debated the dangers and pleasures of the phantasmatic New Women. As the label attached to these novels suggests, for novelists such as Emma Frances Brooke, Mona Caird, Mary Cholmondeley, Jane Hume Clapperton, Lady Florence Dixie, Menie Muriel Dowie, George Egerton, Isabella Ford, Annie E. Holdsworth, "Iota" (Kathleen Mannington Caffyn), Arabella Kenealy, Olive Schreiner, and Sarah Grand, the New Woman—as a character, a set of demands, and a model for female readers—expanded the nineteenth-century imagination by introducing what we would now call feminist issues and feminist characters into the realm of popular fiction.[1] Polemical and assertive in their alliance of readers with a rebellious woman's point of view, the New Woman narratives challenged society's most fundamental and sacrosanct vision of Woman—her desires, her capacities, and the worlds, particularly the world of marriage, in which she might move.

By 1890 long-developing critiques of women's social position in England escalated in tone and pointedness. On behalf of women, men and women reformers demanded improved education, voting rights, equitable divorce laws, employment in all areas, access to the means of sex education and birth control, and in some instances freedom from heterosexual conventions such as monogamy. These activists must have worked with a sense of optimism in light of several contemporary developments. Girton College, for women, had opened its doors in 1873, and Newnham followed in 1876. By 1884 female students were living in Oxford's first women's residence halls, attending classes, and sitting for examinations (although they were not granted degrees at Oxford until 1920 and were not admitted to university membership at Cambridge until 1948). Women had begun to serve as Poor Law guardians in 1875, and Josephine Butler and her followers had succeeded in defeating the Contagious Diseases Acts in England (though not in India), signaled by their final repeal in 1883. After the passage of the Married Women's Property Acts of 1882 and 1891 guaranteed women possession of their earned income, middle-class women more confidently moved into the workforce as teachers, nurses, midwives, clerks, writers, and journalists.² Supporters of the women's movement, after dividing over their disagreements about which issues to fight for first, reaffirmed their shared desire to win votes for women by establishing the National Union of Women's Suffrage Societies in 1897 under the leadership of Millicent Fawcett.³

Late-Victorian women writers contributed to the fight for women's rights by creating representations of women that confronted the self-abnegating, submissive, housebound image of middle-class Ideal Womanhood. This ideal was epitomized at mid-century by William Thackeray's Amelia Sedley from *Vanity Fair* (1847) and Charles Dickens's Esther Summerson from *Bleak House* (1852–53). In particular, the New Women novels of the 1880s and 1890s critiqued prevailing forms of femininity and its superstructure, marriage, by way of editorial analysis and alternative plots. In *Thomas Hardy and Women* Penny Boumelha points out that for many Victorians "womanhood, in contrast to womanliness, is not an ideal or an aspiration, but an immanent natural disposition, originating in a pre-determining physiological sexual differentiation."⁴ Taking issue with the limited opportunities available to women in the 1880s and 1890s, female New Woman novelists forced their readers to question the biological essentialism at the heart of ideal womanhood. The New Woman fiction emerged as one of the most powerful forms of resistance to this ideal.⁵

Sarah Grand (1854–1943) took center stage in both political and literary arenas, popularizing the term *New Woman,* advocating rational dress, lobbying for suffrage groups, lecturing on women's issues in England and America, even serving as mayoress of Bath during the 1920s. In an interview with Athol Forbes, in 1900, Grand brashly claimed to have invented the New Woman in an 1894 *North American Review* article.⁶ Ellen Jordan calls Grand and Ouida (an antifeminist novelist, Marie Louise de la Ramee, whose work Grand greatly admired) the "godmothers" of New Woman fiction because Grand's use of the term *new woman* and Ouida's diatribe against Grand and "New Women" in a later issue of the *North American Review* propelled the term into general usage.⁷ Most important, however, Grand wrote one of the best-selling and most controversial of the New Woman novels, *The Heavenly Twins* (1893). Mark Twain, George Bernard

Shaw, and Thomas Hardy praised Grand's courage, the power of her writing, and her sales figures. Parodies as well as praise signal her prominence in the literary world. For example, she is lampooned for her lecture "Mere Man" in a drawing in which she pinions a squirming male figure on a fork; her fictional twins exercised cartoonists' wits; in 1894 her name appears in a *Punch* parody of Whitman's *Leaves of Grass;* and in 1899 a sendup of a household management guide, titled *The Domestic Blunders of Women,* is published "by a Mere Man."[8]

Grand fascinated her readers because, like many of her female contemporaries, she lived as well as wrote the often self-contradictory role of the New Woman. Born on 10 June 1854, she began life as Frances Bellenden-Clarke, the daughter of Edward John Bellenden-Clarke, an English naval officer and coastguard who was stationed in Donaghadee, County Down, on the northeast coast of Ireland. After her father died, when she was seven, Frances's mother, the former Margaret Bell Sherwood, moved the family to England, near Scarborough, Yorkshire, where Mrs. Bellenden-Clarke had grown up in a prominent farming family. In England Frances briefly attended two schools. First, in 1868 she entered the Royal Naval School in Twickenham. Later she grudgingly endured a finishing school in Holland Road, Kensington, before escaping the miseries of home and unsatisfying girls' schools by marrying at age sixteen. Her husband, David Chambers McFall, was the assistant surgeon of the Thirty-fourth Foot, stationed in India. McFall was a thirty-nine-year-old widower with two sons, Haldane, aged ten, and Albert, aged eight. Together, the McFalls had a son, David Archibald Edward, the same year they were married.[9] After twenty years of life as a military wife and mother living overseas and in Norwich and Warrington, Frances McFall took an enormous step. With the proceeds of her first novel, *Ideala,* which she had privately published in 1888, McFall left her husband, moved to London, and began her writing career in earnest. Following the publication of her best-selling novel *The Heavenly Twins,* in 1893, Frances McFall took the further step of adopting the dramatic and self-aggrandizing pseudonym Madame Sarah Grand.[10] To Sandra Gilbert and Susan Gubar her name change signals "a name of power, the mark of a private christening into a second self, a rebirth into linguistic primacy"; her pseudonym thus transforms the writer's name into an "[icon] of female artistry."[11] The new name certainly signified self-transformation to Grand; for years afterward she defended the change in letters and to interviewers. In 1894 she wrote to the editor of *Truth,* angrily protesting a "paragraph" that claimed she was ashamed of her name. Charging him with ungentlemanliness, she insists she has the right to protect her privacy and distance herself from her family.[12] More practically, McFall was also apparently compromising with her husband. By assuming a new name, she dissociated him from the novel's controversial portrayal of miserable marriages, sexual double standards, and the ravages of venereal disease, all potentially embarrassing topics to a husband who had made his living supervising a quarantine hospital for infected prostitutes. As Grand explained to Frederick Henry Fisher, editor of *Literary World,* in 1898, after her husband's death, "My husband had a grt [*sic*] dislike to having his name associated with my ideas, and in order to save him the annoyance, I changed my name, adopting . . . Sarah Grand once and for all. I could not publish any explanation during my husband's lifetime and the consequence to me has been unpleasant."[13]

Between 1888 and 1920 Grand published eight novels, three collections of short stories, and innumerable periodical essays.[14] As a lecturer in England and America, she became friends with leading members of the women's suffrage and social purity campaigns and with well-known artists and celebrities, such as George Meredith, Mark Twain, Ellen Terry, and Alice Meynell. As a member of women's rights groups committed to women's education, to political participation, and to theoretical analysis as well as to practical action as a means of resisting sexism, Grand gathered the tools to construct popular, politicized fiction for women. She marched on London with the National Union of Women's Suffrage Societies and served as an officer of various women's organizations, including the Pioneer Club, the Women Writers' Suffrage League, and the National Council of Women. Withstanding personal and professional attacks against her novels and her political activities, Grand learned firsthand about the fragility of women's social identities as wife, mother, journalist, novelist, and activist. Long after her literary fame dimmed, Grand reigned as mayoress of Bath for six years. She died on 15 May 1943 at The Grange, in Calne, where she had moved after her home at 7 Sion Hill in Bath was damaged during a bombing raid in April 1942.

Thanks to the current surge of interest in the last turn of the century and in both earlier feminist activists and popular Victorian writers, Grand's pivotal roles within late-Victorian literary culture and women's communities are once again being acknowledged. The University of Michigan Press has reissued *The Heavenly Twins,* first published in 1893, with a new introduction by Carol Senf, and Sally Mitchell's introduction contextualizes the new Thoemmes edition of *The Beth Book,* originally published in 1897.

Grand's New Woman characters cover the spectrum of turn-of-the-century, middle-class, independent women: adolescent hoydens, gender-switching heroines, free love advocates, women of genius, novelists and orators, suffragists and social reformers, teachers and businesswomen, housewives who leave home and single women who create homes for their "fallen" sisters. Like other writers classified as New Woman novelists, Grand wrote novels featuring rebellious female characters and created plots that treated women's sexual and social positions with unusual candor. Her novels, though situated in the increasingly contested tradition of "realist" fiction, in fact imported the popular genres of melodrama, the adventure novel, detective fiction, the drawing-room drama, the idyll, even sensation fiction of earlier decades. And in complex, sometimes ineffable ways her novels participate in and reshape a tradition of woman-to-woman discourse, as illustrated by the sale of her books and the enthusiastic response of women readers. In their diversity the only characteristic all Grand's novels share is that the characters, contexts, and plots invoke the *lived experience* of Victorian middle-class marriage—in contrast with romantic, idealized fantasies of love—as the appropriate matter for fiction and the most compelling challenge to the narrative strategies and structural logic of the long-popular fictional marriage plot.

As I repeatedly demonstrate in this study, until the 1980s British New Woman novels were usually dismissed as "popular" instead of "literary," as political (and polemical) rather than artful, and as topical and limited in focus (they concerned themselves with women) instead of "universal."[15] Since 1980 several important studies that most explicitly address the literary contexts for New Woman fiction convincingly argue that these novels should be read as prequels to modernism as well as sequels to Victorianism. Gerd Bjørhovde's *Rebellious Structures* (1987) takes a formalist approach to the novels of four women writers of the 1890s, including Grand's *The Heavenly Twins,* to argue that what critics read as confused narrative structure was in fact often complex, innovative integration of forms. Ann Ardis's *New Women, New Novels* (1990) maps a rich landscape inhabited by over a hundred New Woman novelists, short story writers, and journalists. Her work provocatively, rigorously examines the position of New Woman novels within debates over realism as she charts the New Woman's anticipation of and eclipse by literary modernism. *The "Improper" Feminine* (1993) by Lyn Pykett compares the surprisingly similar critical responses to the sensation novels of the 1860s and the New Woman novels of the 1890s. Pointing to the shared though differently rendered excesses, detail, and emotional or sensational effects of two subgenres of fiction often assumed to be addressed solely to women readers, Pykett persuasively argues that both chiseled at prevailing fantasies of the "feminine" with their scandalous encodings of impropriety. Sally Ledger considers the New Woman figure in the contexts of other liminal real and imagined communities in the 1890s, locating her as a crucial component of the landscape of the metropolis in *The New Woman: Fiction and Feminism at the Fin de Siècle* (1997).

Rita S. Kranidis's *Subversive Discourse: The Cultural Production of Late Victorian Novels* (1995) is an important examination of the market forces, the competing forms of fiction, and the cross-currents of oppositional writing from which New Woman fiction emerged. Her work joins a number of other studies that return late-Victorian women's writing to telling contexts of readers and market forces, including Terry Lovell's earlier *Consuming Fiction* (1987), Kate Flint's monumental *The Woman Reader, 1837–1914* (1993), essays by Margaret Diane Stetz, and Margaret Beetham's *A Magazine of Her Own? Domesticity and Desire in the Woman's Magazine, 1800–1914* (1996). Together, these studies draw attention to the commercial arena of literary production and the complex interactions among readers, writers, publishers, and texts, a subject I take up in my next chapter.[16]

While broad, encompassing studies offer one kind of context for the study of women's history and fiction and are a necessary beginning for serious discussion of neglected texts, my study of Sarah Grand's work is based on the premise that we also need focused, in-depth, critical studies that test generalizations about the New Woman and her fictions against the particularities of specific writers and works.[17] Grand's prominence and her willing participation in what became as much a social as a fictional movement make her work particularly important for recuperation and concentrated study. In *Darling Madame* (1983) Gillian Kersley has brought forward a fascinating diary written by one of Grand's admirers from the 1920s through the 1940s. The diary tells us much about Grand's late years in Bath, and Kersley's biographical introduction offers helpful speculation about Grand's earlier life. In this study my goal is to provide a systematic study of Grand's writing, her position as a leading New Woman novelist, and the engagement of her New Woman fiction with contemporaneous social movements and political issues. I locate Grand's novels within the fractious debates over women's position in relation to the law, medicine, book publishing, periodical presses, and the multifaceted women's movement from Rational Dress Societies to women writers' organizations to the women's suffrage movement. In particular, I focus on the reasons why Grand, and by extension other women writers, hammered so relentlessly at marriage, that foundational structure of middle-class Victorian social fantasy and formation as well as the staple of popular Victorian fiction addressed to women. I question why these writers wrangled with the long-standing plots of heterosexual love and marriage rather than simply turning to more experimental plots and forms as vehicles for discontented, rebellious female characters, a strategy Modernists would deploy so soon thereafter.

Seeking to understand how writers and readers interpreted and reconciled their political and intellectual aspirations with their personal circumstances in literary works that I will argue develop into middlebrow women's fiction, I examine Grand's literary feminism, expressed in her work as a commitment to an aesthetics based on education, ethics, and activism. Coming into consciousness of the social, legal, and personal oppression of women within the context of her own marriage, Grand, like many pragmatic Victorian reformers, devoted herself to marriage reform in the belief that, if such a central social institution could be made to serve women's interests, then legal, social, and personal transformation of both men and women must follow. Her novels evince stoic acceptance that marriage would persist as a structure, a set of desires and beliefs, and a frame for most women's lives, even as her own experiences drove her to separate from her husband and to live and work with other women. Her vision of reform is unquestionably heterosexist, middle-class, and largely oblivious to anyone except white European, American, and British people living in the British Empire. In other words, while the subjects she incorporated into her fiction of protest shocked 1890s readers, she, like many of her progressive contemporaries, does not escape the blindnesses and biases of the race, class, and sexual preferences that shaped the gender politics she challenged. These very limitations make the cultural work performed by New Women novels all the more intensely important for present-day literary historians, gender scholars, and feminist activists who wrestle with similar problems of tradition, representation, context, competing responsibilities, and inevitable compromises as they, like Grand, try to effect change in a recalcitrant world. Grand did unrelentingly represent the inevitable contradictions between human belief and desire embedded in marriage, which she saw as not only the controlling structure of Victorian women's lives but as potentially the institution women could best use to restructure their society. To that end her novels engage the logic of conventional marriage plots, in which the developing desires of two heterosexual lovers overcome a series of obstacles and a mutually satisfying union forms closure. She invokes this structure, however, only to force it and the assumptions about love, romance, and power relations upon which it depends into confrontation with marriage practices, with the institutions that organize marriage, and with a series of late-Victorian social crises that impinged upon marriage.

In this study I focus on Grand's novels rather than her life, novels that helped break the stranglehold of earlier versions of the marriage plot on fiction and which helped to clarify and promote the goals of turn-of-the-century women's activism. My first chapter, "The Politics of Middle-Class Marriage and Middlebrow Militancy," contextualizes the marriage plot in the perceptions of marriage that guided the political choices and actions of the late-Victorian women's movement. Here I paint a picture of the intricate interconnections among actual marriage practices, public perceptions of middle-class marriage, a long if vacillating history of fictional representations of love and marriage, and the complex exchanges among New Woman readers, writers, and novels, signaled by allusions in the novels to other texts, by reviewers' clustering of texts, and by stories of readers' participation in or reactions to Grand's work.

In the chapters that follow I move from the broader context in which marriage practices, marriage protests, and marriage plots circulate to a closer examination of the place of Grand's novels within those debates. My second chapter, "Gendered Plots and the Search for Feminist Form," deals with Grand's two early novels. In light of late-twentieth-century queer theory the first two novels Grand wrote (though not the first she published) read like what a theorist such as Judith Butler would call performances of gender and what I would call a performance of the gendering of genres.[18] In *A Domestic Experiment* (1891), a reworking of the drawing-room drama, and *Singularly Deluded* (1892), a feminized adventure and detective novel, the roughness of apprentice work only renders more visible married women's personal dissatisfaction and psychological disturbances. In more conventional novels the marriage plot disciplines or ignores marital discord. Both novels disrupt and thereby expose the logic that drives marriage and the marriage plot through their manipulation of gender roles within particular genres. By de-naturalizing masculinity, femininity, and heterosexuality, these novels lay the ideological groundwork for Grand's later "realistic" explorations of the conditions of marriage and their hold on fiction.

Chapter 3, "The Marriage Plot and the Male Narrator," discusses Grand's first published novel, *Ideala* (privately printed in 1888 then issued by Heinemann's in 1893), which inaugurated the New Woman trilogy that also includes *The Heavenly Twins* (1893) and *The Beth Book* (1897). In her first two novels Grand explored the strategies by which social practice and "common sense" unite to create a culture's sense of fixed gender characteristics and, consequently, a culture's means of enforcing gender roles. In *Ideala* Grand began to examine, more closely, the power of aesthetic forms to inscribe those social identities in fiction. These three early apprenticeship novels reach for a language, a range of characters, an interweaving of generic conventions and plot possibilities, that might interrupt the predictable plots of middle-class women's actual and imaginative choices. Therefore, in my next two chapters I focus upon the formal operations of these texts as the crucial location at which the imaginative restructuring, the re-genre-ing so to speak, of the feminine begins. The changes in Grand's novels suggest that, as she began to understand how gendered identities were encoded, she restructured those codes through the formal elements of fiction. *Ideala* marks a crucial turning point in Grand's development as it dramatizes the fundamental problem of representing the experience of women in a culture under the governance of male authorities. To become Grand's first New Woman, Ideala must wrest free from three old-fashioned male characters who represent alternatives that would structure her plot as that available to a dutiful wife, fallen woman, or idealized heroine of romance. She must unlearn lessons of femininity and wifely behavior to escape domestic abuse; she must confront the social consequences of taking a lover; and in the most fascinating twist of the novel she has to resist the narrator by interrupting his idealization of her in order to realize her own ideal. Female desire becomes the means by which Ideala interrupts the dictates of marriage, romance, and narrative intrusions as a formal, politicized intervention in fictional form.

The Heavenly Twins, the subject of my fourth chapter, "Love Triangles," launched Grand's career as a controversial novelist and an advocate of women's rights. Beginning with this novel, Grand's novels became increasingly intertextual: *The Heavenly Twins* incorporates a melodramatic look at the painful, unwilling sisterhood of middle- and working-class women forged by the shared experience of venereal disease; the struggle for power over women waged by religious divines and the medical professionals soon to be labeled psychoanalysts; and the debilitating effects of women's inferior education. The novels in this first trilogy treat social, legal, and medical crises as narratives working in tandem with the marriage plot; consequently, my study of these mid-career novels draws upon those same materials. Ultimately, New Woman novels embrace these social plots as a way to counter, rewrite, and militantly restructure the marriage plot.

The Heavenly Twins splits into three overlapping plots. Two of the plots are rent by the uncompromising portrayal of the third protagonist's death from syphilis. In the novel's highly sensationalized account of Edith's descent into madness, Grand uses the conventions of melodrama, which usually affirm a heroine's self-abnegation, to undermine the definitions of femininity central to the marriage plot and to pinpoint the institutions—the church, the legal system, and the family—that promote and benefit from these definitions. These multiple plots interrupt the focus and linearity of the conventional romance logic; they also use repetition to reveal the tedious uniformity of power relations within marriages despite the seeming differences among relationships. With these three plots Grand debunks conventional femininity by portraying female desire but redirecting it from romance to education, occupation, and community.

The final novel of Grand's first trilogy, *The Beth Book,* stands as an isolated example of a successful nineteenth-century *kunstlerroman*. In chapter 5,

"The Woman of Genius as Wife," I demonstrate still another strategy by means of which Grand resists the claustrophobic marriage plot with an alternative form; here she turns to the female artist plot. Beth begins her career as a writer by reading the literary models of French and British Decadent writers. Dissuaded from the art-for-art's-sake aesthetic, she immerses herself in the woman's movement so that her political work forms the substance of her art. Her aesthetic, which emerges from her attention to women's daily lives, provides forms and language in which to express her political views. Most important (and most intriguing for twentieth-century feminist critics), Beth's aesthetic is unapologetically an ethics driven by her desire to transform society from within the male-dominated world of letters. The promise of Beth's public, political career, juxtaposed with other popular representations of suffragists, demonstrates one of the means by which liberal and radical women's rights supporters were pitted against one another. This context also reveals the interplay of periodical and novelistic representations of women activists in what came to be a contest over the meaning of the New Woman.

After Grand finished this first trilogy, the death of her husband released her from fantasies of feminist political activity to a life of activism. She organized and led a local chapter of the National Union for Women's Suffrage, served as vice president of the Tunbridge Wells Suffrage Society, and became an officer of the National Council of Women; she joined the Women Writers' Suffrage League, the Authors' Club, and the feminist Pioneer Club; she instituted the Women's Citizens' Association in Tunbridge Wells. In 1908 she spoke before the International Women's Suffrage Alliance in London, while she was also publishing essays and short stories. To support herself and family members she performed as a public lecturer in England and America. Her letters during these years wearily document the rigors as well as excitement of lecturing to audiences of up to two thousand people, of incessant travel, and of the ill health and "rest cures" with which she paid the cost of living such a public life. Most poignantly, the letters are also haunted by Grand's constant anxiety that she was left so little time and energy to write. After a decade of struggling to support herself, her stepson Chambers Haldane McFall, and his daughter Beth with her lectures and of devoting great energy and time to political activities, Grand finally carved out the time to begin a second trilogy, one she never completed. She did, however, write and publish the first two novels, *Adnam's Orchard* (1912) and *The Winged Victory* (1916). The second novel pushes toward apocalyptic disaster in the same historical moment as World War I, the event that dissuaded her from writing the third novel of the trilogy. The most compelling, if horrifying, motivation that drives these last novels is the promise for social change offered at the turn of the century by eugenicists. These novels ask whether eugenics might in fact be the biological, cultural, and social expression of the marriage plot, dressed in the trappings of science and governmental bureaucracy. In chapter 6, "The Eugenic Plot: From New Woman to Brave New World," I explore the history of eugenics as a self-styled scientific movement then trace its permutation into a social narrative. Grand turns this social narrative into a perverse literalization of the marriage plot. This chapter considers the reasons why social eugenics appealed to middle-class women reformers, many of whom trumpeted the call to "race motherhood." These social movements and Grand's novels also demonstrate late-Victorian fears of degeneration and attribute those fears to anxieties about the increasingly visible protests of the urban poor, the potential for "reverse colonization," the threat to gender boundaries posed by homosexuals, lesbians, and cross-dressers, and the power of women to withhold sex (and hence hold any "future race" hostage) or, conversely, the power of women whose sexual experiments threatened the dissolution of class and kinship systems.

In the case of Grand's last novels marriage becomes the moral obligation of genetically superior partners; marriage promises not only personal happiness but a future super race. The first novel suggests that marriages like these would produce such a morally and intellectually superior species that its members would recognize the inhumanity of class and gender hierarchies. The second novel plays out this terrifying possibility by exposing the eugenic plot as a Gothic nightmare of incest, suicide, madness, and murder.

In the devastating conclusion of *The Winged Victory* Grand finally seems to condemn not only eugenics but the marriage plot on which eugenics depended. In a sense eugenics narrated the ultimate romance, the reconciliation of gender conflict, class conflict, political struggles, and social upheaval in the matchmaking of a perfect couple and the directing of all of women's energies into the perfection of the "race." The third novel of the trilogy was never written. One hopes Grand recognized the eugenic vision as a nightmare; she lived long enough to see the horrors that eugenic national policy had inflicted upon her world. Our lives are still shaped by the legacies of eugenic nightmares and feminist fantasies that formed the dreamscape but also the social policies and practices of the end of the last century.

Chapter 1

The Politics of Middle-Class Marriage and Middlebrow Militancy

"Marriage," wrote George Eliot, as she concluded *Middlemarch*, "which has been the bourne of so many narratives, is still a great beginning, as it was to Adam and Eve, who kept their honeymoon in Eden, but had their first little ones among the thorns and thistles of the wilderness."[1] Throughout the nineteenth century, subgenres of the novel, including the Gothic novel, melodrama, and the sensation novel, dramatized dark alternatives to, or rather complications of, the marriage plot. Victimized Gothic heroines, fallen women, and terrifyingly feminine murderesses embodied aspects of female psychology that appear marginally in the mainstream Victorian domestic novel. Though some New Woman writers experimented with fantasy or utopian literature, as in Lady Florence Dixie's *Gloriana; or the Revolution of 1900* (1890) or "Ellis Ethelmer's" long poem *Woman Free* (1893), the majority transformed their personal dissatisfaction with the definitions of womanhood structuring the marriage plot into more socially and historically grounded fictions. Even sympathetic present-day critics such as Elaine Showalter, Penny Boumelha, and Rachel DuPlessis have argued that Grand and other New Women novelists are ultimately conservative because in their work the formal, social, and imaginative constraints of the marriage plot create an impasse to serious social or artistic progress that is surmounted only by Modernists' avant-garde work in the twentieth century.[2]

Rather than imposing twentieth-century definitions of radical politics or social progressiveness on the novels, however, I would argue that today's readers must try to imagine the audacity of these novels in light of Victorian conventions of popular romantic fiction and of women's history. In these contexts the New Woman novels represent determined, insistent attempts to synthesize the dramatic, overwhelming social changes in laws governing women, in the sense of possibility posed by educational reform and increasing career opportunities, in the choices offered by birth control or a single, celibate life, and in the organizing of women. As Gail Cunningham explains:

> It was the novel which could investigate in detail the clash between radical principle and the actualities of contemporary life, which could portray most convincingly the stultifying social conventions from which the New Woman was trying to break free, and which could present arguments for new standards of morality, new codes of behavior, in the context of an easily recognisable social world.[3]

Instead of abandoning the marriage plot, Grand and other women writers saw the novel as a concrete and immediate, if fictional, structure within which to begin, at least imaginatively, the transformation they wanted to effect in the public world. Grand embodies the conflicts of the liberal (as opposed to radical) feminists: she could not tolerate her own marriage, so she courageously ended it; however, ever the pragmatist, she understood the power of the institutions governing her world, including the system of marriage. Consequently, her treatment of the marriage plot presumably grows from a political commitment to improve women's lives by changing and reforming them from within the forms of society and within the imaginable limits of her middle-class women readers' world rather than by ignoring, dismissing, or fancifully transcending the realities of marriage in her novels.

To appreciate how Grand reworks the marriage plot and why her revisions are so significant, we need to consider the social, political, and narrative functions the marriage plot serves. Grand's novels document one woman writer's attempt to mediate among literary narratives of women as objects of male desire and men's institutions (or the marriage plot), society's "narratives" of femininity (so often disguised as adulation to ideal womanhood), and the narrative of change activists were continually writing and revising (which was already being called "feminism"). Also, ironically, as Grand's novels evolve into a form both literary and political, her very success in transforming the marriage plot alienated reviewers and critics, which explains in part why works by Grand and other female New Woman novelists have been neglected.

Most studies of the marriage plot take Ian Watt's *Rise of the Novel* as a starting point—whether they accept or reject his thesis. Watt argues that in the eighteenth century the growth of the middle classes into a significant social and economic force in English society together with the impact of the Puritan movement, which opposed the Catholic reverence for celibacy by idealizing marriage, led to the fusion of two previously hostile concepts, romantic love and contractual marriage. Thus, by the nineteenth century marriage functioned as a system of contractual law that organized and defined the range of class and gender relationships most likely to be found in English society.

Ideologically, these practical consequences were legitimized by the developing concept of companionate marriage, the domestication of romantic love that Lawrence Stone discusses in detail in *The Family, Sex and Marriage in England*. Whereas the courtly love tradition depended upon unattainability or illicitness as a condition for love, companionate marriage provided a regulated, codified, and goal-directed structure within which individuals were to experience love. Historians and literary critics agree that this structure is modeled upon theories of sexual complementarity, in which a man and woman are seen as two incomplete halves requiring the union of marriage for completion, an idea harkening back to Plato. The general popularity of this notion is suggested by Grand's own reference to this theory in a footnote in *Ideala*.[4] Marriage, then, depends on the resolving (or dissolving) of potentially hostile, competing oppositions into a union that must, at least superficially, dispel contradictions or conflicts. In fact, these hostilities come to look like enticing obstacles when viewed through the lens of much nineteenth-century fiction.

More recent literary studies of the Victorian marriage plot interpret its function in light of the critical insights of Marxist and feminist narrative theories. Tony Tanner asserts that marriage functions as the central "mediation procedure" between "natural, familial, social and transcendental laws."[5] The bourgeois novel grounds itself in marriage because marriage is the "all-subsuming, all-organizing, all-containing contract. It is the structure that maintains the Structure, or System," in effect, "the means by which society attempts to bring into harmonious alignment patterns of passion and patterns of property."[6] Thus, marriage at once organizes society and provides a screen for the capitalistic and patriarchal structures that produce social conventions. Evelyn Hinz further argues for the operations of marriage both as a legal institution and a code of ethics by defining marriage as a

> social and legal institution with moral overtones or as a conjugal relationship which, if not always ratified by society, nevertheless takes place within a social frame of reference; hence, we are disposed to see it as a subject practically indigenous to the novel, that genre of prose fiction that above all others is characterized by its concern with the depiction of human relationships and moral issues in a social and historical context.[7]

Wedlock creates a system of contractual law to organize and define the range of relationships that will be possible within a given society. The indi-

vidual is ethically constrained into sacrificing unrestrained freedom and a
state of potentiality for socially defined communal responsibilities structured
by marriage. According to Hinz, in the process of representing this transition, novels based on the marriage plot shift from "*romantic* illusion to a *novelistic* sense of reality."[8] This secondary system of belief further obfuscates
the truths women's lives might reveal.

For Joseph Boone the early Modernist novels, particularly those of
Henry James, mark the textual collapse of the marriage plot, as gender tensions burst its formal dam. He sees the Modernists' shift of interest from
character and closed narrative form to technical innovation and the ambivalence of open, inconclusive endings as a partial consequence of what he calls
domestic "warfare" in the form of legal reform of marriage laws and mass
support for female suffrage.[9] Grand's work is a reminder, however, that the
later Modernist rejection of the closure and authority of the Victorian
novel, demonstrated by Boone, is not the only form of resistance to the
marriage plot. The politics of the New Woman, a distinctly personal protest
but one that must be read as integrally connected to the women's movement and the social purity movement (led chiefly by female reformers), also
produced a powerful desire to reform marriage law and practices and to
enable a far greater play of possibilities within marriage plots. Grand's life
and novels were devoted to this project of reform. The very social textures
in her work, used to dismiss her work as topical, popular, and aesthetically
unsophisticated, demonstrate what Leslie Rabine calls the impulse toward
"feminine historicity."[10] As women intellectuals, activists, and authors
struggled to articulate female desire from within the formal restrictions of
masculine plots of desire and from behind their own socially constructed
blinders, writers like Grand turned to their experiences and interpretations
of history—the personal experience of marriage and its failure, wifehood,
motherhood, and opportunities or the lack thereof for education, a profession, and economic independence—to find a social text that would interrupt the only plot they knew. For Sarah Grand this led to a variety of experiments that involved the interplay of literary forms.

In contrast to the conventional marriage plot, structured by the vicissi-
tudes of courtship and culminating in a wedding, Grand's novels, like many
New Woman novels, begin after marriage, follow the gradual disintegration
of a relationship to demonstrate the injustices of the institution of marriage
to women, include an illicit romance not so much to demonstrate the alternatives to marriage but to offer the female protagonist a liberating experience that clarifies the constructive role an equitable relationship could play
in a woman's life, and conclude with the New Woman's uncompromising
"freedom," even at the price of death. By the end of these novels, rather

than being reabsorbed into the social order, as in the marriage plot, the protagonist demands that the social order change to accommodate her.

Though marriage as a topic structured Grand's novels throughout her career, she refines that topic in at least two important ways. First, she politicizes the topic by focusing on the abuse of married women. The punctuating events in Grand's novels that delay and disturb the headlong rush of more traditional novels toward the closure of wedlock include domestic quarrels, women leaving their husbands, dramatizations of sexual double standards, scenes suggesting that romance may be a female delusion, and depictions of women's desire for and idealization of education. Second, these novels not only treat marriage as a theme, but they also reveal ongoing attempts to renegotiate the formal elements that made the marriage plot seem so attractive—and so inevitable. In her study of twentieth-century women writers' attempts to emancipate their fiction from romance, Rachel Blau DuPlessis claims that until the twentieth century the structures of the marriage plot balked women writers' attempts to "write beyond the ending." In the chapters that follow I argue that, if Grand and her fellow New Women writers do not reject or escape the marriage plot, they do tenaciously challenge the cultural assumptions that turned even the most powerful fictional female subjects into objects in the closing moments of romantic and marriage plot fiction, in a sense rewriting the middle so that the "ending" could no longer take on the same cultural and gendered meanings. Drawing attention to the potentially masculinist authority of narration, through intersecting generic structures and conventions, multiple plotting, and "feminizations" of the *bildungsroman* and the *kunstlerroman* plots, Grand's novels depict not alternatives to the marriage plot so much as exposure of the operations of gender privilege and suppression masked as marriage practices. Promoting the interests of women, these novels work to remake marriage, a framework shaping so many women's lives, into a fictional structure and an institution that would give women power, control, authority, security, respect, and, most significantly, agency.

Without ignoring the problems inherent in trying to argue for a direct relation between "real life" and literary representation, I would argue that Grand's novels immerse her readers in the political milieu that became the center of Grand's personal life, her intellectual and activist work, her choice of subject matter, and her understanding of the role fiction could play, that is as a cultural and political intervention. While the fight over the vote dominates histories of late-Victorian women, for many middle-class women marriage, and more specifically the complex social, legal, religious, familial, and daily practices marriage signified, formed the site of the most intensive personal and political struggle for change.

Despite advances made on behalf of women, under Victorian law men still had the right to imprison their wives, to assault them, to deny them access to friends and family, to enforce conjugal rights (i.e., to rape their wives with impunity), to divorce their wives on the suspicion of adultery while committing adultery themselves, to consort with prostitutes with little fear of exposure or arrest, to exploit young girls sexually, even to deprive their wives of their own children, the alleged reward for tolerating such degradation and physical danger. Men's privileges were made painfully clear in 1888, when Emily Jackson refused to live with her husband, and the court supported him when he kidnaped her and kept her locked up in a relative's home.[11] The impossibility of trusting even seemingly benevolent men was repeatedly demonstrated as men in the Liberal Party who purported to be supporters of women's rights compromised with Conservatives by bartering away the vote for women, as they did yet again when Parliament debated suffrage in 1892.[12] Grand's exasperation with the efforts of male politicians colors a wry comment during an 1896 interview: "I tell you what I should like, and that is to do away with the House of Lords and establish a House of Ladies . . . It has often occurred to me that a chamber composed of women qualified to watch legislation as it affects their own sex, and to report their ideas to the House of Commons, would be doing more useful work on behalf of the general community than the present House of Lords is doing."[13]

The various factions of the women's movement sought the vote, in their different ways, because they believed full citizenship promised legal representation that would allow women to set the terms for their personal lives. Only then could they save themselves from such abuses. They also sought the vote as a means to establish legal representation in the multiple senses of that word. Legal and literary feminists could meet on the ground of representation. Grand and her fellow novelists tackled many of the same issues as activists, and with equal fervor, in their representations of "old" women and their struggle to imagine new ones. Herein lies the connection between what I call turn-of-the-century middlebrow fiction and the women's movement.

The phrase *middlebrow* itself highlights the difficulty of mapping present-day categories onto the past as well as the danger of uncritically importing terms and categories from the past without attending to their etymology. Characterizing what she calls the "browing" of literature, Susan Bernstein points out that the term derives from Victorian anthropological categories that judged primates on the basis of their skull development and led to scientific arguments for the superiority of both upper classes and white races.[14] Tad Friend's far more cavalier 1992 essay, "The Case for

Middlebrow," argues that past associations notwithstanding, the long-term "derogation of middlebrow . . . has gone much too far." He defines cultural productions in this category as "distinguished by technical competence, singleness of affect, purity of emotion, tidiness of resolution, and modesty of scope," adding that for all its aesthetic and intellectual limitations, "Where highbrow excludes, middlebrow includes, even welcomes."[15] Caught between these two perspectives, Janice Radway thoughtfully examines her ambivalent responses to middlebrow books that brought her enormous pleasure before graduate school disciplined (in both senses) her taste in books in *A Feeling for Books: The Book-of-the-Month Club, Literary Taste, and Middle-Class Desire.* Confronted with the origins of middlebrow culture, present-day readers who see themselves as either intellectual or progressive on the one hand may want to dissociate themselves from its vulgar premises. On the other hand, mass culture audiences are likely to dismiss "middlebrow" Book-of-the-Month selections as dull or elitist and choose, instead, formula romances, westerns, or novels of espionage, suspense, or horror. And yet for many Victorians this emergent middlebrow literature offered pleasures of language, information, story, and moral vision as precious to them as Radway so honestly recalls her books were to her.

Two of the most rigorous books that explicitly focus on middlebrow literature—Joan Rubin's *The Making of Middlebrow Culture* and the study already noted, Janice Radway's *A Feeling for Books*—argue that this cultural formation was intact in twentieth-century America by the 1930s (although Rubin traces the history of middlebrow literature to turn-of-the-century pursuits such as correspondence courses, lectures, and women's study groups).[16] In contrast, in *The Common Writer: Life in Nineteenth-Century Grub Street* Nigel Cross convincingly argues for an earlier emergence of a body of writing that presumes to fulfill Matthew Arnold's mission for literature, a "browing up" of newly middle-class readers who had aspirations to climb socially by way of a cultural ladder but a ladder available at affordable prices. Moreover, and this point I think is often overlooked, for many Victorian readers, especially women readers, literary value was inseparable from "values" in a broader ethical sense. In discussing novels like *Uncle Tom's Cabin* (with which Grand's *The Heavenly Twins* was compared in regard to its popularity and polemics), Jane Tompkins writes, "I see them as doing a certain kind of cultural work within a specific historical situation, and value them for that reason. I see their plots and characters as providing society with a means of thinking about itself, defining certain aspects of a social reality which the authors and their readers shared, dramatizing its conflicts, and recommending solutions."[17] This preoccupation with doing cultural work for but also with a widespread, middle-class audience distinguishes many

New Woman novels. I would argue that, at the very least, British literary culture of the 1890s shows clear signs of the emergence of concerns and categories that critics and marketing specialists would be routinely calling middlebrow a few decades later.

Cross discusses the founding of the Society of Authors in the early 1880s, a source of financial support for indigent writers to which Thomas Hardy, Sarah Grand, and other "professional" writers subscribed, as an indication of a change in the structure of the English literary establishment. He contextualizes the society in the fierce debates at Oxford over a proposal to institute English literature as a course of study. Proponents, such as J. C. Collins, took the Arnoldian claims for literature to what was seen as an extreme. He insisted that the beneficiaries of the 1870 Education Act, which mandated universal education, should be able to pursue their education further at the university level. Because it was assumed that these men, who came from the upper reaches of the working classes as well as from the middle classes, would not wish to study Greek, Latin, philosophy, or mathematics, Collins proposed that studying the national literature would civilize and democratize the students as they prepared for their futures as civil servants or professionals.[18] While Oxford adamantly refused to revamp its curriculum, the debate marked a shift not only in the larger educational system and the codes designating class distinctions but also in the nature of late Victorian readership. As Cross puts it, "In the 1880s, changes in the price and distribution of books allowed readers to exercise a much more direct choice over their reading matter . . . an irrecoverable schism had occurred in the bourgeois literary world. Where there had been literature there was now middle-brow and high-brow literature."[19]

In part Cross's definition of middlebrow fiction depends upon his assumption that highbrow writers like Henry James and the late-Victorian aesthetes insisted writers should at best set the standard for public taste and at worst simply ignore the public. Writers Cross classifies as middlebrow, for example Walter Besant, not only courted public taste but attempted to reproduce the formulas for success in books such as Besant's *The Art of Fiction* (1884).[20] While Cross's study illuminates the growing desires of diverse readers to find an accessible means of becoming "cultured," a desire generally as amorphous as the word *culture,* he pays little attention to the particular desires of Victorian middle-class women readers and the ways those desires were being met by women writers.

Kate Flint's *The Woman Reader* provides ample evidence of the numbers and variety of women readers, especially from the middle classes, of their importance to the market of literature, and of the attention they received from arbiters of literary culture: theorists of education, literary critics, advisors on etiquette, manners, and hence appropriate reading, even an unlikely but powerful authority, the medical community. Together, Margaret Beetham's *A Magazine of Her Own? Domesticity and Desire in the Woman's Magazine, 1800–1914* and Flint's *The Woman Reader* demonstrate that by midcentury a women's literary culture in all its complexity—as a circuit of readers, writers, publishers, advertisers, specialized publications, and marketing strategies—was flourishing.[21] By the end of the century public and philanthropic educational enterprises and therefore girls' increased access to education in addition to changes in the book trade produced more readers, more publishers, and more books and periodicals. The sheer diversity of kind and price led to endless distinctions and categories—from genre to religious preference to class markets, to name but a few. In this context literary stratification was predictable.

Writers with a constant eye on the market such as Walter Besant believed they could clearly distinguish these hierarchical categories and their correspondent audiences. Besant describes the hierarchies of literary culture in "Literature as a Career" (1892) that anticipate current conceptions of high-, middle-, and lowbrow.

> In literature there is a kind—without doubt the highest kind—which pleases the refinement of five hundred or five thousand who possess the highest culture possible. That is a very rare kind. There are not a dozen living writers of our language who quite satisfy the standard of this small class. But there are lower standards—those which appeal to the better class, the class whose literary taste is not so keen, so subtle, as that of the first class, yet is sound and wholesome. And there are lower standards and lower still, till we reach the depths of the penny novelette, the journal which is a scrap-book, the halfpenny sheet of ballads. Yet it is all literature, the literature of the nation, the literature of the people, from highest to lowest.[22]

For all Besant's appeal to a democracy of tastes, he often found fault with women writers and had to be persuaded to admit them to the Society of Authors. He, like many other critics who accepted the social stratification of literature, routinely attacked New Women fiction, especially by women. Women writers were excluded from democracy or taste or both.

While Besant attempted to shape middlebrow literary culture with how-to books and the Society of Authors, others like Edmund Gosse read the collapse of culture in the rise of middlebrow tastes, which he explicitly associates with newly literate readers and women readers and writers in "The Decay of Literary Taste" (1895). "At the present day," he writes, "the general public has a great deal of taste, and it requires a critic to be a thorough-going truckler to democracy to say that he thinks all of it very good."[23] He laments a past when the exercise of taste "was concentrated in a narrow circle" and complains against New Women novelists who "err grievously against taste" as well as against their readers, "a public as hysterical and vulgar as themselves" that "buys their silly books in thousands and tens of thousands."[24]

This emergent middlebrow culture was explicitly material as well as theoretical. The Author's Syndicate, the nonprofit legal wing of the Authors' Society, fought for authors' remuneration, and literary agents maddened publishers by negotiating to place books with "appropriate" presses.[25] Grand's letters show that she worked with two of the most successful agents, William Morris Colles and James Brand Pinker, to sell her short stories. Similarly, she, like many middlebrow and even a few high-culture authors, organized lecture tours in Britain and America that blurred literary culture, celebrity, and spectacle. Grand herself consulted with two famous agents, James Burton Pond, known as Major Pond, and James Redpath.[26] She also participated in the growing cult of celebrity, complete with glamour photographs, society notes, and magazine interviews, that marked one of the endless points of contact between literary and consumer culture.[27]

Because middlebrow fiction was quickly associated with formula, journeyman work, and crass commercial success, Victorian gatekeepers of culture (academics, intellectuals, reviewers, and even well-educated readers) trivialized such fiction as consumer-driven, popular, escapist, and entertaining rather than improving. As Rita Kranidis, Terry Lovell, and Gaye Tuchman and Nina Fortin, among others, have argued, this denigration of best-selling fiction is linked to the fact that it was often marketed to women and to "the masses," a usefully vague phrase that signifies the growing audience of lower middle-class and working-class readers.[28]

Joan Rubin provides an illuminating survey of writers' attempts, usually disparaging, to define middlebrow taste, beginning in the 1930s.[29] Many of the essayists and critics she cites focus less on literary or cultural texts than on their consumers. Defenders of high culture seem to share Matthew Arnold's earlier ambivalence over the spread of literacy. Fundamentally, high culture requires, on one hand, a sense of tradition (which, despite its representation as stable, is usually a shifting construct), but, on the other hand, high culture also requires the imagined masses and their unrefined tastes against which to invent itself. To the contrary, writers with a social or political agenda require a mass audience both as consumers and converts.

Comfortable with the didacticism of earlier Victorian cultural gatekeepers and increasingly supported by cultural institutions such as authors'

Ⅲⅾⅿе. Ѕага Gⓡаⓝ.

PEMBRIDGE CRESCENT,
LONDON. W.

H. L. Mendelssohn produced the photograph of Sarah Grand that
circulated widely in this *carte de visite* format and is now owned by
the National Portrait Gallery in London. (Courtesy of the National
Portrait Gallery, London.)

societies, literary societies, women's clubs (such as Grand's own Pioneer
Club), and explicitly political literary groups like the Women's Writers Suffrage League as well as by political organizations for women, a writer like
Grand developed a sense of mission along with a desire to write and the
necessity to support herself. While middlebrow culture at large may have
been located in a generalized desire in readers for self-improvement, the

women's middlebrow culture of clubs, societies, ladies' magazines, and fiction marketed to "progressive" women labored to balance self-improvement with arguments for social reform. Women readers would have to change the world in order both to invent the selves imagined by these New Woman writers and to alleviate the injustices that structured the plots of these novels.

Ironically, as early as George Moore's *Literature at Nurse* in 1885 and repeatedly through the rest of the century, the success of writers like Grand as well as the sales of romance writers like Ouida led to attacks on women readers as representatives of tasteless masses, inhibiting the sales of novelists like George Moore.[30] As Lyn Pykett points out in *Engendering Fictions*, notwithstanding the rare exception like George Eliot and Elizabeth Barrett Browning, women writers were disdained by high culture, but they most immediately threatened closer competitors, the male writers equally intent upon cultivating their own middlebrow markets for what Elaine Showalter in *Sexual Anarchy* calls the male romance, for other forms of adventure fiction, and for alternative conceptions of realist fiction, among other struggling literary forms. Like the female New Women novelists, these male writers sought "popular" markets but resisted association with mass culture.[31] They were fighting for a stake in Besant's second tier of literature, territory being ruined by women readers and writers.

New Woman fiction has a crucial relation to women's middlebrow genres that begs a reconsideration of the relationship between middlebrow writers and readers. The commercial success of "women's novels" seemed to be determined by several responses on the parts of readers. As I show in later chapters, we gain glimpses of these responses in reviews published in women's magazines, in minutes of women's clubs, and even in letters and secondhand accounts of individual women's opinions of a novel. Readers valued the capacity of these novels to satisfy politicized yet intensely personal desires for alternative accounts of gender relations, for a woman-centered analysis of the play of power within domestic and institutional landscapes, and for relief from the discontent that, though often dismissed as personal, in fact inspired significant numbers of readers to political action. In other words, what is now generally disparaged as middlebrow fiction was and is derided as the packaging and selling of culture. Yet the successful formulation and transmission of the politics associated with New Women and their social counterparts, women's rights activists, depended upon popular circulation and commercial success. Commercialism strengthened the circulation of women's fiction; however, the taint of the market undermined their cultural capital.

The character of this neglected readership emerges in the vivid and fas-

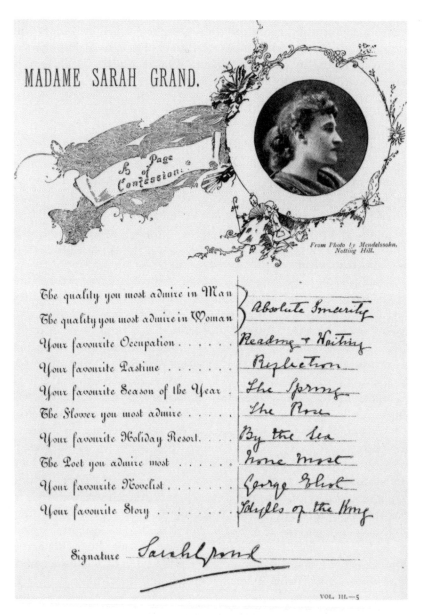

MADAME SARAH GRAND.

A Page of Confession.

From Photo by Mendelssohn, Notting Hill.

The quality you most admire in Man
The quality you most admire in Woman   } Absolute Sincerity

Your favourite Occupation . . . . . .   Reading + Writing

Your favourite Pastime . . . .   Reflection

Your favourite Season of the Year .   The Spring

The Flower you most admire . . . . .   The Rose

Your favourite Holiday Resort. . . .   By the Sea

The Poet you admire most . . . . . .   none most

Your favourite Novelist . . . .   George Eliot

Your favourite Story . . . .   Idylls of the King

Signature   Sarah Grand

Like other writers of the 1890s, Grand was marketed to women readers in magazine articles and fluff pieces. This questionnaire, titled "A Page of Confessions," was a regular feature in *The Woman at Home*. The interview with Grand appeared in 3 (October 1894): 65. (Courtesy of the Library of Congress.)

cinating details Kate Flint mines from the letters, essays, paintings, and fictional portraits of readers she discusses in *The Woman Reader.* Her book challenges stereotypes of women readers as vulnerable, passive, uncritical, and naively absorbed into the identity of any fictional heroine.[32] She argues that, to the contrary, reading, particularly involving the kind of novels I call women's middlebrow fiction such as New Women novels, is

> centrally bound in with questions of authority: authority which manifests itself in a capacity for judgment and opinion based on self-knowledge (so far as this may be possible, both in psychological terms and within the framework of language); and authority to speak, to write, to define, to manage, and to change not just the institutions of literature, but those of society itself.[33]

Sarah Grand's novels claim this authority quite explicitly and take on the educational project of producing feminist readers for whom middlebrow novels might serve as a means to middle-class activism. Grand's novels suggest that the chief task of the novelist was to undertake women's education, a preliminary step to providing women with a feminist critique of marriage and a call to change marriage law and practices. Therefore, Grand gives a privileged place to female readers in her fiction, and she treats reading as part of a progressive education that begins by broadening women's scope. Her characters read physiology, biology, medicine, evolutionary theory, the eugenicist Francis Galton, John Stuart Mill and other social theorists such as John Ruskin and Ralph Waldo Emerson, as well as romances and popular novels. But Grand's novels also argue that the skills of analysis, comparison, and criticism that produce what Judith Fetterley characterizes as *The Resisting Reader* (1978)—a process the woman writer learns and teaches by comparing life experiences to fictional plots—must then be used as a reversed lens with which life is compared to the idealistic promises of romance and sentimental conceptions of the feminine. In determining what kind of novels she would write, Grand exercised literary as well as social and legal politics. Her arguments slip from protests against marriage to restructurings of the marriage plot to revisionings of "culture." Harnessing the Trojan horse of middlebrow women's fiction, Grand sought to infiltrate literary romances with political, issues-oriented, woman-centered critiques of marriage.

The gender of New Woman writers bore profoundly on the gendering of this developing middlebrow literary culture, and the consequences still influence critical characterizations of individual writers and this subgenre of fiction. Novels by male New Woman novelists, such as Thomas Hardy's *Jude the Obscure,* George Gissing's *The Odd Women,* George Meredith's *Diana of the Crossways,* and others, like the literary works of their female counterparts, challenge both the narrative and moral logics of nine-teenth-century marriage plot fiction. Yet they are rarely pinioned or dis-missed with the same ease. Influenced by Henrik Ibsen's plays and the novels of Honoré de Balzac and Gustave Flaubert, these British writers sought what Thomas Hardy called "a new realism," an antidote to the marriage plot that would permit franker treatment of sexuality and heterosexual relationships.[34]

Just as most studies of middle-class writing in the early twentieth cen-tury overlooked women readers, before feminist literary criticism changed the face of literary history in the 1970s, studies of New Woman fiction highlighted these male writers. At best women writers were treated as minor writers whose only significance was that they provide a context for the "serious" literature written by men. Because women writers had a far stronger personal investment in issues that affected women—most of which were bound up in the restrictive roles of wife and mother both in real life and in literature—these writers drew more heavily upon contemporary social issues than did their male contemporaries. Grand speculated about the effects of gender on the New Woman novelists' work and reception as crit-ical fireworks flared following the publication of *The Heavenly Twins:*

> I am just thinking—perhaps women are bolder because they have suf-fered more from these sex matters than men. Most of them write with loathing of the subject—I certainly do—but are impelled to it by the hope of remedying the evils which exist. Men do it because these things are in their minds, and they have not the excuse of the object to be attained.[35]

Grand's comments suggest that New Woman novels by women required a form as hospitable to social issues as to "literary" content and conventions. The women's novels dealt with female desire, male and female sexuality, abandonment, domestic abuse, divorce, illegitimate births, prostitution, venereal disease, the need for female education and access to professions, the current status of women and labor, women's suffrage, and relationships between women of different classes. Driven by their personal experiences and ambitions, female New Woman writers, particularly those like Mona Caird and Sarah Grand who openly supported women's suffrage, departed from the "objective" perspective and omniscient point of view that readers prized in the novels of earlier British writers such as George Eliot and William Makepeace Thackeray. Instead, these politicized writers tended to be polemical and unapologetically didactic, urging their new vision of men's and women's responsibilities and relationships on their late-Victorian world.

Disgruntled by the subjects and the tone of these New Woman novels, the institution of literary producers—the very men and male institutions whom the New Woman novelists powerfully attacked in their fiction—dismissed these novels as distasteful, exaggerated, and even neurotic. The female New Woman novelists struggled against what Grand repeatedly called "a conspiracy of silence," that is, against male and female critics, against more conventional novelists, and against conservative readers, as the writers labored to create alternative meanings of womanhood and consequently the kinds of female characters and plots that would shape the forms of fiction.[36]

Even after the success of *Ideala* Grand's letters vividly document the manipulations of the publishing world that taught her to read conspiracy in the resistance to her work. An 1892 letter to William Blackwood, editor of *Blackwood's Magazine,* informs him that she has decided to publish *The Heavenly Twins* despite his intense dislike of the book. The letter reveals that Blackwood had threatened to stop the serialization of one of her earlier novels in *Blackwood's* if she ignored his advice, surely a case of editorial extortion.[37] Ultimately, the more radical New Woman novelists succumbed to the cultural forces that silence some writers and celebrate others. The hundred-year exclusion of female New Women writers from course syllabi and *Books in Print* resulted from the far-reaching gender and class prejudices that we can trace in every facet of Victorian life, from a university don's refusal to grant women access to degrees to editors' selections of the writers he or she would publish and promote.

Although the women's movement seems a likely source for the New Woman figure, the character, unlike many of the authors who were a part of the women's movement, frequently antagonized rather than impressed feminist activists when she first appeared in the 1880s. Originally, a New Woman was less often a political identity or a literary construct than a character in a social drama staged by journalists who were hostile to the suffragists and educational reformers. Even though Grand took credit for naming the New Woman in 1894, by 1898 she was indignantly protesting conservative exploitation of the figure:

> Where is this New Woman, this epicene creature, this Gorgon set up by the snarly who impute to her the faults of both sexes while denying her the charm of either—where is she to be found, if she exist at all? For my own part, until I make her acquaintance I shall believe her to be the finest work of the imagination which the newspapers have yet produced.[38]

As Ann Ardis points out, before 1895 many of the critical discussions of the New Woman question whether the New Woman existed in the "real world" or merely on paper in an ongoing debate that figures the paradoxes that still plague assessments of New Woman fiction. A reviewer for *Vanity Fair* (1894) declares, "we do not believe in the New Woman's existence. She is a caricature. We read of her in books, and we see her on stage. But we have not met her."[39] A year later a reviewer writing for the *Athenaeum* similarly protests: "The 'New Woman' is a product oftener met with in novels of the day than in ordinary life, where, fortunately, she remains so rare as to be seldom seen in the flesh at all."[40] As these reviews suggest, versions of these female characters with the trappings later associated with the New Woman—the bobbed hair, shortened skirts, spectacles, cigarettes, bicycles, books, and latchkeys—dominated cartoons and caricatures in periodicals of the 1890s.[41] Ardis succinctly summarizes the complex relationship between the journalists, the novelists, and the critics during this decade:

> even as critics are arguing the New Woman never existed as a "real" phenomenon, New Woman novelists are representing the hostility which she encounters in the real world: even as critics are dismissing her as a "journalistic myth," New Women novelists are depicting her "retreat with honour" before a political and social establishment which refuses to recognize her work within its domain.[42]

These parodic images were directed against a variety of emerging "types" of women who challenged conventional female roles, including women journalists and novelists, the increasing ranks of female college graduates, the women intellectuals who were teaching at women's colleges and fighting to insure that their students could take fully accredited university exams and degrees, the aesthetes in their "yallery-greenery" dress, and the increasingly organized and visible advocates for women's rights, in particular the right to vote.

Rather than welcoming the New Woman as a desirable public image, female suffragists were more likely to protest angrily against what they considered a reactionary caricature of their politics. In an 1895 review of Grant Allen's highly publicized New Woman novel, *The Woman Who Did*, Millicent Garrett Fawcett, who became the leader of the National Union of Women Suffrage Societies in 1897, upbraids Allen for defining women's freedom in terms of sexual rather than social issues. She believed that Allen's version of the New Woman reinforced journalistic stereotypes and diverted public attention away from women's political demands because his novel depicts a New Woman whose experiment in "free love" produces an illegitimate child who becomes a conservative young woman and therefore rejects her mother along with her mother's radical theories. Fawcett writes:

"The Woman Who Did" being as a story feeble and silly to the last degree, it may be asked, why take any notice of it? It only seems worthwhile to do so because its author purports to be writing in support of the enfranchisement of women . . . But it is satisfactory to remember that Mr. Grant Allen has never given help by tongue or pen to any practical effort to improve the legal or social status of women. He is not a friend but an enemy.[43]

She concludes, "He purports to write in the interests of women, but there will be very few women who do not see that his little book belongs very much more to the unregenerate men than to women at all."[44] In the foreword to her 1897 study, *Marriage Questions in Modern Fiction,* the more conservative Elizabeth Chapman protests "the interminable flood of gaseous chatter to which the invention of a journalistic myth known as the 'New Woman' has given rise" and adds, "it has become necessary sharply to emphasize the distinction between this phantom and the real reformer and friend of her sex and of humanity whom I would call the 'Best Woman.'"[45]

Not all female journalists agreed, however, with these negative assessments of the New Woman. Unlike Fawcett and Chapman, other women hoped the New Woman might provide a healthy alternative to innocent, passive, dependent, lovestruck literary heroines. More cautious supporters, such as the journalist Mrs. Roy Devereux, promoted a version of the New Woman as eugenic wonder. In a series of articles Devereux wrote for the *Saturday Review* in 1895 and subsequently published as *The Ascent of Woman,* she portrays the New Woman as a better-informed, more able-bodied, more responsible and social-minded mother who could contribute to society by improving the race. The New Woman's more radical promulgators, such as the novelist and journalist Mona Caird, created a more threatening version. The New Woman who appears in Caird's novels and who informs her collection of essays, *The Morality of Marriage* (1897), argues for the overthrow of marriage altogether, advocating sexual freedom instead.

While political feminists angrily denounced the trivializing implications of the parodic New Woman figure and journalists debated the merits of the New Woman, female writers confronted the image with fictions rather than facts. Appropriating the cartoon New Woman figure to serve their own feminist ends, these writers produced counternarratives in answer to society's attempt to conceal the breach between the roles reserved for women and the opportunities that women were beginning to demand. By picturing the transformation of the most womenly women into protesters against social barriers to women's education and economic independence,

New Woman novelists exposed the misogynistic implications of journalistic conflations of all types of New Women into a single, anomalous, absurd female figure. Their novels recast the New Woman as assertive rather than strident, intelligent rather than pedantic, and discriminating rather than man-hating. Thus, these novelists forced a crisis both in social definitions of gender and in the form of the novel, in particular the marriage plot novel, that inscribed those gender relations.

Resistance to change often takes more violent and emphatic expression than attempts at change, in part because reformers struggle to conceive as well as to enact alternatives. Moreover, reactionaries know their audiences; part of the project of reformers and revolutionaries is to create an audience and one that will act rather than merely agree. It is unsurprising, therefore, that the New Woman's early detractors were louder, more emphatic, more lurid, and therefore more capable of influencing the general readers of late-nineteenth-century periodicals than the New Woman's advocates were. Using the increasingly codified and intimidating discourse of psychology, these journalists labeled the New Woman morbid, neurotic, and degenerate. By the 1890s the psychological establishment, a newly instituted authority, had already gained social and intellectual prestige under the aegis of Max Nordau, J. M. Charcot, and Havelock Ellis. Sigmund Freud's work would later fully canonize the new "science" of psychoanalysis. By introducing this new medical language into a literary context, the literary reviewers constructed a means to suppress what Terry Lovell calls the "woman-to-woman forms" of New Woman novels by women writers.[46] Psychological analysis ultimately became the single most powerful force invoked to silence New Woman characters and, by extension, their female creators as well. Repeatedly, journalists like Hugh Stutfield and Janet Hogarth blazoned this version of the New Woman as madwoman, threatening female readers with the dangers of knowledge, sexual experimentation, education, self-reflection, social analysis, and any opinion or action that was not sanctioned, which is to say controlled, by men. From the perspective of the present these reviewers seem to have capitalized upon the most unsavory connotations of middlebrow—primitivism, atavism, mental inferiority, animality, irrationality, and unbridled desire—to shut down the more socially grounded, politically interested texts shaping women's middlebrow culture. Critics of this literature vacillate in their complaints. The novels are too uncivilized or too effete. The readership they address is too exclusive or too vulgar.

This confusion may even be a partial explanation for the tendency of reviewers to turn to the newly emerging social science of psychology as a basis for evaluating New Woman fiction. Psychology lay outside the

periphery of "culture" in a literary sense, but, as a rising profession associated with medicine, it became a critical component in the formation of
middlebrow culture. One of the earliest writers on psychology to attract the
attention of literary critics was the German-Hungarian physician and
author, Max Nordau, who was best known for *Degeneration,* controversial in
England throughout the late 1890s. Janet Hogarth, a writer for the *Fortnightly Review,* established her credibility as a psycho-literary critic by taking
the title of her 1895 article "Literary Degenerates" from the master himself.
This article is especially curious because the first two pages, which characterize the "degenerate" according to Nordau's definition, rely entirely on a
masculine subject and male pronouns for illustration. Suddenly, mid-para-
graph on page 2, Hogarth asks, "Now that we know genius to be a disease
of the nerves, what more normal than that women should use their favorite
fallacy of simple depression?" She continues, "If abnormal nervous excitement can be made to spell genius, what is to hinder every woman from
claiming the coveted distinction?"[47] Describing women's deceptive nature
and dismissing any serious possibility for female genius, Hogarth next attacks
the project of the New Woman novelists:

> With the instinct of a true degenerate, and with wearisome iteration,
> she rings the changes on this single theme. The theory of the marriage
> yoke, the mutual rights of men and women, and their growing mutual
> disgust, the degradation of the wife who is made her husband's play-
> thing, her undue exaltation at the expense of her bolder sisters, who are
> prepared to follow nature and defy convention, and finally the deliri-
> ous fancies of the victims of sex mania; we know the weary round, and
> would fain leave it behind forever.[48]

Hogarth protests that the matter of women's lives and the social forces
that determine women's limited scope are not fit subject matter for fiction.
By representing these plots as tedious and insignificant and characterizing
those who would reform women's lot as "delirious" women undone by an
obsession with sexuality, Hogarth discredits the seriousness of the New
Women characters and their counterparts in the women's movement.
Finally, after matter-of-factly asserting that "most of the newer school of
women writers are undoubtedly insane," Hogarth appeals to yet another
psychological authority, Havelock Ellis, who "has collected a large amount
of testimony as to the peculiar forms which madness takes amongst women;
it goes to prove that 'in all forms of acute insanity the sexual aspect is more
prominently shown in women than in men.'"[49] Collapsing madness, sexuality, and feminist writers into a single category, Hogarth replaces aesthetic
or ethical judgments with clinical condemnation. By discrediting these

women writers, she justifies what is at best a superficial reading of their works.

Another reviewer who drew heavily from the work of Max Nordau was Hugh Stutfield, a literary critic for *Blackwood's Magazine*. Like Hogarth, he too demonstrates the critic's power of erasure as he condescends to, trivializes, threatens, and finally undermines New Woman fiction by labeling its practitioners as well as its protagonists madwomen. In "The Psychology of Feminism," written in 1897, Stutfield conveys his misogyny through the authoritative language of psychology. After denigrating the content of the New Woman novels as an account of "the monotony of her life, its narrowness of interest, the brutality and selfishness of man, the burden of sex, and the newly awakened consciousness of ill-usage at Nature's hands," he then demeans the New Woman writer's serious social critique of such a life. Introducing one of Sarah Grand's characters, he patronizingly explains:

> The glory of the women of to-day as portrayed in the sex-problem literature is her "complicatedness." To be subtle, inscrutable, complex—irrational possibly, but at any rate incomprehensible—to puzzle the adoring male, to make him scratch his head in vexation and wonderment as to what on earth she will be up to next,—this is the ambition of the latter-day heroine.[50]

Here he imposes "the double standard of content," labeling the topic of the New Woman fiction, that is women's lives, insignificant.[51] Stutfield's entire article depends upon the "pollution of agency" as a means of discrediting the fiction he reviews.[52] In his attacks on women writers he reads the political struggles of the New Woman as a new and fairly transparent form of flirtation—a distinctly sexist misreading.

Stutfield postulates that the New Woman is a victim of restless dissatisfaction rather than an agent of purposeful change. Invoking Nordau, he presumes to diagnose the failings of women writers as well as their literary texts: "I remember that Max Nordau classes egomania as among the leading stigmata of degeneration, so doubtless this newly aroused consciousness lies at the root of our modern introspectiveness, and accounts for many of the strange things that neurotic people do both in real life and in fiction."[53] Confident that both the characters and their creators are pathological, Stutfield concludes by accusing the New Woman novelists of increasing the hostility between the sexes and consequently of undermining their own ends: "There is no doubt that the literature of vituperation and of sex-mania, with its perpetual harping on the miseries of married life, and its public washing of domestic dirty linen, tends to widen the breach between men and women, and to make them more mutually distrustful than ever."[54]

Stutfield's analysis provides insight into the defensive nature of his criticisms of New Woman fiction. He revealingly prefaces his statement of injury with a complaint about the male roles in women's fiction that represent man "as a blackguard, an idiot, or both, sometimes diseased, always a libertine and a bully."[55] His pretense at scientific objectivity is undermined by the juxtaposition of these two passages. By the end of his essay Stutfield maligns novels, characters, and women writers alike, using the language of abnormal psychology to discredit the literary work and by extension, in this instance, the political work of the women's movement.[56]

Both of these essayists argue that what they object to is the vulgar representations of female sexuality in New Woman fiction, yet their attention inevitably turns to women's minds rather than their bodies. Perhaps the reviewers sense the complexity of the New Woman's desires, her longing for a freedom that transcends mere rejection of womanhood, domesticity, and the dogma of female frigidity. In fact, it is the power of knowledge itself and of the female mind that can engage ideas and question conventions that most agitates detractors.

The Victorians' increasing respect for science invests a scientific prognosis of madness, however amateurish, with an authority, however undeserved, not available to traditional literary analysis. Accusing the novelists themselves of madness, morbidity, and hysteria, the reviewers drew parallels between the New Women characters and their authors that blocked the novelists' literary careers by many of the same means the social conditions represented in the novels restrain the fictional heroines.

Contemporary reviewers' misrepresentation of the content of the New Woman novels erected another obstacle. Critics' claim that New Women novels by women focus on the single issue of women's sexuality is a misperception that still shadows studies of the novels. In "The Fiction of Sexuality," published by the *Contemporary Review* in 1895, James Ashcroft Noble attacks what he calls the "erotomaniacs."[57] Commenting on the fiction of George Egerton and Sarah Grand, he writes:

> The new fiction of sexuality presents to us a series of pictures painted from reflections in convex mirrors, the colossal nose which dominates the face being represented by one colossal appetite which dominates life. Sometimes it is made as inoffensive as deformity can ever be made; sometimes it is unspeakably revolting; occasionally . . . it is allied with moralising as aggressive as that of a Sunday-school story-book; but everywhere it is a flagrant violation of the obvious proportion of life.[58]

Noble demonstrates through his argument that a feminist writer like Sarah Grand is damned if she does and damned if she doesn't: first he labels her fiction promiscuous; then he condemns her for moralizing. In either case he forestalls a more realistic treatment of sexuality by asking: "Is the persistent presentation of the most morbid symptoms of erotomania a seeing of life steadily and wholly? Is it even a clear, truthful seeing of that part of life which it unnaturally isolates?"[59]

For many of the educators, lawmakers, and literary authorities who were influenced by their interpretations of sexologists of the late nineteenth century, the answer seemed clear. Women who publicly discussed female sexuality, particularly those writers who emphasized female discontent and desire, were exhibiting symptoms of mental or emotional disorder. Many critics clung to the midcentury belief that good women were either inherently frigid or constitutionally reticent. Apparently, many middle-class readers also accepted (or wished) that "normal" women, at least those in literature, would have limited interest or experience in matters of sexuality and believed that this obliviousness had "natural" psychological and physical causes. Even at the turn of the century an influential author of popular medical handbooks like Edward Carpenter who advocated open discussion of sexuality and voiced support for the women's movement argued that normal women had no capacity for sexual response. This belief, of course, added support to the idea that the New Woman novelists were mentally disturbed.[60]

The critics' focus on the topic of sexuality had another function as well. The emphasis on this single, most controversial topic conveniently led critics to ignore other fundamental concerns taken up in the novels. Mona Caird's characters Bessie Saunders and Margaret Ellwood in *Daughters of Danaeus* (1894) and Sarah Grand's Beth of *The Beth Book* (1897) roundly condemn the laws governing marriage. Grand's Evadne in *The Heavenly Twins* (1893) and Iota's Gwen Waring in *A Yellow Aster* (1894) resist the inflexibility of parental authority, and Menie Muriel Dowie's heroine Gallia (in the novel of the same name, 1894) denounces the paucity of education for women, along with Olive Schreiner's Lyndall of *Story of an African Farm* (1883). Nearly all the New Woman characters decry the failure of society to use the talents of women in the public sphere. Though many of the female characters in these novels experience partial or euphemistically portrayed sexual initiations, the characters, like Grand's Angelica, also in *The Heavenly Twins,* or Schreiner's Lyndall, lament that their desires for romance and sexual fulfillment thwart their opposing desires for financial autonomy, work, and an independent and purposeful existence. The analysis of female experience, provided by narrators as well as characters, is far more complex and sophisticated than reviewers like Noble, Stutfield, or Hogarth suggest. In fact, the novels bear little resemblance to their caricatures. In the lines of these literary critics we can read the misogyny, conservatism, and protection of privilege that warp their critical judgments. In this early trivializing and misreading of the New Woman novelists, we can read the critics' efforts to exert power over the increasingly prolific and increasingly successful culture of New Woman readers, writers, and novels.

The chapters that follow explore Grand's politicized, if consistently middle-class and heterosexist, fictional agitation for marital reform and social and institutional changes that would serve women's interests. By exposing the contrary and sexist character of both the worlds of fiction and of lived experience, Grand's novels demonstrate the power of fiction to participate in dynamic processes of social change and remind us that literature as well as law has created the political contexts in which we find ourselves today. She also assumes a role in the history of middlebrow culture, a culture that remains vital in the United States today through the Book-of-the-Month Club, Oprah's Book Club, and the skyrocketing popularity of reading groups, of whom women form the greatest numbers.

Chapter 2

Gendered Plots and the Search for Feminist Form

William Blackwood and Sons published *A Domestic Experiment* in 1891 in response to the sales of *Ideala,* and to Sarah Grand's delight *Blackwood's Magazine* serialized *Singularly Deluded* between August and December of 1892. The order of publication, however, probably differed from the order of production; in a 1923 foreword to *The Heavenly Twins* Grand notes that the success of *Ideala* led to "the acceptance of two other little books, previously written and rejected."[1] Even Grand's promoters have dismissed these two early works as failures best ignored. Grand herself lamented the inadequacies of her early work.[2] In a letter of 1892 she worried to William Blackwood:

> With regard to *A Domestic Experiment.* I think it was ill-advised to publish the book at all in that form . . . It is young work and crude—too literal a transcript from life—and I felt all along I ought to re-write it; but when you, the leading publisher in the kingdom, seemed satisfied with it, I was naturally flattered, and thought you must know best. As a matter of fact I don't suppose now that you ever saw the ms. I had not seen it myself for years, and I should like to have written to you about it when I read the proof sheets. I was disappointed, however, in those days, unfortunately, but riding around on the sides of omnibus's [*sic*] reforming the world has done something for me since, and I am not at all disappointed now. And I want to ask you if you will be so good as to suppress the book either altogether or until I can rewrite it? You have not furnished me with any account of how it sold, which is ominous, but perhaps you will kindly do so now.[3]

Both display the problems of apprenticeship works, including undeveloped characters, a disregard for probability, and patched-up, impossible endings. The *Athenaeum* protested the "intricacies of incident" in *Singularly Deluded,* calling it "the story of a wild-goose chase, arising out of an episode of quite transcendental preposterousness,"[4] while a reviewer for the *Spectator* protested against a scene from *A Domestic Experiment,* "Anything more extravagant we have never seen in literature."[5] Though it seems clear that all three early novels were completed before Grand moved to London, Grand left no clues to indicate the exact dates or sequence of composition. At sixteen she had married an older widower with two children, David Chambers McFall, believing that life with a military surgeon would be an improvement over her unhappy childhood home. At seventeen she had a son, David Archibald Edward. And a year later McFall's military assignments transported the family to a series of exotic foreign posts for five years—Singapore, Japan, Ceylon, China, Malta, and the Straits settlements—before the family returned to England. All through these years Grand attempted to find publishers for the short stories she began writing when she married.[6] Isolated and unhappy in the military community of Norwich, Grand forever after associated these early years, which she called her "black time," with a sense of entrapment that infuses the early novels, lending power to the barely controlled anger of characters who are principally defined, as was she, by their status as wives.[7]

Because the chronology of Grand's writing career is so uncertain at this point, because *Ideala* belongs to a trilogy of novels that share characters and settings and that were not completed until 1897, and because the early novels suggest such a rich period of experimentation before Grand settled on the conventions that came to be associated with the New Woman novel, I begin with these two novels, even though they were not actually published until after *Ideala.*[8] While Grand's late novels treat marriage as an institution determined by social conventions and enforced by public authorities such as the legal system and the church, these two early novels probe the personal, individual, and psychological experience of marriage from a woman's point of view. If the plots are far-fetched and unruly, their very roughness conveys the personal dissatisfaction and psychological disturbances of the married women characters that the marriage plot usually disciplines or ignores. In these novels the main characters do not rail against marriage or even analyze their dissatisfaction with it, but their ambivalence spills over into action.

A Domestic Experiment anticipates the novels of Grand's feminist trilogy in its treatment of a painfully failed marriage. Though Grand claimed not to have read Ibsen before 1890, irascibly insisting in a letter to Frederick Henry Fisher, "Ibsen, in fact, was a name of no significance to me until I saw myself mentioned as a follower of his," this novel uses the structure of Ibsenian drawing-room melodrama to establish a conventional husband-wife-mistress triangle then displaces that plot by offering the female protagonist the choice of either a male lover or a female lover.[9] The novel reaches melodramatic closure when the wife rejects either avenue to romance for a loveless marriage.

Grand's boldest novel, *Singularly Deluded,* plays out a fantasy of action and freedom through a delightfully outrageous near-parody of two conventionally masculine popular genres: the adventure novel and the detective novel. A second *Spectator* reviewer describes the plot:

> A young lady's feverish, helter-skelter pursuit after someone, under the mistaken impression that he is her husband in a state of mental aberration, is the theme of *Singularly Deluded,* which is a very clever and fresh tale, though not perhaps altogether exempt from the charge of "nightmarish," because of the breathlessly rapid succession of obstacles great and small, that hinder the plucky heroine, and cause her to be again and again disappointed when apparently on the verge of success.[10]

The novel highlights the instability of gender categories not only by positioning the heroine in the traditionally male roles of detective and adventurer but also by trapping the husband in surreal femininity. Even as the wife discovers the advantages and failures of "feminine" characteristics to meet the demands of travel and sleuthing, the husband finds his own paternalist, superior, that is husbandly, kindness turned on himself by the affectionate, dictatorial desires of his Neanderthal captor.

The novels differ markedly in form and subject matter, yet both reveal the turbulent, ungovernable emotions, desires, and drives experienced by women who could be defined, but not subdued, by social or literary categories of femininity. In effect these first novels dramatize psychological resistance to the forms of femininity that made the marriage plot imaginable. Moreover, in light of recent studies of what we would now call lesbian cultures and subcultures, the second novel can be seen to offer homosocial, if not overtly homosexual, alternatives to the miseries attributed to marriage and to the confining range of possibilities proffered by the marriage plot. Denaturalizing masculinity, femininity, and heterosexuality—the beliefs and behaviors giving rise to the nineteenth-century marriage plot—these rough novels laid the ground work for Grand's later "realistic" explorations of the conditions of marriage and its hold on fiction. The characters in these early novels experience brief moments of psychological transformation; ultimately, however, social realities drive each character back into an acceptance of conventional womanhood and wifehood. Grand would broach the barriers to her personal development and that of her fiction with her next novel, *Ideala,* by leaving the so-called private sphere for the public and publishing world of London.

Grand wrote *A Domestic Experiment* as a fictional rebuttal to another text. While she lived in Warrington, a curate wrote what Gillian Kersley calls a "squib," entitled *Battleton Rectory*.[11] This squib caricatured a number of locals, including Grand. In the guise of Mrs. Tumbledown, Grand was ridiculed as a pseudointellectual who wore absurd clothing, prated nonsense in the inflated non sequiturs of those who read only enough to confuse themselves, and offended everyone with her self-righteous, self-assumed superiority.[12] Incensed, Grand immediately retaliated with her own fictional portrait of Warrington society. Here only the intelligent heroine is free of prejudices; the clergy are remote and their wives are social climbers who despise both the "sick-poor" and those, like the protagonist, who desire social change and a life of activity beyond female social rituals.

The action is fairly down-to-earth in contrast with *Singularly Deluded*. Belligerently, Paul Oldham invites his lower middle-class "friend," Dolly Cartwright, to call on his refined upper-middle-class wife, Agatha, because Dolly desires an introduction into high society. At first Agatha is shamed and humiliated; however, she quickly turns the tables against her husband by imitating Dolly's outrageous behavior. Dolly is married to a wealthy boor who never appears in the novel. Although vulgar—she "paints," wears a tight-laced corset, and flirts with little discretion—she is also vivacious and generous. Eventually, Dolly's good nature wins Agatha's affection and admiration, and the two delight in tormenting Agatha's repentant husband and the staid, self-righteous older women in their circle (including the curates' wives, of course). Paul ceases to lie and philander; however, his newly adopted methodistical piety makes him more ridiculous than ever. A combination of circumstances finally encourages Agatha to act more circumspectly: a friend of her husband named La Motte shocks her with an insulting proposition; her father's old friend, Lord Alec Graham, takes an interest in her welfare; and she falls in love with an absurdly naive and idealistic young lord. Nevertheless, though she treats Paul more politely than before, she cares nothing for him. The novel concludes after Dolly saves Agatha's reputation by exposing La Motte's villainy then loses Agatha's friendship by warning her to avoid her potential lover, Lord Vaincrecourt, for both his and her sakes. Dolly's fears become reality when Lord Vaincrecourt declares his love, bids Agatha goodbye, then dies defending her honor against La Motte. Her husband quietly pleas for her compassion and companionship, and she unsentimentally agrees to live with him. The husband and wife concede that a long life of loneliness would be more fearful than a flawed but tolerable marriage. Later, Agatha learns that Dolly's wealthy, boorish husband has died and left Dolly a fortune; Dolly now devotes all her time and money to charitable works. The sudden introduction (and execution) of a visionary lord provides an absurd resolution. Nineteenth-century knights aside (Agatha even compares him to Arthur), the novel reflects two preoccupations, one of which would be sustained throughout Grand's career—the nature of woman's position in marriage as constituted by law and social practice. The second issue is particular to this novel: Grand considers then rejects a dream that still inspires feminist ideology, the power of women's love for one another to transcend the usual means of separating women, whether the division is caused by the men in their lives, the social class into which they marry, or by differences a culture defines as obstacles to women's mutual affection.

The first issue, the status of women in marriage, is taken up not only thematically but formally. The married woman's function as her husband's property is made literal; the protagonist is represented as fixed within domestic space and affixed to commodities. Studies of the period often define Victorian culture in explicitly material terms, as in Asa Briggs's *Victorian Things* (1988) or Thomas Richards's *The Commodity Culture of Victorian England: Advertising and Spectacle, 1851–1914* (1990).[13] The materiality of Victorian capitalism may have benefited the middle-class woman, but Grand's novel suggests that "things" also bore heavily upon such women. Like the material objects that form the mise-en-scène of the novel, the protagonist frequently functions as a domestic object signifying gender and class status. Agatha's name, which calls to mind the semiprecious stone agate, locates her as a valuable commodity within the Victorian middle-class gender system and in terms of Victorian marriage law. So intimately married are Agatha and her things—her rooms, furniture, decorations, jewelry, clothing, even flowers—that her moods, desires, and frustrations are projected onto changes in and changed relations toward those things rather than by means of conventional psychological markers of character development. Agatha's relation to elements of her setting acts as a feminine equivalent to the pathetic fallacy, a term that usually signifies the projection of feeling onto natural rather than domestic environs. Setting and character are so inextricable that even the passage of time, like changes in character, is expressed through the setting.

The novel opens and closes in the Oldhams's drawing room, a room that friends praise as one of the most inviting in London. As in Virginia Woolf's *To the Lighthouse,* the room is sentient. The fragmentary quality of the opening paragraph establishes a consciousness apart from human life:

> A sunny summer morning shining into a bright big room. Three broad French windows, wide open, showed a terrace descending by shallow steps into a high-walled garden. Over the terrace a bright striped awning sloped, while all about it, behind a balustrade decorated with

pots of flowers and foliage plants, easy wicker lounging chairs were scattered. (1)

The description of the room continues as the unidentified narrator emphasizes the loveliness of the room and the garden. The perspective then shifts to the table setting, and the husband and wife are introduced. After chapter 3, in which Agatha rebels against her husband (the afternoon of Dolly's visit), the novel breaks abruptly for several months. To emphasize the break, the opening of chapter 4 reproduces the effect of chapter 1. Again, the narrative begins from an unidentifiable perspective with the line "Autumn now." The narrator then describes debris blown into the garden, adding, "There had been storms within as well as without, and the result was quite as apparent to an intelligent observer." Here, however, the narrator provides a clue to the function of the setting. Alluding to the protagonist's name, the narrator explains:

> Our dwellings show the habit of our minds as the soft silk lining of a casket takes the form of the jewel it contains, and Agatha's own immediate surroundings had shown hers as she walked apart above the world in her habit of sweet thought and kindly consideration for others. (61–62)

Though this aside emphasizes the contaminating effect of a bad husband on a "good" wife (the name Agatha derives from the Greek word *agathe,* meaning "good"), an issue Grand turns to repeatedly during her career, the passage also underscores Agatha's position in the house as a possession. She lives in a world of ornaments, but she is not mistress of them. Instead, she herself is the prize gem adorning her husband's home. The ominous overtones of the word *casket* also echo a fear expressed earlier by Sir Alec that Agatha may commit suicide like her Aunt Judith. He compares Agatha to her aunt, who was "energetic, high-spirited, patient up to a certain point; but then, the devil." Creating emphasis through thematic repetition, Sir Alec painfully remembers, as he watches Agatha, that "Judith was generous, all fire and fearlessness; but Judith's life did not arrange itself to please her after she married the wrong man, and Judith was found dead in her bed one morning, killed by an overdose of chloral 'taken to relieve pain'" (24).

Unlike her aunt, Agatha does not literally die; however, her eventual rejection of Dolly, the only constant source of pleasure in her life, and the loss of Lord Vaincrecourt, immediately after her first fantasy of "ecstasy," suggest that she accepts death in life.[14] The opening of the novel is evoked again in chapter 10, just before Lord Vaincrecourt expresses his love and goes off to his death: "The Oldhams' large drawing-room again, and a very different scene" (237). The air is heavy and sultry, and gusts of hot wind presage another storm. Agatha plays the piano for Lord Vaincrecourt as her husband complacently looks on and the more observant Sir Alec fidgets. Once again the perspective shifts to the room:

> The decoration and arrangement of the room had also been restored to the simple, subdued, and costly elegance that had formerly distinguished it. The tawdry tambourines, ribbons, and meaningless draperies, the natural outcome of debasing influences [i.e., Dolly], had disappeared, and Agatha was outwardly herself again. (238–39)

Agatha's final acceptance of her position as an ornament, her willingness to be "outwardly herself again," anticipates her "death," after she rejects potential lovers to care for her now lonely and pathetic husband. In addition, the passage complicates interpretations of the setting, for the apparent moral connection between character and setting fails. Agatha is just as rebellious and resistant to her wifely role as before. Here, however, the setting provides the necessary social facade Agatha needs to hide adulterous fantasy and anarchic impulses. Her exploitation of the setting may suggest a secondary definition of *agate:* the term refers to glass made to appear as a marble, agate surface. We have no indication that Agatha has returned to her former, "innocent" self. She has merely learned her husband's hypocrisy. Like Grand herself during the writing of this book, Agatha yields to the form of the marriage plot, but this choice represents defeat, failure, and irresolution rather than success or closure.

Agatha's status as domestic commodity registers in her clothing as well as in her name and surroundings. Even more than home furnishings, the tiniest nuances of dress defined the social, economic, and "moral" character of the middle-class domestic woman, a point not lost on dress reformers. Philippe Perrot's history of nineteenth-century French dress, *Fashioning the Bourgeoisie,* describes the simultaneous cultural work of Victorian household possessions and clothing:

> Clothes became organized as significative differences within a code and as status symbols within a hierarchy. When this began to affect minds more or less alienated, "intention" and "motivation" in the matter of dress choice and behavior became a problem complicated by the universal semanticization of "utilitarian" objects and by the inevitable intermingling of use-values and sign-values.[15]

Valerie Steele investigates the specific uses and values of nineteenth-century clothing in Britain, America, and France in *Fashion and Eroticism: Ideals of Feminine Beauty from the Victorian Era to the Jazz Age* (1985). From women's magazines and books offering advice on women's fashion, Steele unearthed compelling evidence that designers, consumers, and spectators were well aware of the economic and erotic implications of dress. Steele notes that one commentator, Mary Haweis, argues in *The Art of Beauty* (1878) that dress is "the second self, a dumb self, yet a most eloquent expositor of the person . . . Dress bears the same relation to the body as speech does to the brain; and therefore dress may be called the speech of the body."[16] Self-consciousness about this telegraphic capacity of clothes was just as likely to make women feel nervous as empowered. As Haweis sees it: "It is almost appalling to think of all we may have implied in our dress without knowing it, for so many years. The mind almost quails before a new fashion, lest it should bear some construction contrary to our feelings."[17] Steele's claims are given additional force by Joel H. Kaplan and Sheila Stowell's account of theatrical clothing in *Theatre and Fashion: Oscar Wilde to the Suffragettes* (1995). Kaplan and Stowell show how costume changes were explicitly designed to imply female character development in two New Woman plays, Sydney Grundy's *The New Woman* (1894) and Arthur Wing Pinero's *The Notorious Mrs. Ebbsmith* (1895). Moreover, reviews that meticulously praised or abused details of costume similarly demonstrate critics' knowledge of fashion as a sign system.[18] Both Haweis's nervousness and Kaplan and Stowe's focus on the theatricality of clothing indicate one of fashion's consequences for women that Grand takes up in her novel. When women's fashion becomes art, the female mind-body inside the clothes is perceived at worst as a mannequin and at best as an object of art. In this circumstance the visual display of the female figure represents the tastefulness or vulgarity not so much of the woman as of the artwork's owner, her husband.

The novel teeters between two interpretations of Agatha's "costume changes." The changes register a protest against binding clothes that distort the female body to suit preposterous erotic tastes, but the changes also signal an ultimately useless attempt to protest the wife's function as the sign of her husband's status. In early descriptions of Agatha she affects classical dress, popularized in paintings by Lord Leighton, Alma Tadema, and others in the 1870s and 1880s.[19] All is in "perfect proportion"; "her dress was original . . . shaping itself to the symmetrical lines of her body as she moved . . . all was light, easy, and elegant; and therefore every movement of the unfettered limbs was graceful and unconstrained." She impresses those who see her as one who has "modest self-possession, purity, and health." The narrator pays particular attention to the color of her dress: "It was grey in colour, the softest grey of the sunset, and of that it might have made you think, for she wore a bunch of roses pinned high at the neck, which gave the requisite tinge of pink" (4). In the protagonist's home, her decor, her clothing,

and her bearing, she is an upper-middle-class lady whose refinement contrasts sharply with her husband's boorishness and dishonesty.

As Agatha rebels, she projects her licentiousness through the things—
the elements of the setting—that define her. For example, after she
befriends Dolly, Agatha unconsciously parodies the type of women her husband admires. Steele notes that throughout the century writers on female
fashion worried that "fashions were set by immoral women. If a woman
wanted to look fashionable, she ran the risk of looking immodest" in part
because "courtesans and members of the theatrical profession *were* among
the leaders of fashion."[20] While Steele notes this anxiety to emphasize that
Victorian women used dress to express rather than repress their eroticism,
her claims that "there does not seem to have been a clear distinction
between the clothing of the 'pure,' 'respectable,' 'maternal,' and 'domestic'
middle-class woman" and the woman who was "her sexual counter-ideal"
can also be used to argue that Victorian women who wished to be considered genteel would be likely to scrutinize their dress for distinctions that
would prevent any such confusion.[21] Dressing in imitation of her husband's
mistress, Agatha degenerates into a "tawdry" woman and an unpleasantly
asymmetrical art object:

> The gown she wore now was an unhealthy, degenerate descendant of
> a once rich red, and the very lines of her figure . . . had been deformed
> to the fashion of a vulgar age. She had the regulation small waist now,
> above which her bust bulged up and her shoulders expanded out of all
> proportion, while her arms stood away from her sides as if they had
> been attached too high to her figure. (64–65)

Obviously, Grand uses this negative example to promote "rational dress," a
cause that she publicly championed.[22] More abstractly, Agatha's clothing
emphasizes the grotesquerie of the constructed female form, a deformity
that replicates the deformities of the female character required by middle-
class society. Trapped in her private circle and prevented escape from her
domestic disappointments in work or education, Agatha resorts to futile,
visual gestures of resistance, such as dressing to accuse and humiliate her
husband. She willfully rebels against the fashion laws laid down in guides
such as *How to Dress Well:* "A married woman has to . . . dress not only to
please her husband, but also to reflect credit upon his choice."[23] Another
writer warns in *Etiquette of Good Society* that "there is no easier method by
which to detect the real lady from the sham one than by noticing her style
of dress. Vulgarity is readily distinguished, however costly and fashionable
the habiliments may be, by the breach of certain rules of harmony and
fitness."[24] Thus, Agatha uses her own vulnerability to objectification as a

means to shame her husband, but her dress also becomes a means of identifying herself with his lover.

In the final section Agatha's clothing reveals the erotic impulses that the restored respectability of her home suppresses. This costume change swaths her in the "long loose statuesque draperies" Steele calls "Aesthetic" and attributes to the influence of another group of artists, the Pre-Raphaelites.[25] This change promises a new day in contrast to the earlier description, which had compared her with the sunset: "It was the sunrise she had copied to-night, white and the tenderest grey, the first faint flush of rose and the palest blue." Her clothing accentuates rather than conceals or deforms her figure, as she plays seductive piano pieces for the man she wants to take as a lover: "The robe was cut low at the neck, and her arms were bare except for the only ornaments she wore, a rich gold bangle on each forearm above the wrist, chosen probably to accentuate the colour and roundness" (238). Ornamented as a female slave and imprisoned, once again, in her husband's drawing room, Agatha's clothing and ornaments articulate her anger and desires. When the men who own her—her husband and her relative, Sir Alec—leave, she asserts herself. Melodramatically, she informs Vaincrecourt that he loves her, plots her husband's death, then embraces her lover's pillow after he leaves her. Momentarily losing control, she thinks:

> In olden times a woman would have rid herself of such an incubus, and would have considered herself repaid with an hour of love. Love! She had never known love—pure passionate, ecstatic! . . . She buried her face in the cushion against which his head had rested, she kissed the spot passionately again and again, and then she clutched her hands and moaned. (261–62)

Other female New Women novelists and short story writers attempted to represent female sexual desire, in particular George Egerton and Olive Schreiner. Only a few of Grand's works, however, depict female sensuality as explicitly as this novel. The most forthright treatment occurs in the short story "An Emotional Moment" in which a jaded female playwright loses her conservative lover after telling him of a past passion that ended as soon as requited.[26] And here sexual desire carries heavy moral baggage; the libidinous female character's passionate heterosexual longings incite criminal schemes.

Though less melodramatic than this scene of heterosexual desire, the subtle rendering of passion between the two women friends offers a portrait of quietly erotic affection far more threatening to the marriage plot than Agatha's heterosexual histrionics. The delightful unexpectedness of a wife and a mistress sidestepping their potential obstacle to friendship, the shared husband/lover, to form their own loving relationship invokes the same reaction from the female reader that Virginia Woolf famously described in *A Room of One's Own*. Reading Mary Carmichael's *Life's Adventures,* Woolf is astounded by the words "Chloe liked Olivia," a clause that appears in the midst of a fairly conventional romance plot. As Woolf marvels in the often-cited passage:

> First she broke the sentence; now she has broken the sequence . . . All these relationships between women, I thought, rapidly recalling the splendid gallery of fictitious women, are too simple. So much has been left out, unattempted. And I tried to remember any case in the course of my reading where two women are represented as friends.[27]

Like Chloe and Olivia, Dolly and Agatha form an intimate friendship despite every possible impediment, and in their relationship more than anywhere else in her fiction Grand represents female eroticism and affection within a female friendship as an alternative to heroic individualism or heterosexuality. The vitality of this relationship contrasts sharply with the lifelessness of Agatha's existence within her husband's domain. Lillian Faderman, Carroll Smith-Rosenberg, and Martha Vicinus have written at length of forms of intimacy between nineteenth-century women friends, including a kind of love that Faderman calls "romantic friendship" and that today could be called "lesbian," and Sally Ledger provides a helpful analysis of developments in sexology and medical literature that eventually pathologized such friendships, even going so far as to argue that one potentially useful consequence of the categories that emerged was to make conscious lesbian identity possible.[28] The centuries of poetry, love letters, diary entries, and clinical reports collected in Faderman's anthology, *Chloe Plus Olivia* (1994), provide ample evidence of a textual as well as social history of lesbian intimacy.[29] Moreover, a number of earlier novels by male writers, including Honoré de Balzac's *Girl with the Golden Eye* (1835), Théophile Gautier's *Mademoiselle du Maupin* (1835), Sheridan Le Fanu's "Carmilla," (1872) and later novels by women, such as Arabella Kenealy's *Dr. Janet of Harley Street* (1893), Mary Cholmondeley's *Red Pottage* (1899), and *Diana Victrix* (1897) by the American Florence Converse, demonstrate that the woman-identified woman, however defined by late Victorians, was not invisible in the 1890s. I have found no evidence that Grand was consciously aware of, much less sympathetic to, lesbian subcultures or couples in England or France, but the work of cultural historians like Faderman, Vicinus, and Smith-Rosenberg, among others, convincingly argues that, while overtly sexual relations between women may have been limited, covert, even unknowable in a late-twentieth-century sense, romantic friendship was a pervasive part of even the most conventional Victorian women's culture.[30]

Ann Ardis gets at the problem of insisting particular relationships are lesbian in New Woman novels in her discussion of the homoeroticism of three novels, Edith Johnstone's *A Sunless Heart* (1894), Mary Cholmondely's *Red Pottage* (1899), and Gertrude Dixie's *The Image-Breakers* (1900):

> For one, no male-female relationship is as supportive as the bonding depicted between women in these novels. In all three, a relationship that appears to be peripheral to the main plot line eventually displaces the central male-female dynamic that had seemed to be the dominant interest in the novel. Equally significant, the bonding between women figured in these novels is homoerotic without being lesbian in the conventional sense of that term.[31]

Even so, in *A Domestic Experiment* Grand is unusually frank in depicting the pleasures and the potential explosiveness of a friendship that veers toward the woman-identified pole of Adrienne Rich's lesbian continuum before Agatha retreats to the other end of the continuum into heterosexual misery.[32]

Both Agatha and Dolly depend on men for their livelihood and at times for their amusement; however, the intimacy of the two women provides a haven of trust and affection more dependable than that provided by their relationships with men. The narrator sympathetically registers their mutual affection in the women's forthright discussions of their pasts and their hostility toward men as well as in their love for one another. Though Agatha is by far the more beautiful, talented, and intelligent, Dolly is in some ways more appealing. Originally, Agatha forms her friendship with Dolly both to teach her husband a lesson and to take vicarious, cynical pleasure in Dolly's jabs at society. Ultimately, however, she learns to admire Dolly's generosity and open-heartedness, to respect her good-humored exploitation of the men who wish to exploit her, and to pity the effects wrought by the disastrous marriage arranged for Dolly by her mother while Dolly was too young to protest. During the height of their friendship, in fact, Dolly appears more admirable than Agatha, for Dolly's defenses are callous but not cruel or calculated:

> The evil in her was all on the surface—it was the scum which had collected in an unhappy home. Agatha herself in the same surroundings would have become cold and hard, but Dolly was not to be embittered. Her nature was bright and pleasure-loving; she was born to be

happy, but since happiness was denied her she had tried excitement, its
perilous substitute, and excitement had answered for a time. (67)

Refreshingly, although Agatha improves Dolly, she never completely
"reforms" her. Instead, Agatha, who appears to be the moral and intellectual superior, falls far short of Dolly's integrity and loyalty.

A vengeful La Motte tests Dolly's loyalty to Agatha by threatening to
blackmail Dolly with a note he assumes she has written to Paul, unless Dolly
helps to ruin Agatha's character. This scene is important not only for the
light it throws on Dolly and Agatha's relationship but also for the suspicion
between the sexes that the incident accentuates. When Dolly turns the
tables on La Motte by inviting him to read the note aloud, he passes the letter to Sir Alec, Lord Vaincrecourt, and Paul Oldham. Each refuses to read
it, automatically assuming Dolly's guilt though admiring her self-sacrifice
for Agatha. Infuriated by their suspicion, Agatha bursts out: "Oh! how hate-
ful you men are, all of you! . . . How dare you believe her guilty, and stand
there condemning her in your hearts, without a word of proof!" (225). To
the alarm of the men she then proceeds to read the letter aloud:

> MY OWN DEAREST,—I have just got home and changed my dress, and
> now I feel quite fresh. I shall never forget last night; it was the happiest
> of my life. My old man is going on a long journey on Monday; do
> arrange to be here with me as much as possible during his absence, and
> if you can stay all night, all the better. I can't express myself as you do,
> but believe me I love you dearly, and I am a different woman since you
> loved me.—Ever your own
>
> DOLLY

As the men raise eyebrows at one another, Agatha bursts into laughter,
"'You wretched little Dolly! . . . will you never be cured of your tricks?
Why . . . this is my letter. She wrote it to me . . . What a joke! She stayed
with me that night you spent at Brighton, Paul, and we had a long talk
about—oh, about everything'——" (227). Blinded by masculinist and heterosexist assumptions, the men can only construe the letter as evidence of
infidelity and can only imagine infidelity as heterosexual adultery.

The long sequence of dashes in the text that eclipses Dolly and Agatha's
conversation, leaving the "unnamed" unknown, may be the most revolutionary moment in Grand's shifting negotiations with the marriage plot.
Though Grand probably could not define Agatha and Dolly's friendship so
precisely, our vision of this alternative to marriage promises the most sincere, healthy, generous, honest, and trusting relation in the novel.

Sadly, when Dolly warns Agatha of the danger that only she is loving, perceptive, and attentive enough to see, which is Agatha's growing attraction to Vaincrecourt, Agatha angrily rejects Dolly's friendship. Frightened by her own feelings and resolutely denying their implications, Agatha can only flee Dolly's voice of truth. Ignoring Dolly's concerned pleas that she be honest with herself, Agatha storms out, leaving the person dearest to her. In this scene Dolly collapses into a chair, foreshadowing Agatha's pose and actions after Vaincrecourt leaves her: "'Guinevere going to her doom!' thought Dolly; and then she threw herself into a chair, covered her face with her hands, and moaned—'She is lost—lost—oh, heaven! And I alone am to blame for it'" (236). The love affair between Agatha and Dolly, whatever forms it takes, offers the best hope for happy escape from the institutions of Victorian society that imprison women. One wonders whether the power of such friendships threatened Grand in some way, for, although her fiction frequently portrays communities of supporters of women, groups that include women working together but which often also include sympathetic men, never again do the novels dramatize such a powerful private relationship between women.

The power of this friendship is again emphasized in a secondhand report of Dolly's later life. Agatha drifts into a futile, destructive romance, abandoning all her dreams of improving life for the poor or finding a life's work for herself. Dolly, on the other hand, fulfills the promise of the woman she loved, opening a home for retired servants and devoting her time and money to their care. Thus, the successful female character finds an alternative to the marriage plot in a life of service to other women. (This is also the solution offered in a later novel, *Ideala*.) Agatha finally and perversely steels herself to a stoic friendship with her husband, a relationship they both understand to be a failure, and she does so only to live up to the impossibly heroic ideals of her dead lover. (She literally turns from the lover's body to her pleading husband in the last sentences of the novel.) While neither Agatha nor Dolly explicitly questions the conditions that make their marriages so dreary, the novel argues for their misery through their actions, through the formal fixing of Agatha within the setting and properties of her house, and through the grim conclusion to the novel in which the one path to happiness—female intimacy—fails, due to the interference of the real power figures in the world of the novel, the men.

As Grand moved from *A Domestic Experiment* to *Singularly Deluded,* she also turned from domestic drama to masculinist fantasy. Fleeing the doll's house of the drawing room, the female protagonist of *Singularly Deluded* romps across heaths, oceans, and countries on the trail of an errant husband. Rather than attempting an analysis of marriage in the realistic vein, as in *A Domestic Experiment, Singularly Deluded* dramatizes the fears, angers, resentments, desires, and capabilities of women through fantastic events, emblematic vignettes, and character doubling. The novel also indicates that Grand read the literary market astutely. Her attempts to exploit popular rather than highbrow literary forms suggest attention to the tastes of a mass market and a willingness to use popular forms to communicate her discontent with the position of Victorian middle-class women.

As the novel opens, Mr. Leslie Sommers, his wife, and his young son are vacationing at the seashore so that he can recover from his stressful career as an eminent London barrister. His disorder manifests itself as domestic tyranny: "long periods of depression from which nothing would arouse him, and the succeeding fits of irritability when it was not only impossible to please him, but to move without making him angry" (3). As the family relaxes on the heath, Mr. Sommers plays with a piece of rope; his son chases butterflies, and his wife leans against a telegraph pole near railroad tracks. As they chat, Sommers "playfully" winds the rope around his wife and the telegraph pole "till she stood pinioned like a victim tied to a stake" (14). At first the wife finds this amusing; soon, however, she notices her husband has wandered off, catches sight of him striding purposefully away across the heath, and realizes her child is playing on the tracks. After hours of watching her child miraculously survive the passing of two trains, she is rescued by a stranger, Dr. Mansell. They conclude that her husband's exhaustion has caused a temporary mental disorder, a theory borne out when they learn that her husband bought a train ticket, using the name Laurence Soames, and left for Southampton. With the help of the doctor, his employer Lord Wartlebury, and her sister-in-law, the wife sets off on a search that takes her to London, Southampton, Jersey, St. Malo, Mont St. Michel, and Malta. Finally, Lord Wartlebury lures "Soames" onto his yacht, and Gertrude is shocked to find that he is exactly who he says he is. Stunned, she returns home to her son, where she finds her true husband anxiously awaiting her.

Though the event that motivates Gertrude's plot, her "imprisonment," may seem improbable, this sequence powerfully dramatizes the psychological reversals necessary for a female adventure. The "bonds" of matrimony are made literal when Sommers imprisons his wife, and the "playful" husband reveals himself to be the villain of Gothic melodrama.[33] Moreover, the stark contrast between the pleasant family outing and the description of the woman not only as a victim but as being tied at the stake—in punishment? as a sacrifice?—illuminates the contrast between the public, social lives and the secrets of Victorian women who were not happy with the roles they inhabited. This contrast motivates the wife's quick dismissal of her husband (and the conventions of domestic fiction) after he vanishes: "the impulse to struggle and cry was over, and she drew herself up against the post, and looked about her, a changed woman in these few minutes, in a changed world!" (16). In this changed world the reality of her husband recedes as quickly as the man himself, a point the narrator emphasizes: "And it was strange that during all this time she never once thought of her husband" (27). When "the wife" finally does escape her bonds, through the agency of Dr. Mansell, she also escapes the restraints of Victorian womanhood; the "changed world" she enters is the world usually inhabited only by men, the world of action and adventure. Almost immediately after her escape, Mrs. Sommers demonstrates the changes in herself as she prepares to enter the transformed world. Up until this point the narrator has described the woman only in terms of her function: she marries at eighteen; she puzzles over her husband's ill temper; she feeds and dresses her child. After the woman escapes her bonds, however, she develops into an individuated character.

Adventure fiction encompasses a spectrum of male characters—soldiers, sailors, explorers, castaways, runaways, colonists—although the plot has been described as formulaic. In *Dreams of Adventure, Deeds of Empire* Martin Green attempts to delineate the parameters of Victorian adventure fiction:

> In general, adventure seems to mean a series of events, partly but not wholly accidental, in settings remote from the domestic and probably from the civilized (at least in the psychological sense of remote), which constitute a challenge to the central character. In meeting the challenge, he/she performs a series of exploits which make him/her a hero, eminent in virtues such as courage, fortitude, cunning, strength, leadership, and persistence.[34]

While Green's inclusive pronouns promise that the genre could accommodate female as well as male characters, his examples all focus on male protagonists. John G. Cawelti's characterization of the adventure "formula" offers one explanation: "the hero frequently receives, as a kind of side benefit, the favors of one or more attractive young ladies. The interplay with the villain and the erotic interests served by attendant damsels are more in the nature of frosting on the cake."[35] Paul Zweig is even more explicit. He claims adventurers must flee women in order to reinvent themselves as men.[36] Implicitly, Green agrees, insightfully arguing that adventure fiction becomes a debased form at the same time that the domestic or courtship novel asserts its cultural authority because the later could carry "key values of the ruling mercantile caste, and at the same time protest against the crudest expansive thrusts of the modern system—including imperialism and adventure."[37] Lyn Pykett's *Engendering Fictions* and Elaine Showalter's *Sexual Anarchy* show that beginning in the 1880s the increasing number of these adventure novels is evidence that male writers were fighting to wrest "the novel" from both writers in the French naturalism vein and popular women writers of romance by displacing both with "King Romance." These romantic novels of adventure were explicitly addressed to a male audience, or as Stevenson and Kipling were wont to say, to boys large and small.[38] In attempting to feminize the genre, Grand faced not only gender incredulity but also marketing problems. Yet, because her first successes at publishing had been in the children's magazine *Aunt Judy's*,[39] she was willing to accept critical sneers and marginalization as a novelist for adolescents if the tradeoff would be the financial reward that accrued to adventure novelists like H. Rider Haggard, Robert Louis Stevenson, R. M. Ballantyne, George Borrow, George Henty, and Rudyard Kipling or to novelists who focused on the urban adventurer, the detective.

The oddities of Mrs. Sommers's reaction and the events that follow point to the difficulties of inserting female characters in masculinist plots during historical moments in which gender difference relentlessly constrains fictional probabilities. The tension is registered, in part, in very practical terms: an old-fashioned heroine needs a new wardrobe to be a New Woman. As Marjorie Garber notes in *Vested Interests: Cross-Dressing and Cultural Anxiety:* "Cross-dressing is a classic strategy of disappearance in detective fiction. The lady vanishes by turning into a man—or the man by turning into a woman."[40] Though Garber refers to criminals attempting to escape detection, her comment illuminates Mrs. Sommers's transformation as she prepares to seek her husband. Capitalizing upon the success not only of the adventurer and the male detective but also of other popular Victorian female detective figures such as the policewoman Mrs. Gladden in Andrew Forrester's *The Female Detective* (1864); Wilkie Collins's amateur sleuth, Valeria Macallan, in *The Law and the Lady* (1875); Milton Danvers's detective-wife, who appeared in a series of 1890s novels; or George R. Sims's *Dorcas Dene, Detective* of the late 1890s, among many others, Grand loosely fuses the detective and the adventurer into a figure of literary transvestism.[41] The genre play was not lost on the reviewer for the *Critic* who explains that the heroine must "play detective with a delightfully Fortunatus purse and a *flair* for clews such has made famous the heroes of Gaborieau or Miss Green."[42]

Grand's cross-genre experiment may also owe something to the most famous female cross-dresser of the nineteenth century, George Sand. In this respect *Singularly Deluded* anticipates *The Heavenly Twins,* a novel that prominently features a female cross-dresser. Like George Sand, Mrs. Sommers is a study in the simultaneity of genders. The narrator describes her

from the perspective of her male sidekicks, who are surprised by the transformation in her appearance once she is attired in a practical, manly fashion
appropriate to her new role as adventurer:

> The two gentlemen found her dressed in a plain dark travelling cos-
> tume, ready for any emergency. Her hair was bound round her head in
> thick dark glossy coils, which looked as if they had been arranged less
> for ornament than for neatness, which would last out a long journey
> should she be obliged to take one. Her manner was cool, composed,
> and resolute; her face, pale; her eyes, unnaturally bright, but steady . . .
> she was interesting in appearance and intellectual, two lasting charms
> which a man like Lord Wartlebury would appreciate at once, and pre-
> fer to mere animal beauty, however striking. (43–44)

Though the narrator certainly acknowledges her femininity, the passage
invokes the codes of the strong, silent *man* of action not only in her masculine dress and the binding of her hair (in contrast with the flowing locks traditionally associated with femininity, particularly with female sexuality) but
also in her controlled demeanor. The character may be one of the subjects
wildly parodied in Eliza Lynn Linton's protest against the "bearded chin, the
bass voice, flat chest and lean hips of a woman who has failed in her physical development."[43] Like the man of action and the Holmesian cerebral
detective, she is composed, determined, able, and, most important—given
Grand's own sense of herself as a would-be novelist—intelligent. At the
same time, she retains her femininity. Like other fictional female detectives
of the period, she is motivated by the need of a family member rather than
by her own pleasure or curiosity. Nevertheless, although she accepts men's
assistance, Mrs. Sommers does not degenerate from heroism to heroinism.
Discussing the situation, she speaks "in a steady, self-contained, almost busi-
ness-like tone, which betrayed strong feeling enough, but without a symptom of tears or hysterics" (45). This capable demeanor disturbed one critic
more than the cross-dressing. Defending the book against charges of
"intrinsic improbability," a *Spectator* reviewer notes:

> the two things that are the greatest tax upon credulity in the whole
> book are her extraordinary power of endurance in keeping on as she
> did at high-pressure without breaking down—which not one woman
> in a thousand could have done—and her having been so sanguine as to
> imagine that there was still a possible chance of a Judgeship for a per-
> son mentally afflicted as she supposed Mr. Somers [*sic*] to be.[44]

The husband/wife and hero/heroine reversals are fully accomplished and
sustained during the next three-fourths of the novel. Without explanation
the narrator begins to call Mrs. Sommers by the only name that is truly her

own, Gertrude, and Gertrude becomes the hero of a series of adventures. Learning that her husband has crossed the channel, she follows, but her steamer catches fire, and she calmly leads women and children to safety. Throughout the series of episodes she is a veritable transportation engineer, arranging cabs, trains, steamers, carriages, hotels, and baggage, triumphing over unscrupulous minor characters, the general suspicion of a woman traveling alone, and repeated near-misses as she tracks her husband.

Despite Gertrude's difficulties, she delights in her skill, her intellect, her increasing knowledge, and the sheer freedom of movement so often denied to women:

> Gertrude's anxiety had given way now to a state of excitement that was almost pleasurable. She was on the right track sure enough, and this detective business was easier, after all, than she could have believed possible. She could understand, too, that it must be a very fascinating pursuit when the object of it did not concern you personally. She thought, if she ever had to work for herself, she would be a detective, it was quite interesting to talk to so many queer characters. (83)

Gertrude's musings help to explain what the heroine seeks as hero. By definition the adventurer and the detective must travel alone and unhindered. Only the female detective could take pride in being a woman of the streets—whether as an urban flaneuse or an international explorer.[45] In addition to freedom of movement, a second pleasure Gertrude seeks later motivates all of Grand's New Women protagonists: Gertrude desires knowledge. The "detective business" grants the detective unlimited access to secrets of all kinds and justifies questions, demands, and revelations.[46]

In proportion to Gertrude's heroic ascent her husband embarrassingly falls. In Grand's later novels, written just before or after her separation from her husband, unworthy husbands are carefully analyzed by their wives, by outsiders, and by "society," either in the guise of the narrator or a character who sympathizes with "the Cause." While she was writing this novel, however, Grand still lived with her husband. The psychological doubling of Gertrude's husband and the man she pursues (she believes him to be suffering a temporary mental collapse in the form of amnesia combined with a delusion) powerfully damns the husband Grand may have been trying to protect. Whereas Leslie Sommers is reputed to be a distinguished barrister and a model husband and father, Gertrude's object, who calls himself Lawrence Soames, leaves scandal in his wake. Each time Gertrude speaks with someone who has seen her husband, she hears more horrifying reports of his drinking, cursing, gambling, and debaucheries. One hotel clerk asks if the man she seeks has "a rowdy, rollicking, free-and-easy sort o' happy-go-lucky manner? Drinks brandies-and-sodas all the time, and was sweet on the barmaid" (86). Another clerk mentions his "freshness" (106), and in Mont St. Michel her driver hears that "he has damned the dinner, the wine, the house, the high-tide—everything, in fact, and everybody" (183). Gertrude grows increasingly unnerved at the thought of achieving her purpose as she imagines living with such a man even as she unhesitatingly assumes this *is* the same man she has known for years. Her fears only increase when "Soames" is lured onto Lord Wartlebury's yacht, and she waits for Dr. Mansell and Lord Wartlebury to prepare him to meet her.

The doctor's prognosis confirms what previous reports have suggested. A slyly comic portrait of a politician, Soames suffers from the delusion that he will be a consul working in San Francisco, and he displays a profound loss of both dignity and "self-control" (225). The doctor puzzles:

> He suffered from a perversion of tastes . . . and a radical change of tone . . . He had a craving for drink, and would never have been sober could he have got the liquor; and what he liked best was to gamble all day long. He did not care with whom he played—the novel Earl, his host, or the stoker, it was all one to him . . . Had Dr. Mansell met him casually he would have set him down as an uncultured man of low tastes, with a good brain much weakened by dissipation and drink. (224–27)

The doctor's evaluation, combined with the information Gertrude has unearthed, suggests that what makes her husband frightening, embarrassing, repulsive, in fact mad, is merely the predictable behavior we would today ascribe to the type, "the good old boy." The alleged Leslie Sommers does not steal, kill, or even assault anyone; he simply acts out conventional, slightly seedy pleasures that would have been tolerated in an upper-class man by all but the most puritanical of his peers. Implicitly, then, the novel equates maleness with madness in a witty reversal of the equation between female and madness traced by Susan Gilbert and Sandra Gubar, Elaine Showalter, or Janet Oppenheim.[47] This passage also suggests that transgressions of social class as well as gender might be read as signs of madness, for Soames's willful disregard of class distinctions disturbs the doctor as much as his profligacy disturbs Gertrude.

When Gertrude finally meets Soames/Sommers face-to-face, we learn that appearances are not always deceiving. Soames is indeed the "same-as," but the same as he seems—a lower-middle-class consul headed for San Francisco. When Gertrude screams and her sister-in-law exclaims "What does it all mean?" Soames sarcastically turns the tables: "Well, it means . . . so far as I can make it out, that I've got among a set of staring—lunatics" (239). From Soames's point of view he is the one who has been duped, first by being held on Lord Wartlebury's yacht under false pretenses and second by being charged with insanity. (Since neither the doctor nor Lord Wartlebury had ever seen Sommers, they had accepted Gertrude's claim that Soames is the name Sommers has adopted as a part of his delusion). Soames abuses everyone roundly, more or less blackmails the earl into promoting his career, and demands an unlimited supply of champagne until they reach port. From Gertrude's perspective the search was futile; she turns the case over to professional detectives. The *Spectator* reviewer draws the flat-footed moral, "do not trust to amateur detectives when you want to trace what has become of a missing person."[48] From our vantage point, however, the novel pictures the exciting world of adventure known to so few nineteenth-century women, while it also projects masculinity from a feminine point of view. In Grand's later novels she carefully examines the social conditions that produce masculinity and femininity; here she dramatizes what she will later analyze.

The conclusion of the novel explains Leslie's absence, and his experiences provide perhaps an even more formidable indictment of the power relations between a wife and husband. Whereas Gertrude had cross-gendered and cross-genred her way into the terrain of the adventure and detective novels, her husband stumbles into the maze of the feminized genre of Gothic romance, where he is literally held prisoner by a "deaf-mute, amiable, ignorant, and semi-imbecile" shepherd (247–48) but where he also seems, in terms of fictional form, to be trapped in the role of the besieged Gothic heroine.[49] Leslie explains that, after leaving his family on the heath, he fell through a heavily overgrown bank of heath into a deep pit, where he lay unconscious for hours. He awoke to find himself in a shepherd's hut. Crippled by a dislocated ankle, Leslie had remained a prisoner of the shepherd for about ten days. He finally escaped by crawling several miles back to their cottage.

In a bizarre, fantastic play of Grand's imagination Leslie is imprisoned in the role of womanhood, even "wife," while his wife escapes into the role of hero, which is usually reserved for men, or perhaps more daringly into a full, uninhibited expression of herself, Gertrude. On the day that Gertrude's adventure begins and in a passage charged with female eroticism, the narrator records her impressions as she watches the sun on the heath:

> And on a day like this, too, everything was throbbing with an answering throb to the heat of the summer sun, glowing responsive to his ardent kiss; the whole broad bosom of the heath outspread, as it were, a thymy couch for him to rest upon, warmed into life and rapture by

his rays, and uttering, in the joy of his caress, a low, varied, blissful, inarticulate sob of deep ecstatic pleasure. (11)

The corporeality and sexual effusion of the heath prepare the reader for the mysterious events that Leslie narrates after he and Gertrude are reunited. After Leslie abandoned his wife, he fell through "a perfect jungle-growth of weed and fern" into "a sort of gully or rift in the heath, the presence of which nothing indicated until you were in it" (244–45). Plunged into this vaginal enclosure, Leslie lost consciousness and wakened to find himself the powerless prisoner of the shepherd.

Leslie Sommers's captivity dramatizes the most painful dynamics of even loving marriages, for it is the shepherd's longing for company and companionship that transforms the pathetic creature into a benevolent despot. While Soames seems a caricature of masculinity in his misconduct, the shepherd may be a burlesque of masculinity in its alien physicality. As Leslie characterizes the shepherd to Gertrude, he speaks from his new feminine perspective, emphasizing the distortions of maleness as they might first appear to the uninitiated female eye. His description is embedded in popularizations of Darwinian evolutionary theory reinforced by primitivism, anticipating Grand's later fictional investigation of eugenics:[50]

> It was a man apparently, but he was more like a huge monkey. He had short misshapen legs, long body, broad at the shoulders, with great depth of chest betokening strength, abnormally long arms upon which the muscles stood up suggestively, and small grizzled head looking out of all proportion to the rest of the body, with close-cropped hair standing up on end all over it as a monkey's grows. (245)

Ironically, Leslie expects when "the creature" turns that he will be confronted with a monster. Instead, he views "a sensitive expressive mouth and a pair of soft brown eyes, speaking and pathetic as a stag's." Moreover, the shepherd's expression is vaguely intelligent and entirely "gentle and caressing" (246). Gradually, Leslie realizes that his captor, like Mary Shelley's monster in *Frankenstein* or Emily Brontë's brooding Healthcliff, is motivated by loneliness, affection, and the desire to possess another. He refuses to understand Leslie's hand signals or drawings only when they communicate the prisoner's desire to escape. Kindness becomes cruelty as personified in the shepherd's husband-like assumption that he knows best and that he has the right to exert control and possessive protection over a being who has no other means of survival. In this picture we have one of Grand's most bizarre but most stirring representations of the strangely mingled exercise of kindness and cruelty, protection and privilege, affection and suppression, that characterized marriage within a culture that privileged men's rights. The simultaneous sympathy and repulsion the shepherd inspires implicitly argues that the dynamics of marriage would pose one of the greatest obstacles to changes in gender relations and to progress toward women's desires and rights, balking women's desires to form alternative sexual, affectional, professional, or legal identities and relationships apart from or even in concert with heterosexual marriage.

The action and energy of such a plot sets *Singularly Deluded* apart from most nineteenth-century women's fiction; Gertrude's adventure is not confined to the family circle or the society of a drawing room. Nonetheless, in her character's struggles and triumphs Grand foreshadows the central drama of the New Woman fiction that follows: the exposure and eventual disintegration of the marriage plot.

Grand's early novels suggest the excitement and energy that fired the public to read New Woman novel after New Woman novel. Grand addresses topics that titillated some, outraged others, and probably intimidated a good many readers: domestic abuse, adultery, the relations between sex and class, "fallenness," the nature of women's relationships, women's anger, and women's determination. Moreover, her early novels challenge readers not only thematically but formally. Like other New Woman writers, she twisted and turned the structures of fiction with which her readers were familiar to fashion narrative strategies and forms through which she might articulate her own discontent, frustration, fears, half-formed questions, and constantly evolving analyses of women's lives in the last years of the nineteenth century. These novels also convey a sense of skepticism and a consciously revolutionary stance, even here, at the outset of her career.

Chapter 3

The Marriage Plot and the Male Narrator

"The anonymous author of *Ideala,*" wrote a critic for the *Saturday Review* in 1888,

> describes his or her work as a Study from Life. Without departing widely either from accuracy or from the character of the phrase selected by the author, we might describe it as a modest essay in Naturalism, using that word in the modern French sense. It is the story of a nasty-minded woman. It is unhappily the fact that there are some nasty-minded women about—not counting those who do not prate about their "purity." They are noisy out of all proportion to their numbers, and odious out of all proportion to their noise.[1]

Success in the literary arena, in the case of Grand and many other New Women novelists, had to be read between the lines of rejection and condemnation, and the publication history of *Ideala* testifies to Grand's determination. From 1881 until 1883 she searched doggedly for a publisher. A writer for the *Woman's Signal* offers an intriguing, angry analysis of the gatekeeping function of press readers: "The tone of superiority affected by some of them, as I flip through those grim letters of refusal, read in the light of to-day like the lines of a farce."[2] The writer claims that George Allen, Ruskin's publisher, was prepared to take the book if Ruskin approved. Instead, Ruskin "used his giant strength after reading only a few pages of the manuscript which has since borne its writer to fame, and pettishly scribbling on it that he 'didn't like the title' and 'couldn't bear queer people, however, nice,'" to reject the novel.[3] Grand gave up hope and put the novel away. Many years later she recalled:

> Both *Ideala* and *The Tenor and the Boy* were written in Warrington, when my husband was serving there at the Regimental Depot. I suffered terribly from want of encouragement; it was a black time . . . I was thrown back for years . . . *Ideala* was put away in a drawer for seven

years . . . I determined to print it myself . . . It made, to me, an astonishing literary sensation.[4]

Despite her discouragement, in 1888 she did print the novel, anonymously
and at her own expense. She later explained in a letter to Frederick Henry
Fisher that she chose to remain anonymous because "my husband had a gt.
dislike to having his name associated with my ideas."[5] She was amply
rewarded for the financial risk. E. W. Allen, a London publisher, marketed
a yellow-back paperback for three shillings and sixpence;[6] it sold well
enough to encourage Richard Bentley, who had earlier rejected the manuscript, to print a second, more durable edition. During 1889 the novel was
reprinted three times.[7]

   Being Grand's first novel to condemn conventional marriage practices
openly, *Ideala* marked a significant turn in her personal as well as professional fortunes: she abandoned her marriage and her biological son and
entered the literary arena. The 1882 Married Woman's Property Act guaranteed Grand rights to the receipts of the novel, and by 1890 the sales from
Ideala permitted Grand to leave her husband. A letter dated 9 April 1890
indicates that she and her stepson were living in a "temporary abode" at 24
Sinclair Road in Kensington; she later moved to 60 Wynnstay Gardens in
the same neighborhood.[8]

   Ideala launched the trilogy of novels that includes Grand's two best-
known works, *The Heavenly Twins* (1893) and *The Beth Book* (1897). The
principal setting of each, a cathedral town called Morningquest, reworked
the landscape of Norwich and its surrounding countryside. Grand's comments about her uses of the setting illustrate her desire to couch social problems in the particular, local details associated with realism. In a 1923 letter to
Walter Powell, Grand explains: "It was Norwich. I invented the chime and
placed the Tenor's cottage on the site of the house which was occupied
. . . when I lived in Norwich. I have also introduced a Castle dominating
the city, but otherwise the descriptions are as accurate as I could make
them."[9] The novels employ a range of narrative techniques and plots, but
they share, in addition to the setting, a host of characters and an array of topical and thematic issues: the double sexual standard, the inadequacies of the
marriage contract, the dangers of the separate spheres theory of gender relations, domestic abuse, venereal disease, prostitution, and women's socialization, psychology, and rights.

   In its own distinctive fashion each novel weaves these topics into a critique of the conventions of the marriage plot, training presumed female
audiences in the art of reading then rewriting those conventions as a preliminary, literary, step toward marriage reform. *Ideala* establishes the crucial

problem for progressive women. How does one begin to tell women's experiences, or a "woman's story," from a female character's perspective and to women readers when the available shapes, forms, narrative structures, and speakers are generated from and reinforce a masculine position of cultural privilege? The friction between masculine and feminine perspectives on "reality" register in *Ideala* as a problem of narration. A central male character, Lord Dawne, is identified as the narrator; however, muted alternative perspectives raise questions about the limits of his understanding. Authority becomes detached from comprehension, an untethering that leaves gender hierarchies intact while making space for feminine experiences that the narrator misses, ignores, misunderstands, or resists. The voices of two female characters, Ideala and Lord Dawne's sister Claudia, interject this alternative knowledge. In discrete textual moments the first-person narration is fissured by narrative disturbances arising when the details of women's lives interrupt the male character's characterizations and interpretations. This disjuncture becomes the present absence, the subject rather than the secret, in Grand's next novel, *The Heavenly Twins*. There the fates of three female protagonists are dependent upon their learning not only to read critically but also to transfer the interpretive skills of astute reading to the circumstances around them. Unlike the protagonist in *Ideala,* in the later novel characters learn to "read" the patriarchal assumptions that adhere in their culture's understanding of gender and in gendering institutions such as the family, schools, religion, and ultimately the social institution of marriage, because they have learned first to read books by men. In the process of reading *The Heavenly Twins,* the audience is guided toward critical, comparative, resistant reading strategies by the repetition and variation of female experiences structuring the triple plots. Finally, in *The Beth Book* the trilogy takes a step further by shifting its focus from the process of reading culture to the act of producing it, a goal shared by women writers and suffrage leaders alike. In creating Beth, a fictional "genius" who commands language in both its written and spoken forms, Grand authorizes an imaginative space of choice, freedom, and change that she, like other writers who assume continuity between fictional and "real" worlds, believed was the foundation from which actual social change could be first fantasized then initiated.

The chronological progression of Grand's trilogy suggests that before women could invent a new world for new women, even in fiction, they would have to map the contours and boundaries of the old world. Therefore, while the protagonist of *Ideala* is ostensibly the young, intelligent, artistic Ideala, the real *subject* of the novel is less "Ideala" herself than the "feminine" as it is projected by three male characters. The conflict between the two—the character as constituted by her actions versus the character as idealized by an unreliable narrator—is anticipated by the preface, presumably spoken in the voice of "the author," though not signed. The preface warns readers that, apart from vicious gossips and harsh judges, even "the best of us, and the best intentioned among us . . . are apt to make some one trait in the character, some one trick in the manners, some one incident in the lives of people we meet the text of an objection to the whole person" (vii). Armed with this admonition, the audience is encouraged to read the novel in a way that repudiates the implications of Ideala's name, that is, not in search of static ideals but in nonjudgmental appreciation of "not a perfect, but a transitional state." Ideala's opinions, warns the preface, are "the mere effervescence of a strong mind in a state of fermentation" (v). The preface thereby puts the reader somewhat at odds with the narrator; he judges Ideala unhesitatingly and in light of his own fixed ideals of femininity, of marriage, and of a form of male honor that blinds him to the realities of women's social position.

This narrator, the idealist and philanthropist Lord Dawne, is one of three significant male characters in the novel. Lord Dawne describes Ideala intimately and refers to himself as "me" and "I" from the first sentence of the novel, but he only gradually reveals the gender and class identity of that "I." Most important, the narrator waits until very late in the novel to disclose the secret that belatedly provides the key to his construction of Ideala. He deeply loves his narrative object but feels bound by honor and duty to uphold marriage, even her miserable marriage; therefore, he hides his passion from Ideala. This admission complicates readers' responses to the narrator, whatever their own desires for the female protagonist. His submissiveness to convention led even a conservative critic for the *Saturday Review* to imagine the narrator in ageist, emasculated terms: "It is narrated by an elderly man of aristocratic birth, considerable means, and, as we are expressly told, of the male sex. He once insinuates that he cherishes a senile and unrequited passion for his heroine, and it seems likely, upon the whole, that this was so."[10] (Neither this novel nor the next two portray him as elderly.) For readers principally concerned with the female character's fate the narrator's confession casts his claims of narrative objectivity into doubt. This narrative ambiguity registers in the dissonance between his enforcement of Ideala's marriage, on one hand, and key moments of domestic abuse and her consequent despair, on the other.

The reader's attention is drawn to a second important male character, the husband himself, in only a few scenes, and even these incidents are recorded secondhand and in retrospect. The narrator reveals the husband has locked Ideala outdoors overnight for her stubbornness, that he strikes her, that Ideala has seen him embracing a barmaid, that she sees him escorting a notorious member of the "demimonde" about town, and that he all but abandons her after sending their only child, an infant, to a wet nurse, leaving the baby to die of diphtheria.

Halfway through the novel the third male character enters the plot, when, in desperation, Ideala seeks advice from a medical doctor, Lorrimer, whom friends have praised for his work with the mentally ill. She chooses Lorrimer as her confidant under the impression that he will be an older man, a kind of father figure. Instead, he turns out to be young, intelligent, and passionate, and they soon fall in love. Although the plot details the failure of Ideala's marriage and her escape from a vicious husband, in a larger sense, the novel tells the story of a woman's struggle against all the men who wish to control and bind her—even the men who would bind her with genuine love.

In effect, to become a New Woman Ideala must wrestle free from three old-fashioned men. First, she must unlearn all that she has been taught about femininity and wifely duty in order to escape a destructive and dangerous marriage. Then, she must subdue her attraction to her lover, Lorrimer, after realizing that a life with him would make them both social outcasts and create new problems rather than solving existing ones. And, finally, in the most intriguing twist of the novel the female character's voice must break through the male narrative of "idealization" in order to realize her own ideal. This novel, then, represents an important step in Grand's creation of the New Woman figure, for its structure isolates crucial conventions of literary form and social practice that must be overcome by women fashioning woman-centered stories and histories. In Grand's novel Ideala's husband embodies the legal authority men wield over women; her lover suggests the tempting but dangerous attractions of romance; and, most significantly, the narrator represents the power of narrative authority, that ability to control women by idealizing them, by romanticizing their suffering, and by imposing helpless forms of femininity that trap female characters in the marriage plot and in heterosexual fantasies of marriage. To become a New Woman Grand's protagonist must escape the objectification imposed by these three men's desires and by masculinist readers and must find a means of articulating desires of her own.

To translate one's intuitive sense of competing voices into a critical vocabulary poses difficulties, particularly when the normative voice has the bewildering omnipresence of white noise. Mikhail Bakhtin's discussion of what he calls "heteroglossia" in the novel as a genre illuminates the multiple meanings available—from the level of the individual word, subject to interpretative contexts in and out of the text, to competing genre conventions (as in *Singularly Deluded*) to the status of the "narrator." Bakhtin points out that

> the author manifests himself and his point of view not only in his effect on the narrator, on his speech and his language (which are to one or another extent objectivized, objects of display) but also in his effect on the subject of the story—as a point of view that differs from the point of view of the author. Behind the narrator's story we read a second story, the author's story; he is the one who tells us how the narrator tells stories, and also tells us about the narrator himself.[11]

This "dialogic" relation is further complicated by the voices of characters: "each character's speech possesses its own belief system, since each is the speech of another in another's language."[12] Moreover, each character exists in a "character zone,"[13] a zone of language mutually created by the character, the narrator, and the author. In *Ideala* this dialogic interplay invites the reader to listen for brief interruptions. The voice of liberal Victorian sentiment, ventriloquist-like, speaks through the male narrator, whose authority is then contradicted by the perspective of a female character, his sister, Claudia. Claudia's commentary on the narrator's enactment of *his* text is reinforced by textual cues that Ideala's actions are being forcibly interpreted by the male narrator rather than "objectively" recorded. This novel, then, grapples with masculine narrative authority by playing out a woman's fantasy of a man's fantasy of a woman (character's) fantasies.

In *Reading the Romantic Heroine* Leslie Rabine addresses these narrative tensions with explicitly feminist questions. She suggests that the fictional origin of language within the formal world of any given novel, that is the narrator, may be a place to begin disentangling the patriarchal language of authority that Victorian male and female writers believed to be a property of the novel:

> We automatically agree to see what the dominant masculine voice of narration shows us and to ignore what it masks because the narrator tells his story through codes of interpretation which readers have already internalized, and which seem as natural as the ideologies of linear narrative and romantic heterosexual relations.[14]

Accommodating themselves to this inequitable distribution of power in language, women writers sometimes seize narrative authority by appropriating the male voice. New Women novelists seem to have found this tension both a frustration and an inspiration.

As Penny Boumelha points out, using narrative strategies to unsettle an

ostensibly objective, anonymous, omniscient narrator is a hallmark of New
Woman fiction. Breaking the traditional boundaries between author and
character, the female author interrupts the "male" voice of authority in
many of these novels: "It is as if at moments there is no mediating narrator;
the writing of the fiction becomes for a time its own action, its plot, enact-
ing as well as articulating the protest of the text."[15] Rabine's reading strategy illuminates the role of the reader in relation to the interplay of these
narrative voices: "I have sought to separate the stories narrated from the
charm of the narrator's voice that frames them in what seems a necessary,
natural, and factual interpretation, and to discover to what extent the stories
exceed this frame and its implicit value system."[16] Feminist narratologist
Susan Sniader Lanser also offers a useful characterization of the complex
nature of the authority a novel needed to be effective as a social text: "Discursive authority—by which I mean here the intellectual credibility, ideological validity, and aesthetic value claimed by or conferred upon a work,
author, narrator, character, or textual practice—is produced interactively; it
must therefore be characterized with respect to specific receiving communities."[17] Together Rabine and Lanser's representations of the process by
which narrative authority accrues to a text suggest why Grand employs a
male narrator: she sought a position of authority within the world of publishers (and their gatekeeping readers), within communities of women readers, but also within progressive male-dominated circles that could provide a
platform for legal change.

Considering these narrative "addresses," the choice of a male narrator
was sensible. Rita Kranidis cites Alice Kahler-Marshall's study of 2,650
women writers who used pen names. Kahler-Marshall claims that nearly all
late-Victorian women published under names other than their own at some
point: "protected by their masculine pseudonyms they would presume to
have opinions on matters more intellectually challenging than those
believed suitable for women."[18] The political as well as the literary relations
between gender and authority in the Victorian period may have influenced
Grand's narrative gender crossing. In her study of British men who fought
for women's suffrage Sylvia Strauss discusses "feminist fathers," male writers, and activists who supported women's rights in several arenas. Strauss
argues that because women had so little political power before the twentieth century, men inevitably took central roles in the early feminist movement. Only men could present petitions before the British and American
governments; only men could change the institutions of law, medicine, religion, and most professions, over which they retained exclusive control.[19] If
we consider Strauss's thesis in relation to literature, it seems likely that Victorian women understood the importance of sanctioning and promoting

their feminist views in fiction as well as in politics either by catering to or invoking male authority. Grand's shift from assertion to conciliation in an 1896 interview speaks to this necessity:

> When the weaker of our sex are subjected to great wrongs we, as women, are bound to look after them, and if that brings us into opposition to some men we cannot help ourselves, but I always feel very sorry when it occurs. I entirely deprecate rivalry and the spirit of war between the sexes; what we want is to work together for the good of each. And after all it is very cheering to find so many good men willing to aid in the uplifting of women.[20]

At the same time, many women must have shared the frustration that Grand expressed much later (in 1923) when their political and personal fates depended so heavily upon the goodwill of men:

> Speaking generally, the chivalry of men towards the women they did not love or admire and were not bound to protect was limited to little acts of politeness on public occasions. Once the door of her home was shut on her, a woman was not safe from insult to the end of the street in which she lived. There were plenty of high-minded men: right-hearted it might be, but wrong-headed; victims themselves, many of them, of custom, ignorance, prejudice, and lack of imagination.[21]

The novel reveals a paradox at the heart of middle-class women's struggles for authority, whether in the guise of fictional form and voice or in the public, political arenas of law and representation. To court male sanction and particularly to ask men to speak for women might achieve a limited, particular end, but the power dynamics—men speaking to men about women—remained intact.[22] The response of the *Critic* reviewer suggests just this failure. The reviewer rejects the "story" while applauding its teller: "The story . . . is ridiculous often, and morbid and unwholesome always, but it is redeemed occasionally by Lord Dawne, who is an exquisite creation. His influence over Ideala is all for good, and his exceptional sweetness and strength of character brighten the book and keep us from condemning it utterly."[23] Elsie Michie's account of Charles Dickens's monopoly over the stories of prostitutes who sought refuge at Urania Cottage provides a real life reminder that the narrator of stories can possess a terrible power over the subject of a story. The prostitutes were required to tell a board of men their stories upon entering the refuge then forbidden ever to speak of their stories to the women in the house, whether inmates or volunteers. As Michie points out, narrative authority here becomes "masculine surveillance."[24] The narrator of *Ideala* treads a fine line between the two.

Marital duty is the law that justifies this narrator's exercise of authority. Though the narrator comments that Ideala occasionally hints at her marital problems, he often refuses to hear (or record) either her husband's abuses and infidelities or her own extramarital romance because these events have no place in the life of any heroine *he* can imagine. Ideala's interfering accounts and actions hover as a shadow story that dramatizes a version not just of her marriage but of marriage more generally, before which men's notions of honor pale. As Joseph Boone, Penny Boumelha, Jane Miller, and others have explained, in novels developed along the lines of the marriage plot marriage itself becomes the object, the logic for plot development, and the source of reader expectation.[25] In the antimarriage plot marriage becomes the obstacle. What then is the interest? What desire leads the reader forward, and what ultimate goal produces titillating delays and digressions? For Sarah Grand and other New Woman novelists the problem was not merely to represent motivations prompted by female desire, but to imagine what those longings could be, given the limited social options for middle-class women.[26] Without easy access to education or employment, and with little hope for economic security unless a marriage provided it, women had little impetus to define female desire beyond the necessity of finding a marriage partner.

Ideala's discontent first manifests itself as "recklessness" then as romantic passion and ultimately as feminism, at least in nineteenth-century terms. As her husband's abuses escalate, Ideala begins acting and speaking impetuously, unexpectedly challenging ideas about marriage and morals in the "inappropriate" context of frivolous social occasions. The narrator trivializes this recklessness as a mere safety valve: "I soon began to recognise the sign, and to judge of the amount she had suffered by the length to which she afterwards went in search of relief, and the extent to which suffering made her untrue to herself" (54), a view starkly contradicted by contemporary studies of domestic violence.[27]

Ideala not only dislikes marriage, but she is also distinctly unlike the heroines of the conventional marriage plot in her obliviousness to most men. Though she is attractive, particularly to men, she is also indifferent to their approval. The narrator muses about the reason: "it was noticed that men who took her down to dinner, or had any other opportunity of talking to her, were never very positive in what they said of her afterwards. She made every one, men and women alike, feel, and she did it unconsciously" (12). When her power of influence is pointed out to her, presumably as a compliment, she replies: "I do not think I am conscious of anything that relates to myself, personally, in my intercourse with people. They are ideas to me for the most part, men especially so" (56). In her emotional independence from as opposed to feminine dependence upon others, Ideala becomes an indecipherable surface prompting projections that reveal more about her interpreters, such as Lord Dawne, than herself.

Throughout the novel men construe Ideala's inability (or refusal) to pay homage to sexual difference in one of two ways. One group, feeling slighted and vaguely humiliated by her refusal to flirt, to indulge male privilege, or to strike a submissive pose, decides that she is unwomanly and pays her little attention. The second and more potentially threatening response comes from those characters who interpret her lack of feminine deference and her inability to flirt as a kind of looseness that marks her as sexually available. In fact, in the course of the story both Lorrimer, who loves her, and the narrator, who worships her silently, assume that she invites inappropriate attentions of men by failing to obey codes of behavior, social or moral, which are supposed to insulate women against indiscreet male attention. These inconsistencies between Ideala's character and that of the ideal heroine create ambivalences that cannot easily be accommodated by the marriage plot. When Ideala resists the idealizing fantasies of men, disavows the social institutions men have created, and refuses both romance and marriage, she exceeds the boundaries of the marriage plot. None of its mutations, versatile as they are, quite contain her contradictions or demands.

Yet even a protagonist who is dispassionate about men finds her life structured by the marriage plot. Based on her experience and anticipating a pivotal theme of *The Heavenly Twins,* Ideala describes the coercion within the family that leads to unhappy marriage:

> but have you never been conscious of the tender pressure that is brought to bear when a desirable suitor offers? Have you never seen a girl who won't marry when she is wanted to, wincing from covert stabs, mourning over cold looks, and made to feel outside everything— suffering a small martyrdom under the general displeasure of all for whom she cares, her world, without whose love life is a burden to her; whom she believes to know the best of everything? (251)

When Ideala succumbs to this pressure, she suffers physical abuse and the intense loneliness of an unhappy wife who, like Dickens's prostitutes, can tell no one her story. Looking back over Ideala's past, the narrator acknowledges the effects of such mental abuse: "She could never bear to be alone, and I always thought the worst trial of her married life was the mental solitude to which it had reduced her by making her feel the necessity for reserve, even with her best friends" (242). Ideala's loneliness, the antithesis to the promises of marriage, is intensified by her husband's manipulations of her through motherhood, the estate guaranteed to women by the supposed distribution of power within the separate spheres theory.[28] Because in reality she has no jurisdiction over the child, her husband can leave the baby to die at the hands of a wet nurse. Denied the stability of a good marriage and the supposedly redeeming joys of motherhood, Ideala struggles to maintain the appearances of ideal womanhood while suffering as a victim of that ideal.

Ideala also fears the power of her husband's influence to degrade her as a consequence of her daily association with his low-mindedness and depravity. Grand's novels begin to explore the psychological consequences suffered by women married to disreputable husbands in *A Domestic Experiment,* and she continues to make an argument for an inferior husband's contaminating influence through the rest of her writing career, both in fiction and nonfiction. In an 1899 essay, for example, she passionately pleads the case of women like the character Ideala:

> Tied to a man who, from obtuseness or selfishness or principle, not only does not assist her development, but refuses to recognise either the necessity or the possibility of further development, the married woman finds her intellect shut in a dungeon from which there is no escape. And added to the blight of the ghastly constant fact of uncongenial companionship, she learns to her cost that it is just this type of man who, while forever prating of the unfitness of women for the work of life, thrusts upon her every sordid and wearisome detail of tedious labour in the house.[29]

Elaine Baruch offers reasons why a woman writer would insist that a female heroine's moral fate depends so heavily upon her husband: "Traditionally, for women at least since Eve, the devil has merely been the husband or lover and not the real thing, for it is to the husband or his imago that the woman is to entrust her soul. Thus women's fall as well as their development has been vicarious."[30] Arguing that "marriage grafts [women] to the man's moral being no less than his intellectual one," Baruch reiterates Ideala's claim that she has not only a right but a duty to break her marriage contract in order to save herself morally as well as emotionally.[31]

As one consequence of her husband's vices, Ideala learns with horror of the existence of the demimonde, portrayed as a carefully structured, upper-class system of prostitution. Grand would present the encounter between the "wife" and the mistress more sympathetically in *The Heavenly Twins.* Other New Woman novelists also depicted the meeting of the "good woman" and the fallen woman, for example in Ella Hepworth Dixon's *The Story of a Modern Woman* (1894), treating the good woman's sympathetic commitment to the victim of her husband or lover as a formative moment of feminist cooperation that transcended barriers of class, sexual transgression, and loyalties to men. Here the socialist-feminist argument that the law made marriage no better than legalized prostitution is carried a step further, since this fictional mistress of the demimonde has an enviable class position as well as more freedom and control over a relationship than a legally married woman. Although Ideala fears her exposure to her husband's carnality, later in the novel she identifies with a working-class woman he has exploited. As her life's work, she ultimately chooses to help incorporate "fallen" women such as these back into society.[32]

Grand extends her critique of marriage from the personal to the social realm and from a focus on sexual monogamy to civil law through several discussions in which Ideala challenges other characters' defense of marriage. At a dinner party with a bishop and a lawyer Ideala creates a comic tumult by requiring the two men to define "social law." She begins by asking:

> "I want to know if a thing can be legally right and morally wrong . . ."
> "Of course not," the Bishop rashly asserted.
> "That depends," the lawyer said cautiously. (199)

Obviously, Grand is spoofing these two professions; however, the conversation seriously addresses marriage as a contract that should be negotiated (and voidable if conditions are not met). Ideala describes signing a contract only to learn that the parties who drew up the contract withheld important clauses:

> "But suppose there was something in the clause to which I very strongly objected, something of which my conscience disapproved, something that was repugnant to my whole moral nature; and suppose I was forced by the law to fulfill it nevertheless, should you say that was a moral contract? Should you not say that in acting against my conscience I acted immorally?"
> We all fell into the trap, and looked an encouraging assent. (199)

Here, as elsewhere, Grand's novel refines the notion of duty, particularly for women. It also clarifies the relation between unhappily married women and civil law; for Grand these women are forced by legal codes of the government and the church *into* immorality. Ideala argues that "only love that lasts can sanctify marriage, and a marriage without such love is an immoral contract," but in the end she rejects both love and marriage and seeks self-definition completely apart from men (200).

Grand also addresses the economic position of married women. In the area of economics Ideala insistently rebels against convention. When she returns to her husband for appearance's sake after her first attempt to leave home, she does so on the condition that she remain economically independent; she "would accept nothing from him but house-room, for she held that no high-minded woman could take anything from a man to whom she was bound by no more sacred tie than that of a mere legal contract" (179). Later Ideala understands that accepting financial favors from her lover, Lorrimer, would destroy what she characterizes as their "masculine" camaraderie, an equitable relationship that gives her great pleasure. In both cases Ideala tries to revise the marriage contract in ways that would allow her greater participation in and control over her relations with men. Only after she sees the impossibility of rewriting social roles does she abandon both marriage and romance plots, resisting the closure each would impose.

As a woman writer, it is not surprising that Grand would also consider the usefulness of art as an expression of personal unhappiness and political analysis. Early in the novel Ideala describes writing poetry as "the one safety-valve I have to ease the pressure" of feeling (90). At the end of the novel she refers again to her poetry, explaining, "it is a means of expression that satisfies when nothing else will. I always carry my last about in my pocket. I know them by heart, of course, but still it is a pleasure to read them" (249). The narrator clearly reveres Ideala's poems; in fact, one of the clues that reveals his secret love for Ideala is that he keeps one of the poems she discards as a memento. The reader, however, sees only one of Ideala's poems and that one Ideala denounces because of its idealized if tragic treatment of romantic love. The novel implies that in these excluded poems Ideala finds a language and voice for the desires that can only be hinted at in the text of her male narrator.

The creative power inherent in Ideala's "nervousness" is also reflected in her artistic temperament. The novel elevates maternity while justifying art as a female occupation in the description of Ideala's talents:

> She loved music, and painting, and poetry, and science, and none of her loves were barren. She embraced them each in turn with an ardour that resulted in the production of an offspring—a song, a picture, a poem, or book on some most serious subject, and all worthy of note. But she was inconstant, and these children of her thought or fancy were generally isolated efforts that marked the culminating point of her devotion, and lessened her interest if they did not exhaust her strength. (39)

Though Grand does not fully explore the development and nature of the female artist until *The Beth Book*, Ideala's sensitivity to beauty and her creative imagination quicken the discontent necessary to force her out of the role of the idealized, conventional heroine. When the narrator first meets

Ideala, she voices her dissatisfaction with the passive, dutiful female role by objectifying herself, identifying herself not with but *as* a work of art: "People always want to know if I write, or paint, or play, or what I do . . . They all expect me to do something. My function is not to do, but to be. I make no poetry. I am a poem if you read me aright" (11). A protagonist's function as an agent within the plot is to act, to propel events forward. Yet as a representation of ideal womanhood, the idealized heroine's function can only be decorative. She faces the same objectifying constraints that destroyed the character Agatha in *A Domestic Experiment*. Until Ideala is rudely shaken by incontrovertible evidence of her husband's cruelty and adultery, her passion, her sensitivity, her imagination, and her impulse to shape her own identity are molded to her notions, that is society's notions, of wifely duty. Being outside the sphere of action and unable to imagine an alternative social role, Ideala, like other balked heroines in Thomas Hardy's *Jude the Obscure,* Olive Schreiner's *Story of an African Farm,* or Grant Allen's *The Woman Who Did,* grows ill, libidinous, and self-destructive.

Ideala's most threatening challenge to the obstacles imposed by marriage is her contemplated escape into dreams of illicit romantic happiness. Impelled by her passion for Lorrimer, Ideala firmly resists the narrator's attempts to coerce her into an empty respectability, rejecting his subtle encouragement that she *pretend* her marriage is satisfying, or perhaps that she unobtrusively (and uncomplainingly) live apart from her husband. (This kind of advice receives sharp attack in Grand's later novels as she came to understand the power of "reasonable" men and "good" women to subjugate women by encouraging them to accommodate quietly even to the most cruel marital circumstances.) When the narrator argues that passion never lasts, Ideala vehemently argues that "there is no degradation in love. It is sin that degrades, and sin is something that corrupts our minds is it not? and makes us unfit for any good work, and unwilling to undertake any" (217). Ideala's assessment of marriage and love results from her personal education in marriage. For her marriage is a fairly mercenary arrangement, as evidenced by the fact that her first impulse when she begins to discover her husband's cruelties is to refuse money from him rather than to withdraw acts of affection.

Ideala also bucks the imposition of the narrator's idealized version of her. He wants her to be silent, stoic, and devoted to charity and good works, but Ideala argues that, while work is essential for a full, vital life, it is not an alternative to the abuses of her marriage or a substitute for woman's bondage under the civil, religious, and social laws that make her subject to her husband's will. Again, the narrator argues that "moral laws" define the duty of individuals who must "sacrifice themselves for the good of the community at large." Ideala, however, resists the narrator's narrow social definition of morality. For Ideala love, and some synthesis of responsibility to oneself and one's desires, must be taken into account when defining morality. She answers the narrator by saying, "I do not understand your morality . . . Do you think that, although I love another man, it would be right for me to go back and live with my husband?" (219). Thus, she forces the narrator and the reader to consider the explicit consequences of the marriage plot: dishonesty, emotional adultery, and erasure of Ideala's "true" story, the assertion of her desires.

While art and romance fail the female protagonist, the novel offers alternatives that will structure the next two novels of Grand's first trilogy: education and work. From the earliest pages of the novel Ideala longs to be educated, to understand how to reason and make judgments. Ironically, the most powerful form of her education results from her husband's debaucheries. Though she repeatedly says that woman's "inborn desire" (260) is to submit to a man worthy of her, by the end of the novel she dedicates herself to "mak[ing] women discontented" (262). Thus, she intends to unite women to reform society, which for Grand meant revising the roles of both men and women, as a consequence of the undesirability of the structure of heterosexual relations at the time.

Ultimately, the novel also suggests that female desire may be expressed through meaningful work, particularly work within a community of women. When Ideala devotes herself to less fortunate women, the narrator praises her lavishly. At this point Grand seems least in control of the narrator's (and perhaps her own) voice. He describes Ideala with such excessive adoration and idealization that neither he nor Ideala seems believable. On the other hand, the contradiction between masculinist and feminist views of work is suggested by the narrator's description of the differing responses to Ideala's project. While "Other women . . . do not doubt but that she has chosen the better part," men assume there "must be something wrong in the world when such a woman misses her vocation, and has to scatter her love to the four winds of heaven, for want of an object upon which to concentrate it in all its strength" (266). Grand's own ambivalence or confusion about Ideala's options may be read in the vagueness with which Ideala's work and her future are described. To imagine the revisions of womanhood that might be required by the eruption of female desire was perhaps impossible for Grand at this stage of her life and literary career. But already calls for education, for female expression, and for work form the basis of Ideala's plot, even locked as she is within the constraints of the narrator's fantasies. And Grand circumvents the closure of that fantasy and of what Joseph Boone calls the "erotic dynamic of the traditional love plot" (376), for

Ideala ends with the beginning of her commitment to prostitutes, the women most reviled by society and exploited by men. Moreover, her career continued to develop as the next two novels of the trilogy took shape. In these next novels Lord Dawne recedes into the background as a sympathetic supporter of the work of Ideala and other characters. He becomes an auxiliary to the women's cause rather than its spokesman. The textual ambivalence his authority creates in this novel suggests why Grand declined to seek cultural authority for her reformist agenda by using a male ventriloquist in her later novels.

The character of this kindly, controlling narrator is revealed gradually through the first several chapters. Being an unmarried aristocrat, he lives with his sister, Claudia, moving back and forth between their various houses. He first meets Ideala at a garden party and comes to know her intimately at a series of house parties; he and Claudia agree to take her under their wing after each notices Ideala's rare intelligence and generosity, coupled with her tendency to make unexpected and often disturbing comments in public about religion, morality, class distinctions, and scientific or political matters. Despite his acknowledgment of Ideala's unconventional behavior, Lord Dawne repeatedly nails the square pegs of her character into conventional circles: he frames her in the language of "ideal womanhood" as prescribed by courtesy books, journal articles, and literature of previous decades. Like the subject of Coventry Patmore's *Angel in the House* or the vision of femininity in John Ruskin's "Queen's Gardens," Ideala's "character zone" is suffused with the self-negating characteristics of idealized femininity: passivity, domesticity, purity, chastity, piety, innocence, forbearance, gentleness, submission, docility.[33] Beautiful, charming, and whimsical, Ideala at first seems what her name might suggest, an idealized heroine who finds herself uncomfortably situated in a novel that attacks the romance of marriage. Character and plot collide in discursive impasses between Lord Dawne and his sister. He interprets Ideala's changes as evidence of superficial, childish, and tentative femininity; readers learn from Claudia and Ideala's contesting murmurs that inconsistent behavior may also signal disagreement or resistance, apparent to but not decoded by the narrator.

Lord Dawne's control over the representation of Ideala is granted as a matter of course due his social as well as sexual birthright.

> I was a privileged person, allowed to be intimate with her from the first, partly because I insisted on it when I saw how matters stood, and partly because my position and reputation gave me a right to insist. I never had occasion to brave insults for her sake, but, like many others, I would have done so had it been necessary. (53)

The narrator's aristocratic status guarantees privileged gender access; however, he inadvertently describes the kind of relation between Ideala and most men in the novel. First, the narrator has access to Ideala not so much due to Ideala's desire as to her husband's sense of his own success in being associated, through Ideala, with a man of importance. Second, both of the men accept, to a large extent, Ideala's function as a possession of one man or another. Though the narrator would fight for access to her, he acknowledges her presumed position of subjection to a husband. The narrator's access is a variation of the social transaction Gayle Rubin has described in social practice and that Eve Sedgwick calls a foundational structure of fiction. In a culture that regards a woman as the property of her father, lover, or husband, homosocial bonds between men are forged through not only the exchange of a woman but also, as Sedgwick points out, through competition over a woman.[34] Whether he sets himself up as Ideala's defender or becomes her lover, the male narrator inevitably speaks about Ideala to other men—rather than speaking to or, more important, listening to *her*.

The narrator's passion for Ideala motivates his insistent desire that she present an image that will allow him to love her, though from afar. The idealization upon which his love depends is evident in one of the few passages in which he explicitly confesses his feelings, although only to the reader:

> But I hold that all men who have felt or inspired great love will be sanctified by it if there be any true nobility in their nature; and I knew that one man, whom Ideala did not love, had been so sanctified by love for her, and held himself sacred always. (235)

This kind of rhetoric undoubtedly appealed to readers of the popular romance in the 1890s (as it would to Harlequin devotees today), yet his love is often coercive and inflexible. In order to sustain the vision of Ideala he has constructed in the early stages of their acquaintance, the narrator cannot permit her to tell him anything about herself that would conflict with his image. First, he encourages her to silence her fears and complaints about her husband's abuses: "The trouble was her husband. She rarely spoke of him herself, and I think I ought to follow her example, and say as little about him as possible. He was jealous of her, jealous of her popularity, and jealous of every one who approached her" (53). He admires her stoicism and restraint; however, he also records the painful effects of the silence he encourages as he shows Ideala growing restless, bitter, irrational, and then physically ill from her loneliness and suffering. Later the narrator makes it impossible for Ideala to do anything other than maintain her silence and thus fails to learn about her relationship with Lorrimer in its early stages:

"What am I to do?" she said. "Will it always be like this?"

But I could not help her. I turned to the picture I was working at, and went on painting without a word. By-and-by she recovered herself, and began to talk of other things.

I blamed myself afterwards. I ought to have let her tell me then; but I had no notion of the truth. I only thought of her husband, and I selfishly shrank from encouraging her to speak. Complaint seemed to be beneath her. (178–79)

The narrator turns to his painting, the artificial, deliberate reconstruction of a fragment of his world, which inevitably stylizes, limits, and transforms the painted object through the alchemy of the artist's vision and freezes that vision in time, just as he resolutely turns away from the woman before him to his carefully constructed vision of ideal womanhood. Though his definition of the ideal woman differs somewhat from the Victorian stereotype in that he would have her actively participating in and reforming the world and he would allow her education and greater freedom of thought and movement, still the ideal woman is an arrested, visionary creature in conflict with the character Ideala. As I noted in beginning this chapter, this impulse toward stasis conflicts explicitly with the preface to the novel. To return to the quotation in which "Grand" addresses her readers directly, the speaker in the preface admonishes readers:

I warn you that it would not be fair to take any of Ideala's opinions, here given, as final. Much of what she thought was the mere effervescence of a strong mind in a state of fermentation . . . The imperfections must be studied, because it is only from the details of the process that anything can be learned. (v–vi)

In direct contradiction to Grand's claims for Ideala's changing character, the narrator fixes an image of Ideala as his ideal woman, a habit that leads him to think of her in conventional, limiting terms made available by the marriage contract. For example, when he learns of her desire to live with Lorrimer, he can only imagine her love affair in the most hackneyed terms of what Amanda Anderson calls the rhetoric of fallenness.[35] Believing that his arguments against Lorrimer have failed, he thinks: "I could say no more. Baffled and sick at heart, I left her, wondering if some happy inspiration would come before it was too late, and help me to save her yet" (197).

The narrator's relation to Ideala and his reading of her words and behavior are inevitably structured by his secret love for her. Though he carefully hides his romantic feelings from Ideala, they color his reactions. When she announces her plan to elope with her medical counselor, Lorrimer, he responds: "'You are infatuated' . . . And then my heart sent up an exceeding great and bitter cry: 'Ideala! Ideala! how did it ever come to this?'" (196). Despite his insistence that he objects on moral grounds, jealousy reveals his self-interest. On the last evening before she is to go to Lorrimer, Ideala sits with her head on the narrator's knee. Suddenly, his repeated protestations end: "In all the years of my love for her she had never been so close to me before, and I was glad to let her rest a long, long time like that" (214). This gentleness affects her more deeply than his arguments. Ultimately, Ideala breaks with Lorrimer, not as a consequence of moral arguments or concern for her own reputation but because the narrator insidiously argues that Lorrimer's reputation, as the man who took another man's wife, will be damaged, probably to the extent that he will be unable to practice medicine. In fear for her lover Ideala sacrifices her hope of trading a miserable marriage for a relationship based on intellectual compatibility and mutual attraction; however, she asks that the narrator take the news to Lorrimer, as partial penance for the narrator's harsh criticisms of the man she loves. This experience reveals the most unique form of the narrator's jealousy, for he establishes a disconcerting sense of identity with Lorrimer in yet another alliance of men and their interests over the body of a woman, the woman each presumes to "speak for."

The most unusual and telling manipulation of the conventional marriage plot is the meeting of Ideala's male lovers, during which they determine the female protagonist's fate in a peculiar moment of male bonding.[36] Paradoxically usurping the husband's authority only to shore it up, the two "lovers" collaborate to rewrite the romantic narrative of escape and passion proposed by Ideala. In a self-congratulatory celebration of masculine honor the two men admire themselves for forfeiting their desires and thereby keeping Ideala's name respectable, thus condemning the protagonist to misery rather than "saving" her. Their actions demonstrate the dangers faced by women who depend upon men to think, speak, and act for them.

The limits of the narrator's vision are most obvious when we see how he defines Ideala's relation to her lover, Lorrimer, and how he ends that relationship. In the narrator's first response to the idea of Lorrimer he acknowledges unreasoning jealousy, which precedes his moral objections to the match. The narrator questions: "But, Lorrimer—what sort of man was he? I own that I was strongly prejudiced against him from the moment she pronounced his name, and all she told me of him subsequently only confirmed the prejudice" (191). Yet, after his first encounter with Lorrimer, the narrator accepts Ideala's love for the other man by projecting himself onto the lover. He recalls the meeting: "—a tall, fair man; self-contained and dignified; cold, pale, and unimpassioned—so I thought—but my equal in every way: the man who was 'all the world' to Ideala. When I saw him I understood" (227). The narrator seems unaware of the odd arrogance that permits him thus to accept Lorrimer when he had earlier despised him.

The process of identification continues through their conversation. Recalling the "delightful discourse" he had with Lorrimer, he remembers particularly, " 'She has had so little joy!' he said; using the very words that had occurred to me." After several days of wrangling over Ideala's decision, the two men assume a strangely proprietary air about the woman both love. The narrator conveys this presumption when the two agree that they cannot agree about the proper life Ideala should now follow:

> This was a point upon which we differed. He would have given her the natural joys of a woman—husband, home, children, friends, and only such intellectual pursuits which are pleasant. *I* had always hoped to see her at work in a wider field. But she was one of those rare women who are born to fulfill both destinies at once, and worthily if only circumstances had made it possible for her to combine the two. (229)

On one level the narrator's conclusion works toward an indictment of a society that prevents women from functioning in both the domestic and public spheres and as such is a tempered version of more vehement arguments that appear in the later novels. The passage clarifies the kind of relationship each of these men imagines having with Ideala. Each assumes he can predict or prescribe Ideala's greatest happiness. Ironically, Lorrimer's prescription, idyllic domesticity, comes from an illicit lover who would have caused Ideala to be socially ostracized and who probably would have burdened Ideala with illegitimate children. The narrator's view must also be read skeptically, for he had repeatedly encouraged Ideala to stay with her husband, despite his knowledge of the husband's vices. Ideala's means of escaping the prescriptions of both of these men is to leave for a yearlong, solitary overseas tour during which she can reach her own conclusions without the "help" of either.

Bakhtin's model of dialogic perspectives and Sedgwick's model of the male-female-male triangle together suggest the importance of a third character in the novel, Lord Dawne's sister, Claudia, who could otherwise be easily overlooked. Sedgwick examines the social and formal power established by a triangular relationship that bonds men over the exchange of women; *Ideala* quietly destabilizes that stable structure. The textual interventions of Claudia together with the resistant interventions of Ideala—in relation to the male narrator—draw a second triangle that shimmers in and out of the reader's view like the vase and face (or duck and rabbit) one sees alternately in a common visual illusion. Claudia, a descendant of the figure Judith Fetterley describes in *The Resisting Reader,* functions as a feminist corrective, a female reader who has little function in terms of the plot yet who provides frequent revisionary readings of the narrator's interpretations of Ideala's motives and feelings.[37]

The narrator first describes Claudia in a patronizing if affectionate tone, making it easy for the reader to discredit or simply read over Claudia's subsequent rereadings of his narrative. Yet, despite her status as a middle-aged single woman, Claudia seems to have the respect of all the other characters in the novel. Economically independent, she has created a circle of friends who are intelligent and interested in social concerns. Though she remains a minor character, her presence provides a qualifying function; she constantly reminds the reader of the narrator's gender by contrast and resistance. Since she has little plot function in the novel, other than to make a socially acceptable and harmless relationship between the narrator and Ideala possible, her comments, in their very excessiveness, seem especially significant. The narrator introduces Claudia in her relation to Ideala:

> She was a good deal older than Ideala, whom she loved as a mother loves a naughty child, for ever finding fault with her, but ready to be up in arms in a moment if any one else ventured to do likewise. She was inclined to quarrel with me because, although I never doubted Ideala's truth and earnestness, no one could, knowing her weak point, I feared for her. I thought if all the passion in her were ever focussed on one object she would do something extravagant. (59)

The narrator's predictions foreshadow Ideala's falling in love with Lorrimer, but this passage also asserts his authority over women's stories. In this case he pigeonholes Claudia as a biased defender of Ideala, whose version of her story is therefore not completely trustworthy. The irony of qualifying Claudia as a biased, undependable narrator only becomes clear late in the novel when the narrator admits his unrequited romantic desire for Ideala to the reader, belatedly undermining his own credibility as narrator.

Claudia adamantly challenges the narrator on the grounds that he "silences" Ideala's marital difficulties. Contrary to the narrator's views, Claudia's feminist analysis of the husband's abuses requires exposure as a first step toward correction of Ideala's problems:

> My sister was one of the people who thought it would have been better for Ideala to have talked of her troubles. When I praise Ideala's loyalty, and her uncomplaining devotion to an uncongenial duty, Claudia says: "Loyalty is all very well; but I don't see much merit in a lifelong

devotion to a bad cause. If there were any good to be done by it, it would be different, of course, but, as it is Ideala is simply sacrificing herself for nothing—and worse, she is setting a bad example by showing men they need not mend their manners since wives will endure anything." (58–59)

In this passage, as in others, the narrator appears to be the voice of "reason." Holding the utilitarian line that "no petty, personal mishap" should influence the individual to reject an institution such as marriage that is designed for the greater good of society, the narrator at once fixes Ideala in the position of passive, enduring, and therefore conventionally heroic womanhood and reveals his own patriarchal, conservative protectionism as he defends marriage (99). His defense is suspect even at this point because neither he nor Claudia is married; Ideala's marriage is miserable; and other married couples in the novel appear briefly and inconsequentially. Claudia argues from her observation of Ideala's personal experience, while the narrator argues from historical precedents and conventions structured to serve the comfort of men. Thus, Claudia's reading of Ideala's story conflicts sharply with his idealization of her stoicism:

> It is immoral for a woman to live with such a husband. I don't understand Ideala's meekness; it amounts to weakness sometimes, I think. I believe if he struck her she would say, "Thank you," and fetch him his slippers. I feel sure she thinks some unknown defect in herself is at the bottom of all his misdeeds. (59)

Claudia's astute analysis reverses the narrator's definition of morality. Moreover, she makes a point more recent audiences still resist, even when therapists who work with abused women—generally accepted psychological authorities—raise the issue. While reviewers from mainstream journals applauded the narrator as a character and harangued Ideala's "nasty-mindedness," the feminist voice of the *Woman's Signal* adamantly reinforced Claudia's perspective, arguing that Ideala is "governed by a mistaken sense of duty" that leads her "to live cheerfully beside the noisome being to whom she is tied, and from whom our revolting man-made social laws give her no means of escape except disgrace.[38] (This claim is supported by the *Saturday Review* writer's Jimmy Carter–like judgment that "she commits adultery in her heart with the first cleverish man she comes across after the rupture with her husband, and fails to do so in fact only because she lacks the courage of her appetite.")[39] Claudia realizes that the endurance revered by the narrator is, in fact, a kind of emotional paralysis of self-blame, self-abuse, and shame, which is nurtured by the precepts of ideal womanhood and the social plot of marriage. Behavior praised as "duty" by the narrator is defined as degradation and self-destruction from Claudia's perspective.

Throughout the novel Claudia encourages the narrator, and by extension the reader, to question superficial assessments of Ideala's story. While Ideala is still living with her husband, the brother and sister receive an uncomplaining letter from Ideala that the narrator accepts at face value. Frustrated by his obtuseness, Claudia asks, "Can you read between the lines of that letter?" (99). Claudia, unlike the narrator, realizes that when Ideala writes with desperate cheerfulness she is vigorously hiding her misery behind the trivialities and vagaries that amuse other characters as feminine charms. Similarly, Claudia questions the whimsicality for which Ideala is famous, asking, "Who knows what pain is at the bottom of it all?" (89). When the narrator applauds Ideala's restraint, arguing that "silence is best" for Ideala, Claudia turns the terms of his argument back upon him by revising his notion of "duty":

> "But why *should* she bear it?" Claudia demanded.
>
> "It is her duty."
>
> "I know she thinks so, and is sacrificing her life to that principle. But will you kindly tell me where a woman's duty to her husband ends and her duty to herself begins? I suppose you will allow that she has a duty to herself? And the line should be drawn somewhere?" (99–100)

Claudia questions not only the narrator's portrayal of Ideala but the centrality and inevitability of the marriage plot as well. If woman's duty to herself assumes a central position in Ideala's story, clearly the marriage plot will be disrupted, as will the courtly love fantasy that characterizes the narrator's relation to the marriage plot. One of Grand's admirers, Mona Caird, argued in the pseudoscientific discourse that shaped Grand's later novels:

> Men are living lives and committing actions day by day which imperil and destroy the well-being of the race; on what principle are women only to be restrained? Why this one-sided sacrifice, this artificial selection of victims for the good of society? The old legends of maidens who were chosen each year and chained to a rock by the shore to propitiate gods . . . seem not in the least out of date. Sacrifices were performed more frankly in those days, and nobody tried to persuade the victims that it was enjoyable and blessed to be devoured.[40]

The dialogic interplay of voices within a text described by Bakhtin illuminates the tensions in the novel between Grand's own experience of male authority and her deeply enculturated respect for men's views, particularly those of concerned men like the "feminist fathers" who supported the women's movement and, in the case of the narrator, who sympathize, if only in a limited way, with women's plight.[41] The struggle among these various camps is, in part, a problem of "address."

In comparing novels by women that survive time versus those that quickly disappear, Terry Lovell sees a distinct difference between novels' types of address. Successful novels (she cites Elizabeth Gaskell's *Mary Barton*) use a "woman-to-people/men" address, which guarantees a broader readership.[42] Novels (or, to use one of Lovell's examples, soap operas) that center on "the private, domestic, and personal, the 'woman's world'" tend instead to be perceived as using woman-to-woman address.[43] Lovell says that New Woman novels by women often have two strikes against them. These novels are polemical (and thereby unlikely to last "beyond the moment of controversy") and are limited to an audience of women. Lovell describes their fate: "woman-to-woman fiction is coded out of 'literature.' While feminist fiction in the eighteen-nineties was widely read and was not necessarily addressed exclusively to women, women were the preferred readers. Woman-to-woman forms are not permitted to become part of the general stock of 'cultural capital.'"[44] Given the relationship between a woman author and male authorities and institutions (publishers, reviewers, circulating libraries), the novel *Ideala* represents a structural compromise between these two forms of address. By pleading Ideala's (and women's) case through the approving voice of a socially respectable, upper-class male narrator, Grand may have hoped her political/fictional message might reach the ears of those who held the power to change laws governing marriage and women's education. Invalidating the narrative contract of the marriage plot and undermining the authority presumed by the first-person narrative voice, *Ideala* also permits imaginative space for more abstract questioning of conventions and authorities.

Having tested the uses of a male narrator and having experimented with popular fictional genres such as the adventure novel and the detective novel, Grand turned next to another of the nineteenth-century's principal plots in search of a medium for her feminist vision: the bildungsroman. In its finest moments the female bildungsroman promised radical revision to the marriage plot because it required expression of the unimaginable: female desire defined, expressed, and pursued without reference to male-defined pleasure. Joseph Boone compares the sequencing of the reader's responses in the marriage plot to the phases of sexual arousal, specifically male sexual arousal. After demonstrating that the marriage plot moves from "excitation" to "deferral and disease," Boone explains:

the reader hypothesized here is male; the pattern of desire being evoked follows a linear model of sexual excitation and final discharge most often associated in both psychological and physiological terms, with men. If this is so, the erotic dynamic of the traditional love plot, however much it may play to female desire, nonetheless would seem to encode at the most elementary level of narrative a highly specific, male-oriented norm of sexuality fostering the illusion that all pleasure (of reading or of sex) is ejaculatory.[45]

Ultimately, Boone argues that this thrust of the plot is so forceful and possesses such totalizing momentum that it concludes in a "final stasis that not only suspends all action but . . . cuts short any serious or prolonged questioning of the social ethos of marriage underlying the fictional construct."[46]

As Boone himself points out, the popularity of this structure is curious given Victorian readership. If women formed the greatest part of the reading audiences of the romance, then as now, why should a plot organized according to masculine sensibility, especially male sexual sensibility, satisfy feminine fictional desire, assuming that the distinct differences in men's and women's socialization would lead to different constructions of fictional desire?

Leslie Rabine offers one answer. Like other feminist critics who discuss female desire, Rabine argues that the romance plot, like the language itself in which it speaks, is constructed out of a discourse that is male. She traces the romantic plot to the story of the courtly hero who seeks transcendence through idealized love. In the novel the hero depends upon idealized love within the context of marriage for this transcendence. Female characters are thus denied a position within the historic process encoded into romance. In effect the lack of cultural codes for what Rabine calls "feminine" experience makes the woman author's relationship to the marriage plot extremely problematic:

> The forms of narrative and language in which she must speak are themselves obstacles to the realization of those desires. She must speak in a borrowed tongue and use forms that are constructed to exclude the very history, subjectivity, and sexuality she wants to express.[47]

Just as the female character is confined to a plot structured upon female discontent, the female writer must speak through a language alien to her experience in the world.

Susan Winnett goes even further, arguing that, literally and metaphorically, our pleasures as readers are modeled after bodily pleasures. Responding to Peter Brooks's (and implicitly to Joseph Boone's) claims that the trajectory of male sexual pleasure predicates the form of the nineteenth-century novel, Winnett offers what can be seen as an elaborate (and very witty) dissertation on woman-to-woman address (or at least writer-to-woman address). She tries to imagine how we might read novels differently if we followed a trajectory of female bodily pleasure:

> Without endangering her partner's ultimate "success," she can begin her own arousal at whatever point in the intercourse her fantasy finds exciting. She can take as her point of arousal the attained satisfaction of her mate. Without defying the conventions dictating that sex be experienced more or less together, she can begin and end her pleasure according to a logic of fantasy and arousal that is totally unrelated to the functioning and representation of the "conventional" sex act. Moreover, she can do so again. Immediately. And, we are told, again after that.[48]

Rabine's and Winnett's characterizations of the relation between reader and text are arresting when we consider the implications of Sarah Grand and other women writers deliberately choosing male narrators to articulate female stories. In part the choice represents a clever manipulation of the power of language that a woman writer is denied. Is Grand submissive to linguistically coded gender inequities in her choice of a male narrator, or does she take on the role of dominatrix (over masculinist conventions)? In this and her later novels female desire defines itself *not* specifically in terms of sexuality but in far more diffuse, diversified forms of discontent.

Grand's next and most popular novel, the *Heavenly Twins,* builds upon the fictional possibilities of multiplicity suggested in the earlier novels as Grand weaves three female plots, narrated by two distinctly contrasting speakers, into a literary battle cry for the women's movement. Winnett's wonderfully daring proposal for narratology may explain why Sarah Grand's baggy monster, *The Heavenly Twins,* would be so infuriating to male and male-identified critics and so wildly popular with a generation of women readers in Britain, America, and Europe.

Chapter 4

Love Triangles

"Tell me, Mrs. Sarah Grand
(What I ill can understand),
Why your men are *all* so horrid,
All with a 'retreating forehead'?

Why your women *all* are decked
With every gift of intellect,
And yet—invariably wed
These knights of the retreating head?

She, as bright as a geranium;
He, a simian type of cranium,—
Why, with decent chaps all round her,
Choose an atavistic Bounder?

We are Apes,—well, let that pass;
Need she, therefore, be an Ass?
Tell me, tell me, Sarah Grand,
For I do not understand.[1]

When Grand arrived in London in 1890, she immediately began to seek a publisher for *The Heavenly Twins*. She tells the story of the long, discouraging three-year search in the foreword that she wrote to the 1923 edition of the novel. From her letters and reminisces, as well as the foreword, a fascinating picture emerges of the intimate connections among publishers, the in-house readers at publishing houses, the critics writing for periodicals, and the writers themselves. Grand skirmishes with, even counterattacks, dismissive readers' reports and snide reviewers with the aid of her friends and fellow writers. Writing about the success of *The Heavenly Twins,* a reviewer for the *Critic* characterizes the novel's publishing history as itself a social melodrama in which Grand plays first victim then victor: "Some returned the

MS. without a word, others proffered courteous excuses and thought the book calculated to cause great indignation among women. Mme. Sarah Grand thought exactly the other way—naturally—as she had written the book for women, and finally she decided to publish it at her own expense."[2] George Meredith, as a reader for Chapman and Hall, complained about Grand's characterization, structure, style, and her claim to "ideas":

> The author is a clever woman and has ideas; for which reason she is hampered at present in the effort to be a novelist . . . Evadne would kill a better work with her heaviness. It matters little what she does—she has her ideas; the objection is the tedium in the presentation of her. The writer should be advised to put this manuscript aside until she has got the art of driving a story. She has ability enough, and a glimpse of humour here and there promises well for the future—if only she would practise, without thought of publishing, until she can narrate and sketch credible human creatures without harping on such trash as she gives them.[3]

Meredith's final rejection of the manuscript is based on his desire to protect an imagined culture of readers. As Elaine Hadley points out in discussing resistance to popular forms, Meredith acted as a defender of "intellectual culture," a culture threatened by the excesses of the feminized genre of melodrama and by the political incursions of women writing novels about issues and ideas.[4] Meredith writes:

> The subject of the novel, and the tone which necessarily springs from it are such, however, as will cause great pain to the majority of novel readers; and even "advanced thinkers" who may be presumed to be in sympathy with your view of social subjects will in our opinion regard the book as too bold and daring an attempt to revolutionize established ideas of Marriage Relations. Our own experience of "advanced thinkers" has been that however latitudinarian they may be in theory, they are conservative enough in practice with respect to their female belongings, and would probably be the first to repudiate their abstract views presented in such concrete form as is to be found in your novel.[5]

Grand's revision process involved reading portions of the novel to the advanced, principally female audience of the Pioneer Club (with its membership of over five hundred women); the club members responded with enthusiastic applause. Clearly, this readership sympathized with Grand's objectives in ways critics antagonistic to the politicizing of middlebrow fiction could not.[6] Margaret Shurmer Sibthorp, a reviewer for the feminist journal *Shafts* (which routinely reported on meetings of the Pioneer Club), later captured the spirit of the club's listeners in an 1893 review that contrasts forcibly with male press readers' responses:

> It is an inexpressible joy to a woman, to know that a woman's pen has done this deed of grace, has given to society a work which even the most prudish may read and be greatly exalted. The refined purity of the mind and heart which has guided the fearless pen, is seen plainly by eyes that desire to see, in every word which is written, even in the most painful portions of this human tale, of human life as it is lived, under conditions infinitely lower than its possibilities.[7]

The contrast suggests that Meredith's conception of what I have called an emerging middlebrow culture presumed a separation of art and politics, or at least gender politics, which excluded the very readers to and for whom Grand understood herself to be writing.

In the foreword Grand also quotes what she calls "a thunderclap of a letter" that she received from William Blackwood when she sought his advice about her unpublished manuscript.[8] Blackwood, like many later reviewers, was horrified by Grand's focus on venereal disease:

> We do not say that the ideals you employ are coarse, though we have no doubt critics will be less scrupulous, but we venture to assert that they are antagonistic to all culture and refinement that do not rest upon a purely physical basis. All delicately-minded women must feel themselves aggrieved, if not insulted, by the prominence which is given to the physical ideal of marriage in Evadne's resistance to her husband; and the sad fate of the bishop's daughter is too loathsome to be of artistic merit.[9]

He returns to the problem of audience and, implicitly, to his notions of literary culture, writing, "Even had I not the traditions of my House to go by in the case of *The Heavenly Twins,* I could not, and would not dare to place your work in the way of ladies, who compose so large a proportion of the novel-reading public."[10] It is a tribute both to Grand and to Blackwood that his criticism initiated a long-term friendship. Even as she answered his arguments, she sought his advice. Acknowledging that "I rather expected *The Heavenly Twins* would make your hair stand on end," she turns that admission into strategic common ground: "That is the effect it has upon me when I think of its even being read by anybody, and I ought to be inured to the subject."[11] In answer to his concern for women readers' sensibilities, Grand explains, "I have been urgently incited to write the book by other women, who send me accounts of cases so horrifying and heartrending that I believe if you knew but a little of them you would take up the subject yourself."[12]

In retrospect Grand's determination is astonishing. After three frustrating years of rejections, she decided once again to publish a novel at her own expense at the Guardian Office in Warrington. In fact, when she decided to give one last publisher, William Heinemann, a try, she submitted the manuscript to him in printed form. Heinemann had opened his business in 1890, and Grand feared that inexperience would make him hesitate to publish a little-known woman writer. A house reader, Daniel Conner, gave the book a favorable review, however, even though he, too, failed to anticipate the novel's appeal to a middlebrow female audience. He noted the book was "admirably written" as well as "daring and original . . . and so unconventional, so altogether outside the ordinary track of fiction that, in the absence of anything with which it can be compared, any criticism of it becomes difficult," but he also recommended "the passages of medical detail ought to be cut out or, at any rate, softened. The whole subject of these chapters is extremely unpleasant."[13] Heinemann's successes in marketing inexpensive editions of foreign fiction, including early translations of Ibsen, further encouraged him to publish *The Heavenly Twins*. The consequences astonished everyone involved. In just one year Heinemann reprinted the novel six times, selling nearly twenty thousand copies in Britain. Cassell's had sold five times as many copies in the United States. Although Grand had sold the copyright to Heinemann for one hundred pounds, when the novel's success was assured, he tore up her first contract and gave her "most favoured royalties," handing her a check for the twelve hundred pounds she had already earned under the new terms.[14] Gillian Kersley speculates that Grand eventually made about eighteen thousand pounds from *The Heavenly Twins* alone.[15]

While sales of *The Heavenly Twins* leave no doubt that it was a tremendous popular success, Grand's work was taken far more seriously, at least for several decades, than shilling shockers or formulaic fiction. I first became interested in Grand's work because Victorian reviewers repeatedly characterized *other* writers' works by comparing them to *The Heavenly Twins*. Ironically, many of the writers who most admired her were the male novelists whose literary reputations outlived hers. Mark Twain filled the margins of his edition of *The Heavenly Twins*, now owned by the Berg Library in New York, with admiring (as well as abusive) commentary. When Grand toured the United States, she stayed at Twain's home, and Grand and Twain apparently had long discussions about the uses of twins in fiction.[16] Despite George Meredith's criticisms of *The Heavenly Twins*, he and Grand became good friends, and both he and Thomas Hardy applauded her bravado. Writing to a female friend, Hardy encouraged her:

Sarah Grand, who has not, to my mind, such a sympathetic and intuitive knowledge of human nature as you, has yet an immense advantage over you in this respect—in fact of having decided to offend her
friends (as she told me)—and now that they are all alienated she can
write boldly, and get listened to.[17]

Perhaps her greatest male advocate, however, was George Bernard Shaw.
Shaw repeatedly referred to *The Heavenly Twins* in reviews of plays with
similar themes. In 1895 he wrote:

But now see what has happened. A terrible, gifted person, a woman
speaking for women, Madame Sarah Grand to wit, has arisen to insist
that if the morality of her sex can do without safety-valves, so can the
morality of "the stronger sex," and to demand that the man shall come
to the woman exactly as moral as he insists that she shall come to him.[18]

Moreover, if Stanley Weintraub is correct in assuming that Shaw's play *You
Never Can Tell* owes a great deal to his reading of *The Heavenly Twins,* then
Shaw paid her the most sincere compliment of all.[19]

Suddenly, unexpectedly, Frances Clarke McFall had become a
celebrity. Significantly, as she wrote about these early days of her success
from the perspective of 1923, Grand recalled the network of friendships with
feminists such as Emily Conebeare, Lady Elizabeth Cust, Mrs. Fawcett, Mrs.
Massingberd (founder of the Pioneer Club), Lady Henry Somerset, and
Constance Wilde that she formed in London between 1890 and 1893 with
the same warmth as she did her literary acclaim: "With these new friends I
was in a new world. To hear them talk was like having doors opened and
light shed on all that was obscure to me."[20] The delight in hard-won acceptance of her work, her optimism that her feminist fictions could contribute
to the fight for women's rights, and her relief at finding herself at home in a
community of like-minded women all resound in the name, Madame Sarah
Grand, that she chose for herself and used exclusively thereafter.

Grand's New Woman trilogy—*Ideala, The Heavenly Twins,* and *The
Beth Book*—triumphantly charts the growing sophistication and power of
the New Woman character. In *Ideala* the main character fights to win her
story away from a male narrator who would write her into the marriage plot
regardless of her desires or the circumstances of marriage. Ideala's obstacle-
ridden path to any serious knowledge of her world, her rights, and her alternatives leaves her in a miserable marriage for years after she realizes its
destructiveness. Structured as an experimental bildungsroman, *The Heavenly
Twins* offers a further argument for female education both as a right and as a

defense against misery and injustice. Marriage functions as an obstacle along the female character's path to education and self-fulfillment rather than as a goal. By pitting the logic of the bildungsroman against the logic of the marriage plot, *The Heavenly Twins* demonstrates that to survive the New Woman must learn first and foremost to be a critic of her culture. Her failure or success depends upon how well she learns to read—men's books, men's reasoning, men's means of control, and the masculine privilege that organizes the marriage plot.

To emphasize the necessity for women to learn to critique their culture if they want to resist it or transform it, the novel depicts not one but three plots, each of which develops the story of a separate female protagonist.[21] Though these three plots develop independently, they often overlap because the families of the three female protagonists are friends and because each has some association with the cathedral town of Morningquest. Together, Kate Flint's study of reading practices, *The Woman Reader,* and Margaret Beetham's investigation of periodical literature, *A Magazine of Her Own,* admirably document the centrality of reading to the formation of feminine identities in the nineteenth century. By 1890 literacy rates would support this claim for many working-class women as well as women with easier access to formal education. Despite the passage of the Education Act of 1870 and of improving education for girls, reading (especially books that were not included in the lists recommended for girls or in the conventional curricula of girls' schools) offered women the likeliest means of grasping cultural authority in the absence of political representation. As Flint shows again and again, the pleasures and potential power women experienced as readers led to lengthy debates about the dangers of reading, the appropriateness of particular kinds of reading material, and the consequences of misreading, and nowhere was represented reading more prominent than in New Women novels. Perhaps the preoccupation of the novel with reading explains why, as Flint points out, *The Heavenly Twins* appeared in so many cartoons and illustrations of the New Woman: "The image of a woman reading this novel became, together with references to her fondness for Ibsen, E. F. Benson's *Dodo,* and learning by heart quotations from *The Second Mrs. Tanqueray,* a cliché in the description of the 'New Woman.'"[22]

Not surprisingly, then, the theme of reading knits together the three plots of *The Heavenly Twins.* Edith, an old-fashioned womanly woman and the subject of the central line of action, marries a man who turns out to be a villain, and his villainy is highlighted by Grand's treatment of this marriage as a grisly melodrama. The fate of the other protagonists, two New Women figures, depends on their ability to "read" the implications of Edith's melodrama. Therefore, the novel traces the course of their educations and analyzes the way in which they interpret and respond to Edith's death. In the end, though each of these characters plays out the plot of her bildungsroman according to her reading of Edith's story, we, the audience of the novel, are the readers who have received the fullest education by reading the counter-readings, misreadings, and attempts at rewriting women's stories that this multiplot novel offers in a collective exploration of and resistance to the marriage plot.[23]

Edith, the protagonist of the first plot I discuss, is the epitome of the romantic female heroine: blond, blue-eyed, sheltered from all knowledge of the world, trusting, loving, and childlike. Her marriage to the worldly Sir Mosley Menteith, a union blessed by her loving parents, ultimately reveals to Edith the deadliness of the sexual double standard to innocent women after both she and her child contract syphilis. Thematically and structurally, the death of this romantic heroine is crucial to the entire novel. Although Edith dies in the first half of the novel, she presides as both martyr and plot motivation throughout. When other, more assertive, even "unwomanly" female characters have doubts about the fairness of their demands for education or for a place in the public sphere, they invoke Edith's memory as unanswerable testimony in support of their arguments. Edith's disease serves a metaphoric function; it becomes an infectious metonym for the moral illness Grand attributed to the ruthless, irresponsible, destructive exploitation of women, whether by individuals or institutions. Grand feared the threat of the disease quite literally as well. In a letter of 1894 infused with the eugenic rhetoric adopted by social purity feminists from Josephine Butler to Christobel Pankhurst, she writes:

> I have myself known 8 of those dreadful Edith cases. Don't you think it a disgrace to our civilisation that such a thing should be possible? It ought to be made a criminal offense, and will, I expect, when men themselves wake up to the fact that the numbers said to be diseased by dissolute living in Europe are one in three and in America one in five, and also that the disease is incurable and has been known to recur twenty years after it has apparently disappeared . . . Doctors advise these men to marry, and only the most consc'tious acknowledge that the disease is incurable. The marriage certificate should be a certificate of health.[24]

Edith's plot provides Grand with a means to convey messages to her readers so threatening to the social order that the realistic, regulated, mannered style and content of the marriage plot could not contain them.[25] The excesses permitted by melodramatic form, including one-dimensional villains, sensational details of disease and decay, impossible coincidences, and emotional logic, free the novel to vent feminist outrage at the sexual double standard, to denounce "good women's" quiet acquiescence to that standard, and to insist that all women must combine forces against male exploiters regardless of the antagonisms that separate women of different classes.

Elaine Hadley's definition of the "melodramatic mode" helps to explain why a feminist like Grand would turn to the conventions of melodrama as a vehicle for political fiction. Melodrama is marked by "familial narratives of dispersal and reunion, its emphatically visual renderings of bodily torture and criminal conduct, its atmospheric menace and providential plotting, its expressions of highly charged emotions, and its tendency to personify absolutes like good and evil" in social contexts as well as the theater; the genre also possesses an "uncanny responsiveness to its audience."[26] Peter Brooks's earlier characterization of melodrama also illuminates both the features of Edith's unfortunate career and the play of melodrama within the confines of "her" plot. Brooks particularly notes the indulgence of strong emotionalism; moral polarization and schematization; extreme states of being, situations, actions; overt villainy, persecution of the good, and final reward of virtue; inflated and extravagant expression; dark plottings, suspense, breathtaking peripeteia.[27] Yet, whereas Brooks emphasizes the psychological character of melodrama, feminist studies like Hadley's suggest how the effects of melodrama extend beyond Edith's story, motivating Evadne and Angelica's plots and vicariously acting upon Grand's readers. Hadley argues that as a communal, expansive, emotional form associated with mass rather than high culture, melodrama could be adapted to explore social and political issues with audiences who were outside the mainstream of cultural authority. In the nineteenth century these audiences would be primarily women and laborers. Focusing on the latter audience, Martha Vicinus maintains that the "binary world view" of melodrama inevitably favored the powerless: the lower classes, women, even criminals presumed redeemable.[28] Melodrama provides

> a psychological touchstone for the powerless . . . a means for exploring social and political issues in personal terms . . . By insisting on the ultimate triumph of social and personal justice, melodrama is able to provide consolation and hope without denying the social reality that makes goodness and justice so fragile.[29]

Unfortunately, the soothing restoration of order at the conclusion of the usual melodramatic plot, whether in the vindication of the hero, rescuing of the heroine, or punishment of the villain, usually leaves the audience with a palliating sense of relief rather than a desire for change. Often, therefore, melodrama reinforces self-sacrifice and resignation as positive, if passive, heroism. Vicinus explains this interaction of the revolutionary and reactionary impulses by pointing out that the central paradox of melodrama is that it defends the domestic ideal against a malign society under the belief that a larger moral order will prevail, yet in fact this moral order is a reflection of current social values.[30] E. Ann Kaplan also makes a case for the power of melodrama at once to subvert and oppress. Though Kaplan discusses films made primarily for female viewers, her analysis of melodrama helps to explain how *The Heavenly Twins* negates the consequences of melodrama while exploiting its psychological power. Noting that in the "family melodrama" the fictional world of good and evil polarizes according to the position of the woman in the film, Kaplan points out that "the work of the film centers on the problem *she causes* within the narrative."[31] Thus, the melodramatic plot may subvert the social order by representing a female character who is being treated unfairly on the basis of her sexuality, as in the case of Edith and her disease, but melodrama usually reinforces female acceptance of a subordinate position in that society. To restore order the abused heroine (who is in this case literally tainted by a disease) may die with the narrator's assurance that she will go to heaven as in the fallen Aunt Esther's death of alcoholism in Elizabeth Gaskell's *Mary Barton,* or she may inspire good in her seducer or accusers as Little Emily does in Charles Dickens's *David Copperfield,* as Hetty does in George Eliot's *Adam Bede,* as Tess does in Thomas Hardy's *Tess of the D'Urbervilles,* or as does the protagonist of another Gaskell novel, *Ruth.* The best she can hope for is a case of mistaken identity that proves she is still pure so that she can be rescued by the hero. Kaplan argues that, while male spectators leave melodrama "temporarily convinced of a 'just' universe," the female spectator recognizes that she is controlled by a moral universe which demands her sacrifice. As Kaplan says, "Her 'morality' is limited to sacrificing herself for the 'good' of her husband and family," a conclusion *The Heavenly Twins* adamantly resists.[32] In answer to this supposed limitation of the melodramatic form, Hadley offers a qualification that bears upon the politics of the New Woman: "the melodramatic mode was a reactionary rejoinder to social change but not, it must be stressed, necessarily a politically reactionary response."[33] The New Woman writers, when incorporating melodrama, often affirmed the status quo but only in order to demand that society live up to its own claims of honor, fairness, justice, truth, and decency, a demand that shifted the responsibility for creating an equitably gendered universe onto those who possessed the political power to effect changes in law or social practice.

Grand both uses and refuses the dictates of good and evil, individual and social culpability, and upheaval and restoration of order in the melodramatic plot associated with the character Edith. Edith does not "fall"; she follows the prescribed path by marrying; she even marries for love. Yet neither goodness nor social correctness can save her, and in the end she herself denounces the social order. As Norma Clarke points out, Grand's thinking "can be conservative, but the novelist in her is able to explore dimensions of woman's experience which in her lectures and speeches she did not address. One example of this is woman's anger."[34] Just as the fantastic logic of *Singularly Deluded* permitted Grand to exaggerate and elaborate the facets of masculinity that repelled her, the emotional tenor of melodrama allows her, through Edith's mad ravings, to describe and decry the misogyny masked by society's construction of and seeming reverence for ideal womanhood.

Like the endings of all good melodramatic plots, Edith's terrible fate is foreshadowed by events that we can only understand fully after the tragedy strikes. The scene in which Edith's danger is first suggested foreshadows the reversal of expectation that occurs in her later death scene, when the usually gentle, passive girl explodes into vituperative fury. After the announcement of Edith's engagement, her story recedes in the background; she reappears about two years later. In the meantime Edith has given birth to a son, the "one hope of happiness left for Edith," who instead "only proved to be another whip to scourge her" (277). The structure and content of the scene magnify Menteith's villainy. Edith sits in their seaside cottage, confusedly pondering her illness and unhappiness, while Menteith stands on the porch ogling a flirtatious young girl on the beach. The narrator comments, "She had been weakened into dependence by excess of sympathy, and now was being demoralised for want of any" (280). Though Edith tensely maintains the pose of conventional femininity, she fights for the rigid self-control necessary to remain quiet and submissive:

> her spiritual nature had been starved in close contact with him; only her senses had been nourished, and these were now being rendered morbidly active by disease. The shadow of an awful form of insanity already darkened her days. The mental torture was extreme; but she fought for her reason with the fearful malady valiantly; and all the time presented outwardly only the same dull apathy, giving no sign and speaking no word which could betray the fury of the rage within. (281)

The overlapping discourses of disease and morality in this passage invite comparison with ideas stirring among feminist groups during the 1890s. For Grand and other members of what came to be called the "social purity movement," lechery was a moral contagion as damaging to women as the potential physical consequence, venereal disease.[35] Elaine Showalter has shown that in the popular imagination of the 1890s syphilis was associated most with its last phases, insanity and paralysis. Her research reveals that literary representations of syphilis usually focused attention on the sufferings of men, as in Ibsen's *Ghosts*.[36] In an exercise of literary denial female characters who did contract syphilis, such as Émile Zola's main character in *Nana,* occupied the position of the prostitute, and the disease was treated as a predictable, even a just, fate for their transgressions. Grand's novels use the same strategy that many fund-raisers for AIDS research use today. The novels argue that "innocent" middle-class women could physically, mentally, and "morally" degenerate into this same condition. While the immediate or implied assumption is a reactionary (and untenable) suggestion that *anyone* could deserve to contract a disease, Grand's novels do something the AIDS fund-raisers sometimes fail to do. These plots connect women of middle and lower classes as well as wives and mistresses or prostitutes, all of whom are treated as the victims of unscrupulous men. Since insanity was a medical reality for victims of syphilis, this early glimpse of Edith's barely repressed anger can hardly be read as gratuitously sensational. Exhausted by Menteith's coldness (he is petulant at the loss of her good looks), Edith returns home to her parents.

Once Edith returns to Morningquest, the narrator (who is never identified but speaks as a member of the community) focuses on Edith's parents' and friends' readings of her degeneration. Here melodrama reveals that even the kindest and best-intentioned people in a woman's life share responsibility for the terrible consequences of her vulnerability to her husband and to the social structure that produced both husband and wife. Edith's gentle, naive parents are stunned by their daughter's haggard appearance and frightened by its implications. Mrs. Beale watches in horror as Edith alternately curses and whimpers forgetfully:

> Then all outward sign of Mrs. Beale's agitation subsided. Some shocks stun, and some strengthen and steady us. The piteous appeal in Edith's eyes, the puzzle and the pain of her face as she made an effort to recall her words and understand them, had the latter effect on her mother. (285)

Outwardly optimistic, the terrified mother summons Dr. Galbraith, insisting that "Weakness makes people unhealthy-minded. You must see the doctor, and have a tonic" (285). Mr. Beale (a bishop) is also profoundly disturbed; he feels deeply responsible as Edith's father, "protector," and spiritual advisor. When Edith ceases to fight against her fury and collapses into madness, the bishop stands by helpless and ashamed, confronted by a "stream of horrid imprecations." Her illness produces near-madness in her father: "He was trembling. He was at a loss. Nothing he had ever studied either in theology or metaphysics had in the slightest degree prepared him for the state of things in society which he was now being forced to consider" (297). After the Bishop hears Dr. Galbraith's prognosis, his anguish deepens; "every nerve was jarring in response to the horror that had come upon him. His heart was wrung, and his conscience did not acquit him" (298).

At the same time that the narrator attributes blame to Edith's parents, the novel also extends the responsibility outward into the reader's world. As the narrator makes clear, the restricted education and overprotection of women, the other-worldly emphasis of the Anglican Church, the irresponsibility of traditional education for men and women, and even the dangerous smugness of good people—all are at fault. The mythology of the long-suffering melodramatic heroine is drained of romance when the reader sees Edith from Angelica's perspective:

> Edith was lying on her back, with her face turned toward Angelica. There were deep lines of suffering marked upon it, and her eyes glittered feverishly, but otherwise she was gray and ghastly, and old. It was the horrible look of age that impressed Angelica . . . Edith was looking at her father. "That is why I sent for you all," she was saying feebly— "to tell you, you who represent the arrangement of society which has made it possible for me and my child to be sacrificed in this way. I have nothing more to say to any of you—except"—she sat up in bed suddenly, and addressed her husband in scathing tones—"except to you. And what I want to say to you is—Go! go! Father! turn him out of the house. Don't let me ever see that dreadful man again!" (300)

Edith's youth and innocence give way to unnatural age and awful knowledge, as she wildly denounces her husband, marriage, and the "arrangement of society" that victimizes women like her. After Edith pronounces her terrible judgment, madness overwhelms her, though periodically she awakens to agonizing awareness of her insanity. Alternately begging for release from the pain and laughing uncontrollably, she tortures her family with the inner truths of her anger:

> "I am quite, quite mad!" she said. "Do you know what I have been doing? I've been murdering him! I've been creeping, creeping, with bare feet, to surprise him in his sleep; and I had a tiny knife—very sharp—and I felt for the artery"—she touched her neck—"and then stabbed quickly! and he awoke, and knew he must die—and cowered! and it was all a pleasure to me. Oh, yes! I am quite, quite mad!" (304)

Probably this Ophelia-like, melodramatic self-reflexivity illustrates the stereotype of feminine madness that, Showalter argues, the asylum directors actually promoted.[37] In any case, in Edith's determination to name and repay Menteith's crime the novel insists that neither promises of salvation for submission to duty nor social pretenses should ever again silence women's stories of abuse.

The novel also emphasizes the dangers of deception to the poor and working-class sufferers whom good women ignore in order to protect their worldview. Both *The Heavenly Twins* and *Ideala* insist that social barriers prevent women of different classes and even different nationalities from perceiving their shared oppression. This second work links the fates of the angelic, upper-class Edith and a French former servant. Early in the novel, just before Sir Mosley Menteith first marks his preference for Edith, she and her mother encounter this Frenchwoman for the first time. While taking a drive, they see "a beggar, a young, slender, very delicate-looking girl, lying across the footpath with her feet toward the road. A tiny baby lay on her lap" (160). Shocked, Mrs. Beale sends her driver to examine the woman then drives on to the workhouse to ask someone to look after her. Twice, when the driver tries to tell Mrs. Beale and Edith the girl's story, Mrs. Beale firmly cuts him off, refusing to hear him, apparently because she assumes that the child is illegitimate and that therefore the pathetic young mother would blight her and her daughter's purity.

Yet the narrator connects Edith to the suffering servant woman in a striking passage that reminds readers of the French woman's suffering even as Edith forgets her. The passage contrasts the onset of Edith's attraction to Menteith with a disavowal of romance conveyed through the French servant's situation. After the Frenchwoman has been carried to the poorhouse, Edith and her mother return home to find that Menteith has arrived for a visit, and he shows a decided partiality for Edith. When he leaves Edith

> felt as if she could be eloquent, but no suitable subject presented itself, and so she said little. She was very glad, however, and she looked so; and naturally she thought no more for the moment of the poor French girl—who was just then awaking to a sense of pain, mental and physical, to horror of the past, and fear for the future, and the heavy sense of an existence marred, not by reason of her own weakness so much as by the possession of one of the most beautiful qualities in human nature—the power to love and trust. (167)

Following the pattern of social reformers who worked (however paternalistically) to "save" prostitutes rather than to punish them, the novel argues that prostitutes are victims of men, of economics, and of their feminine social training, on one hand, and that, on the other hand, if only from self-interest, middle-class women must protect the interests of poorer women—issues taken up more explicitly in *The Beth Book*.[38]

The melodramatic implications of the contrast between Edith and the Frenchwoman only become clear two years later. In the meantime, of course, Edith has married Menteith, given birth to a sickly, malformed child, and returned to her parents' home in Morningquest in search of treatment for her son and for her own mysterious illness. Before she is completely overwhelmed by syphilis, Edith goes out for another drive and once again encounters the young mother, now partially recovered and bent on revenge. The appearance of the Frenchwoman's child, as ill and wizened as her own young son, startles Edith.

The melodramatic doubling of the children would have intensified the Victorian audience's reactions by forcibly reminding them of "syphilis of the innocents," which caused retardation and deformity in children and which is believed to have killed fifteen hundred children annually. Showalter quotes one doctor's account of a "small, wizened, atrophied, weakly, sickly creature," who looked like a "monkey or a little old man"; she suggests, moreover, that Thomas Hardy's enigmatic Father Time may be based upon popular conceptions of the syphilitic "mad child," whose breakdown is the "signifier of the conflicts, lies, and hypocrisies of the sexual system."[39] When Edith asks the servant her child's name, the woman snaps, "Mosley Menteith," then begins a tirade against her seducer, which confirms all of Edith's worst fears.[40]

Edith's education exacts its harshest sentence in this scene. By avoiding a simple personal act of kindness she might have done the servant in her illness, Edith has missed an opportunity to save her own life. The selfish innocence of a "good woman," thrown into explicit relief here by the extreme consequences of melodrama, destroys her. Although neither of these pathetic children retaliates with the brutality of Father Time, Edith's child haunts the other female characters long after Edith herself dies and thus functions as a physical reminder of the exploitation at the heart of the marital system and the double sexual standard it reinforces.

The incident connecting Edith and the French emigrant is foreshadowed by an event in Grand's earlier novel *Ideala,* when Ideala is mysteriously summoned to a stranger's sickbed in a London slum. There she learns that her husband has seduced and abandoned an impoverished working-class girl. This former mistress is now dying of scarlet fever, and, as an act of atonement, she wishes to warn Ideala of her husband's unfaithfulness. The narrator recalls: "it was the old story, the old story aggravated by every incident that could make it more repulsive—and her husband was the hero of

it" (152). Ideala risks her own health to comfort the girl then to take charge
of her burial. Penny Boumelha points out, in discussing a number of New
Woman novels, that "the solidarity of wife and mistress, or of virgin and
whore, is often recognised as a crucial element in the struggle against the
double standard of sexual morality."[41] In *The Heavenly Twins* melodrama
provides this connection between a particular instance of sexual exploitation
and the larger framework of power relations that victimize women, particularly women outside the partial protection of middle-class rules of conduct. By suggesting the possibility that women might break the barriers of
class to unite on gender issues, Grand followed the lead of Josephine Butler,
whose work on behalf of prostitutes she had deeply admired from her girlhood.[42] In the 1923 foreword to *The Heavenly Twins* Grand wrote:

> It was time someone spoke up, and I felt that I could and determined that
> I would . . . It was torture to think of it and shame to mention it. But it
> had to be brought in some how . . . One and all thought it impossible to
> do more or better than Josephine Butler was doing. The brutal way in
> which she had been treated was quoted as an example of the result on
> public opinion of any effort a woman might make to change it.[43]

Grand's sense of responsibility and culpability forms a consistent refrain
in late-nineteenth-century feminist arguments across the spectrum from
moderates to militants. Elaine Hadley's rhetorical analysis of Josephine Butler's speeches documents Butler's repeated attempts to create a conception
of family that incorporated prostitutes as "fallen women," sisters and daughters who had been victimized by failed patriarchs who were thereby
destroying the family.[44] Two decades later Christobel Pankhurst would
mobilize similar arguments in her collection of scathing editorials, *The Great
Scourge* (1912). In her analysis of Pankhurst's politics Janet Lyon challenges
late-twentieth-century critics who dismiss social purity feminists as misguided reactionaries. Lyon argues that Pankhurst reverses the rhetoric that
equates women with disease by insisting that literal and metaphorical
degeneration would not cease until men acknowledged their responsibility
for economically exploiting women who had no economic or political control over their fates. Pankhurst's strategy, claims Lyon, was to convince the
public that "moral" issues were in fact economic and political issues by
uncovering the connection between "patriarchal economic coercion and
sexual subjection."[45] Grand invokes Butler's rhetoric and anticipates
Pankhurst's arguments by pitting the cross-class gender interests of exploited
women against what she and other purity feminists saw as the sexual rapa-
ciousness of wealthy men. In *Ideala* as well as *The Heavenly Twins* Grand
exploits a middle-class, middlebrow, feminist strategy, erecting a realistic

scaffolding of social issues upon which to build melodramatic action. Through these connections the novel argues that women encouraged to be enemies due to class differences or competition for men must form an altruistic bond strong enough to militate against the victimization each has experienced. The contrasts tenable under the logic of melodrama juxtapose a gendered fantasy of moral wholesomeness with the very real social problem of physical contamination.

The conventional marriage plot promised to liberate women from the evils of the public sphere into the pleasures and spiritual powers of the domestic realm. Grand stands these assumptions on their heads. Edith's plot threatens readers that marriage visits the consequences of a woman's past— a past of poorly prepared parents, miseducation, mindless religiosity, separation of the sexes, tolerance of the sexual double standard—upon the present. The marriage contract quite literally binds Edith to death, hardly the social regeneration promised by the end of even skeptical marriage plot novels like Jane Austen's *Pride and Prejudice,* George Eliot's *Middlemarch,* Thomas Hardy's *Far from the Madding Crowd,* and so many others. This shocking conclusion to Edith's plot, an innocent heroine's death portrayed in such gruesome detail, also refuses the affirmation or social consolidation offered to audiences by conventional melodrama. Edith has committed no mistake to necessitate forgiveness; instead, she has obeyed the rules of society by marrying (even for love). She also differs from the traditional heroine of melodrama by unrelentingly charging her villain with full responsibility for her death. The Christian stoicism of earlier expiring heroines encourages readers to reconcile themselves to melodramatic deaths, as with Charles Dickens's Little Nell in *The Old Curiosity Shop* or Harriet Beecher Stowe's Little Eva in *Uncle Tom's Cabin.* Rather than pitying or reforming Menteith, however, Edith furiously orders him from her house. Edith recognizes that goodness is no guarantee against the reality of evil as it manifests itself in disease. Therefore, she denounces the ignorance imposed upon her and the social constraints that shaped her character, including the misused powers of good women such as her mother.[46] Pivotally placed near the center of the novel, Edith's collapse and death establish an immoral, immutable benchmark against which the other female characters define their ethics and actions for the rest of the novel.

The story of Edith's friend Evadne begins while Evadne is a young girl, educating herself by reading her father's and brother's books. At nineteen she becomes infatuated with an older military man, Colonel Colquhoun; however, on the day of their wedding she receives a mysterious letter about his past sexual encounters. Against her better judgment, Evadne finally gives in to her family and friends' insistence that she live with the Colonel, but only after he agrees to a celibate marriage. The strain of such an "unnatural" arrangement so damages Evadne's physical and psychological health that even after the Colonel dies she never fully recovers. Though the first five books of *The Heavenly Twins* are narrated by a third-person omniscient narrator, the final book is a medical record of Evadne's failing health, written by Sir George Galbraith, a doctor and psychologist, who becomes Evadne's second husband.

Grand emphasizes the centrality of reading to Evadne's development throughout the novel. During Evadne's girlhood the narrator carefully details her eclectic reading from John Stuart Mill's *The Subjection of Women* to philosophy, medicine, anatomy, mathematics, poetry, and physiology. In particular the narrator describes Evadne's naively radical readings of male novels. The other characters only learn of the seemingly quiet, demure young woman's dangerous ideas when she begins to use her reading techniques to interpret the actions of her family and friends. Later, Evadne's sense of duty forces her to remain married to the Colonel even though she believes his previous sexual experience should invalidate the marriage contract. Her disillusionment with a social order that demands her toleration of immorality as a duty is represented through her changing relationship to her reading as well as to her husband. Her independent habits of thought conflict with her emotional and economic dependence on others, and she "evades" the moral paradox in which she finds herself by suppressing mental activity, even burning her books, in symbolic capitulation to a society which requires women to serve rather than to think.

The mythological source of Evadne's name foreshadows her plot.[47] Readers are reminded of the story of female self-immolation associated with the name when one of the twins, Diavolo, playfully but perceptively describes Evadne as he finds her several years after her marriage to Colonel Colquhoun: "The name means Well-pleasing-one, as nearly as possible, and it suits her sometimes. Evadne—classical Evadne—was noted for her devotion to her husband, and distinguished herself finally on his funeral pyre-expyred [*sic*] there" (603). The Greek Evadne was the daughter of Poseidon and Pitane; she was most famous in her role as loyal wife to Kapaneous, an Argive general. When Kapaneous attacked Thebes despite the gods' warnings, he and his men were killed by Kreon (with the gods' assistance) and left unburied as a mark of their disobedience and defeat. In revenge the Argive forces launched a second battle to rescue their dead, and when the troops returned the dead were honored by public funerals. During the oration in praise of Kapaneous,his wife, Evadne, threw herself upon his funeral pyre in an act similar to sati, a practice that perversely fascinated and horrified late Victorians. Sati, like Chinese foot-binding, was also exploited by Englishwomen reformers as a sensational analogue for the destructive effects of legal and social constraints upon women (just as North American women and sometimes British women compared "womanhood" with slavery).[48] The classical Evadne sacrificed her life to show her respect for her husband and to accompany him to the underworld; the Evadne myth introduces a question Grand indirectly asks throughout her literary and activist career: what is woman's "duty"?

The myth not only functions as a commentary on duty, the focus of Evadne's plot, but it also fearfully anticipates the outcome. Defeated by the "duty" society imposes upon her, Evadne finally uses her skills as a reader to reinterpret herself, since her readings of others offer no solutions to her problems. In an ironic twist of the female bildungsroman Evadne reads/ immolates herself into the repressed, passive (or passive-aggressive), and self-destructive role of the hysteric.

Both Kate Flint in *The Woman Reader* and Linda Petersen in *The Determined Reader* demonstrate the prevalence of reader-protagonists in the nineteenth-century novel and particularly in the bildungsroman. Petersen notes that younger reader-protagonists often turn to books in search of "cultural facts," a process that presumably inspires the reader's quest for identity.[49] The reader fetishizes the book, consciously demanding that it fill an unconscious desire for a sense of unity and/or identity. In the process the reader-protagonists of the nineteenth-century British novel may bring upon themselves the very alienation that outcast characters, including women, long to escape. Without a teacher or guide, the reader-protagonist "cannot see texts as meaning continually displaced or as dialectical."[50] Consequently, "reading becomes misreading," as the protagonist withdraws from the possibility for accommodation and community in the social world.[51] Petersen goes on to discuss the problems for actual (as opposed to fictional) female readers who seek an identity, particularly a sexual identity, in the women characters of male writers' texts. Because Evadne's father does not believe in women's education, Evadne's only recourse is self-guided, solitary reading, which leaves her heavily dependent on the very male intellectual authorities she must challenge to understand the gender dynamics that threaten her as an adult. Acknowledging this problem, John Kucich suggests that Evadne's complex, changing relation to reading brings into play a larger conflict between feminist politics and "fiction":

> Evadne is linked to literary practices despite herself when she is revealed to be an excellent reader of the narratives of other characters. But her rejection of fiction signals a widespread problem, noted in many New Woman novels, with the aesthetic consequences of

women's demand for "real" truth. When taken to extremes, feminist realism—as male reviewers never tired of pointing out—could include a contempt for art.[52]

While the narrator applauds Evadne's ambition, the novel also dramatizes the dangers of reading, including those that Petersen and Kucich discuss—as alienation, misreading, identity crises, and the loss of art as a means of expression or community building—when the reading experience is structured as an alternative to education rather than a means to education.

In contrast with the male bildungsroman, Evadne's education is the product of a delicate paradox sustained between her and her father.[53] As a young girl, she molds her thoughts upon her father's patronizing and conservative views, developing her powers of reason by silently disproving each of her father's assessments of female intellect and by unraveling the contradictions of his thought even as she sustains her respect and affection for and duty to him:

> He was one of those men who believe emphatically that a woman should hold no opinion which is not of masculine origin . . . But these precepts of his were, after all, only matches to Evadne which fired whole trains of reflection, and lighted her to conclusions quite other than those at which he had arrived himself. In this way, however, he became her principal instructor. (5)

In Grand's depiction of this father/daughter-teacher/amanuensis relationship, Evadne (and by extension inquisitive women of the nineteenth century) becomes a thief who plunders the male hoards of knowledge. To educate herself Evadne must ferret out her brother's discarded textbooks from the attic, pick up books that adults leave lying about, or rifle her father's library. The rebelliousness of illicit reading is beautifully illustrated in two paintings Kate Flint discusses, Auguste Toulmouche's *Dans la Bibliothèque (Les fruits defendus)* (1868) and Alexander M. Rossi's *Forbidden Books* (1897). In both, unsupervised girls plunder family libraries: Rossi's painting shows an older woman surreptitiously listening to adolescent girls discussing a book through a half-open door, while the girls in Toulmouche's painting have actually appointed a lookout who bends toward the keyhole, listening for intruders, as three other girls plunder the shelves. As Flint's work demonstrates, both the act and the fear of girls' illicit reading stretched across time and continents.[54]

The cultural custodian in Evadne's home is her father. The contradictions between Evadne's talents and her father's contempt for the female intellect reveal how men use rhetorical tactics to turn any evidence of female potential or accomplishment into proof of female inferiority. In a scene reminiscent of Maggie Tulliver's struggles to educate herself in *The Mill and the Floss,* Evadne carefully works through her brother's "Colenso" and "Barnard Smith" to test her father's claim that women cannot learn arithmetic because "they have no brains" (11). Instead of changing his views, Mr. Frayling (like Tom's misogynist tutor, Mr. Stelling, in *Mill and the Floss*) changes his tactics to explain away a girl's accomplishment. Thus, he insists that women "pick up things with a parrot-like sharpness, but haven't intelligence enough to make any practical application of them" because Evadne has not yet learned to work accounts. When she astutely asks, "Can men keep accounts who have never seen accounts kept?" she provokes ridicule rather than changing her father's opinion of women's intellectual abilities (12).

Evadne's love and respect for her father prevent her from admitting to herself, much less drawing to his attention, the illogical propositions that bolster his contempt for women. But, in the silence of her reading and her thoughts, Evadne constructs an alternative reality to her father's:

> coming across so many sneers at the incapacity of women, she fell insensibly into the habit of asking why. The question to begin with was always: "Why are women such inferior beings?" But, by degrees, as her reading extended, it changed its form, and then she asked herself doubtfully: "Are women such inferior beings?" a position which carried her in front of her father at once by a hundred years, and led her rapidly onto the final conclusion that women had originally no congenital defect of inferiority, and that, although they have still much way to make up, it now rests with themselves to be inferior or not, as they choose. (13)

In the gap between Mr. Frayling's knowledge, gained in public schools and in the conversational diversity of the male sphere, on one hand, and his limited use of that knowledge, on the other, Evadne's own formidable intellect develops. By her nineteenth year Evadne herself recognizes that "her mind returned from every excursion into no matter what abstruse region of research, to the position of women, her original point of departure." Based on her stolen moments in men's books and secret pilferings of her father's thoughts, Evadne forms her own notions of evil: "'Withholding education from women was the original sin of man'" (24). At the same time, the novel shows that the qualities cultivated in women and valued by Evadne make the shift from analysis to resistance nearly impossible, even for exceptional women. Feminine reticence, passivity, submission, and respect for male authority, particularly in that most personal, domestic, and potentially tyrannical space of the childhood home, prevent Evadne from questioning either her father's contradictions or her mother's toleration of her father's abuses. Even if only silently, however, Evadne's incursions into men's stores of knowledge train her to be a duplicitous reader as she negotiates with male representations of women.[55]

Written in the nineteenth century, Grand's novels stoically acknowledge the patriarchal character of literature as well as life. When first characterizing Evadne's response to her reading, as recorded in a "commonplace book," the narrator notes:

> Some of the criticisms she wrote in her "Commonplace Book" are quite exhaustive; most of them are temperate, although she does give way occasionally to bursts of fiery indignation at things which outrage her sense of justice; but the general characteristic is a marked originality, not only in her point of view, but also in the use she makes of quite unpromising materials. In fact, the most notable part of the record is the proof it contains that *all the arguments upon which she formed her opinions were found in the enemy's works alone.* (14; italics mine)

Here the act of deciphering and decoding masculinist messages distinguishes women's quest for knowledge from men's; it also provides a means of tapping the anger and energy beneath the surfaces of ideal womanhood. Evadne struggles to develop the skills necessary to read the signs of patriarchy in men's novels as well as in her father's pompous lectures; to use Jane Miller's terminology, Evadne learns "the questions of an imposter, a practiced liar, schooled to a double vision and bilingualism."[56] The contradictions she discovers teach her a great deal, yet, like many twentieth-century as well as nineteenth-century women, she lacks the confidence either to pursue the conclusions she draws from this decoding process or to share her gleanings with her hostile audience. Consequently, even though she *is* exceptional, her hesitancy in asserting and acting on her knowledge confirms others' belief in female inferiority, for her reticence (or restraint) passes for ignorance.

The most significant insight into Evadne's analysis of male texts comes from her reader's journal. In effect, "we," as Grand's readers, participate in the educational process; we learn to read "the enemy's works" by reading Evadne's readings. In one instance Evadne charts her progress by *re*reading Oliver Goldsmith's *The Vicar of Wakefield,* "an early favorite," in order to compare "her childish little synopsis, very quaint in its unconscious irony" (14), with a second response written three or four years later. In both entries Evadne chastises the vicar for refusing to let his wife and daughters read his books. She draws an unconscious parallel between the vicar's family and her own as she records the vicar's unjust criticism of his wife's inanity after he discourages her from reading or thinking. Over time, Evadne's assessments remain consistent; however, her powers of analysis (like Grand's) grow sharper, more precise, and more dangerous.

Evadne exposes the gender biases of the male bildungsroman in her response to two "classics," *Roderick Random* and *Tom Jones*. She expects great things of these books after overhearing her father praise the novels, calling them "true to life" in their lifelike rendering of "human nature" and prosing about the "education in moral philosophy on every page." Silent as ever, Evadne slips the novels out of her father's library and begins to read. Grand's condemnation of the male picaresque plot surfaces in the narrator's wry summary of the reading experience: "They did not please her, but she waded through them from beginning to end conscientiously, nevertheless, and then she made her remarks." Evadne begins with a summary of *Roderick Random* that foreshadows her own future:

> The hero is a kind of king-can-do-no-wrong young man; if a thing were not right in itself he acted as if the pleasure of doing it sanctified it to his use sufficiently. After a career of vice, in which he revels without any sense of personal degradation, he marries an amiable girl named Narcissa, and everyone seems to expect that such a union of vice and virtue would be productive of the happiest consequences. (19)

She concludes her review with equal asperity: "The fine flavour of real life in the book seems to me to be of the putrid kind which some palates relish, perhaps; but it cannot be wholesome, and it may be poisonous. The moral is: Be as vicious as you please, but prate of virtue." Equally hostile to *Tom Jones,* Evadne disposes of both novels with the angry ambivalence born of feminist ideas and feminine social training. Annoyed with the fictional marriage of a "spotless heroine" to Tom, who is "steeped in vice," she writes: "The two books taken together show well the self-interest and injustice of men, the fatal ignorance and slavish apathy of women; and it may be good to know these things, but it is not agreeable" (20).

These journal entries impress readers even a hundred years later for their distinctly feminist character. Where masculinist readers even now perceive adventure, bravado, maturity, growth, and romance, Evadne discovers exploitation, indulgence, and excuse of male privilege. Evadne's response to these novels seems less a revision of a masculinist reading than a genuinely alternative interpretation of the codes and conventions of a masculinist narrative.

While Evadne's plot encourages sympathy and admiration for her heroic efforts, the narrator also warns of the disadvantages and dangers consequent to the isolated and undirected study that for Evadne and her nineteenth-century counterparts was too often the only available form of education. We see the isolating effect of Evadne's education not only in her stealthy reading but also in the association of reading with the room of one's own Virginia Woolf so longed for twenty years later. While Woolf describes such a room as a feminist fantasy, Grand's representation of Evadne's education, as she reads dusty, forgotten books in the attic or studies in her room only after her duties to the family are done and they are asleep, provides another view.[57] The novel's treatment of Evadne implies that for women's education to be balanced and productive their minds must be cultivated in space and time provided within the larger, public world.

We first see Evadne in her private retreat when Mrs. Orton Beg, a beloved, widowed aunt, visits her there. Evadne's aunt compares her room to Elaine's bower before the disastrous arrival of Lancelot. Aunt Beg's comparison between Evadne and Tennyson's Elaine, "a lily maid high in her chamber up a tower to the east guarding the sacred shield of Lancelot" provokes Evadne's scorn for such foolish self-sacrifice (35). Yet the analogy is prophetic; eventually, she too is lured from the safety of her attic room by her infatuation for the Colonel.

Evadne becomes conscious of the tension between her private life of revolutionary ideas and her public life of conventional acquiescence when her aunt, as a representative of that public world, enters and examines the interior of her private life. As Aunt Beg questions Evadne about the "peculiar views" she usually confines to her journal, Evadne explains that, after years of being bored in her childhood schoolroom, she began to explore her ideas alone: "Having a room of my own always has been a great advantage. I have been secure all along of a quiet time at night for reading and thought—and that is real life, auntie, isn't it?" (36) Evadne is alarmed when her aunt questions the benefits of this solitude (sounding like a present-day feminist activist berating an academic colleague): "The room to yourself has been a doubtful advantage, I fancy . . . It has made you theoretical" (37).

Their exchange dramatizes the New Woman's paradoxical position. To investigate ideas she must retreat from an intolerant society into silence and solitude, where her interpretations will be skewed, at best. Should she succeed in educating herself, the act of attainment ensures social ostracism. For the intellectual woman success can only be failure. Evadne's anxious response poses a dilemma that is not lost on today's female reader. She fears learning that she *is* exceptionally bright perhaps more than learning that she isn't:

> But, auntie, don't use such an ominous expression as "peculiar views" about anything I say, *please;* "views" are always in ill odour, and peculiarities even peculiar perfections, would isolate one, and that I *do* dread . . . I don't want to despise my fellow-creatures. I would rather share their ignorance and conceit and be sociable than find myself isolated even by a very real superiority. The one would be pleasant enough, I should think; the other pain beyond all bearing. (37)

Evadne's earnest denial of reality reminds the reader that, for all her exceptional qualities, Evadne inhabits the same universe as Edith. Though Evadne contrasts with Edith's unquestioning acceptance of women's social roles, her intellect cannot free her from the longing to be what her society most values in a woman: cooperative, tolerant, accepting, even unintelligent. These longings explain the secrecy surrounding her self-education. In the very act of pursuing this desire for knowledge, Evadne learns the oldest of feminine strategies for success—suppression.[58]

In many ways Evadne's insular education dooms her to her first marriage. After years of indulging her intellect but ignoring her emotional life, Evadne is suddenly overwhelmed by the tumultuous feelings and sensations of puberty: "Her intellectual activity was suspended—her sense awoke" (46). (As John Kucich helpfully points out, Grand consistently celebrates sensuality regardless of how much distrust her novels express toward sexuality.)[59] The narrator characterizes this dizzying phase, once again, in relation to Evadne's reading. Exhausted by weeks of coming-out parties in London, Evadne gladly returns home to books. Now, however, she turns to

> inflated fiction . . . sweet stimulants that soothed and excited, but did not nourish: tales that caused chords of pleasurable emotion to vibrate while they fanned the higher faculties into inaction—vampire things inducing that fatal repose which enables them to drain the soul of its life blood and compass its destruction. (45)

Though Evadne forestalls such a fate by balancing "sweet stimulants" with the "wholesome" works of Oliver Wendell Holmes, the narrator blames her difficulty in balancing sensation and intellect on the lifelong silence imposed by her parents. For Evadne the room alone, with both its literal and metaphoric implications, is not a luxury but a furtive necessity, attendant with debilitating consequences. The greatest of these is her first marriage, as she herself realizes only after her experience in the world reveals that she was unable to discern between a partner compatible to her tastes and intelligence and "a mere affair of the senses" (78).

During the period of courtship Evadne's confusion over her implausible attraction to the Colonel (she knows little about him and seldom looks at, much less speaks to, him) temporarily overwhelms her so that she accepts his proposal of marriage and her family's delighted congratulations without question. On the day of her wedding, however, she is startled out of her romantic reverie when she receives a mysterious letter that reveals the Colonel's profligate past. She abandons the wedding party, travels alone to ask the never-identified informant for details, then seeks sanctuary with her Aunt Beg. At first Evadne naively assumes that her parents had also been deceived about the Colonel's previous life and that when they learn the truth her marriage will quickly be annulled. When her family ridicules her fastidiousness and demands that she return to the Colonel and humbly apologize, Evadne startles everyone by attacking the illogic that enforces gender differences in her world. She turns her reading strategies from literary constructions of masculinity to her "real-life" husband. This crucial shift, from textual to cultural reading and from the seemingly passive position of the reader of books to the pragmatic, activist stance Evadne assumes as a reader of men, is marked by Evadne's answer to their demands:

> he is not at all a proper person for a young girl to associate with . . . in point of fact his mode of life has very much resembled that of one of those old-fashioned heroes, Roderick Random or Tom Jones, specimens of humanity whom I hold in peculiar and especial detestation. (84)

Evadne's unexpected assessment of her own relationship in conjunction with her reading of literary relationships may be refreshingly humorous from the reader's point of view (though hardly from hers or for different reasons from her father's or husband's); however, she soon learns that reading masculine privilege is one thing, escaping its effects is quite another.

Evadne had previously resisted male fictions in confessions to her journal; she now launches a rebellion against male privilege by writing, turning her increasingly astute reading strategies onto a new text, her mother's letters. The positioning of readers and writers in this passage is complex. Evadne's father refuses to write and instead employs Mrs. Frayling, her mother, who filters his directives through the sieve of her own anxieties. Indirectly, the letters record paternal threats, which extend to Evadne's mother because she has produced such a disobedient child; explicitly the letters chastise Evadne in her mother's voice. Consequently, Evadne must read through her mother's anxieties to her father's dictates so that she can adequately respond to both.

The Fraylings's arguments clarify the obstacles facing Evadne; the letters also implicitly and explicitly name the social forces that repressed and restricted women in the late-Victorian years. Moreover, though Grand may not have been prophetic (or suspicious) enough to anticipate the eventual disappearance of her own work, the letters employ many of the strategies with which literary critics discredited the fiction of the New Woman novelists. One of the key letters encompasses all of these issues:

> YOU MOST UNNATURAL CHILD:
>
> We shall all be disgraced if this story gets out. So far the world knows nothing, and there is time for you to save yourself. I warn you that your father's anger is extreme. He says he shall be obliged to put you in a lunatic asylum if you do not give in at once, and consent to live with your husband. And there is the law, too, which your husband can invoke. And think of your five sisters. Will anybody marry them after such a business with you? Their prospects will be simply ruined by your heartless selfishness. No girl in my young days would have acted so outrageously. It is indecent. It is positively immodest. I repeat that your father is the proper person to judge for you. You know nothing of the world, and even if you did, you are not old enough to think for yourself. You do not imagine yourself to be a sort of seer, I hope, better informed by intuition than your parents are by wisdom and knowledge, for that would be a certain sign of insanity. Your father thinks your opposition is mere conceit and certainly no good can come of it. All right-minded women have submitted and suffered patiently, and have had their reward. Think of the mother of St. Augustin [*sic*]! Her husband returned to her penitent after years of depravity. "Every wise woman buildeth her house; but the foolish pluck it down," and that is what you are doing. "A continual dropping on a rainy day and a contentious woman are alike." For Heaven's sake, my child, do not become a contentious woman. See also Prov. viii. If only you had read your Bible regularly every day, prayed humbly for a contrite heart and *obeyed your parents,* as you have always been taught to do, we should never have had all this dreadful trouble with you; but you show yourself wanting in respect in every way and in all right and proper feeling, and really I don't know what to do. I don't indeed. Oh, do remember that forgiveness is still offered to you, and repent while it is called today. I assure you that your poor husband is even more ready than your father and myself to forgive and forget.
>
> I pray for you continually, Evadne, I do indeed. If you have any natural feeling at all, write and relieve my anxiety at once. (90–91)

For Evadne, Colonel Colquhoun's sexual promiscuity is an unforgivable reminder of unacceptable double standards, standards enforced by her par-

ents. The colonel himself personifies moral and physical contagion. Therefore, to deny her wedding vows and her parents' authority becomes a moral
imperative. When she rejects the authority of family, the law, and her religion in answer to the demands of her own conscience, however, Evadne
relinquishes their protection and provokes their enmity. Whereas Lord
Dawne simply refused to see conflicts between the "real" woman and "his"
Ideala, Mrs. Frayling must turn unwilling clay into a womanly woman. In
her letter Mrs. Frayling retaliates with every possible authority contributing
to the definition of Ideal Womanhood. She threatens Evadne with the loss
of respectability, legal coercion, indecency (the gravest threat to the ideal of
womanhood), parental authority, guilt for her selfish inconsideration of her
family, historical and biblical precedents, and unnaturalness.

From the distance of a century the letter is also startling in its incisive
summary of the techniques used to discredit women's ideas, including their
literary ideas. Joanna Russ's *How to Suppress Women's Writing* provides an
astute overview of the discrediting strategies that Grand weaves into this letter. For example, when Mrs. Frayling claims that Evadne's flight is "inde-
cent," this "pollution of agency" implies that the mere act of expressing
anger—whether anger takes the form of resistance to the law (as in this
case), public complaint, or political art—is immodest and therefore could
only be the work of a woman who lacks decency.[60] Mrs. Frayling also
applies what Russ calls a "double standard of content," which labels "one
set of experiences as more valuable and more important than the other," a
common practice of reviewers of New Woman fiction.[61] By implicitly
defining male experience as "normative," a society prevents serious consideration of female experience or the knowledge it produces. Mrs. Frayling
insists that Evadne knows "nothing of the world" and must consequently
obey her father and her husband. As she echoes her husband's opinions,
Mrs. Frayling personifies a society that has been deafened to a woman's
analysis of marriage by the roar of male opinion. She also dramatizes the
most effective weapon in the masculinist artillery, womenly women.

Evadne unwittingly acquiesces to her own destruction when she
accommodates her principles to society's expectations by agreeing to live
with the Colonel in a state of celibacy. Grand contextualizes Evadne's capitulation in the most overtly masculinist arena imaginable, the military. Leaving girlhood behind for wifehood, Evadne moves to the foreign terrain of a
Maltese military settlement. Grand's choice of setting has biographical as
well as metaphoric significance. Grand's letters and reflections characterize
her own experience of being a military wife as particularly miserable. Being
herself far from a silent intellectual, Grand was ridiculed by members of her
husband's military community as a bluestocking and an eccentric. As I men-

tioned in discussing *A Domestic Incident,* the resident curate even parodied her as a fatuous pseudo-intellectual in a vignette of military society.[62] Moreover, she must have experienced firsthand the utter dependence of a wife upon her husband's rank for social status and public identity. Myna Trustram's study *Women of the Regiment* gives some indication of the harsh conditions Grand might have experienced as the daughter of a petty officer and the wife of a military surgeon.[63] Grand probably felt intimately the dislocation of being defined by connection with a man within an inflexible hierarchy that only exaggerated the social conditions outside the military.

Reviewers of *The Heavenly Twins* were generally hostile to Evadne's marital compromise without being particularly sensitive to its costs to her. An anonymous review, "The Strike of the Sex" (1894), is generally attributed to William Barry, although Grand's letters indicate that she believed it was written by the staunch antifeminist Mrs. Humphrey Ward. The review interrupts an all-out attack on New Women to charge, contradictorily, that "after all, *la pruderie anglaise* . . . has cut short Mrs. Grand's argument in the middle, and ruined her story. The scientific Evadne went too far, unless she intended to go a long way farther."[64] The review continues:

> [the] young lioness replies that she is not bound to Colonel Colquhoun and will not go back to him. Why, then, did she go back? Was not her return a "silent abject submission to vice," such as patient Grizzelda might have commended? . . . But, alas for the strong woman's consistency! Evadne was sacrificed; or rather, both were offered up as a holocaust to these moral axioms imperfectly fulfilled . . . the author felt that a consistent Evadne would have taken her first marriage to be null and void, dismissing the offender with a caution . . . To promote, in her own person, the doctrine of liberty would have been logical but she never could have ventured so far without losing caste.[65]

At one moment the reviewer attacks the New Woman and accuses Grand of indirectly encouraging divorce; in the next moment he scorns "an Evadne, an Ideala, whose principles allowed them a freedom which they were too demure and British to take."[66] A series of angry letters Grand wrote to Frederick Henry Fisher about what she believed to be Ward's review reveal her suspicion that Ward went even further by exerting her influence with the *Times* to prevent its reviewing *The Heavenly Twins,* as when Grand fulminates, "Mrs. Ward is bitterly determined to show no favour to any other authoress."[67] For Grand, Ward embodied a literary version of the repressive "good woman" who would withhold lifesaving information from real women and would exclude feminist politics from the developing field of middlebrow women's literature. The ongoing duel of words between Grand and Ward (as well as between Grand and Ouida, Grand and Janet Hogarth, or Grand and Eliza Linton) provides a crucial reminder that the formation of a woman's middlebrow culture incited internal struggles to define that culture as well as "external" struggles with masculinist forms—from the adventure novel to decadent poetry—and a masculinist publishing industry intent on protecting the heights of high culture as well as the lucrative depths of low culture.

Late-twentieth-century critics name the "duty" that undoes Evadne more explicitly. Elaine Showalter calls Evadne story's "realistically unheroic" and argues that, while the Colonel "finds other outlets," Evadne "sickens from sexual frustration and a sexless marriage."[68] Norma Clarke disagrees, noting Evadne's exceptional health, which the narrator attributes to her having "none of the trials peculiar to married life." Instead, Clarke blames Evadne's decline on "aimlessness for which the cure is work."[69] Ironically, both arguments would have been easily encompassed by the contradictory claims of late-nineteenth-century psychological studies of neurosis, even insanity, in women. As Janet Oppenheim's study richly documents, women who did too much or too little, as well as women who indulged in sexual pleasures or who abstained or who declared themselves free of sexual desire altogether, were equally liable to be labeled and interpellated as ill and abnormal.[70]

Grand's treatment of Evadne's deterioration is complicated by her refusal of sexuality or even sexual feeling as a distinct category of experience. Like most New Women writers (and female romance novelists today), Grand acknowledges no divisions among female sexuality, emotionality, and morality. In her girlhood Evadne lived in the world of ideas; in her adolescent years before marriage she lived in a dream state of unfixed, abstracted sensory experience. After her marriage Evadne can content herself with neither of these possible worlds; consequently, she deliberately numbs sense and senses alike. When the Colonel complains of Evadne's continued indifference to him, the narrator defends her to us as Evadne defends herself to her husband:

> The shock of the discovery which had destroyed her passion for him had caused a revulsion of feeling great enough to subdue all further possibilities of passion for years to come . . . All the energy of her nature had flashed from her heart to her brain in a moment, and every instinct of her womanhood was held in check by the superior power of intellect . . . Her senses had been stunned, and still slept heavily; but there remained to her a vivid recollection of the entrancing period which had followed their first awakening. (339)

At the same time, though the Colonel is characterized as a rather obtuse, boorish, military "type," he never becomes a villain. Evadne's father denounces and disowns her for refusing the Colonel his conjugal rights, but the Colonel himself is surprisingly respectful of her dilemma: "She was not cold-blooded, and he knew it as well as she did. She was only a nineteenth century woman of the higher order with senses so refined that if her moral as well as her physical being were not satisfied in love, both would revolt" (345). Even in the moments when Evadne's own affectionate nature and sexual impulses make her vulnerable to him, the Colonel honors the conditions of their arrangement. In a painful near-parody of the "companionate marriage" Evadne and Colquhoun eventually develop a tolerant friendship that largely consists of staying out of each other's way and of forming separate friendships.[71] Ironically, their pretenses are so convincing that they are considered by most observers to be a uniquely well-suited couple.

Though Grand makes scapegoats of several male characters, for example, Mosley Menteith and Belliot, a lecherous sea captain whose physical repulsiveness resonates in his name, she is too sophisticated politically to focus on the symptoms rather than the causes of Evadne's problems. Remembering her early passion for Colquhoun, Evadne blames the social system for her marital predicament more than she blames her husband (although her choice of words offers carrion comfort): "Don't blame yourself. I have never blamed you since I was cool enough to reflect. It is the system that is at fault, the laxity which permits anyone, however unfit, to enter upon the most sacred of all human relations" (340). Like all but the most radical feminists of her day, Evadne never denies the *potential* for a healthy, mutually supportive marriage. Grand explicitly and repeatedly defended the perfectibility of marriage as an institution—for example, in essays such as "The Modern Man and Maid" and in interviews—at the same time that she attacked marriage practices in her fiction. Though the resistance to divorce seems reactionary to many late-twentieth-century feminists, the majority of Victorian feminists would have shared Grand's view.[72] In both fiction and nonfiction Grand defended marriage as the only possible protection for women and children who might otherwise be abused and abandoned by men. This argument suggests several simultaneous assumptions: that the majority of women desired heterosexual marriage and children; that, apart from that desire, most women recognized men as their likeliest guarantees of social position and financial security; and that, finally, men simply could not be trusted.[73] Because the novels operate on the premise that marriage must be made to protect women, Evadne's arguments point to the institutions that dictate the forms of marriage. Thus, she blames the church for its failure to nurture rather than to cloister virtue, and she blames the double standard that produces the inequitable positions of ignorant chastity for women and knowing promiscuity for men. Again, it is important to remember that even as she urged "Votes for Women! Chastity for Men!" twenty years later, the self-styled militant feminist Christobel Pankhurst argued, in her own way, that men and institutions should be temporarily abandoned (or attacked) so that women could cure them rather than ultimately escape them.

As Evadne retreats further and further from her questions and her principles, the changes in her character are again described in relation to reading. The Colonel uses Evadne's love of reading in an unconventional attempt at seduction: in Malta he arranges a study for her that includes books by social Darwinist Herbert Spencer and by eugenicist Francis Galton. Ironically and unbeknownst to him, these books would likely have contributed to Evadne's views on social purity. In addition, he leaves a host of novels by French writers, but, instead of being aroused by their sensuality, she weeps over the pain and misery (presumably of the women characters in the novels she admits to reading: *Nana, La Terre, Madame Bovary,* and *Sappho*). Eventually, the Colonel comes to see himself as a casualty of Evadne's education, for, even as he sympathizes with her principles, he bemoans their origin: "I wish from the bottom of my soul you had never been taught to read and write, and then you would have had no views to come between us" (341). His dull-witted wish locates the bulwark of ideal womanhood: ignorance. The Colonel's solution to the sexual double standard that hampers his marriage is not to change the system but to continue to blind women to the system. Thus, he reverses the Pygmalion fantasy: he wishes to uncreate the life of Evadne's mind and with her cooperation. In lieu of a sexual commitment he appeals to her sense of justice by asking her to make another, equally unfair vow (the same vow exacted by Sarah Grand's husband): "Will you promise me that during my lifetime you will not mix yourself up publicly—will you not join societies, make speeches, or publish books, which people would know you had written, on the social subjects you are so fond of?" Despite Evadne's irritation at his trivialization of her beliefs as a "fondness" for issues and despite her remonstrance that "ignoring an evil is tantamount to giving it full licence to spread," Evadne concedes (342).

The narrator invokes the demons created by the psychological establishment in the late nineteenth century—morbidity and hysteria—to impart the seriousness of Evadne's choice. In fact, as Gerd Bjørhovde points out, characters describe cases of hysteria throughout book 6, "amounting almost to a sub-text or discourse on sex and sexual drives in the novel," a discourse that emphasizes connections among sexuality, emotions, and intellectuality.[74] To avoid action Evadne learns to act but in the theatrical sense. As Kucich points out, she resorts to a series of masks more debilitating than the guise of a silent young girl that was her chief protection from her father's small tyrannies.[75] At the same time, Evadne realizes she must resist knowing: "She gave up reading; and by degrees there grew upon her a perfect horror of disturbing emotions" (349).

As a girl, Evadne feared being an exceptional woman; as an exhausted adult, she cooperates in trying to "unknow" all that has made her exceptional to compensate for her husband's disappointments. Like Thomas Hardy's Sue Bridehead in *Jude the Obscure,* she removes all the pictures in her home that depict human suffering and burns books she associates with painful thoughts. The narrator summarizes the symptoms of her change:

> She would look at nothing that was other than restful; she would read nothing that harrowed her feelings; she would listen to nothing that might move her to indignation and reawaken the futile impulse to resist; and she banished all thought or reflection that was not absolutely tranquilizing in effect or otherwise enjoyable. (350)

After months of stoically and symbolically annihilating past ambitions and future hopes for work and community, Evadne is consumed in the flames of Malta fever. Rejected by her family, deprived of the imaginative and intellectual escape of reading, and devoid of purposeful action in work, Evadne regresses into a sad burlesque of ideal womanhood, a process that culminates in the final book of *The Heavenly Twins.*[76] Reinforcing a sense of the "doubtful advantage" of a room of one's own, Evadne further secludes herself in a dismal English country house of the Colonel's choosing. Even after the Colonel dies and an "ideal" lover appears to rescue Evadne, any expectation that Evadne's virtue will be rewarded is disappointed.

Evadne's domestic role typifies the confused status of nineteenth-century women once female leisure became a mark of middle-class success. Her servants fulfill the routine duties of the household; she has no children; and her husband's social life is confined to male military friends. Isolated from her friends because she lives in the country and because she refuses to discuss her marriage or her dissatisfaction, Evadne deliberately steels herself to repetitious, frivolous tasks, chiefly decorative needlework.[77]

Critics have offered various and contradictory responses to the shift from an omniscient narrator to the first person "casebook" approach of book 6. Dr. Galbraith is present as a family friend of the heavenly twins throughout the novel. Yet in the final section, book 6, entitled "The Impressions of Dr. Galbraith," he assumes a far more privileged status as narrator. Most critics express suspicion that this limited perspective obscures rather than reveals information. Lyn Pykett says "the feeling female subject becomes the object of the male, medical gaze," arguing that, while the third-person perspective of other books provides sympathetic, "privileged access to the character's subjectivity" and suffering, the first-person perspective of Galbraith "scrutinises those feelings as hysterical symptoms."[78] On the other hand, Bjørhovde sees this shift as evidence of New Women writers' protomodernist sense of complexity: "It is as if these writers do not trust their vision with one, authoritative voice; as if they realize that the world is too complicated, too complex, to be interpreted to the readers by one voice only."[79] Similarly, despite sharing Pykett's suspicions that Dr. Galbraith unjustly dismisses the seriousness of Evadne and other female characters' mental distress, John Kucich also points out that the final book can be understood in the context of the larger literary field as Grand's astute capitalizing on one of the predominant "patterns of decadent aesthetics," the use of an unreliable narrator.[80] In large part the response to this narrator depends upon the degree to which the reader trusts medical authority, an authority fraught with difficulty for a nineteenth-century feminist.

What Bjørhovde would call Grand's "vacillating" relation to the reader strikes one with particular force in the transition to this book.[81] Once again, as in *Ideala,* Grand attempts to wrest cultural authority for both her fiction and her politics. Whereas the earlier novel drew upon both masculine and class authority (the narrator Lord Dawne is a male aristocrat), *The Heavenly Twins* weighs in on the cultural front with a male authority figure deemed an expert in the increasingly revered professions of medicine and psychiatry (or psychology). Grand's feminist readers may have felt she was making a pact with the devil, a possibility she herself explores in *The Beth Book.* As Susan Kent points out, after the publicity surrounding the Contagious Diseases Acts, many women saw doctors as an incarnation of the worst abuses of male and state authority.[82] Animosity toward the medical establishment was also fueled by the use of medical arguments against middle-class women's demands for education and employment. From treatments such as ovarectomies to restrictions based on women's skull measurements, the medical profession repeatedly asserted control over the bodies and options of women. Later in the century large numbers of feminists also resisted the characterizations of female sexuality from sexologists.[83] On the other hand, several arguments can also be made for Grand's confidence in such a narrator. As various letters indicate, she suffered frequent bouts of what her generation called neurasthenia, particularly after she finished each novel (and as she braced up to reviews). She depended upon medical help, in part, because doctors offered the prescription she wanted, giving her permission to escape to Europe, to spas, to the seaside, to her bicycle. She was so pleased with a treatment called the Salisbury Cure that she tried to persuade a magazine to publish an article about it.[84] Moreover, as she had in *Ideala,* Grand here attempts to subsume potentially oppositional authority to her own ends. In terms of literary antecedents George Eliot's Dr. Ludgate in *Middlemarch* seems an obvious source, and Grand saw Eliot as a role model. In terms of political connections, once again, Pankhurst offers an interesting comparison, though of course her popularity follows the novel. Janet Lyon reads a similar sleight of hand in *The Great Scourge and How to End It:* Pankhurst "drops Butler's melodramatic narratives and turns the discourse of physicians into a tool *against* the misogynistic state." Pankhurst does this by depicting physicians as "willing allies in women's battle against conspiracy and vice," a strategy Grand deploys here.[85]

To introduce this section the previous narrator (presumably) inserts a "Note" to explain the change in narrators. First, the change offers the fresh perspective of someone who knows less than "the reader" (who is "better informed than himself with regard to the antecedents of his 'subject' "). Second, the change allows the reader to "note both the accuracy of his insight and the curious mistakes which it is possible even for a trained observer like himself to make." Third, the shift will make "apparent the changes of habit and opinion and the modifications of character that had been brought about in a very short time by the restriction Colonel Colquhoun had imposed on [Evadne]" (554). Though this introduction lends verisimilitude to Galbraith's case history, this shift in point of view also signals the dangers of unquestioningly accepting the authoritative male account of female experience. The first lines of Galbraith's entry reiterate the inadequacy of his perceptions at the same time that they assert his authority as an observer:

> Evadne puzzled me. As a rule, men of my profession, and more particularly specialists like myself, can class a woman's character and gauge her propensities for good or evil while he is diagnosing her disease if she consult him, or more easily still during half an hour's ordinary conversation if he happens to be alone with her. (555)

Once again Grand links morality and disease, but here she uses male authority largely as reinforcement rather than as an enemy of her view. In relation to the development of Evadne's character, what promises to be her salvation (the intervention of a rescuing hero in the guise of a modern psychologist) in fact foreshadows her defeat.

In her girlhood Evadne's aunt had compared her to Elaine waiting hopelessly for her knight. After she settles in England, Dr. Galbraith prophetically compares her to the heroine of another Tennyson poem "The Lady of Shalott," in which "the lady" awaits the fulfillment of a curse as she weaves in her tower (586). When the doctor first meets Evadne, the Colonel is still alive, and Evadne is more interesting as a psychological study than as a lover. As an antidote to her morbid fancies, he recommends that she read books that are "true to life." Evadne abruptly replies that on the few occasions when she reads she prefers escapist fiction, particularly supernatural literature, adding curtly, "my ideal of perfect bliss in these days is to know nothing and believe in ghosts" (560). The mere suggestion of "ghosts" in 1893 would no doubt summon associations with syphilis. If Evadne's comment is an ironic reference to Henrik Ibsen's *Ghosts,* which appeared in London theaters beginning in 1891, Evadne cryptically defines her torment.[86] Her ghosts, like Oswald Aveling's sins, are incited by her parents, in particular by a mother who, like Mrs. Aveling, is willing to sacrifice a child to preserve social appearances. Within the world of the novel the reference links Evadne to Edith's final days because Evadne also begins to create her own ghosts from the passionate anger and murderous impulses she nurses as she sits in silence, seemingly content with her seclusion and her needlework.

Once again, this time through a negative example, Evadne's plot links the liberating act of reading to women's liberation. Proportionately, as Evadne rejects her education, she fosters an antipathy to the women's movement from which she has promised to dissociate herself. During a discussion of politics the usually stoic Evadne erupts into a bitter harangue:

> I hear women say that they are obliged to interfere just now in all that concerns themselves because men have cheated and imposed upon them to a quite unbearable extent. But they will do no good by it. Their position is perfectly hopeless . . . You need not be afraid to give us the suffrage . . . After the excitement of conquering your opposition to it was over we should all be content, and not one woman in a hundred would trouble herself to vote. (559)

Evadne displaces her own anger and sense of helplessness onto the life of the activists. But her diatribe also suggests how hopeless she feels, having been manipulated not only by the laws of marriage but also by the pressure of those she most trusted: her father, mother, and aunt, among others. Evadne's sense of impotence also helps to explain why she so resolutely refuses to continue to seek answers through reading. Rather than saving her from an unhappy marriage and an unproductive life, her education only clarifies the extent of the failure and futility of her life.

Ultimately, Evadne's inner conflicts are manifested through mental and physical symptoms; she joins what Barbara Ehrenreich and Deidre English call "the cult of invalidism."[87] As a semi-invalid, she is absolved of responsibility and can unapologetically rely upon the strongest male authority over women's minds and bodies during the nineteenth century—the medical establishment. Ironically, when she surrenders the active role of reader, she assumes the passive, objectified role of "text" (566), as her medical doctor reads her history of suffering in her symptoms. Ideala begins a life of energy, direction, and work once she refuses to "be" a poem; Evadne's life is filed away as yet another neurotic woman's case history. As Bjørhovde explains:

> More than ever before in the novel Evadne becomes a *case* or an *object:* she is a medical case appealing to the doctor's curiosity and scientific interest; she is the object of the friend and would-be-lover's care and concern. And since he in fact "knows" Evadne less well than the reader at the time he begins to write down his impressions, she seems at this stage in a way more distant to the reader than in earlier parts of the novel.[88]

Thus, when Dr. Galbraith first sees Evadne in the role of patient, the symptom that strikes him as most significant is her acceptance, even relief, at being ill. He puzzles:

> My impression was that she enjoyed being ill. I never saw a symptom of depression the whole time; but when she had quite recovered . . . no sooner did she resume her accustomed habits than that old unsatisfactory something in her, which it was so easy to perceive but so difficult to define, returned in full force. (581–82)

Kucich reads the doctor's role with sensible skepticism, pointing out not only that the doctor earlier describes hysteria as "shamming" but also that "Galbraith's scrutiny of Evadne's hysteria follows all the classic patterns of late-century psychoanalytic colonization of the feminine—at one point, he even compares his observation to the exploration of a cave."[89]

Even more troubling is the connection between love and madness. As Galbraith becomes absorbed in the complex intersections between her physical and mental state, the doctor's love for Evadne grows in direct proportion to the degree of her illness. He frames his desire in the professional wish to cure her of unhealthy preoccupations and avoidances, yet her unhealthiness and potential dependency quicken his affections. Like his sympathetic but misguided predecessor, Lord Dawne, he nearly kills Evadne with his kindness.

In light of the invention of the "talking cure" by Josef Breuer's patient Berthe Pappenheim some years later, it is significant that Evadne herself analyzes the interrelations of her physical and mental states. Sounding like George Eliot's young Dorothea Brooke as she too turned to a young doc-

tor for confession and comfort in *Middlemarch,* Evadne explains the phases of
her misery to Galbraith, outlining the stages by which she has slipped into
continual and terrifying dreams:

> I tried to work out schemes of life in my head, as I would do a game of
> chess; not schemes of life for myself, you know, but such as should save
> other people from being very miserable. I wanted to do some good in
> the world . . . but before the impulse to act came upon me I had made
> it impossible for myself to do anything, so that when it came I was
> obliged to resist it, and then, instead of reading and reflecting, I took to
> sewing for a sedative, and turned the trick of thinking how things
> might be different into another channel. (626)

Repressing her desire for work and activity, Evadne internalizes her plans
and dreams. The "dream friends" of earlier fantasies become "demons" who
master her. Once again Evadne articulates her psyche in supernatural terms,
suggesting that religion has failed or turned malevolent: "By degrees they
mastered me; and now I am their puppet, and they are demons that torment
me. When I awake in the morning, I wonder what the haunting thought
for the day will be" (627). Eventually, she confesses to Dr. Galbraith that the
demonic thoughts are often murderous impulses toward her husband in an
illustration of Carroll Smith-Rosenberg's observation that hysteria may
have been one of the few available forms for nineteenth-century women's
anger.[90] Before Evadne acts on those impulses, however, the Colonel dies
of a heart attack, and the Hamilton-Wellses, the twins' parents, whisk
Evadne off to Europe in an attempt to restore her mental and physical
health.

  One of the greatest stumbling blocks for a later generation of feminist
critics who work with nineteenth-century women's texts is the preponder-
ance of male-female relationships that fit too neatly into Freudian schemes.
Here the male characters who earn the narrator's deepest sympathy are profoundly paternal. Evadne's pet name for Dr. Galbraith after they marry is
"Don," with all the implications of a student/teacher relation intact. (One
feels even more squeamish about Angelica's pet name for her elderly husband, Daddy.) Wendy Langford's study of Valentine personals in the 1993
Guardian wittily illustrates that we have hardly escaped such foolishness. She
argues that romance often depends upon the construction of alternative
realities in which the participants attempt "an escape from, or an attempted
resolution of, the contradictions of heterosexual love in patriarchal society—the paradox of the romantic ideal of intimacy within a relationship
which is one of structural and psychic inequality."[91] As Bjørhovde points
out, Grand seems to attempt such an alternative reality in her construction

of Galbraith and Evadne's relation as both doctor and patient and husband and wife:

> It is hardly unusual for an author to give a medical man a prominent place or a voice of authority: again and again doctors have been chosen to represent some sort of ideal, of reason and common sense, of a scientific and hence a more rational, as opposed to for instance a religious or superstitious, attitude; in general of a better understanding of the forces that shape our lives.[92]

Though the late-Victorian medical and psychological establishments look oppressive from a distance of a century, for women like Grand the psychologist must have been a tentative alternative to the religious divine. Unlike a religious counselor, he at least might acknowledge the importance of female sexuality and might listen seriously to accounts of women's physical and social ills. Moreover, by offering her interpretation of the causes of Evadne's decline in a voice carrying the authority of a medical man and a titled aristocrat, Grand uses her character's masculinist power to support her feminist cause, an intriguing revision of the function of the male narrator in *Ideala*.

In the novel Dr. Galbraith consults the preeminent London authority on female mental illness, Sir Shadwell Rock, about Evadne's case. The ponderous weight and fixity suggested by this expert's name in addition to the sternness of several of his prescriptions emphasize his patriarchal status. In the novel, however, he is characterized as a genuine friend to Evadne and later to her son, and he is associated with the steadfastness and strength as well as the sternness of rock. One can at least speculate about Grand's view of members of the psychological profession from Sir Shadwell's own description of his role, a description that illustrates Bjørhovde's point:

> the clergy have had a long innings. They have been hard at it for the last eighteen hundred years, and society is still rotten to the core. It is our turn now . . . I suppose eventually morality will be taught by medical men, and when it is much misery will be saved to the suffering sex. My own idea is that a woman is a human being; but the clerical theory is that she is a dangerous beast, to be kept in subjection, and used for domestic purposes only. (639)

Here Grand entrusts the cause of women to medical men; she also uses these medical characters to express anger that women characters could not voice without alienating many of her readers. In *The Heavenly Twins* the doctor figures make the powers of patriarchy available to, in fact subservient to, the needs of women, although the next novel, *The Beth Book,* treats the "doctor" with deep skepticism.

Even here, although doctors are portrayed sympathetically, they also fail, at least in treating Evadne. After Evadne and her Don marry, he and Sir Shadwell anxiously observe Evadne, particularly through her first pregnancy. Soon before the birth Evadne muses over Edith's fate, imagining her child's potential danger. When Galbraith returns home from attending a patient, he finds Evadne on the brink of suicide. This time Evadne justifies preventive suicide and child murder from her reading of male texts: "Christ committed suicide to all intents and purposes by deliberately putting himself into the hands of his executioners; but his motive makes *them* responsible for the crime; and my motive would place society in a similar position" (671). When her husband remonstrates with this reading, Evadne clarifies her object in a terrifying revelation of the true nature of ideal womanhood. As he asks her to think about the implications and consequences of her actions, she bursts out:

> All my endeavour is not to think. Let me live on the surface of life, as most women do. I will do nothing but attend to my household duties and the social duties of my position. I will read nothing that is not first weeded by you of every painful thought that might remind me . . . Don, help me to that kind of life, will you? And burn the books. Let me deserve my name and be "well pleasing one" . . . I can be the most docile, the most obedient, the most loving of women as long as I forget my knowledge of life; but the moment I remember I become a raging fury; I have no patience with slow processes; "Revolution" would be my cry. (672)

In this desperate, melodramatic plea Evadne reveals the elements of female psychology at war within the New Woman. Her intellect contradicts her notions of social and domestic duty; her education reveals the injustices of ideal womanhood; and her anger and appeal for change consume her potential for love.

Evadne's plot closes with a scene reminiscent of those scenes of sex and horror that electrified audiences of the "sensational" novels of the 1860s.[93] After Evadne accidentally encounters Mrs. Beale with Edith's pathetic child, she suffers yet another emotional breakdown. Thus, the novel concludes with a bizarre relationship that comments on romance in the same way Evadne's retreat into passivity and dependence comments on ideal womanhood. In a sense Evadne *has* accepted the boundaries of marriage and the hierarchies of the healer, yet what a dreadful accommodation this is. Her husband/healer knows he has failed. In the future the most he can hope for is to isolate and protect her from the unpleasant realities of the outside world. The closing words of the novel grimly define the limits of love for men and women who accept the tenets of ideal womanhood. Bewildered and hopeless, Galbraith tries to comfort Evadne:

> "So long as you will let me be a comfort to you, you will not be able to hurt me again; but if at any time you will not listen to my words, if nothing I can do or say strengthens or helps you, if I cannot keep you from the evil that it may not grieve you, then I shall know that I have lost all that makes life worth having . . ."
>
> She looked up at me in a strange startled way, and then she clung closer; and I thought she meant that, if she could help it, I should not lose the little I ask for now—the power to make her life endurable. (679)

The conclusion of the novel abandons the humor of the twins, the moral lesson of Edith's suffering, and the enthusiastic praise of women and their future delivered throughout the novel by minor characters. Despite the reviewers' representation of the novel as a romance or a comedy, Grand's conclusion uncompromisingly damns the society Evadne fears even as it reverences the consistency of love. The only hope left to the reader is a lesser-known part of the mythological Evadne's story in which she gives birth to Apollo's son, Iamus, a celebrated prophet and leader of the family of Iamidaes of Olympia. And even this possibility suggests the hopelessness of women's condition, for it seems that only a male child can succeed.

While Edith's death contributes to Evadne's collapse, it inspires other female characters to action, particularly the third protagonist, Diavolo's twin, Angelica, who fights for women's education and for an end to the sexual double standard and the injustices that standard represented and reinforced. Both Edith and Evadne serve as negative examples, exposing the dangers of the ideal of womanhood and the constraints upon women that ideal was used to justify. In quite different ways their plots are negations of the notion of gender relations that structure the marriage plot. Trained by her reading of Evadne's misery and Edith's death, however, Angelica characteristically elbows her way through twinship, marriage, and flirtation to politics and power, wantonly defying the subject position of wife as she does that of daughter or sister.

Ironically, those reviewers who praised the novel to some degree also misrepresented it, for they drowned its feminist message with deafening laughter at the antics of the twins. Grand herself described the book's fusion of comedy and horror as "an allopathic pill" that would be "mistaken for a bonbon and swallowed without a suspicion of its medicinal properties."[94] A reviewer for the *Athenaeum* applauds characters so "humorous yet true, that one feels inclined to pardon all [the novel's] faults and give oneself up to the unreserved enjoyment of it."[95] Even in vituperative essays, for example "The Strike of a Sex," the characters Angelica and Diavolo are excused: "the 'Heavenly Twins' play such pranks before high Heaven, as make the serious smile with undesigned amusement."[96] *Punch,* with its usual bluntness, says the other characters are "wearisome intruders . . . I should have liked the Twins, and only the Twins, and nothing but the Twins."[97] Accounts of the twins' popularity with the public read like a Barnum publicity campaign, and their notoriety may be attributable to showmanship as well as literary taste. Frederick Whyte recalls in his biography of Heinemann:

> The publication of the book had synchronised with the notoriety of Mrs. Ormiston Chant and her crusade against London's music-halls. "The Empire" in particular. Heinemann, walking one day down the Strand, stood for a moment to watch a man who was disposing rapidly of a stock of funny-looking dolls in short paper frocks to the cry of: "One penny for the Empire lidy! One penny for Mrs. Ormiston Chant!" A few yards further on another man was having much less luck with a tray-full of bladders which when blown out took the form of a fat-faced baby. "Who wants a biby?" he was crying . . . Presently Heinemann had an idea. "Your business is bad, my friend . . . I will advise you in your affairs. Hold up two of your beautiful babies together and offer them for twopence as *The Heavenly Twins.*" The man did so and with triumphant results. The "Empire Lidy" was completely eclipsed!"[98]

In *Darling Madame* Kersley records an undated news story in the Bath archive that claims that a young woman left a copy of the novel on a train and caused great consternation when her telegram requesting the return of the Heavenly Twins received the answer, "No trace of twins, wire description."[99]

Long after the first stir occasioned by the novel subsided, the twins themselves remained popular. In an 1899 *Idler,* above the caption "Famous Book-Covers as They Might Have Been," we find a parodic sketch of the twins by T. E. Donnison.[100] Still later, in 1938, Amy Cruse recalls in *After the Victorians* that

> it created one of the greatest sensations of literature; it certainly caused tremendous excitement in the ranks of the Feminists and the Anti-Feminists, and the upholders of the new and the old morality. The general public read it with interest and pleasure, mainly because of the pranks of the irrepressible twins, Angela and Diavolo. These two

formed the chief attraction of the story, and "the Heavenly twins" came into common use to denote any partnership in fun and mischief.[101]

The twins do serve an important comic function in an otherwise serious political novel. Yet, in the best tradition of comedy, their plot is at once counterpoint and underscore to the tragic fates of Edith and Evadne. Edith's body and Evadne's intellect fall victim to the forces that determined Victorian gender roles: the family, schools, the church, and the increasingly powerful medical, legal, and political institutions. The twins' comic experiments with gender switching, even gender blending, illustrate the power of individuals to unsettle the dichotomous logic that reproduced sexual difference as gender roles, a structuring process that, as the twins' insights make clear, benefits men. Angelica's childhood pairing with her biological twin, Diavolo, inspires her unconventionality. Later, drawing upon her experience of twinship, she also uses relationships with two other characters, the mysterious "Tenor" and the man she marries, Mr. Kilroy, in her struggle to understand not only why she experiences gender largely as prohibition but what gender is.

Though twin characters frequently appear in literature, Carolyn Heilbrun claims that opposite-sex twins seldom appear after Shakespeare until the late nineteenth century, perhaps in response to women's increasing visibility in traditionally male arenas. She notes the Platonic account of opposite-sex twins that presumes "an original unit which has split, a unit destined to be reunited by sexual love, the ultimate symbol of human joining" as well as the Shakespearean pretense that opposite-sex twins could be as easily be mistaken for one another as those who were identical.[102] Charlotte Goodman includes "psychic" twins, such as Catherine Earnshaw and Heathcliff of *Wuthering Heights,* in her analysis of twins as a device women authors used to explore the effects of education on gender identities. She finds that the structure of the bildungsroman breaks down when the opposite-sex twins reach adolescence, and gender roles force the twins into different lives. As in the case of earlier psychic twins—Bronte's Healthcliff and Catherine and Eliot's Tom and Maggie Tulliver—the terrible loss the characters experience drives the plot toward reunion and regression as the twins search for a return to childhood. Though she suggests that women writers may have used opposite-sex twins to criticize patriarchy and the gender roles it imposes, she concludes that these plots reveal "only art can heal the fragmentation of these characters by patriarchal society."[103]

The twins in Grand's novel raise many of these same questions and possibilities; however, the twins demand a surprising degree of control over

The Heavenly Twins inspired endless jokes and parodies, including this cartoon in the *Idler* 14 (1899): 703, by T. E. Donnison, entitled "Famous Book Covers as They Might Have Been." (Courtesy of the Library of Congress.)

their "gendering" by structuring how they *look,* in both senses of the word. By dictating the terms of their education, they determine how they will look *at* others. Moreover, in the best Shakespearean style they put gender on and off not like, but as, clothing, thus controlling how they are looked at *by* others.

As children, Angelica and Diavolo frequently escape prescribed sexual categories by slyly slipping in and out of behaviors society labels as masculine and feminine as a consequence of being twins. Angelica first rebels against the constraints of femininity when her parents hire a tutor for Diavolo and a governess for her. Unlike Diavolo, Angelica has an active, curious mind and a determination to learn. She receives the education Evadne and Edith are denied because she has developed such confidence from her upbringing as a twin that she holds to her convictions and demands that she and her brother continue to share life's experiences equitably. As the narrator wryly explains, "she was consumed by the rage to know, and insisted upon dragging Diavolo on with her" (126). When the twins are separated, they launch a campaign (under Angelica's direction) to break the educational barrier. True to their gender-reversed behaviors, Diavolo hesitantly asks, "Do we like having different teachers?" and Angelica resolutely responds, "No, we don't" (123). First, they do one another's homework; next, they simply exchange places: Angelica appears before the tutor and Diavolo before the governess. In a comic revision of Catherine Earnshaw's famous speech in Emily Brontë's *Wuthering Heights,* Angelica finally informs the tutor:

> there must have been some mistake. Diavolo and I find that we were mixed somehow wrong, and I got his mind and he got mine. I can do his lessons quite easily, but I can't do my own; and he can do mine, but he can't do his . . . It's like this, you see. I can't learn from a lady, and he can't learn from a man . . . You don't understand twins, I expect. It's always awkward about them; there's so often something wrong. With us, you know, the fact of the matter is that *I* am Diavolo and *he* is me. (124)

When teachers and parents alike give up hope of separating the two, authority gives way to cooperation. Thus, their father, Mr. Hamilton-Wells, "had recourse to a weak expedient which he had more than once successfully employed unknown to Lady Adeline. He sent for the twins, and consulted their wishes privately." Angelica specifically states her terms, foreshadowing her determination as an adult to grasp opportunities equal to men's: "it is beastly unfair . . . to put me off with a squeaking governess and long division, when I ought to be doing mathematics and Latin and Greek." What for Evadne are silent, ineffectual conclusions become for Angelica arguments and assertions: "Men are always jeering at women in books for not being able to reason, and I'm going to learn, if there's any help in mathematics" (124–25). Repeatedly described as brighter, more determined, healthier, stronger, more energetic, more adventurous, and far more wicked than Diavolo, Angelica finally triumphs and joins him in his schoolroom.

Even as a child, Angelica realizes that gaining male privileges herself, in the form of a good education, may end her immediate frustrations but will not change the world's view of women. From childhood, therefore, she assumes responsibility for Diavolo's education, according to her own lights. Most important, she trains Diavolo to support women's rights:

> Angelica was naturally the first to draw definite conclusions for herself, and having made up her own mind she began to instruct Diavolo. She was teaching him to respect women, for one thing; when he didn't respect them she beat him; and this made him thoughtful. (255)

Here we see one of many instances of Grand's droll humor; nevertheless, Angelica's recognition (and Grand's) that men must change before women can turn revolutionary knowledge into political practice continues to influence Angelica's relationships with men.

The novel also specifies why women require reason to see through male logic. One of the running jokes in the novel involves Angelica and Diavolo's periodic comic battles over primogeniture. When Evadne remonstrates, Angelica explains, "You see, I'm the eldest, but Diavolo's a boy, so he gets the property because of the entail, and we neither of us think it fair; so we fight for it, and whichever wins is to have it" (28). Reasoning that society believes biology is destiny, Angelica and Diavolo challenge society by unsettling destiny with disguises.

Though not specifically about twins, the recent work of critics like Judith Butler, who characterize gender as a performance rather than a set of biologically or even socially instilled characteristics, suggests an additional means by which Grand's opposite-sex twins challenge the operations of gender.[104] Significantly, their first public gender masquerade takes place at that costume party that fixes gender as well as heterosexuality in love and law, a wedding. To their parents' horror the children switch clothes moments before the service:

> so Angelica obtained the coveted pleasure of acting as page to Evadne, and Diavolo escaped the trouble of having to hold up her train, and managed besides to have some fun with a small but amorous boy who was to have been Angelica's pair, and who, knowing nothing of the fraud which had been perpetrated, insisted on kissing the fair Diavolo, to that young gentleman's lasting delight. (61)

The dangers of cross-dressing are rendered comic by the assumption that children are "sexless" if not without gender identities. But the exchange only reinforces the ironic reversal of the twins' characters and names: Diavolo has already begun to drawl, to plead his ineptitude at mathematics, to follow Angelica's lead and accept her authority. Ironically, their socially acceptable dress disguises their true natures.

Grand uses the grammar of repetition to emphasize the difference between sex and gender and to address the question: is anatomy destiny? Once again the occasion is a wedding, but this time the twins, now adolescents, find that gender play no longer provides the same sense of escape and pleasure:

> for the truth was that they were not as they had been. Angelica was rapidly outstripping Diavolo, as was inevitable at that age. He was still a boy, but she was verging on womanhood, and already had thoughts which did not appeal to him and moods which he could not comprehend. (150)

Though friends and family continue to treat the twins as their younger comical selves, the twins themselves experience separation in their bodies as well as their relationships. Angelica finds herself "just on the borderland, hovering between two states," while Diavolo remains a child (243).

The crisis arises in another form of repetition, a second allusion to Emily Brontë's "psychic" twins, Heathcliff and Catherine. Once again clothing acts as metonomy for gender positioning.[105] Despite prodding by parents, aunts, and uncles, Angelica resists the marks of adult femininity: "Although she was over fifteen, she had no coquettish or womanly ways, insisted on wearing her dresses up to her knees, expressed the strongest objection to being grown-up and considered a young lady, and had never been known to look at herself in the glass" (245). Angelica's will, however, cannot subdue her body. Diavolo complains that their chief form of entertainment, fighting, is coming to an end: "you used to be hard as a nail. When I got a good hit at you it made my knuckles tingle. But now you're getting all boggy everywhere. Just look at your arms" (255). Standing before the glass together, they observe their bodies: "Hers was round and white and firm . . . his was all hard muscle and bone" (256).

When Angelica finally concedes to her physical changes by costuming herself in adult clothes, the effect devastates Diavolo. His tutor discovers him, like Heathcliff before him, sobbing out his sense of exclusion. And, like Catherine, Angelica seeks him out in their secret retreat, amid "old books and playthings," with "her hair down, and in the shortest and oldest dress she possessed" (274). True to the comic quality of their relationship, the twins analyze their differences and absorb change rather than dooming themselves to fantasies of regression in the manner of Brontë's tragic "twins." Reassured that sexual difference does not necessitate gender division, Diavolo exasperatedly acknowledges the absurdity of the dress Angelica has outgrown. The grounds of her acceptance of the changes society demands as visible symbol of her femininity reassure both twins. She decides: "Well, if I *do* wear a long one . . . it shall only be a disguise. I promise you I'll be just as bad as ever in it" (275). She also offers the possibility that even biological symptoms of sex difference may be disguise rather than destiny. Noting that Diavolo will also soon feel the pressures of adolescence ("You'll get a moustache in time"), she offers what we can read as a double entendre by way of a solution: "But when it comes it will make you look as much grown up as my long dresses do me, and then we'll study some art and practise it together, and not be separated all our lives" (276). Both children have aspirations to be musicians, a form of art Angelica will later insist requires a union of both sexes in one person. The twins' experiences in cross-dressing and disguise, however, also teach Angelica the arts she will need to survive the conflicts adolescence provokes from without as well as within.

Grand presents female adolescence as a miserable montage of moods, disappointments, confusion, and conflicts with adult authority. In itself this description sounds both normal and true to life; however, in relation to the traditional Victorian heroine, Angelica's angry awkwardness (though reminiscent of Maggie Tulliver in George Eliot's *Mill on the Floss* or of Jo March in Louisa May Alcott's *Little Women*) is still fairly unusual. The novel attributes Angelica's behavior to the hard-won knowledge that comes with puberty of the dangers men pose to the female body, rather than to a failure of femininity. She learns, quite literally, of the paralysis and insanity that threaten innocent and ignorant women from the lesson of Edith's syphilis. Grand draws upon the public's perhaps exaggerated fear of venereal disease to reiterate the vulnerability of women to men so adamantly depicted in Edith's death. The secret at the heart of *The Heavenly Twins* is that patriarchy disciplines women through sexual exploitation and abuse of the female body, whether that body belongs to an upper-class, respectable woman, an exploited working-class woman, or a prostitute. Angelica is goaded into her adolescent experiments with gender disguise—when the playful antics of childhood become a daring venture into the "masculine" sphere—after she learns how dangerous the world is to women who have not learned what men see when they look at women.

The melodramatic style of Edith's death cruelly forces Angelica's development, but it also provides a fantastic context in which Angelica can register outrage at the social reality of venereal disease in prophetic, mythic terms that would violate the norms of domestic realism. To Angelica, Edith's death signifies sexual difference and sexual abuse. Angelica witnesses Edith's ravings when she inopportunely arrives for a visit to punish her fam-

ily for their threats to separate her from her twin. Confronted with the horrors of Edith's death, Angelica has what Norma Clarke calls "an epic
dream."[106] The dream opens with the shadowy form of a lover; Angelica
senses that, "if their two lights could be added in equal parts to each other
and mingled into one, their combined effulgence would make a pathway to
heaven." When the phantom materializes into an unnamed figure and kisses
her, she knows "love" for the first time. This perfect union (of lovers? of
twins?) is prevented by "a chorus of men from earth" who begin to shout:
"You're beginning to know too much. You'll want to be paid for your
labour next just as well as we are, and that is *unwomanly*" (294). As she
watches, her lover turns into a series of legendary heroes, while a group of
women begin dividing Solomon among them, "cherishing the little bits in
the Woman's Sphere of their day." Angelica refuses her portion, demanding all or nothing, which infuriates the choric males, who evolve into the
pope and various cardinals. "Slamm[ing] the doors of the Sphere in his
face," Angelica leads the women in revolt as the men are reduced to peer-
ing through the keyhole. Together, the women begin "revising the moral
laws," as Angelica "arm[s] herself with the vulgar vernacular, which was the
best weapon, she understood, to level cant" (295).

In her gender-blending role as twin, Angelica can be the heroine or the
hero, whatever she needs to be in order to "save" these women. For support the women call on their saints, the popular women romance writers
Ouida and Rhoda Broughton. When the men declare the women
"UNWOMANLY" and abandon them, Angelica finds that she has only confused the women and realizes she will have to save them in spite of themselves. Rejecting the self-abnegating role of "Esther," she turns, instead,
into one heroine after another, Judith, Jael, "all the heroic women of all the
ages rolled into one, not for the shedding of blood, but for the saving of suffering." Yet, when Angelica turns to address the crowd, she finds "men,
women, and children crowding like loathsome maggots together" and
wakes crying, "'All this filth will breed a pestilence . . . and I shouldn't be
surprised if that pestilence were ME!'" (296). Perhaps her flexibility in don-
ning and discarding gender roles as part of her play with Diavolo anticipates
Angelica's shape-shifting powers in her dream. She also imagines herself as
the actress Vashti, who had such a hold on the Victorian imagination, as
well as Lady Godiva, who was famous for using her revealed body to
demand tax relief for the poor. Yet the bodies in this dream, couched in the
real nightmare of syphilis, are diseased and disgusting.

Clarke suggests that Edith's deathbed ravings, which awaken Angelica
from her dream, as well as Angelica's violent reaction, actually constitute a

second part of the dream.[107] I would argue that Grand indulges in a fantasy of feminist melodrama by allowing Angelica to act out the implication of her dream at the "literal" level of the plot. To escape Edith's rantings Angelica ducks into the library, and Edith's husband, who has just arrived at the Beales's but is always on the prowl, follows her. Galvanized by the dream, Angelica takes revenge: "seizing the heavy quarto Bible from the table, she flung it with all her might full in his face. It happened to hit him on the bridge of his nose, which it broke" (301).

The dream is a far more radical attack on Grand's society than the larger novel. Drawing upon her years of observing society's gendered responses to her and Diavolo, Angelica connects sexual and economic freedom and allies the religious constraints of the church with the larger patriarchal resistance to women's participation in a man's world. Here, too, her feminism becomes a positive, transformative force rather than a critical, deconstructive methodology. In some respects the dream identifies sources of power: in the female literary tradition, in the cataloging of powerful women, and in the separatist potential of the women's movement. But the dream also acts as a kind of initiation, either, or perhaps both, into the potential for heterosexual love and/or into the illusory division of gendered spheres that delegates desire, characteristics, possessions, and power and that will soon divide the twins.

The dream also, comically, wrestles the power of language, of myth, and of the "separate sphere" back from those who wish to separate Angelica from Diavolo and his future. Driven by these images, Angelica turns from the intimacy of her relationship with Diavolo to an exploration of masculinity in other guises.

Angelica's unladylike behavior, along with several mischievous episodes that follow, convince her elders that she and Diavolo should finally be separated. When the Hamilton-Wellses announce that Diavolo will attend Sandhurst and Angelica will be "brought out" at Court, she rebels. Unhinged by Edith's death and all it implies about the world's cruelty to women and frightened by the prospect of losing her brother, who is also in a sense herself, she desperately, impulsively grasps at a ritual that promises adult liberties, a ritual that she believes will provide her with another version of her twin relationship and this time one that social custom and the law will support—marriage.

To gain the protection while avoiding the responsibilities of marriage (apparently including sexual duties), she selects Mr. Kilroy, a kindly neighbor twenty years her senior, as her groom. The proposal is unconventional and violent. Storming through the woods, Angelica encounters Mr. Kilroy:

When he saw her he dismounted, and Angelica snatched the whip
from his hand, and clenching her teeth gave the horse a vicious slash
with it, which set him off at a gallop into the woods.

Mr. Kilroy let him go, but he was silent for some seconds, and then
he asked her in his peculiarly kindly way: "What is the matter, Angelica?"

"Marry me!" said Angelica, stamping her foot at him—"Marry me,
and let me do exactly as I like." (321)

The narrator repeatedly recounts Angelica's futile attempts to find satisfactory freedom within marriage. Mr. Kilroy remains kind in the face of
Angelica's moods and romps, partially because they spend most of their time
apart. He holds a Parliament post in London, and Angelica remains at home
to avoid him.

In some ways Angelica and her husband's relation reveals a profounder
if subtler criticism of marriage than Evadne's miserable marriage or, from
the earlier novel *Ideala,* Ideala's abusive marriage. Though Angelica possesses all that should satisfy the ambitions of ideal womanhood—that is, a
kind, caring husband, a beautiful home, wealth, position, and family—she
feels miserable. Mr. Kilroy is the embodiment of masculinity in its kindest
forms, but he is no Diavolo:

> She was conscious of some change in herself, conscious of a racking
> spirit of discontent which tormented her, and of the fact that, in spite
> of her superabundant vitality, she had lost all zest for anything. Out-
> wardly, and also as a matter of habit, when she was with anybody who
> might have noticed a change, she maintained the dignity of demeanour
> which she had begun to cultivate in society upon her marriage; but
> inwardly she raged—raged at herself, at everybody, at everything.
> (477–78)

Angelica's struggle replicates Evadne's, but Angelica's determination and
commitment to action forestall Evadne's fate. Grand extends the analysis of
marriage and womanhood begun in Edith's plot and problematized in
Evadne's by suggesting an escape from the limited sphere of action in
Angelica's plot. Angelica alone possesses potential for resistance because she
has experienced the formation of gender and the systematic devaluing of
women it enforces firsthand as an opposite-sex twin.

As a child, Angelica learns the delight of cross-dressing by exchanging
places with Diavolo. When biological developments and social constraints
impose femininity along with a female body on her in adolescence, she
turns to masquerade once again, this time in resistance to the life of idleness

and domesticity Diavolo escapes when he leaves for Sandhurst. For a brief, dreamlike period Angelica exists not as man or as woman but as a "sexless thing," as what she calls a "bright particular spirit" (403, 393). When her disguise is discovered, she loses the power of the triangulated third self she feels she's become—as Angelica, Diavolo, and the third "being" in between.

Book 4 constitutes the most bizarre and imaginative form of Angelica's resistance to marriage. As Gerd Bjørhovde points out, this book differs significantly in style and tone from the other books that form *The Heavenly Twins,* for Grand weaves mystery, fantasy, comedy, and poetry into what she demarcates as "An Interlude," in the subtitle to book 4.[108] Linda Dowling and John Kucich read this stylistic shift as another adaptation from decadent writers, the use of stylized "pastoral" that permitted freedom from the constraints of "nature" or realism.[109] Grand must have felt strongly that "The Tenor and the Boy" was important. She tried to publish book 4 as a separate, autonomous novel in 1890, and eventually Heinemann did publish the narrative as a separate work with an introduction contextualizing it in 1899.[110] After the success of *The Heavenly Twins* Grand co-wrote a playscript of "The Tenor and the Boy" with Robert Buchanan, but when British and American copyright claims clashed the project was abandoned.[111] In book 4, separated from her twin and disappointed in her marriage, Angelica becomes Diavolo. Splitting her existence between a daytime life as Angelica and a nighttime life as Diavolo, she seeks to invent an entirely new form for a relationship, a form equal to the desires of the "feminine" and "masculine" facets of her split, twinned self. Disguised as Diavolo, she forms a secretive, nighttime friendship with a talented singer known only as "the Tenor."

Angelica's dual life begins after she packs Mr. Kilroy off to his parliamentary responsibilities in London. Restless and bored, she roams the streets of Morningquest at night, dressed in her brother's clothes and wearing a curly blond wig. As Angelica, she hears the Tenor sing in church; that same evening she encounters him in the market square, when she is dressed as Diavolo. S/he adopts the Tenor as an older brother, pestering him, haranguing him, debating the position of women with him, and delighting in a friendship with a man who treats her as an equal. The oddest feature of their friendship is that the Tenor adores the "real" Angelica from afar, based solely on his vision of her in church, and the "Boy" teases him unmercifully, first fueling the Tenor's infatuation then puncturing the romance with stories of "Angelica's" temper and eccentricities. The narrator explains, "He saw in the girl an ideal, and had found soul enough in the laughter-loving Boy to make him eager to befriend him" (385). Through this deliberate splitting of selves the novel renders the contradictions of femininity as a secret self who moves and speaks openly but only in the dreamlike world of night versus the flattened character who exists in daylight only as a vision. This self-division also dramatizes the disorientation of women who imagine themselves not as subjects but as objects of the male gaze, a form of female alienation described by Laura Mulvey.[112]

The deception is comic, absurd, intriguing, and sometimes discomfiting for the reader. As the Boy, Angelica plies the Tenor with innuendoes and clues to which he remains oblivious, despite his own remarks about her effeminacy, her girlishness, her unshapely head, and her vampirish tendency to appear only at night. The Tenor and the Boy both attribute the Boy's artistry (s/he plays the violin) to a kind of androgyny. Calling the Boy a "genius," the Tenor compares him with the "Witch of Atlas":

> A sexless thing it was, and in its growth
> It seemed to have developed no defect
> Of either sex, yet all the grace of both.

> (403)

The Boy qualifies the Tenor's view of the artist and of androgyny: "Is that what you call genius? . . . I believe it is the attributes of both minds, masculine and feminine, perfectly united in one person of either sex" (403). This exchange provides the rationale for this entire fantastic sequence. The twins liberate themselves from education based on gender through their shared upbringing and swapping of behaviors as well as clothes. But Angelica now seeks a model to counteract the limits of romance, proscribed by sexual domination and rigid sexual roles within the family. Quite simply, Angelica wants friendship between men and women on terms unimaginable to the Victorians (and to us as well probably). The sequence certainly has homoerotic overtones, which Grand's audience countered by calling her men hopelessly effeminate, ineffectual, and lifeless, despite her protests that "there are nineteen men in *The Heavenly Twins,* and only one of them is an out and out bad lot. I can think of no mere male man's novels with so low a percentage?"[113] The "Interlude" argues for a relationship that would permit honest, unselfconscious, nonhierarchical friendships between men and women that sexual attraction usually prevents.

The moment of unmasking exposes not only Angelica but also Victorian fears of flexible sexual identities; the Tenor's reactions suggest why society so rigorously prescribes and enforces sex roles. Although the Tenor feels horrified, shocked, repulsed, abused, and deceived when he discovers the Boy is Angelica, she blames his lack of imagination and open-mindedness as much as her own deceitfulness. First, she describes the joyful freedom of movement, from "the restraint of our tight uncomfortable clothing" (456). Next she defends herself through analogy, arguing that, if George Sand and the legendary female doctor, James Barry, could pass as men, so can she. This genealogy is particularly significant because these women cross-dressed with such great effect. Sand's access to the public world gave her the knowledge and experience English critics claimed women lacked to be great writers. Masquerading as a man, James Miranda Barry attended medical school in Edinburgh then worked her way up from staff sergeant in 1817 to surgeon and major in 1827 to inspector general of the army.[114] (Perhaps Barry's fame influenced Grand's willingness in this novel to portray the medical doctors as a refuge for women.) Finally, Angelica broaches her real need, to escape the manacles of male desire, after the Tenor asks if she loves him:

> The charm . . . has all been in the delight of associating with a man intimately who did not know I was a woman . . . Had you known that I was a woman—even you—the pleasure of your companionship would have been spoilt for me, so unwholesomely is the imagination of a man affected by ideas of sex. The fault is in your training; you are all of you educated deliberately to think of women chiefly as the opposite sex. (458)

The equation between sexual desire and immorality, even illness, was a radical observation that produced conservative effects. Grand, like many middle-class feminists, supported the social purity movement a few years later. As I have noted, she shared the view of many women that equality could not be won on the grounds of free love because women would inevitably have to contend with children. Therefore, no sex before marriage rather than uninhibited sex before, apart from, or after marriage, became the battlecry. Grand tried to clarify her position on free love in an 1896 interview, in an example of the interplay of conservatism and reform that shapes her feminism:

> Laxity in the marriage tie would eventually lead to the younger women constantly changing their lovers and refusing to have children, and when they became old and *passé* men would neglect them. The position of women in middle life and old age would be very sad and desolate, whereas with binding marriage the majority have an honoured position and a fair share of happiness . . . women have nothing to gain and everything to lose by renouncing the protection which legal marriage gives . . . We want progress, not retrogression. Men could be taught the self-restraint which women have had to learn, and we want the same law for men as for women in these matters."[115]

This quotation again signals that Grand's premises about reform are grounded on her assumption that active agents in the world are middle-class, male, and heterosexual and that, therefore, women will inevitably be deeply dependent on the responsible behavior of largely self-interested men. Though it is perhaps too optimistic a claim, however, the cross-dressing and ambiguous gendering of book 4 suggest that in the interlude world of the Tenor and the Boy a radical revision of gender roles would permit far more flexible human relations. Juxtaposed with the predictable structures of romance, the turns of the plot are certainly innovative. Here we see a married woman, dressed as a man, rejecting an idealized lover, and finally growing exasperated with his predictable behavior even under such fantastic circumstances. When the Tenor discovers her identity and silently reproves her, Angelica rebukes him for his absurd idealization of her daylight, feminine incarnation:

> If you are deceived in me you have deceived yourself . . . You go and fall in love with a girl you have never spoken to in your life, you endow her gratuitously with all the virtues you admire without asking if she cares to possess them; and when you find she is not the peerless perfection you require her to be, you blame her! oh! isn't that like a man? (459)

Stunned and uncomprehending, the Tenor escorts her home through the rain then conveniently dies of pneumonia. It almost seems that Grand so fears capitulation to romance that she has to kill off the potential lover. Refreshingly, Angelica soon recovers from his death. Though his parting words, "you will be a good woman yet," encourage her to live more purposefully, she never succumbs to guilt or self-abnegation (462). (Perhaps this last detail, above all, marks this segment of the novel as fantasy.)

Grand's narrator uses the Romantic poets' concept of androgyny to explore the potential for cross-dressing and gender switching. The relationship Angelica-as-boy forms with a musician, on the basis of his fantasies about Angelica-as-girl, challenges conventional representations of heterosexuality and homosexuality. This self-division dramatizes the alienation of women who can imagine themselves only as objects of the male gaze; through her cross-dressing Angelica appropriates that gaze, and with sight comes speech.

Having seen the world with a man and as a man, Angelica finally understands the message of her earlier dream. As she sits in her grandfather's centuries-old home, grieving over the Tenor, she envisions the series of male inheritors, including her grandfather and her brother, who will share "the horrible monotony" of patriarchal ownership. But now the patriarchy is under siege by the women of her vision:

> the vulgar outcome of a vulgar era, bred so, I suppose, that I may see through others, which is to me the means of self-defence. I see that in this dispute of "womanly or unwomanly," the question to be asked is, not "What is the pursuit?" but "What are the proceeds?" No social law-maker ever *said* "Catch me letting a woman into anything that pays!" It was left for me to translate the principle into the vernacular. (534)

Her childhood struggles with Diavolo over family property, her family's refusal to grant her a career, and everyone's insistence that Diavolo live up to his masculine responsibilities and Angelica subside into her feminine duties suddenly coalesce into a political vision that gives Angelica's life, even her marriage, purpose. Her dream suggested that women's words had transformative power and offered "the vernacular" as a tool of resistance against the mysteries of the clergy. Once Angelica sees what men see, she translates the masculinist codes she has discovered into a political strategy. Having learned that clothes make the woman a man, she reconciles herself to marriage by consciously adopting a new disguise as "wife." In reality she spends the rest of the novel (and of Grand's next novel, *The Beth Book*) like George Eliot's Dorothea Brooke before her, writing speeches on behalf of women that her husband delivers as a willing mouthpiece. In effect Angelica once again disguises herself as a man, but this time she becomes, one removed, a nearly invisible spy, disguised as a sober, kindly, elder statesman to Parliament.

The character Edith seems to exorcise Grand's affection for the conventional heroine; Evadne functions as a study of female psychology when an exceptional woman tries to accommodate her "new" ideas to archaic forms of femininity; and Angelica points the way to the "androgynous" life of action, transformation, and subversion of the more optimistic New Women. One of the many interesting minor characters in *The Heavenly Twins*, however, most clearly anticipates the direction Grand's New Woman fiction would take in her next novel, *The Beth Book*. Like Grand, this character, Mrs. Malcomson, is a novelist who is married to a military man and living in Malta, where she becomes friends with Evadne. Her presence marks an important shift in the trilogy from women readers to women writers, and this transformation promises women agency. Learning strategies of reading misogyny in their culture merely teaches women to survive. Learning to rewrite the dominant culture and its plots and even to invent

unimagined, utopian plots shifts women from the object to the subject position. The female characters cease to be behind-the-scenes subversives and
become active agents. The woman reader may be a cultural critic, but the
woman writer promises to create "culture." The similarities of Grand's
experiences and that of her character Mrs. Malcomson are indicated by an
anonymous newspaper article of 1901:

> "Mrs M'Fall" [*sic*] was quite a misunderstood personage in Warrington.
> She was an idealist—an exotic in a strictly mercantile atmosphere—a
> pioneer of the feminist movement, when it was thought unwomanly
> to make any claims on behalf of women. But Mrs M'Fall went her own
> way. She was brimful of ideas; and ideas, like murder, will out. She was
> unconventional in dress and in habits, and the narrow-minded little
> coteries around her covered their faces with their hands—metaphori-
> cally speaking—and . . . kept a strict look out through their fingers.[116]

Mrs. Malcomson's unapologetic and irreverent analyses of Maltese society
represent the views of a small group of male and female characters in Malta
who support women's rights. Like Evadne, Mrs. Malcomson takes the
"enemy's" pronouncements as her text and reads the general resistance to
women writers in their specific complaints.

The fictional author's object is to "represent things as she saw them,
things real, not imaginary" (334). When Mrs. Malcomson publishes her
novel, however, few of her readers accept her definition of reality. Alternately intrigued and outraged, these local readers, the English enclave in
Malta, justify their intolerance of women writers by unfairly and contrarily
attacking Mrs. Malcomson's novel:

> the book had been a success from the first; but as people had hastily
> concluded that she was setting up for a social reformer and would fail,
> they were naturally disgusted. They had been prepared to call the sup-
> posed attempt great presumption on her part; but when they found
> that she had merely her own interests in view, and had not let their
> moral welfare cost her a thought, they said she was not right-minded.
> (334)

Mrs. Malcomson's readers devise categories for the woman novelist then
react with anger if she will not inhabit those categories. Judging women's
art by allegedly "objective" criteria, rather than allowing an individual work
to elaborate its own aesthetic, these readers freely revise their judgments to
prevent any favorable reading of women's writing.

The readers' reactions to Mrs. Malcomson's representation of "true to
life" subject matter provide an ironic contrast with their responses to com-

parable "realistic" fiction by men. (Recall Evadne's earlier dismay at her father's admiration for *Tom Jones* and *Roderick Random*.) Not only do readers attack Mrs. Malcomson's fictional characters, but she also suffers personal attacks on her own character. Such displaced judgments became a commonplace tactic of literary critics who were angered by New Woman fiction:

> It was said, among other things, that she evidently could not be moral at heart, whatever her conduct might be, because she made mention of immorality in her book. Her manner of mentioning the subject was not taken into consideration, because such sheep cannot consider; they can only criticise. The next thing they did, therefore, was to damage her reputation, and declare that it was autobiographical. There was one man who knew exactly when the thing had occurred, who the characters were, and all about it. (334)

Targeting the author rather than the book, these readers reverse the usual process of reading. In a perversion of biographical criticism they read Mrs. Malcomson in light of an incident in her novel rather than the reverse, so that the author becomes the text, and the text is condemned to obscurity. In a final ironic twist the novel turns the disparaging views of women to serve a woman writer's interests. Thus, Mrs. Malcomson does find an audience for her novel among the Maltese community, a surprising consequence of their malice. Mrs. Guthrie Brimston, a woman of ambiguous morals whose name refers to her penchant for gossip, attacks the novel publicly. When she announces, "I consider it *improper* simply," the narrator describes the unexpected result:

> Such an objection from such a quarter was considered too funny, and when it became known, there was quite a run upon the book; for Mrs. Guthrie Brimston's stories were familiar to the members of all the messes . . . not to mention the club men, and the curiosity to know what she did consider an objectionable form of impropriety in narrative made Mrs. Malcomson's fortune. (335)

Grand's characterization of the attacks upon Mrs. Malcomson's politics, morals, and authority as a would-be writer proved only too prescient. Following the spectacular sales of *The Heavenly Twins,* the novel was heaped with equally extreme critical praise and blame. At one extreme were outraged moralists like Billy T. Saunders of *Open Court: A Weekly Journal Devoted to the Religion of Science,* who denounced the novel's medico-political content as crass commercialism: "the degrading and prurient suggestions in which it abounds are wholly gratuitous. The story, such as it is, could very well have been told, and might have been told with a sense of reserve and decency; but then, of course, as the authoress must be perfectly aware, it would have failed to attract such wide notice."[117] As if in answer, Frederick Bird of *Lippincott's Monthly Magazine* agrees: "She does use plain language, and a good deal of it; but everybody knows that the offences which rouse her wrath are by no means products of her imagination. They have a very real and wide-spread existence; they are shocking to a pure mind, frightful in their occasional consequences, and a festering sore in the body politic."[118] Grand's constitution of a middlebrow feminist audience galvanized disdain, envy, and admiration in equal measure. As late as 1901, Walter Besant churlishly damned the work and its female readers as politically correct and culturally inept. Comparing *The Heavenly Twins* to a novel with a similarly complicated reception history, Harriet Beecher Stowe's *Uncle Tom's Cabin,* Besant recalls the novel was

> equally famous and notorious, was a fierce onslaught which, it is safe to say, made a fearful breach in the walls of the Home—that demure fabric so long and faithfully defended by Charlotte Yonge and Miss Rhoda Broughton. The reactionary who fails to see that *The Heavenly Twins* did not leave public opinion, and particularly feminine public opinion, where it found it, has put the telescope to his blind eye. The book was eagerly and gratefully accepted by women, who perceived in it not only the bold utterance of their timid aspirations, but also a distant hope of release from the somewhat Ottoman codes of men. It was a bad novel—artistically vicious in its crudity, violence, unfairness, literary indecorum, improbability, impolity—but it was a brilliant, though unscrupulous, argument against the "criminal repression of women" for the selfish ends of men.[119]

The contrast between reviews like Besant's and too often lost voices of those women readers he describes so contemptuously reminds us of the prejudice against which Grand and other New Women fought. Drawing upon her memories of Grand's novel, which she must have followed from Grand's early readings to the Pioneer Club, Margaret Sibthorp remembered

> how strengthening also and inspiriting to those of us who have long endured evils we have been too cowardly to resist; or too apathetic to think of the harm thus perpetuated—to hear through the pages the sharp crack! like a rifle shot, of the lash of a noble-hearted woman's righteous wrath, coming down upon the soul-killing vices which society cherishes under the name of virtues, or at least, necessary conditions.[120]

As Grand learned too well, even success for women writers turns upon the personal, the sensational, and the delight in hostility among women. Yet Grand also learned from personal experience that, although this sort of publicity might create a temporary audience for women novelists, the same notoriety forestalls serious critical consideration of their work. In the character and the struggles of Mrs. Malcomson, Grand's readers caught a glimpse of the female artist figure who would dominate Grand's autobiographical novel a few years later as the New Woman evolves into a writer of women's plots and a leader of the women's movement.

Chapter 5

The Woman of Genius as Wife

Writing to Frederick Henry Fisher in 1897, Grand exasperatedly denied that the final novel of her feminist trilogy was autobiographical: "I see the papers are announcing that *The Beth Book* is an autobiography. As they have said the same of every book I have written yet, and as the heroine of each is entirely distinct and different, I should think the announcement must begin to fail of its effect."[1] In later years Grand contradicted this claim, acknowledging that she had adapted scenes from her girlhood, and, indeed, the similarities between her life and her fiction are striking.[2] Like Beth, Grand was born in Ireland, later moved to England, complained of a difficult relationship with her parents, was asked to leave one of the girls' schools she attended, and married a military surgeon at a young age to escape unhappiness at home. Most important, joining a number of other women writers of the nineteenth century, Grand dramatizes the story of an aspiring female artist. Madame de Stael's *Corinne* (1807) and Elizabeth Barrett Browning's narrative poem, *Aurora Leigh* (1857) laid the groundwork for late-nineteenth-century women's treatments of the artist plot. In the 1880s and 1890s many women writers of New Women narratives self-reflexively examined the obstacles, the successes, and too often the tragic failures of women artists and writers, as in Olive Schreiner's *Story of an African Farm* (1883), Mona Caird's *Daughters of Danaus* (1894), Ella Hepworth Dixon's *The Story of a Modern Woman* (1894), Edith Johnstone's *A Sunless Heart* (1894), "C. E. Raimond's" *George Mandeville's Husband* (by the American living in England, Elizabeth Robins, 1894), W. S. Holnut's *Olympia's Journal* (1895), "George Paston's" *A Writer of Books* (pseudonym of Emily Morse Symonds, 1899), and Mary Cholmondeley's stunning *Red Pottage* (1899).[3] *The Beth Book* stands out for several reasons. First, Grand's novel is unusually audacious in that *The Beth Book* springs from Grand's and Beth's shared experiences as female artists. Second, Grand is one of the very few late-century women writers who fantasized overwhelming, if complicated, triumph for her female artist figure. The novel even goes so far as to ridicule the methods of a literary establishment that made success difficult for a woman writer, in particular one interested in women's rights.

Grand seems to be taking stock in this third novel, looking back upon her career and asking the question that still plagues feminist literary critics: can feminist politics cohabit with aesthetics? In writing *The Beth Book*, Grand rebelled against the predisposition of Victorian readers to undervalue female artists on the basis of a prevailing belief in an equation between creativity and masculinity. A passage from Arthur Waugh's "Reticence in Literature," which appeared in the first issue of the *Yellow Book* in 1894, is symptomatic of the public's prejudice against female artists on the basis of assumptions about gender:

> The man lives by ideas; the woman by sensations; and while the man remains an artist so long as he holds true to his view of life, the woman becomes one as soon as she throws off the habit of her sex, and learns to rely on her judgment, and not on her senses.[4]

In other words, a woman could only become an artist by first becoming "unwomanly." The passive, nurturing traits many Victorians associated with womanhood would presumably prevent women from understanding or experiencing the individualistic, self-serving, unaccommodating requirements commonly associated with an artistic temperament. Put in aesthetic rather than social or psychological terms, the constitution of a woman writer would presumably make it impossible to meet the criteria demanded of the high-culture novel, which Pykett, drawing from reviews in the 1890s, describes as "rigorous impersonality, classical reticence, and transcendence of the merely local and particular.[5] Current studies of the female artist plot explore the problems women artists faced in a culture that tended to imagine the figure as male and as behaving in an often antisocial fashion that would only be tolerated in men. For example, in her groundbreaking study of the female artist-protagonist, Grace Stewart argues that, as the embodiment of "motherhood, purity, fear of experience, domesticity, selflessness, and the status quo," women were discouraged from participating in the public world, yet also, paradoxically, denied the luxury of "selfish" solitude that Romantic characterizations of the artist deemed essential to the male artist's success.[6] The plot of *The Beth Book* dramatizes these tensions and the suffering they cause through phases of Beth's life; however, Grand also shows how Beth uses these tensions to construct a feminist aesthetic that leads to private and public "success." *The Beth Book* attempts to answer the question—what would a feminist aesthetics be?—by detailing the many influences that shape a feminist artist's character, her motivation, the forms or genres in which she works, and the ways she defines (and defends) the

People I Have Never Met.

By Scott Rankin.

THE MAN OF THE FUTURE.

The Man of the future—*Loq.* :—"I *will* be good! Oh, I *will* be good' "

Scott Rankin provided this satire of the "New Man," surrounded
by New Women novelists who are rebuking him with their best-
selling novels. The cartoon appeared as part of a series "People I
Have Never Met" and was subtitled "The Man of the Future," in
the *Idler* 9 (1894): 212. (Courtesy of the Library of Congress.)

products of her labor. In this novel Grand turns more explicitly to "life stages"—an increasingly popular approach to conceptualizing personal development in the last decades of the century—to investigate the social, cultural, and biological forces that inspire (or inhibit) the formation of artistic genius. Specifically, she focuses upon childhood and adolescence as crucial to the formation of what we would now call an adult feminist subjectivity. In this respect, as Flint points out in her illuminating discussion of women's autobiographies, the novel also takes on a form especially common to Victorian women's writing about their lives.[7]

This chapter explores several related issues that surface in each of the three major phases of the novel: the sources, form, and kind of aesthetics that the novel endorses. The novel begins, like *David Copperfield,* hours before Beth's birth, and the first third of the novel locates the origins of feminist art in the friction between a mother bound by tradition and a daughter with unusual talents and a searching, critical intellect. Ironically, while Beth suffers at the hands of her mother, her resistance to her mother's conservatism teaches her the nature of women's abuses. The second phase of the novel develops along the lines of the marriage plot. Beth marries a doctor, then she learns he is a vivisectionist, an administrator involved in the quarantining of prostitutes, and a philanderer. His career isolates Beth from respectable society, and she teeters on the brink of a nervous breakdown until Evadne's husband, Dr. Galbraith, now ambiguously positioned as a healer, sympathizer to women, yet medical manager of women, befriends her and encourages her ambitions to be a writer. While Edith's death theatrically renders the horrifying physical consequences of venereal disease to a *single* woman, *The Beth Book* shifts the analysis of the marriage plot to a political register, embedding marriage practices in the language of medical law to show how the marriage plot exploits not one but all women. In the last third of the novel Beth abandons her husband, moving to a garret in London, where she writes her first book and meets the American male artist who will become her lover. This third phase of the novel explores the forms of art available to a female character with a feminist mission. The novel constructs a portrait of turn-of-the-century literary culture, and, after depicting Beth's triumph in that world, it then fantasizes an expansion of literary middlebrow feminist culture beyond the boundaries of print and into the public, "political" world. Breaking a path for a feminist artist, the novel navigates between biology and environment in each of these phases of the novel. Beth resists her biological mother's tyranny while "inheriting" inadvertent gifts of other women who share the childhood spaces of domesticity. The character develops political arguments from the biological script provided by her husband's lurid stories of his work in a state-funded hospital. And, ultimately, Beth's presence—her body—as well as her ideas are called into the service of her vision of feminist art.

Each phase of the novel emphasizes Beth's special attention to language: its nuances, its abilities to subdue and to control, and its power to name and thereby structure perception. Therefore, in the last phase of the novel Beth struggles to shape language into representations of women that expose rather than conceal their desires as well as the obstacles they face. Seizing upon a timely quarrel in literary circles as a means of playing out an imagined conflict between content and form, the novel grounds its aesthetic platform upon distinctions between the "Decadents" and the New Women writers. Like the New Woman writers, the Decadents, or Aesthetes, were amorphously defined and constituted. As a unified group, they, like New Women, were largely a critical fantasy.[8] The Aesthetes, or "Stylists," in the novel appear to be a compilation of Algernon Swinburne, Walter Pater, Oscar Wilde, Arthur Symons, and, in the references to early death and suicides, perhaps Ernest Dowson, Aubrey Beardsley, and John Davidson. While the late-Victorian stereotype of the effeminate aesthete seems at first distinctly dissimilar from the mannish stereotypes of the New Woman, *The Beth Book* argues that critics' characterizations of both groups of writers as "erotomaniacs" threatened to sweep the particular feminist politics addressed in New Woman fiction, of which sexuality was but a part, under the cultural carpet. Like New Women literature, Decadent literature was a short-lived phenomenon, and the two literary movements intensely engaged critical attention at the same moment. Consequently, despite the fact that these were only two currents among many widely circulating literary forms—adventure, detection, literary journalism, nonfiction, and self-styled realist and naturalist fiction—Grand's determination to construct a middlebrow feminist literature was served by reducing readers' choices to an overly simplified "either-or" in the novel. In the process of the complex, evolving plot in *The Beth Book* the New Woman writes herself out of the marriage plot and out of what the novel reveals to be a masculinist artist plot; she writes herself into an ending that is a series of new beginnings for what the novel's subtitle calls "the woman of genius."

To try and define a feminist aesthetics is a dangerous if not impossible enterprise, for the history of women's writing shows the many ways literary criteria may be used to denigrate or exclude writers whose work is unconventional or explicitly political. The agenda of *The Beth Book,* however, at least clarifies key questions for artists with feminist political objectives. In Grand's earlier novels the first obstacle for the feminist author is the traditional structure *of* the novel. Beth's interest in daily lives, presumably of the female audience she imagines, in addition to her ultimate decision to use her talents as a feminist leader, suggests that mere resistance to the marriage plot is not enough. Countering the immobility of both the love story and the late-nineteenth-century Decadent aesthetic, Beth must be accountable to an ethics of transformation. Most feminist studies of aesthetics and of literary representations of women artists fasten upon the connection between what I would call the "ordinary extraordinariness" of women's lives and an aesthetics of transformation.[9]

Of the many insightful studies of the female artist figure Jane Marcus's characterization of "an aesthetics of political commitment" offers a particularly useful way of looking at the artistic goals established for the character Beth:

> This model of art, with repetition and dailiness at the heart of it, with the teaching of other women the patient craft of one's cultural heritage as the object of it, is a female poetic which women live and accept. Penelope's art is work, as women cook food that is eaten, weave cloth that is worn, clean houses that are dirtied. Transformation rather than permanence is at the heart of this aesthetic, as it is at the heart of most women's lives.[10]

The female artist Marcus describes finds her inspiration, as does Beth, in her own experience. To create she must become vulnerable to her own struggles and must sincerely represent the ethical and social conditions of that struggle. Rachel Blau DuPlessis's description of such an aesthetic objective reiterates Marcus's vision:

> The fictional art work, distinctively described in these works, has a poetics of domestic values—nurturance, community building, inclusiveness, empathetic care. The poetics of the fictional art work begins with its ethics, not its aesthetics; it has its source in human ties and its end in human change. The work is described as having a clear ethical function and is not severed from the personal or social needs that are its source.[11]

Writing with "a critical purpose," such an artist character articulates the conditions of female life, resists the masterpiece status that would remove the work from "everyday connections" and "the realm of necessity," and consequently insures the artist a functional role in a social group no longer constrained by the limits of the conventional marriage plot.[12] In Grand's case, for example, the writing of *The Beth Book* was so intimately tied to the life of the feminist community that vacillations within the women's movement affected her creative process. Writing to her publisher, William Heinemann, in 1896, Grand apologizes for her slow progress: "You know

it is the fluctuation of the Woman Question—the new evolutionary movement—that affects my success; and it has been low tide with us of late. But
the tide will turn about the beginning of the year, and *I* must come in on
the flood."[13] Though DuPlessis argues that the female artist only achieves
this status in twentieth-century novels, her profile of a feminist aesthetic
helps to explain the final twist of *The Beth Book* as Beth turns her back on
literary fame for a far less prestigious, less socially and culturally sanctioned
vehicle for her genius and talent—oratory.[14]

As the subtitle, "Being a Study of the Life of Elizabeth Caldwell
Maclure, A Woman of Genius," suggests, *The Beth Book* portrays a female
writer and orator who not only succeeds in escaping many of the constrain-
ing Victorian roles for women but who takes up as her mission finding a
message, a voice, and a form that will inspire others to fight for women's
rights. Because the protagonist, like Grand, is a writer, critics frequently
refer to *The Beth Book* as an important example of the nineteenth-century
female artist novel. The novel deftly negotiates, however, the distinction
between a woman of genius and a female artist in a subtle challenge to conventional categories.[15] The etymology of the word *genius* suggests some of
the reasons why Grand and other nineteenth-century women writers were
predisposed to use this term rather than *artist* and also raises questions about
Grand's view of her own role as a political novelist. According to the *Oxford
English Dictionary,* the English word derives from the Greek *genus,* which
means to be born or to come into being. In classical mythology a "genius"
was the divinity that each person is assigned, a sort of guardian angel who
protects an individual in this world then escorts her or him to the next. In
the seventeenth and eighteenth centuries, as divine explanations for human
behavior gave way to the secular, *genius* came to refer to an inherent capacity or inclination, usually an exceptional inventiveness, brilliance, or creativity that seemed natural, even instinctual, rather than learned. By the late
eighteenth century *genius* was used regularly as an antonym for *talent,* which
implied a developed, studied skill. *Genius* is usually considered superior to
talent because it results from "instinctive perception and spontaneous activity, rather than by processes which admit of being distinctly analyzed."[16]

The narrator of *The Beth Book* emphasizes this distinction between
genius and talent through quotations from and allusions to English Romantic writers and American transcendentalists who are allied with intuitive,
instinctive, mystical ways of knowing.[17] The novel also compares types of
writers:

> As the sun rises, as the birds build, so would she work when the right
> time came. Talent may manufacture to order, but works of genius are

the outcome of an irresistible impulse, a craving to express something for its own sake and the pleasure of expressing it, with no thought of anything beyond. It is talent that thinks first of all of applause and profits, and only works to secure them—works for the result, for the end in view—never for love of the work.[18]

Though at first reading the phrase "with no thought of anything beyond" seems to preclude a connection between aesthetics and activism, one could also argue that Grand equates professionalism rather than politics with *talent*. The choice of the verb *manufacture* and the references to "applause and profits" are crucial. Beth's careers as artist and orator depend on her independence, first, from the male literary establishment, represented in the novel by the Stylists, presumably the Decadents of the 1890s, and, second, from the circles of literary journalism, personified in the character Alfred Cayley Pounce.

In considering the significance of the term *genius,* it is also important to remember that Grand simultaneously held a strong belief in her powers as a novelist, a powerful commitment to the struggle for women's rights, and an astute understanding of the literary politics that distinguished high and low forms of culture and controlled the emerging, lucrative cultural space between the two, the middlebrow market. Until quite recently, literary reviewers have shown little tolerance for literature that embraces "topical" political or social issues too enthusiastically, precisely the kind of literature Grand believed should dominate that cultural space. A review from the *Athenaeum* (which Grand parodies in *The Beth Book*) illustrates the general dismissal of political fiction:

> We know it is no good expostulating with Sarah Grand about having a purpose in the sense of a doctrine to preach in her novels; she would say quite frankly that she cares nothing about novel-writing as an art, except in so far as it can be used as a vehicle for her doctrines.[19]

By insisting that Beth is a woman of genius driven by irresistible impulse, Grand circumvents this facile dichotomy between art and politics with an alternative aesthetic that can encompass both. "Purpose" motivates art; language ceases to be art unless driven by purpose. Art without purpose—art for art's sake—thus ceases to be an aesthetic category.

Another practical advantage of the term *genius* is that Grand's exploitation of Romantic conceptions of the term excuses, even exalts, Beth's (and her own) lack of a formal education, although, as both Wim Neetens and Christine Battersby point out, this association raises problems as well as offering solutions for a woman "genius."[20] In earlier novels Grand stresses the disadvantages women suffer because they have no access to formal education. In *The Beth Book,* however, Grand focuses on the sources of inspiration that *are* available to the female artist, particularly in the relationships that shape her personal history. Even when the novel does address the limitations of female education, the narrator defends women's powers of knowing. In one instance the narrator prefaces a critique of one of the girls' schools Beth attends by paraphrasing Rousseau's comment in *Emile,* "genius will educate itself," adding, "had the development of her genius depended upon a careful acquisition of such knowledge as is to be had at school, it must have remained latent forever." The narrator even goes so far as to take the Romantic view that "theoretical knowledge would have dulled the keenness of her insight probably, confused her point of view, and brought in accepted commonplaces to spoil the originality of her conclusions" (119–120). Not only is male education unnecessary for the woman of genius, but it might even endanger her potential as an artist.

Grand also plays upon the spiritual connotations of the word *genius,* for the artist we find in *The Beth Book* guides and protects the community of women for whom she speaks. In the end Beth's aesthetic may be produced in resistance to the male literary establishment, but ultimately it is Beth's determination to bring a new and better world into being for her community, made up of women whose problems she understands as a consequence of the daily realities of her life with a conservative mother and an unscrupulous husband, that produces the woman-centered, *feminist* aesthetic that she acts out in her life as well as in the artistic and political expression of her genius. In its treatment of the power structures of the family, of marriage, and of the world of publishing, *The Beth Book* develops an ethical aesthetics, an artistic vision grounded in female experience and devoted to the improvement of women's lives yet also capable of transforming male and female readers alike.

The depiction of Beth's childhood is startling even today for its unflinching representation of the cruel, confusing, petty tyrannies children suffer. In writing *The Beth Book,* Grand may have had Dickens's anguished portrayals of childhood in mind, for the night before Beth's birth her father reads "the last number of Dickens" aloud to the family (6), and Beth's development is every bit as complex as Pip's in *Great Expectations* or as the protagonist's in *David Copperfield*. To discuss fully the feelings and impressions of childhood that Grand captures in *The Beth Book* would require a separate chapter: we see, for example, Beth's early awakening to sensation, the fascinating talent at mimicry that educates Beth into class difference, the growth of Beth's mythic and visionary fantasy life, and the child's fascination with and terror of sex and death. To justify this wealth of detail the narrator addresses the reader in an unusual aside that positions the narrator as an interrupting "author" who momentarily permits a fictitious rhetorical veil to fall in order to record minutely Beth's early memories and impressions. In light of the male narrators of *Ideala* and *The Heavenly Twins* the clinical perspective of this voice also eerily suggests the continuing presence of a controlling male narrator:

> To me . . . these earliest impressions are more interesting than much that occurred to her in after life, and I have carefully collected them in the hope of finding some clue in them to what followed. In several instances it seems to me that the impression left by some chance observation or incident on her baby mind made it possible for her to do many things in after life which she certainly never would have done but for those early influences. It would be affectation, therefore, to apologise for such detail. Nothing can be trivial or insignificant that tends to throw light on the mysterious growth of our moral and intellectual being . . . It was a Jesuit, was it not, who said: "Give me the child until it is six years old; after that you can do as you like with it." (11)[21]

Although twentieth-century studies of the novel like Penny Brown's praise Grand's perceptive representation of childhood, her contemporaries had mixed reactions. Some railed against "the prodigal expenditure of personal details."[22] A writer for the *Spectator* protests:

> In the whole range of English fiction there never was a heroine who was described at greater length or in a greater variety of situations than Beth Maclure, née Caldwell. We are even told why she disliked catsup . . . In no ordinary sense of the term can *The Beth Book* be regarded as a novel. It is a prodigiously elaborate study of a temperament merging into an impassioned and polemical pamphlet on the marriage question.[23]

In the same vein an *Academy* reviewer complains: "The first two hundred pages about Beth's early childhood are simply dull. She is a precocious nuisance—that is all. Maggie Tulliver shines immortal beside this clay."[24] In contrast, just as earlier reviewers had repressed the political arguments of *The Heavenly Twins* by focusing on the children's antics rather than the struggles of older female characters, other reviewers praised the unusual realism with which the novel treated childhood. While the *Woman's Signal* reviewer complained that, "from the moment the purpose enters in, the art is destroyed," the writer offers high praise for the characterization of Beth's childhood.[25] Curiously, none of the reviewers seem to make the connection between Grand's novel and what art historian Susan Casteras calls the "hyperbolic biographies that increasingly appeared in the nineteenth century chronicling the lives (especially the formative childhood influences) of 'great men.' "[26]

The Beth Book uses detailed psychological study of the formative events and relationships that shape female genius because this "excess" challenged the critics' implicit assumption that women's lives are dull and trivial matters, hardly worthy of such elaboration despite the comparable abundance of detail in male bildungsroman novels such as *David Copperfield, Oliver Twist,* or *Henry Esmond.* Comparing the sensation novelists of the 1860s and the New Women writers of the 1890s, Lyn Pykett points out that "both groups of writers focused minutely on individual women's lives, demonstrating or exploring the contradictions of the dominant ideology of the feminine, by charting the conflict between 'actual' female experience and the domestic, private angelic feminine ideal."[27] Pykett explores critics' and readers' contradictory responses to the meticulous detail, in particular of feelings, that she finds in these very different subgenres of the novel.[28] Ironically, both critics who were bored by women's lives and those outraged by their fiction attack the excessive detail in women's writing. As Pykett explains, "The gendered critical discourse thus perpetuated two main ways of viewing women's writing, or feminine writing: it was seen either in terms of a limited detailism—a world of surfaces and sympathy—or as a riot of detail and promiscuous emotion."[29] Yet this wealth of detail also provided imaginative spaces for women readers, for Grand's multifaceted characterization of Beth seems to insist that, despite Beth's uniqueness as a female genius, the experiences that produce and develop that genius are common to many of her middle-class women readers.[30] Of course, a novel about a genius can be seen as elitist fiction rather than a lightning rod for feminist activism. Penny Brown notes that Grand risks alienating her readers by depicting childhood genius in such intimate, personal, painful (and egotistical) detailing of Beth's "isolation," "estrangement," "shame," and "dread."[31] In addition, Terry Lovell points out, that because the "woman-as-genius" excels through the accumulation of cultural capital, she is represented as a "natural aristocrat of her sex." This characterization too easily had "the unfortunate effect of opening up feminism to some pretty dubious companions, such as eugenicism and racism" (a problem I address in the next chapter).[32] While genius, by Grand's definition, should transcend social differences of class, as in characterizations of the male genius—from Thomas Carlyle's hero to Friedrich Nietzsche's Ubermensch—the genius figure tends to be positioned outside the social order rather than within the social order. Grand attempts to address this problem by devoting Beth's genius to the service of a community of women by the end of the novel.

Grand's protagonist, then, *is* exceptional; she is articulate, stubborn, determined, and emotionally tempestuous. Yet, by connecting Beth's experience to that of other women, the novel argues that Beth is not an isolated success, a token woman in a world of "real" (i.e., male) artists. Instead, these "personal details" about Beth's childhood ground Beth's developing aesthetic in the personal, practical, social realm of "ordinary" (i.e., middle-class) women. Among the many influences upon Beth's development, her relationships with women pinpoint the first task of the fledgling nineteenth-century female artist. To succeed Beth must negotiate some kind of compromise between Victorian notions of women and of artists.

In *The Heavenly Twins* Grand employed a tripartite plot, myriad genres, and alternating narrators to represent the effects of oppression on different kinds of women. In *The Beth Book* she again uses the principle of multiplicity, though in a different form, to show how female genius develops from the particular affections and anxieties experienced among members of a community of women. Because Beth's father dies when she is a girl, in her youth she is surrounded by women: relatives, female servants, and long-dead ancestors, kept alive by the stories Beth hears about them. In Beth's case her mother, Mrs. Caldwell, and her Great Aunt Victoria-Bench are particularly important. The novel is structured chronologically to emphasize the stages of Beth's career; however, the novel also synchronically details relationships, particularly in the first section of the novel. This structure of repetition with variation emphasizes comparisons between women's experiences, reinforcing the inhibiting effects of child rearing and education on the young female artist that form the obstacles of the *kuntslerroman*. We see how definitions of feminine behavior change over several generations and how one generation insinuates its notion of femininity into the succeeding generation; a variety of "femininities" emerges in the conflicts among women as they negotiate their sometimes antithetical views of what being a woman requires of an individual.

Beth's often troubled relationship with her mother most powerfully externalizes the inner struggles of the developing female artist whose ambitions war with her longing to be accepted by a society hostile to ambitions in women. Adrienne Rich's definition of *matrophobia* in *Of Woman Born* crystallizes the tensions produced in a daughter whose search for identity takes the form of resistance against the traditions her mother embodies: "Matrophobia can be seen as a womanly splitting of the self, in the desire to become purged once and for all of our mothers' bondage, to become individuated and free. The mother stands for the victim in ourselves, the unfree woman, the martyr."[33] Despite the occasional Mrs. Jellyby, Dickens's parody of a mother who neglects her own children for the career in philanthropy she pursues outside the home, Victorians tended to romanticize the loving, supporting role of the mother in courtesy books, women's magazines, and magazine illustrations as well as in literature. (Perhaps one reason we find so many orphans in Victorian novels is that the impulse to romanticize foundered upon the reality of writers' own experiences.) Then, as now, children who desire lives similar to their parents' lives generally cause far less family upheaval.[34] Beth wants something quite different, though, as a child, she can hardly articulate alternatives. While she longs for the affection Mrs. Caldwell unstintingly lavishes on her older and far more traditional daughter, Mildred, Beth must ruthlessly resist many of the feminine values prized by her mother (docility, self-effacement, and self-denial) because these values are incompatible with artistic ambition. In Beth's struggles with her mother the novel searchingly explores the ambivalence produced when one tries to effect change from within a culture. Such ambivalence is particularly clear in the lives of children, who are absolutely dependent upon their parents and who must, at some level, believe their parents are "right" in their actions and their judgments, even as they are driven to rebel against parental authority.

The Beth Book carefully structures the portrait of Mrs. Caldwell so that her conservatism, impatience, narrow-mindedness, and ineptitude in running a household and educating children become a condemnation *not* of the mother but of the forces that shaped her character and that of women like her. Even before Beth's birth the narrator builds sympathy for Mrs. Caldwell. Faced with mountains of wash and mending and with supper for six to be cooked, Mrs. Caldwell mourns her ineptitude and her weakness, and the narrator sympathizes: "Worn and weary working mothers, often uncomplaining victims of the cruelest exactions, toilers whose day's work is never done, no wonder they welcome even the illness which enforces rest in bed, the one holiday that is ever allowed them." As Mrs. Caldwell sits darning, cold and miserable, the narrator asks: "The fire and the book—who knows what they might not have meant, what a benign difference the small relaxation allowed to the mother at this critical time might not have made in the temperament of the child?" (2).

Mrs. Caldwell is a middle-class woman who disappointed her family by marrying "beneath" their social standing, and her unfitness for life as a military officer's wife portrays the domestic misery that Beth ultimately blames on middle-class women's impractical, inadequate education and their ignorance of human nature and economic realities. Mrs. Caldwell has too many children, rebellious servants, and a hot-tempered husband who is too seldom sober and too often in pursuit of "the moon-faced Bessie" or other female servants (7). After her husband's death Mrs. Caldwell's difficulties multiply. Along with Beth and her other daughters Mildred and Bernadine, Mrs. Caldwell travels from Ireland to England, hoping to live with her brother. When the Caldwells arrive in England, however, Mrs. Caldwell finds that her brother, the selfish, social-climbing James Patten, has confiscated her inheritance. James keeps the family estate, Fairholme, for himself; the name of the estate suggests the comfortable elegance of the house and spaciousness of the grounds. He removes the Caldwells to a small, uncomfortable cottage in the neighboring village, Rainharbour. (The name is similarly indicative of the damp, harsh conditions the Caldwells face.)

Despite the grueling conditions of her own life, especially after her husband dies and leaves her with no income and no clear social position, Mrs. Caldwell has no sympathy with her daughter Beth's rebellion. Instead, Mrs. Caldwell, like Evadne's mother Mrs. Frayling and other "good women," demands the same passivity and ignorance that made her so vulnerable to her husband's petty cruelties and to financial ruin at the hands of her brother. Thus, Mrs. Caldwell too often serves as Beth's chief antagonist and silencer, and the novel portrays Beth's interactions with her mother in a number of startling, violent scenes. Repeatedly, Mrs. Caldwell loses her temper and roughly shakes Beth for one infraction or another. Beth's lessons invoke particularly brutal punishment. When Beth does not attend to directions or simply does not understand how to calculate a sum or read a piece of music, her mother resorts to harsh physical punishment. Though Beth attempts to respond with dignity, the pressure of her tempestuous environment constantly threatens her dignity as well as her health. In one particularly painful scene, as Mrs. Caldwell "teaches" Beth to play the piano, Beth inwardly rebels, in cruel imitation of her mother:

> "Oh, you don't know it!" her mother said, now fairly fuming, and accompanying every word by a hard thump of her clenched fist. "Then I'll teach you. I've a great mind to beat you as long as I can stand over you."
>
>   Beth was a piteous little figure, crouched on the piano stool, her back bent beneath her mother's blows, and every fibre of her sensitive frame shrinking from her violence; but she made no resistance, and Mrs. Caldwell carried out her threat. When she could beat Beth no longer, she told her to sit there until she knew [the music notation], and then she left her. Beth clenched her teeth, and an ugly look came into her face. There had been dignity in her endurance—the dignity of

self-control; for there was the force in her to resist, had she thought it right to resist. What she was thinking while her mother beat her was: "I hope I shall not strike you back." (160)

Here we see not only the tensions between Beth and her mother but both the hypocrisy of womanliness and a test of the value systems of the "womanly woman" and the New Woman. Beth has been trained to accept authority, to "endure," to exercise "self-control." The description of domestic violence reveals Grand's unflinching honesty about the painful, even brutal means by which a mother may enforce social law. The passage also depicts the indoctrination of the daughter. As Adrienne Rich points out, matrophobia is not so much fear "of one's mother or of motherhood but of *becoming one's mother*."[35]

In a later passage the narrator clarifies this conflict between old women and new, aligning the "implied reader" with the New Woman. Reader and character are figured as being caught in a painful transition between generations:

The extraordinary inefficiency of the good-old-fashioned-womanly-woman as a wife on a small income, the silly pretences which showed her want of proper self-respect, and the ill-adjusted balance of her undeveloped mind which betrayed itself in petty inconsistencies, fill us with pity and surprise us, yet encourage us too by proving how right and wise we were to try our own experiments. (175)

Mrs. Caldwell's angry confusion in the face of Beth's rebellion against her authority encourages our sympathy with a character whom we might view as obstinate and egotistical rather than misguided and misunderstood. Their relationship helps to clarify the values of the womanly woman and to convince us that Beth *must* rebel. In effect Beth's evolution from a female child raised by a traditional mother to a New Woman depends upon her refusal to become her mother. This apparently clear-cut choice, however, is complicated by a further necessity: Beth's success as a feminist artist depends upon her understanding and forgiving her mother even though she repudiates her mother's beliefs.

As the mediator between the mother and daughter (and between the events and the audience), the narrator tries to explain the tensions sustained between generations of women and played out in female education. Noting that Mrs. Caldwell "was an admirable person, according to the light of her time," the narrator sheds her own light:

To us she appears to have been a good woman marred, first of all, by the narrow outlook, the ignorance and prejudices which were the result of the mental restrictions imposed upon her sex; secondly, by having no conception of her duty to herself; and finally, by those mistaken notions of her duty to others which were so long inflicted upon women, to be their own curse and the misfortune of all whom they were designed to benefit. (280)

Though "highly intelligent," Mrs. Caldwell "had carefully preserved her ignorance of life, because it was not considered womanly to have any practical knowledge of the world"; moreover, she suppresses even her love of reading because "intellectual pursuits were a pleasure, and she did not feel sufficiently self-denying if she allowed herself any but exceptional pleasures" (280). The consequence of this suppression and denial, and its repetition as played out in relation to her daughters, is to reproduce the model of the relationship Rich describes. As Beth comes to some degree to recognize,

> it is the mother through whom patriarchy early teaches the small female her proper expectations. The anxious pressure of one female on another to conform to a degrading and dispiriting role can hardly be termed "mothering," even if she does this believing it will help her daughter to survive.[36]

As Beth grows older, this "pressure" becomes more profound and more obviously debilitating. First, Mrs. Caldwell cajoles Beth to sacrifice her small inheritance from Aunt Victoria to pay for her worthless brother's education rather than going to school herself. Later, she emotionally blackmails Beth into marrying Dan Maclure, even though they know next to nothing about him.

Even the benefits Beth gains from her mother's system of education are tainted by the unrest fomenting in a household of women who cling to old-fashioned notions of femininity while suffering from the poverty, hunger, and degradation that the inadequacies of Mrs. Caldwell's feminine education prevent her from overcoming. A love of literature is one of the few bonds that Beth shares with her mother and her sisters. In *The Woman Reader* Kate Flint documents the moral authority invested in the Victorian mother as the guide to her children's reading. Flint's sources corroborate that the breakdown of mother-daughter relationships was perceived as a widespread problem among nineteenth-century readers of women's journals. One often-cited example is the series of articles called "The Revolt of the Daughters." She points out that 1890s commentators on girls' reading such as B. A. Crackanthorpe urged mothers to read with their daughters as a means of overcoming the very generational conflict *The Beth Book* represents.[37] Contrary to the advice in many of the articles and conduct advice

books for mothers that Flint discusses, but, fortunately for Beth, Mrs. Caldwell cannot afford to buy children's books, so she reads "adult" books aloud
to her children, and Grand carefully catalogs the literary influences that
shape Beth's taste: "Scott, Jane Austen, Dickens, Thackeray, Bulwer Lytton,
and even some of Shakespeare, well; besides such books as 'The Woman in
White,' 'The Dead Secret,' 'Loyal Heart; or, The Trappers,' 'The Scalp
Hunters,' and many more" (119). The character of these readings is turbulent, however, reminding the reader again, of the strange tensions within
the Caldwell household:

> There were lively scenes during the readings. They all wept at the
> pathetic parts, laughed loudly when amused, and disputed about pas-
> sages and incidents at the top of their voices. Mrs. Caldwell forgot that
> Harriet was a servant, Harriet forgot herself, and the children, unaccus-
> tomed to wordy warfare, forgot their fear of their mother, and flew at
> each other's throats. (130)

Jenny Bourne Taylor, Kate Flint, and Lyn Pykett all provide extensive doc-
umentation of the many articles written in protest of the psychological and
even physical consequences to which young girls who read titillating fiction
were subject.[38] Scenes of reading in *The Beth Book* substantiate these fears.
Family readings are charged with stormy, anarchic pleasure. Both an escape
from the sufferings brought on by their poverty and an outlet for power
struggles in the household, the readings liberate characters from conventional hierarchies between mother and daughters, among the children, and
between employer and servant. Thus, even Mrs. Caldwell's gifts to Beth, a
love of literature and astute literary judgments, are complicated. These readings unleash suppressed narratives of family and class tensions as well as ini-
tiating Beth into literary culture.

Despite the generally harsh portrait of Mrs. Caldwell in her role as
mother, criticisms of Mrs. Caldwell soften much later in the novel when the
narrator describes the adult Beth's reaction to her mother's death. Several
years after Beth marries and leaves home, she receives word by mail that her
mother, whom she has not seen since her wedding, has suddenly passed
away. The bleak landscape of Beth's childhood fades into kind memories:

> She had understood her mother better than her mother had understood
> her, had felt for her privations, had admired and imitated her patient
> endurance; and now to think that it was too late, to think that she had
> gone, and it would never be in Beth's power to brighten her life or
> lessen the hardship of it! That was all she thought of. (384)

The play of Beth's memory signifies the power of the *idea* of maternity
regardless of actual family circumstances. Beth's mother is superficially

responsible for Beth's painful and inadequate education. Indirectly, however, Mrs. Caldwell inspires Beth's interest in women's social position. Mrs.
Caldwell attempts to teach the child Beth values and skills that would ultimately undermine her daughter's hope for a better life, lessons that Beth
rejects. Long after Beth leaves home, however, her mature analysis of and
sympathy with her mother train her attention upon the cruelties masked by
Victorian notions of femininity, and this knowledge determines the direction her genius eventually takes.

Although the first third of the novel emphasizes the conflicts between
Beth and her mother, the larger community of women who surround and
influence Beth during the years she lives with her mother somewhat com-
pensates for the limitations of the mother/daughter relationship. Moreover,
Grand's representation of the relationships of girls and women within the
household resists generalizations about class relations in the New Woman
novel, for the formation of the New Woman artist depends heavily on her
engagement with working-class women, especially the servants, who are
developed as complicated characters in their own right and whose sufferings
are generally depicted with at least some degree of sympathy and respect.
Like many middle-class Victorian children, in her infancy Beth has more
intimate relationships with female servants than with her own parents. During Beth's infancy she has an Irish nurse, whose name Jane Nettles betokens
her impatience and harshness. Jane chastises Beth so vigorously for her normal childish questions and chatter that Beth learns to observe carefully,
rather than to ask questions, a skill that becomes vital to her career as a
writer. (As John Kucich points out, Grand's nationalism often manifests
itself in stereotypical treatment of both French and Irish characters.)[39] A
kinder nurse, Kitty, gives Beth access to a vocabulary rather than silencing
her. Mr. and Mrs. Caldwell believe emotional excesses of any kind are
intolerable: "Displays of religious emotion in everyday life they regarded as
symptoms of insanity." Kitty, on the other hand, is a fervent Irish Catholic.
Under her tutelage Beth develops a passion for expression, praying nightly
to the Virgin and singing Catholic hymns. When the Caldwells fire Kitty
for proselytizing, Beth is brokenhearted; "her whole being would have
stirred to speak her emotion, even though speech meant martyrdom" (47).

Of the several working-class women who help to shape Beth's character as a developing woman of genius, Harriet, the maid-of-all-work
employed by Mrs. Caldwell after the Caldwells move to England, wields
the greatest influence. First, she cajoles Beth into cleaning and cooking with
her so that Beth develops the practical skills that Mrs. Caldwell reviles, even
in their poverty, as unladylike. Lyn Pykett argues persuasively that sensation
fiction and New Woman share crucial aesthetic concerns, and indeed Harriet's love of narrative, particularly of harrowing tales and implausible stories

from *The Family Herald,* thoroughly absorbs the character Beth.[40] The contrast between Beth's relationship with Harriet and Harriet's relationship with Mrs. Caldwell illustrates the upstairs/downstairs stereotypes that plagued discussions of the "servant question" in women's journals. To Beth "Harriet was a woman of well-marked individuality and brilliant imagination. She could never separate fact from fiction in any form of narrative, and narrative was her specialty." Beth willingly undertakes Harriet's tasks in return for "a thrilling incident, or . . . a speech impressive with suitable gesticulation" (122). Before Mrs. Caldwell, Harriet appears "in the character of a respectable, vigilant domestic, more anxious about her mistress' interests than her own" (124).[41] Eventually, Beth views Harriet's behavior as duplicitous and manipulative; nevertheless, she never forgets the difficulties of servants' lives, and the position of these women as well as of middle-class women continues to interest her (as well as Grand) in later years. Grand's conflicted treatment of Harriet also points to the aesthetic problem for the New Woman that overwhelmed Evadne in Grand's earlier novel and that John Kucich has so helpfully described. As political analysis, the literature of the New Woman sought "truth"; fiction, on the other hand, was a fabrication, dependent on Harriet's pleasures in invention, in sensation, and in strategic manipulation. Both Kitty and Harriet, as women of the lower classes, are depicted as far more at ease with the what Kucich calls the "lies" of narrative and emotional truth than the novel seems finally able to allow Beth to be.[42]

This same tension between learning to take on cultural authority—a form of role-playing—and "acting" plays out in the dramas into which Beth inserts herself. Like most imaginative children, Beth seeks her identity in literary or imagined characters. She pretends to be "Norna of the Fitful Head," who "made charms, and talked poetry, and people were afraid of" or "a heroine of romance, now, going to do a great deed" (137). As Lady Bountiful, she adopts Emily Bean, a working-class neighborhood child, sometimes as her pupil, sometimes as her parishioner, as she plays teacher or preacher. Fearful of embarrassing herself before Emily, Beth educates herself: "This gave her the first real interest she had ever had in school-work, and inspired her with some slight confidence in herself. She felt the dignity of the position of teacher too, and the responsibility" (139). Even as these incidents register a kind of unthinking class superiority, the scenes also foreshadow Beth's future success as a feminist orator who will speak to and for both middle- and working-class women in an intricate union of privilege and responsibility.

The most important female figure, however, aside from Mrs. Caldwell, is Beth's great-aunt. As the narrator notes, "For two years after Beth was outlawed by her mother, Great-Aunt Victoria Bench was her one link with the civilised world" (185). When Uncle James banishes Mrs. Caldwell and her daughters to the cottage in Rainharbour, he also discreetly evicts Victoria Bench, who is his and Mrs. Caldwell's maiden aunt. He has suffered Aunt Victoria's presence in his home as long as the stocks he has invested for her promise his reward. When the stocks fall, sharply, he "invites" Aunt Victoria to live with the Caldwells. Known for her perfection in manners, her self-discipline, and the impeccable posture that embodies both, Aunt Victoria also represents the best of those virtues generally associated with her name and her century: dignity, self-restraint, forbearance, loyalty, and dutifulness.

The novel self-consciously admires the qualities of Aunt Victoria's life that, in another novel, would doom her to absurd idealization as a too-sweet elderly aunt or to ridicule as a penniless spinster dependent on her relatives' mercy.[43] When Beth meets her aunt, she notices that the older woman is intelligent, self-possessed, and respectable; however, Beth also sees "one of those forlorn old ladies who have nobody actually their own to care for them, although they may have numbers of relations, and acquire odd habits from living much alone" (144). The narrator briefly assumes Aunt Victoria's point of view to register the "poverty and obscurity" that follow her loss of income (186). Abandoned by fair-weather friends and condescended to by Mrs. Caldwell, Aunt Victoria feels the pain of disillusionment as keenly as the longing for decent, sufficient food and a warm, comfortable home. Using Aunt Victoria as the text, the narrator again turns from the moment of the narrative to the presumed New Woman of the present:

> In Aunt Victoria's day old people were only too apt to be selfish, tyrannical, narrow, and ignorant, a terror to their friends; and they were nearly always ill, the old men from lives of self-indulgence, and the old women from unwholesome restraint of every kind. This is the age of youthful grandmothers . . . their vitality is so much greater, their appearance so much better preserved; their knowledge so much more extensive, their interests so much more varied, and their hearts so much larger. Aunt Victoria nowadays would have struck out for herself in a new direction. She would have gone to London, joined a progressive women's club, made acquaintance with work of some kind or another, and never known a dull moment. (186–87)

The disjuncture between Aunt Victoria's capabilities and the opportunities open to her are matters both for regret and optimism. Perhaps because Aunt Victoria and Beth both feel like such misfits, they take to one another immediately. What Victoria Bench cannot achieve for herself, she does make possible for Beth. Significantly, she is not a stand-in for Beth's mother, for her childlessness is a distinct part of her character. Considering that so few of Grand's New Woman characters have children, the future that Aunt Victoria "could have had" holds important implications for Beth.

Precisely because Aunt Victoria does not have children, she has the most to offer Beth. During her lifetime she imparts bits of wisdom and encouragement and teaches Beth self-discipline along with more conventional lessons in sewing and French. She also embodies a way of life that may later explain Beth's decision to leave her husband. When Beth argues that her grandmother (Aunt Victoria's niece), who allegedly went mad due to her husband's cruelties, should have fled, Aunt Victoria praises the joys of spinsterhood in a passage which must have surprised Grand's readers, accustomed to newspaper and journalistic head-shaking over "redundant women":

> Ah, my dear child . . . I have observed that no woman who married and becomes a mother can ever again live happily like a single woman. She has entered upon a different phase of being and there is no return for her. There is a weight of meaning in that expression: "the ties of home." It is "the ties of home" that restrain a loving woman, however much she suffers . . . There is habit too . . . but above all, there is hope—the hope that matters may mend; and fear—the fear that once she deserts her post things will go from bad to worse, and she be to blame. (202)

Even after her death Aunt Victoria's influence continues, for she bequeaths to Beth her room (that longed-for room of one's own) and a small income from stocks for her education. Many years later the value of the stocks improves, and the earnings are enough to make Beth financially independent so that she can pursue the career of her choice.

The transition from childhood to "wifehood" is strongly marked by changes not only in Beth's circumstances but also by changes in her character and by an opening up of the novel to the political, legal, and social contexts absent before the marriage. Beth's husband, Dan Maclure, is a doctor who works for the military. From the first days of her marriage Dan forcefully initiates Beth into "the realities of vice and crime"; as a man and a doctor, he has privileged access to both. He delights in telling Beth about prostitutes and other forms of "depravity" and "degradation" and accuses her of disingenuousness when she recoils from his stories (339). (In a witty reversal of expectation he also infuriates her by forcing her to read cheap romances aloud to him.) Although the novel details more mundane miseries of domesticity (Dan reads Beth's mail, rifles her drawers, steals her insignificant income, repeatedly accuses her of infidelity, and eventually takes a mistress), the revelation of Dan's mysterious career is the crisis that destroys the marriage. After two years of being shunned by neighbors, acquaintances, and even Dan's medical colleagues, Beth learns her husband is as unscrupulous in his professional life as in his personal life. The failure of Beth's marriage functions in the plot somewhat as the failure of Ideala's and Evadne's marriages had in the earlier two novels. Beth is forced into action; she must find a way of life of her own, some form of work to make her life meaningful, since the promise of marriage failed. Yet this marriage is also connected to Edith's death through the topic of venereal disease. In *The Heavenly Twins* Grand uses melodrama to highlight the oppression women from all classes share. In *The Beth Book* she uses the past and anticipates a feared future for the same purpose, for she makes explicit reference to a chapter in British medical history that had just come to a close in England but which was about to be opened in India, the Contagious Diseases Acts. Combining history and fiction, Grand connects the personal and public lives of women, for Beth's marriage shows her (as well as her readers) that the injustice at work in her personal relationship with her husband is not the consequence of her failure as a womanly woman but, instead, is a reflection of the exploitation of women written into the social and medical laws that should protect women. Beth's painful marital education also provides her with a metaphor that helps her to describe the double standard, for she begins to see her husband's immorality as a disease with the same properties as the venereal disease he is supposed to be treating.

Beth's shocking discovery about her husband (which she learns from Angelica) is that he runs a "Lock" hospital. By merely mentioning the name, Grand could be sure that her readers would understand that she was referring to one of many hospitals established by the British government as part of a series of laws called the Contagious Diseases Acts, even though by the time Sarah Grand wrote *The Beth Book* the acts had been repealed in Britain. In fact, several of her reviewers criticized her outdated references to the acts.[44] In 1864, 1866, and 1869 Parliament had instituted a series of laws in an attempt to control the increase of syphilis and gonorrhea among military men. Eventually, these laws covered eighteen military districts throughout England and provided a special division of plainclothes policemen who accosted women suspected of prostitution and required them to submit "voluntarily" to an examination for venereal disease. If the woman was ill, she was held in quarantine for as long as nine months at one of the state-run Lock hospitals with special quarantine facilities. Thereafter, the woman had to register with medical authorities and appear for fortnightly examinations.

What made the laws particularly untenable is that men were neither examined nor imprisoned. Constance Rover, in *Love, Morals, and the Feminists,* quotes a report from the Royal Commission that established the first act in 1864. The report limits the provisions of the acts to cities in the southern counties close to military installations:

> We may at once dispose of this recommendation [that soldiers and sailors should be subject to regular examination], so far as it is founded on the principle of putting both parties to the sin of fornication on the same footing by the obvious but not less conclusive reply that there is no comparison to be made between prostitutes and the men who consort with them. With the one sex the offence is committed as a matter of gain; with the other it is an irregular indulgence of a natural impulse.[45]

Authorities had attempted to examine soldiers in the early 1860s, but the men became so angry and resisted so violently that military leaders feared desertion. Consequently, the military authorities turned all of their attention to women who were allegedly prostitutes. By insisting that only women be examined, quarantined, and treated, the medical authorities (or at least their actions) reinforced the general belief that men's sexual drives excused their uses of women. Moreover, the medical authorities seemed to suggest that, because men could not be held accountable for their sexual desire and consequently their sexual acts, the spread of venereal disease was somehow a female pestilence.

When Parliament attempted to extend the acts from southern military towns to the more industrialized northern cities in 1869, a group of nonconformist ministers and working-class men established a committee to fight the acts. This group excluded women due to the "distastefulness" of the issue. In response, a number of women, led by Josephine Butler, formed the Ladies' National Association. The women's organization shocked the public by publishing the "Women's Manifesto of 1870" in the *Daily News.* Although the document was addressed to the House of Commons, it forced the people of England to consider the acts' legalized inequities. The complaints of the Ladies' National Association provided a crash course in the sexual double standard: the acts robbed women of civil rights; provided for state regulation of prostitution (thereby implicitly condoning the practice); gave the police unmitigated power against women; exploited the poorer classes; and failed in their putative purpose of halting the spread of venereal disease because the partners of prostitutes were not treated. Finally, in 1888 the acts were repealed and the Lock hospitals closed. Judith Walkowitz discusses the consequences of this feminist protest in her book *Prostitution and Victorian Society: Women, Class, and the State.* Topics that had formerly been suppressed erupted into public discussion: women's health, women's challenges to the medical field, the injustice of the sexual double standard (and the role of the medical professionals and politicians in maintaining it), and the dangers of the state's paternal disciplining of England's poor.[46]

Ironically, through the public discussion of the Contagious Diseases Acts many women received a least a partial education in human sexuality. Middle-class women also began to see frightening implications in their lack of power and protection as they learned about the spread of the diseases, for venereal disease attacked married women in the intimacy of the home, despite society's insistence that women's only security resided in the domestic sphere. Venereal disease also affected women in their most venerated function—reproduction. As I mentioned in the last chapter, Josephine Butler had long been enshrined as a feminist heroine by Grand and other women's rights supporters, and her status as a heroine continued long after the repeal of the acts. Moreover, while Grand's critics protested the revisiting of this past as gratuitous sensationalism, *The Beth Book* appeared in the same year as a series of articles debating the reinstitution of the Contagious Diseases Acts in India and England. Elizabeth C. Wolstenholme Elmy was so incensed by this proposal that she reprinted the 1870 "Protest of the Ladies' National Association for the Repeal of the Contagious Diseases Acts" in the journal *Shafts,* urging women to write to Dr. Elizabeth Blackwell for a privately printed pamphlet on the acts.[47] In her several articles Elmy quotes writers from the *Humanitarian,* the *Westminister Review,* and the *Times* who advocated reinstitution. The *Humanitarian* writer even argues that the acts should apply to "every garrison town."[48] Elmy sounds the same alarm that Grand rings in *The Heavenly Twins* and *The Beth Book:*

> this legislation is not merely, like so much of English legislation, sex-legislation of the basest kind, intended expressly to preserve a *privlegium* of vice for the male half of the community, but is also class legislation of the cruellest character; since practically it touches most keenly and closely the poor working woman. Every woman, be her position what it may, is morally outraged and degraded by the very existence of such enactments, seeing that they tend to intensify in the minds of men the horrible notion that woman is merely an appanage to man for the purpose of the gratification of his basest sensuality. But poor women suffer directly and individually, and for their sake I appeal to the sisterhood at large to prevent the very possibility of the re-enactment of such infamous measures.[49]

Like Grand, Elmy warns that the implications of the acts are not only that women are embodiments of physical disease but that the good of the "nation" is endangered by the "moral disease" unleashed by this exercise of masculine authority.[50] As Janet Lyon's analysis of purity reformers demonstrates, by using reverse discourse, feminists like Elmy and Grand reject the characterizations of themselves as diseased, inferior, or in need of discipline. The danger of their arguments, of course, is that the gender hierarchy these writers protest is inverted (and thereby sustained) at the same time that it is questioned.[51]

In *The Beth Book* Grand uses memories of the past and the future threat of the acts to create another wedge with which to destabilize fantasies of separate gendered spheres. She transforms the plot and discourses of these social and legal debates into a rewriting of marriage as a social and political disorder rather than an idealized private and personal relationship. Grand's novel suggests that she read the Contagious Diseases Acts as society's response to women's appeals for education, improved marriage laws, employment, and the right to move from the private sphere to the public. Her version of this social crisis identifies the culpable parties as Parliament, the medical profession, the legal system, and clerics, all of whom enforced a mutual interpretation of the venereal plague as a social disorder and pestilence spread by women's uncleanliness and misconduct. Grand's feminist narrative exposes the Contagious Diseases Acts as a patriarchal society's attempt to conceal the breach between the roles that society reserved for women and the opportunities women were beginning to demand.

Grand herself knew about the Contagious Diseases Acts and the Lock hospitals from personal, painful experience. Her biographer Gillian Kersley speculates about the progress of Grand's disillusionment with her own husband:

> To his already reprehensible habits of opening her letters, drinking, smoking in her bedroom, piling up debts . . . and telling her lewd stories, his sexual demands on her—usually late at night and reeking of alcohol and tobacco—continued and she also suspected he had a mistress. When she locked her bedroom door he demanded she open it saying: "I've a legal right to come here whenever I choose": she felt contaminated by him.[52]

As a military doctor, McFall treated men with venereal disease and was probably involved with the Lock hospital in Lancashire.[53] Dan Maclure holds a similarly mysterious medical post in the novel, and in the fictional account of the wife's discovery and distress the revelation exposes the political structures that organize gender inequities Beth had heretofore experienced chiefly as personal degradation. The confrontation between Beth and her husband over his role in the Lock hospital also clarifies the implications of Ideala's encounter with her husband's mistress and Angelica's witness to

Edith's madness in the earlier two novels of the trilogy. Beth is shocked when Angelica explains "the whole horrible apparatus for the special degradation of women" (398), but she is outraged when her husband defends his position at the Lock hospital. Dan describes his work in "revolting details couched in the coarsest language" then dismisses Beth's concerns for the women when she asks: "what means do you take to protect those poor unfortunate women from disease? What do you do to the men who spread it? What becomes of diseased men?" Dan replies that "doctors can't be expected to preach morals" and echoes Colonel Colquhoun's protests in *The Heavenly Twins* that "it's a deuced awkward thing for a man to be suspected of disease. It's a stigma, and might spoil his prospects. Women are so cursedly prying nowadays. They've got wind of its being incurable, and many a one won't marry a man if a suspicion of it attaches to him" (400). Unwittingly, Dan reveals to Beth the larger implications of the Contagious Diseases Acts when he tries to separate the operation of the acts from the realm of ethics. In an attempt to be fair-minded, Beth carefully compares Angelica's version of the Lock hospitals with Dan's:

> Her own sense of justice was too acute to let her accept at once the accusation that so-called civilised men, who boast of their chivalrous protection of the "weaker sex," had imposed upon women a special public degradation, while the most abandoned and culpable of their own sex were not only allowed to go unpunished, but to spread vice and disease where they listed. The iniquitous injustice and cruelty of it all made her sick and sorry for men, and reluctant to believe it. (401–2)

Beth's analysis, which reads almost like a definition of patriarchy, startles her yet also relieves her because it helps Beth to see her personal dissatisfaction with her husband in a larger context of exploitative relationships.

On a personal level Beth ceases to be such an easy mark for her husband's demands for money and his tendency to blame her for their lack of friends and social attainment. More important, however, Beth's knowledge of the Contagious Diseases Acts forces her attention from the murk of her personal life to the public sphere, as she realizes that her marriage mirrors the relative positions of women to men and their institutions in the larger world, in this case, particularly in the field of medicine. As Beth explains to her husband:

> It is precisely in order to make vice safe for men that such appointments are made . . . Medical etiquette would not stop where it does, at the degradation of those unfortunate women, if you were honestly attempting to put a stop to that disease. You would have it reported,

irrespective of the sex of the sufferer, like any other disease that is dangerous to the health of the community. It is not contrary to etiquette to break your peculiar professional secrecy in the case of a woman, but it would be in the case of a man; so you punish the women, and let the men go free to spread the evil from one generation to another as they like. (442–43)

She weakens the usual claim of medical "ethics" by calling the practice of protection "etiquette." This substitution also suggests that the medical community's method is social practice rather than scientific necessity.[54]

None of Beth's questions is nearly as damning as Dan's own assessments of his role as a doctor. Unlike Dr. Galbraith, who uses his medical knowledge in attempts to heal the New Woman, Dan's cruel and trivial oppressions are magnified to grotesque proportions in the parallel between his execution of domestic and medical law. Repeatedly, Beth's responses to his arguments, his revelations, and his touch are described in terms of disease, corruption, and illness, metaphorically pairing the moral contagion at a national level with Beth's domestic experience of marriage. As Beth tells Dan when he disclaims the moral responsibilities of men and of doctors: "you cannot attend to the health of the community properly without also minding its morals. The real old devil is disease" (444).

The significance of Grand's use of the Contagious Diseases Acts as a context for her analysis of gender relations and the kind of doctor this plot calls into being are suggested by Lorna Duffin and Sarah Delamont. Whereas the doctor, if tentatively, wields the power to heal in *The Heavenly Twins,* the institution of medicine in cooperation with the state is thoroughly demonized in *The Beth Book.* Dr. Galbraith, the "male feminist" who attends to women's mental health, is set up against Dr. Maclure, the embodiment of state manipulation of women through Foucauldian surveillance of their bodies. The medical field's management of women, repressed in *The Heavenly Twins,* erupts melodramatically in *The Beth Book.* By midcentury women had proven they could do the unthinkable, such as manage property and control capital, and the multitude of single women without financial resources could not be denied the means to make a living. Duffin and Delamont argue that in the late nineteenth century the medical establishment first began to exercise significant social power as a "precarious, usually contradictory and inconsistent, and ultimately self-defeating" response to changes in women's position in English society.[55] The shift in Grand's perspective on doctors may have to do with economics and affiliation. Dr. Galbraith's research is funded by his private fortune in contrast with Dan Maclure's practice of medicine as his livelihood. Duffin and Delamont point out that many doctors depended on the patronage of the mid-dle-class women who employed them. Administering to these women not only paid bills but also provided doctors with improved social status. There-fore, many medical practitioners served their own interests by keeping women out of medical professions and encouraging popular beliefs about women's frailty and delicate health. Such doctors easily slipped into a pater-nal role, defining female norms, classifying women's diseases and limita-tions, prescribing debilitating treatments, such as ovarectomies and rest cures, reinforcing the belief that cranial size correlated with gender and intelligence, and shutting women out of medical schools and professional organizations.[56] The misogyny and protection of male privilege that informed the medical profession's rise to power were named and resisted by the groups who fought the Contagious Diseases Acts and their adherents. While Galbraith remains a sympathetic character, this novel targets the medical *profession* as an institution. And, just as a painting or photograph of a few details of a landscape may train the eye to see the landscape itself, so Grand's feminist narrative of one of England's most infamous medical crises, looming again on the horizon, teaches her audience to reread the narratives of misogyny and class bias that continued to structure women's experiences at the turn of the century.

Even though Beth escapes the immediate corruptive influence of her husband and gains emotional independence from him after she learns who and what he really is, she cannot get a divorce because, again, masculine privilege is protected by law. Beth's friends attempt to arrange a divorce for her, only to learn that "there was little chance of that as the acute mental suffering her husband had caused her had merely injured her health and endangered her reason, which does not amount to cruelty in the estimation of the law" (518). Grand emphasizes the connection between the autocratic power of a man over a woman within the context of marriage and the dominion of patriarchal authorities over the lives of all Victorian women, using the metaphor of disease to convey the immorality of the political order. Yet Beth, like Grand, grasps at least limited freedom. Beth separates from her husband, becomes an important member of Ideala's community, accepts a leading role in the larger women's movement, and finds strength and fulfillment working for all classes of English women.

Grand's use of this social crisis, in the midst of a novel detailing the development of the female artist, or the woman of genius, again demon-strates her ambition to construct an image and definition of the artist that accommodates rather than avoids the intersections of art and politics. On one hand, Beth's marriage is an initiation into vice; on the other, this period becomes a quest for the appropriate language and form through which Beth may educate others by revealing connections between personal and political forces. Grand's novel demonstrates the interaction of art and ethics as she casts the traditional matter of the novel—the development of characters, the complexities of relationships, the working out of conflicts between the individual and the social order—in a political crisis that is in large part a crisis of social ethics. As Grand insisted, repeatedly and emphatically, in particular in the 1923 foreword to *The Heavenly Twins,* she was committed to a belief that middlebrow fiction should militantly intervene not only in representations of women but in social debates about women. To that end Grand fashioned an aesthetic accountable to systems of value or ethics that late Victorians gendered as feminine. *The Beth Book* is both an embodiment of and an argument for such an aesthetic. This conflict becomes overtly self-reflexive in the final section of the novel as Beth comes into her own as a writer. Having examined the personal register of Beth's childhood and the political and social register of her marriage, the novel takes on the bastion of male power whose privileges and prejudices Grand knew well—the world of letters and literary publishing.

In the final third of the novel Beth's struggles through an unhappy childhood and a debasing marriage are rewarded, for she becomes the author of a tremendously successful work of social theory and the chief spokeswoman of the London woman's movement. In this section of the novel Grand explores Beth's developing means of expressing a feminist ethical and social vision. For Grand the feminist artist's goal is to forge a synthesis of ethics and aesthetics in a form that inspires the audience to take action. This objective pits Beth and other New Woman writers against the self-proclaimed Aesthetes, also referred to as Decadents, whom Beth calls the "Stylists" (374). Grand's attention to this group of writers is important for historical as well as literary reasons; critics' tendency to conflate the New Woman writers and the Decadents together as "sex problem" novelists or "degenerates" promoted misreadings and misperceptions that threatened the cause of New Woman writers and women leaders who saw themselves as committed to political rather than specifically sexual reform. Similarly, this confusion obscured the radical challenges to representation and sexual essentialism so often clothed in the Decadents' extravagant wit and costume.[57]

Inspired by their own interpretations of the art-for-art's-sake doctrine of Walter Pater, the art criticism of John Ruskin, and the Pre-Raphaelite movement, the Aesthetes figured prominently on the literary scene throughout the 1890s. The *Yellow Book* was first published in 1894, and several of the female New Women authors who wrote of the need for female sexual rather than solely social liberation, including George Egerton and

Victoria Cross, were included in the *Yellow Book*. Many publishers of one group of writers also published the other: John Lane made the reputation of the Bodley Head with both New Woman and Decadent fiction, and Aubrey Beardsley designed illustrations for Lane's editions of both.[58] By the mid-1890s the two groups of writers were being reviewed together regularly, and the titles of the reviews suggest the reviewers' basis of comparison: "Sex in Modern Literature," "Literary Degenerates," "The Gospel of Intensity," and "Tommyrotics."

Linda Dowling's groundbreaking essay examines the causes and consequences of the critics' confusion. The Aesthetes and the New Women novelists did, in fact, share similarities. As Dowling explains:

> The New Woman . . . was perceived to have ranged herself perversely with the forces of cultural anarchism and decay precisely because she wanted to reinterpret the sexual relationship. Like the decadent, the heroine of New Woman fiction expressed her quarrel with Victorian culture chiefly through sexual means—by heightening sexual consciousness, candour, and expressiveness.[59]

Critics who connected the two movements charged the literature of both with being egoistic, emotionally exaggerated (the terms *hysteria* and *morbidity* were often used), morally corrupting, sensational, unnatural, and degenerate.[60] Moreover, as Dowling, Rita Kranidis, Ann Ardis, and Sally Ledger have all demonstrated, though their motives differed, New Woman writers and Decadents both often wrote about what Dowling calls "unfortunates," the poor, alcoholics, seduced women, prostitutes, street people.[61] The socialist sympathies of many New Woman writers like Isabella Ford and the liberal sympathies of writers like Grand led New Women to address the sufferings of poor and working women, while for the Decadents these characters possessed a "mysterious otherness."[62] The crossing of class boundaries, particularly when those others were invested with sexual appeal, further fueled middle-class conservative critics' ire. Constructing what Dowling calls a "lurid vision of cultural apocalypse,"[63] these reviewers nervously retaliated against the sexual implications of the effeminate male Decadents' dress and behavior and the "unwomanly" sexual and social demands of the New Woman by accusing both of threatening the survival of the race. Although public images—such as drawings, cartoons, and caricatures—of both Decadents and New Women suggest they were conspicuous because of their dress, their various props, their forms of slang, and their denunciations of society, the differences were as telling as the similarities. Images of the Decadents depict men lounging in exotic clothing and experimenting with pleasurable excesses; in drawings of the New Woman she pedals furiously on her bicycle or lectures to hostile audiences about the rights of women.[64] This superficial exchange of gender-marked behaviors prompted some critics to read members of the two groups as similar, despite obvious differences, in particular between the Decadents' conscious ennui and the shock value of their eroticizing of sexuality as opposed to the more political New Woman writers' didactic demand for an end to the sexual double standard and criticism of men's exploitation of female sexuality without regard for women's desires or needs, sexual or otherwise. One writer for the *National Observer* discriminates between the decadents of the previous generation and decadents of 1895, the year of the review, by warning readers of the supposedly increasing similarities between male decadents and New Women. The review expresses alarm that the new decadent is an "invention as terrible as, and in some ways more shocking than, the New Woman."[65] Similarly, many of the *Punch* cartoons of the period abound with satiric renditions of the comic mistakes that were alleged to occur when women cross-dressed. Discussing the influence of Victorian anthropological theories of decadence both on social thought and on literary analysis, Sandra Siegel explains the source of one reviewer's anxiety:

> So long as the words "civilization" and "masculine" were conceived as conceptual cognates, the New Woman *was* shocking and the new decadents *were* "an invention as terrible." The New Woman, like her mirror image, the new decadent, who was always male, confused what was essential to her nature. She not only moved in the public sphere, but behaved like a man, even as the new decadents, in their self-absorption and inaction, behaved like women, lost their masculine vigor.[66]

Despite the fact that many of the New Woman writers took regeneration as their political and literary platform, their association with the Decadents obscured their specific political critiques and activist objectives.

While the connection with the Decadents had annoyed New Woman writers in the first half of the 1890s, the association became far more threatening in 1895, when Oscar Wilde, who became the human icon of English decadence (despite his Irish origins), was accused of sodomy, counteracted with a libel suit, and thereby instigated the now-famous trials that culminated in his conviction. In the previous ten years the effeminate, dandyish dress of the Aesthetes, the public posturing, the literary preciousness, the alleged apolitical, asocial, amoral standards for art and life, and the valuation of style over form had been fodder for the caricaturists and cartoonists of periodicals such as *Punch*. For the most part the public had laughed or sniffed at the Aesthetes themselves, though journalists such as Hugh

From a photograph by R. W. Thomas Cheapside.

MADAME SARAH GRAND.

Grand appears in the character of the New Woman in this photo-
graph, which accompanied the essay "Some Famous Lady
Cyclists" in the *Lady's Realm* 2 (September 1897). (Courtesy of the
Library of Congress.)

Stutfield and Janet Hogarth had condemned the Aesthetes' ridicule of Victorian morality. But in 1895 journalists turned Wilde's trials into a highly
sensationalized and homophobic condemnation of Wilde, his associates, and
his imitators. Afterward, the appearance, lifestyles, and literature of the Aesthetes were taken more seriously as a threat to heterosexuality and to gender difference, and this fear inspired apocalyptic warnings and cries of
degeneracy.[67] By association the New Woman's threat to the social spheres,
gender roles and duties, and sexual restrictions that bolstered the Victorian

social system also provoked fierce criticism. Sally Ledger points out, for example, that Wilde was sentenced on 25 May 1895, and on 21 December 1895 *Punch* announced: "THE END OF THE NEW—THE CRASH HAS COME AT LAST."[68] Similarly, John Stokes notes that during Wilde's trials the *Speaker* called the New Women "creatures of Mr. Oscar Wilde's fantasy."[69] The aftershocks were felt throughout the literary community, and charges of degeneration assumed a new significance. Ann Ardis offers fascinating evidence that Grand's publisher Heinemann, known to operate a liberal press, took immediate measures to separate his company from the Decadent writers in 1895. Ardis describes an advertisement in the 27 July *Athenaeum* that acknowledges a "slight reaction against a recent tendency in literary criticism." The advertisement promises that Heinemann's new fiction series will provide "the classics of each country rather than its oddities and . . . obsolete features," which she reads as "a defensive move" to reassure readers who had been following the trials.[70]

In the moment of 1895 a diversity of New Women were at work. As Chris Waters and Ann Ardis have shown, writers like Isabella Ford continued to focus upon women who lived outside middle-class protection, and, as Talia Shires and Kathy Psomiades's forthcoming anthology on female Decadents shows, many women writers could not continue their careers if they distanced themselves entirely from this literary movement.[71] Sadly, however, many middle-class New Women writers did work aggressively to dissociate themselves from the Aesthetes. In the process they clarified an explicit reformist agenda; at the same time, in the inscription of middle-class, heterosexist feminist biases many of these same authors helped to write a still proliferating social script for homophobia.

Grand plays out these conflicts between New Woman writers and the Decadents in the last chapters of *The Beth Book.* Just as Evadne produced a feminist reading of the male bildungsroman in her assessments of *Tom Jones,* Beth produces a feminist aesthetic in resistance to what might be termed a crisis of masculinity—the reaction to the Decadents and their work in the context of the trials—that threatened to subsume the feminist writers' fictional critique of patriarchy. Beth first becomes acquainted with the Decadents' experiments in fiction by reading French novels. Then literature and life come together in the person of her would-be suitor, Alfred Cayley Pounce. Though Pounce lecherously pursues women, he clumsily struggles to perform as a Decadent in his manners and dress. As a would-be sensualist and a moderately successful stylist, Alfred espouses the apoliticism of the Decadents and aspires to their amorality. Through the intersections of literary theory and character, the novel intimates that literary aesthetics as well as personal morality, even when articulated as negations of action and opinion, have social consequences. By dramatizing the conflict between the New Woman and the Decadent, Grand shows how Beth's life—including her personal experience of the lives of women, her reading of the political in the personal sphere of marriage, and her literary education—combine to produce the ethical aesthetic of the New Woman artist. In answer to the concern with style and form that characterizes the Decadent aesthetic, Grand offers an alternative aesthetic both through Beth's evolving artistic vision and through the plotting of Beth's career.

Beth's struggles to define what we would now call a feminist aesthetic are first revealed when she confesses her artistic ambitions to Sir George Galbraith, Evadne's husband. The most striking features of the emergent aesthetic are its self-reflexive attention to biographical sources, its privileging of social topics, or content, over "imaginative" narratives and over style, and its overtly didactic motive—to transform its audience.

Appropriately, Beth is introduced to the Decadents by way of the French writers, who were heralded as the literary forefathers of the British Decadents. In "The Decadent Movement in Literature," published in *Harper's New Monthly Magazine* in 1893, Arthur Symons claims that France is where "this movement began and has mainly flourished," as though it were not a matter that required discussion. His tone toward the popularizers of the Decadents suggests the ambivalence (even of English intellectuals involved in literary experimentation) toward what Symons defines as "an intense self-consciousness, a restless curiosity in research, an over-subtilizing refinement upon refinement, a spiritual and moral perversity . . . really a new and beautiful and interesting disease."[72] Along with many of the writers of her day, the character Beth (and by extension Grand) suffers anxiety of influence as she contemplates the works of Balzac, Zola, and Gautier. Like the Decadents, the New Woman writers were indebted to the French for leading the way in representing sexuality in fiction. Rita Kranidis discusses critics' tendency to blur categories when discussing these novels and the English novels they influenced; depending on the taste of the critic, such novels might be either as the "new realism" or "degenerate."[73] Similar ambivalence surfaces when Sir George introduces Beth to French novels. Although he suggests that she read them, he distances both himself and *The Beth Book* from the project of these novelists:

> If France is to be judged by the tendency of its literature and art at present, one would suppose it to be dominated and doomed to destruction by a gang of lascivious authors and artists who are sapping the manhood of the country and degrading the womanhood by idealising self-indulgence and mean intrigue. (367)

Like most nineteenth-century feminists, Grand maintains the distinctions between "manhood" and "womanhood," even as she argues that both concepts require revision. Her purpose here, however, is also to refute the public's tendency to associate the New Woman novel (and feminists) with the supposed sexual promiscuity and degeneration of the Decadent writers. Grand also plays on the English sense of *national* superiority to foreigners by aligning her work with "Britishness."

Given the semiautobiographical status of *The Beth Book*, Beth's privileging of biography over the novel, or at least honoring biography as a inspiration for her own writing, should hardly be surprising. In addition, Kate Flint's research on female reading patterns shows that autobiographies and biographies served not only as moral models for girls but also as a curious kind of girls' adventure fiction.[74] Exhausted with French novels, Beth instead turns to

> the people who wrote them; biographies, autobiographies, and any scrap of anecdote about authors and their methods . . . Life as they had lived it, not as they had observed and imagined it, seemed all-important to her; and as she read and thought, sitting alone in the charmed solitude of her secret chamber, her self-respect grew. (370)

For Beth these texts provide the simplicity, directness, character, and usefulness that she seeks in her own writing. Pouring over George Sand's *Historie de ma vie,* the lives of the Brontës, and essays by Emerson, Macauley, De Quincey, Carlyle, and Ruskin, Beth begins "forming a code of literary principles for herself" (371). Grand's specific detailing of Beth's reading is significant for several reasons. The list foreshadows Beth's eventual choice to write social analysis. Also, with true "Grandian" bravado, the list places Beth in a long line of distinguished writers of prose who qualify as literary "greats," even though they wrote in other genres besides (or in addition to) the traditional literary forms, poetry, drama, and fiction.

Drawing upon her reading of biography and her resistance to the popular novel, Beth begins to plan her first book-length project. Her objectives are at times so radical that Grand apparently felt impelled to temper her judgments with a framing, qualifying commentary from the trustworthy Sir George. Like George Eliot's Maggie Tulliver, Beth begins by rejecting the "faultlessly beautiful heroine . . . as repulsive as a barber's block" with her "golden hair yards long, a faultless complexion, and eyes of extraordinary dimensions" who appears "so often in the weary ways of fiction." Beth also denounces writers who "make a pivot of the everlasting love-story," for these novels reveal "a want of balance in the author, such an absence of any true sense of proportion, as if there was nothing else of interest in life but our sexual relations." Instead of the idealized heroine or the predictable love story, Beth wishes to write about "the normal—the everyday. Great events are not the most significant, nor are great people the most typical" (373). But the most striking point of Beth's artistic plan is that she wishes to write this "simple story" for an audience of women (reminding us of the importance of Beth's childhood community of women):

> And I'm going to write for women, not for men. I don't care about amusing men. Let them see to their own amusements, they think of nothing else. Men entertain each other with intellectual ingenuities and Art and Style, while women are busy with the great problems of life, and are striving might and main to make it beautiful.

This last assertion is too much even for the liberal Sir George, who gently but condescendingly remonstrates, "It is only when we are extremely young that we indulge in such sweeping generalisations" (376). Formulating her aesthetic and finding her voice at last, Beth begins "to write with decision," replacing "foreign phrases" and "eccentric" effects with "her own language, strong and pure" (423). Like Angelica in *The Heavenly Twins,* Beth takes up the "vernacular" as her aesthetic tool.

Having begun to shape her own aesthetic, Beth even more firmly rejects that of the French novelists. Once the voice of male and class authority (Sir George's) has positioned the novel morally in reference to the French novelists, Grand raises the issue of form in the French novel. This again is an important strategy, for the conscious superficiality and emphatic focus on style that were associated with the British Decadents' work overrode concerns of content, particularly didactic content. Given the political agenda of the feminist New Woman writers, content was an all-important consideration. Thus, Beth complains, "The works of our smartest modern writers, particularly the French, satiate me with their cleverness; but they are vain, hollow, cynical, dyspeptic; they appeal to the head, but the heart goes empty away" (374). At this point the discussion slips from the French writers to the Stylists, presumably the Aesthetes, who were probably the targets of Grand's literary darts all along, and the novel addresses the relation between style and form directly.

Couching the conflict between the Decadents and the New Woman writers as a matter of style and content, Grand identifies the crisis of aesthetics and ethics that must confront any writer with a political purpose. Linda Dowling argues that contrary to the general assumption that the Decadents were a group of writers identifiable by their unconventional clothing, exotic mannerisms and habits, and uninhibited sexual lives, Decadence, in fact, was almost purely a matter of style. She traces the movement to Continental studies in philology, to

> a story, not of cultural decline, but of linguistic demoralization, of the silent subversion of a high Victorian ideal of civilization by the new comparative philology imported from the Germany of Bopp and Grimm. The same displacement of cultural ideals and cultural anxiety onto language explains why we also glimpse in the background of Victorian Decadence no lurid tales of sin and sensation and forbidden experience but a range of stylistic effects, of quiet disruptions and insistent subversions in the prose of Walter Pater.[75]

For a feminist novelist the suspicion that language has no "meaning," that, in fact, the surfaces of language and the style of utterance are more "real" than the "content," or ideas, one presumes to articulate or represent in language, must have posed then, as it does now, a profound dilemma. Beth's quest for a form appropriate to women's experience thus becomes part of a larger dilemma for the writer, and a dilemma most forcibly rendered by the Stylists who adamantly rejected the very notion of content, even when they could no more escape signification than the political artist could escape the effects of style. Given this underlying anxiety about the relation of expression to the matter to be expressed, Sir George's complaint is amusing (if absurd):

> Most of the stylists write as if they began by acquiring a style and then had to sit and wait for a subject. I believe style is the enemy of matter. You compress all the blood out of your subject when you make it conform to a studied style, instead of letting your style form itself out of the necessity for expression. (374–75)

Not only does the argument validate the superiority of the novel of ideas, but the language of the entire passage promotes "woman-centered" values emphasized throughout the novel. For example, Sir George prefaces these remarks by comparing the Stylists' work to a photograph as opposed to a painting, and "the lifeless accuracy of the machine" as opposed to "the nervous fascinating faultiness of the human hand" (374). Rejecting the academic, mechanistic, technical "studied style" of the Decadents, Sir George privileges instead the life-affirming, purposeful, "human" literature that Beth will eventually write. We see the dichotomy even more clearly in Sir George's concluding appeal for "a style that is the natural outcome of your subject, your mind, your character, not an artificial but a natural product . . . Be prepared to sacrifice form to accuracy, to avoid the brilliant and the marvellous for the simple and direct" (375). Once again, a male ventrilo-

quist figure, albeit a sympathetic and sympathizing one, speaks as the New
Woman, simultaneously naming and valorizing her inarticulate desires and
obscuring her still-forming objectives. Sir George's outline for an alternative
aesthetic to that of the Decadents recasts the feminist fictional project: rather
than sharing the superficial excesses, the shock value, the sensationalism, the
eroticism, and the degeneracy of the Decadents, Beth's book and reflexively
The Beth Book are presented as simple, direct, and natural fictions. In light of
twentieth-century skepticism about any text that pretends to be transparent
and unmediated, the novel's claim rings false. Moreover, as Dowling and
Kucich point out, Grand actually often adapts stylistic elements from Decadent writers.[76] Yet, in the context of late-Victorian charges that real or
fictional women asking the questions Beth does must be degenerate and
abnormal, reclaiming the New Woman's script as simple and natural is a
curiously, if ambivalently, radical displacement of conventional style, plot,
and character (at the expense of another group of writers).

Ideala, a female authority figure in all three novels, also affirms
moral/female values by juxtaposing books like Beth's to the works of the
Stylists. She couches her criticism in narrative and uses one center of middlebrow literary authority, the library, to denounce the Aesthetes. In what
must be an allusion to Wilde and perhaps to Arthur Symons, who died pre-
maturely of alcoholism, Ideala warns: "The works of art for art's sake, and
style for style's sake, end on the shelf much respected, while their authors
end in the asylum, the prison, and the premature grave" (460). Ideala draws
on personal observation (and the library) to justify her dismissal of the Decadents, explaining that, when a friend took her to the library, they looked to
see which books were heavily read. Unlike those that were well thumbed,
even written in, the Stylists' books were untouched:

> But we came at last in our wanderings to one neat shelf of beautiful
> books, and I began to look at them. There were no marks in them, no
> signs of wear and tear. The shelf was evidently not popular, yet it con-
> tained the books that had been specially recommended to me as the
> best worth reading by my stylist friends. "There is style for you!" said
> my friend. "Style lasts, you see. Style is engraved upon stone. All the
> other books about us wear out and perish but here are your stylists still,
> as fresh as the day they were bought." "Because nobody reads them!"
> I exclaimed. "Precisely," he said. "There is no comfort in life in them.
> They are the mere mechanics of literature, and nobody cares about
> them except the mechanicians." (460–61)

Ideala's "story" reinforces Sir George Galbraith's critical judgments; the
passage also elaborates further the poetics that will produce Beth's book.
In addition to simplicity, directness, and purpose, the feminist aesthetic

requires immediacy, usefulness, and comfort. Ideala implicitly confirms the necessity for art, and presumably language, to fulfill a practical, timely function, even to inspire action (here reading and responding in writing), all objectives and effects of art that would be dismissed as bourgeois by the Decadents.

Obviously, these terms, particularly *natural,* are problematic. Can novels as complex and dense as *The Heavenly Twins* or *The Beth Book* be called simple or direct? And, given twentieth-century understandings of the interactive operations of ideology and discursive formations—including the novel—what could *natural* mean? In Grand's case it seems that, when she urges a return to character as the primary focus of fiction, she is advocating fidelity to women's experience and to the values the Victorians (often derisively) associated with femininity. Here the language of gender-marking traits merges with the terminology used to describe "moral" fiction, and both are counterpoised against the alleged values of the Decadent writers— the inaccessibility, elitism, amorality, apoliticism, and, as is now painfully obvious, not just homosexuality but even what we might call homosensuality.

The novel breathes life into these abstract discussions of aesthetics by personifying the conflict in the relationship between Beth and another character, a journalist, would-be novelist, and assistant editor, whose predatory nature is suggested by his name, Alfred Cayley Pounce. Beth's progress to literary success is juxtaposed with Alfred's failure. As her childhood suitor in Rainharbour, Alfred showed promise as a sculptor and fought against his parents' demands that he become a man of business. By the time Beth encounters Alfred again, at one of Angelica's "at-homes," she is completing her book, and he, as Angelica wryly explains, is "by way of being a literary man" (451). Neither recognizes the other; however, his appearance as an "old-looking young man of Shakespearian aspect" draws Beth's attention (446). When Beth asks Angelica and her husband about him, Mr. Kilroy describes her childhood sweetheart:

> He's precious, of course, and by way of being literary—that is to say, he is literary to the extent of having written some little things of no consequence, upon which he assumes the right to give his opinion, with appalling assurance, of the works of other people, which are of consequence. There is a perfect epidemic of that kind of assurance among the clever young men of the day, and it's wrecking half of them. (452)

One can hardly help glossing this sketch with Arthur Symons's condescending description of comparable French "literary men" as "noisy, brain-sick young people who haunt the brasseries of the Boulevard Saint-Michel, and exhaust their ingenuities in theorizing over the works they cannot write."[77]

Alfred seems almost a parody of the classic male artist that Maurice Beebe describes in his study of artist figure.[78] Drawn along Byronic lines, the male artist character tends to be sensitive, suffering, misunderstood, otherworldly, and brilliant. Alienated from society, in particular from the bourgeois world of commerce and domesticity, such a hero can only fulfill his artistic promise

> after he has sloughed off the domestic, social, and religious demands imposed upon him by his environment. Narrative development in the typical artist-novel requires that the hero test and reject the claims of love and life, of God, home and country, until nothing is left but his true self and his consecration as an artist.[79]

The artist-hero's primary conflict is his struggle between the inner conflict occasioned by his sensual, worldly desires and, at least in his view, his more spiritual impulse to create. Like those artists who constitute what Beebe calls the "Sacred Fount" tradition, Alfred justifies any excessive desire or demand as necessary inspiration or as materials for his art.[80]

In Beth's conversations with Alfred the battle lines between a liberal, middle-class feminist artist and the male Decadent artist are sharply drawn. When Beth praises character over social position, Alfred calls her sentiments "bourgeois" (449). When she expresses her interest in "social subjects," he accuses her of having exhibiting "a feminine point of view" (451). Indifferent to Beth's preference for work as opposed to romance, Alfred plays what Ellen Moers calls the "Decadent dandy."[81] He foists bouquets bought for another woman onto Beth, conspicuously haunts the street where she lives, and writes her absurd literary letters, which she pitches along with his flowers. When Beth steers his attempts at lovemaking to literary topics, their differences erupt, and they quarrel. Beth asks the "purpose" of Alfred's novel-in-progress, and he recoils in horror: "'purpose!' he ejaculated. 'Had you said pur-port instead of pur-pose, it would have been a sensible question. It is hardly likely I shall write a novel with a purpose. I leave that to the ladies'" (455).

The seriocomic conclusion to the *personal* relationship between Alfred and Beth combines love, literature, and lessons, as Alfred urges Beth to become his mistress and his muse, yielding both her social and literary reputation up to him in the sacrifice of the female artist's self. Alfred's sophistries interest Beth, but his sensibilities are gravely wounded when she devours sandwiches as he tries to make illicit love. When she tells him to

mind his duties to his wife rather than "expressing exceptional selfishness
and excusing exceptional self-indulgence," which he espouses in the name
of his "exceptional temperament," Alfred accuses her of being "a mere slave
to social convention" and conflates Schopenhauer's theories of genius with
Darwinian rhetoric in defense of his desires (467). Undaunted by her coldness, Alfred insists:

> Allowance *must* be made for exceptional natures. Look at me! I tell you
> if I had met the right woman, I should have been at the top of the tree
> by this time. I have the greatest respect for woman. I believe that her
> part in life is to fertilise the mind of man; and if the able man does not
> find the right woman for this purpose, he must remain sterile, and the
> world will be the loser. (469)

Unmoved by his procreative metaphors (which, like many Victorian discussions of male genius, slyly reverse biological roles to suit Alfred's arguments), Beth queries, "And what is the man going to do for me?" When he
protests that he will surround her with comfort, luxury, and jewels, she
turns the tables on him by accusing him of being "old-fashioned" and treating her "like a ballet girl" (469).

Alfred's second line of argument provides insight into the popular
understanding of the phrase *exceptional woman*. Masking his selfish desires in
analogies with famous public figures, he reminds Beth of the affair of
Georges Sand and Alfred de Musset. When Beth tries to change the subject
with an unfortunate reference to "George Eliot's serener spirit" (471),
Alfred grasps at this second example by arguing that as exceptional artists, he
and Beth, like George Eliot and George Henry Lewes, transcend ordinary
moral categories. Alfred's tactics reveal his egotism, but this particular comparison may also have made him look ridiculous to readers during the 1890s,
as suggested by an article William Stead wrote for the *Review of Reviews* in
1894. Stead recalls the startling revelations of a" modern woman" who is
trying to make her own living:

> Why not do as George Eliot did? If I have had that said to me once, I
> have had it said to me twenty times by men in London . . . And always
> it was George Eliot . . . Why don't you do as George Eliot did? See
> how happy she was living with Lewes—he was a married man. Why
> not let me be your Mr. Lewes? You would be far happier than strug-
> gling for bare life."[82]

Despite Alfred's pleas and his threats that he will use his position as a
reviewer to destroy Beth's literary reputation, Beth disgustedly disposes of
him in a final severing of her own work from that of the Decadent coterie.

The conclusion to Beth's *literary* relationship with Alfred provides a dose of feminist humor as well as female victory. Grand certainly pays off her own angry debts to unsympathetic critics in her portrayal of Alfred's career as a reviewer. Anticipating the publication of Beth's book, he prepares "an elaborate article upon the kind of thing he expected it to be," condemning her unread work "from the point of view of art, and for the silly ignorance of life displayed in it"; moreover, he criticizes the writer "for taking herself too seriously" (517) and concludes with "a bitter diatribe against the works of women generally, as being pretentious, amateur, without originality, and wanting in humour." Grand drives her attack on reviewers home by noting that Alfred's review is to appear in the *Patriarch*, a journal modeled on the *Athenaeum;* then Grand caps this cynical portrait of the Victorian reviewer by beating the pompous critic at his own game:

> Unfortunately for him, however, the book appeared anonymously, and immediately attracted attention enough to make him wish to discover it; and before he found out that Beth was the author, he had committed himself to a highly eulogistic article upon it in *The Patriarch,* which he took the precaution to sign, that the coming celebrity might know to whom gratitude was due, and in which he declared that there had arisen a new light of extraordinary promise on the literary horizon. (518)

Secure in her modest fortune, her literary fame, and her community of friends and comrades, Beth seems to have reached the pinnacle of feminist success. Why then does Grand write a second and yet a third conclusion "beyond the ending" of the marriage plot?[83] Beth's rejection of marriage secures her independence from social strictures. Her triumph over Alfred and the literary establishment he embodies asserts the right and ability of the woman artist to take her place *within* the traditionally "male" world of letters. An artist motivated by a feminist ethic must inevitably do more, however, than simply make room for women in society; she must also use her artistry to transform that world. As a speaker, Beth fulfills this third objective.

Grand's interest in women who lectured publicly may again be attributed to autobiography. As I mentioned earlier, from childhood Grand had fervently admired Josephine Butler's courage as a public speaker. Grand herself earned money by lecturing in both England and America, but women's rights supporters in the States found her lectures disappointing; in the vein of many popular speakers Grand lectured to entertain rather than to educate. During her four-month tour of the United States a *Harper's Weekly* reviewer wrote that her "lectures are as impregnated with the spirit of fun and sly humor, not to speak of sarcasm, as was her latest book, *Babs the Impossible.*"[84] Noting the 1884 essay "Platform Women" in *Nineteenth Century*, Sally Ledger points out that, even when they were vilified, women speakers had become part of the urban landscape by the 1880s.[85] Even in the 1890s a woman speaking in public, especially on political topics, was a noteworthy spectacle. As a character whose activities asserted women's rights to participate in public discourse as well as their right to a place in the public sphere, Beth as a fictional female orator represented the New Woman in one of her most threatening guises. Other novels of the period also thematize the social confusion and change brought about when a woman quite literally finds a public voice. Henry James portrays women orators condescendingly in *The Bostonians*. The talents of the young speaker Verena Tarrant receive less attention than the struggles between Basil Ransom and the latently lesbian Olive Chancellor and her fellow women's rights supporters over Verena's fate. Florence Dixie's cross-dressed heroine in *Gloriana; or the Revolution of 1900* (1890) foments national rebellion when she lectures to laborers and middle-class women, while Mrs. Humphry Ward's protagonist fails miserably when she attempts to speak before a working women's audience in *Marcella* (1895). Elizabeth Robins's *The Convert* (1907) offers a behind-the-scenes looks at an upper-class woman's initiation into street corner suffrage oratory.[86] Robins's novel, unlike Grand's, pays careful attention to both the style and the message of each woman speaker, noting differences attributed to class, party politics, the imposing presence of largely male and largely hostile audiences, as well as to personality.

Beth's progress, as an artist, from writing to speaking is somewhat surprising given the novel's (debatable) assumption that Decadent art held pride of place as high culture in the 1890s. Despite the popularity of other forms of fiction, particularly of the other realistic and naturalistic novels that increasingly threatened to displace "high art" with something much closer to the kind of middlebrow aesthetic Grand advocated, critics (if not audiences) were inclined to favor the style, structure, and nuance of carefully crafted and often ornamental prose. This bias would inevitably privilege the written word over the spoken word. In the case of women the disjuncture between writing and speaking would have been even more dramatic. In *The Beth Book* Grand conveys the public's hostility to feminist speakers in particular. After Beth leaves her husband she moves to an attic flat, hoping to support herself by writing. Instead, she spends most of her time and all of her money caring for Arthur Brock, a young American artist who has the flat across the hall from her. Arthur assumes that she is using his money for food and medicine, but the supplies cost far more than he suspects, and Beth (like Louisa May Alcott's Jo in *Little Women*) is finally forced to sell her clothes and then her hair. When Arthur sees Beth's short bob, even he, a man who knows and cares for Beth, forgets his gratitude and gives way to suspicion, asking—in the language of one of Grand's great antagonists, Eliza Linton—"Are you going to join that unsexed crew that shriek on platforms?"[87] Annoyed, Beth replies: "I don't know any unsexed crew that shriek on platforms . . . and I am surprised to hear you taking the tone of cheap journalism. There has been nothing in the woman movement to unsex women except the brutalities of men who oppose them" (509). Despite the increasing numbers of women speaking out against a range of social ills, a woman speaking to a mixed crowd in a public forum and about a political topic continued to provoke the public's anger and hostility.

Having longed for the solitude of a quiet life of writing in the Kilroys' cottage, Beth is shocked to learn, quite by accident, of her own talent as a speaker. Filling in as a "stopgap" at one of Angelica's meetings, she speaks as few have

> spoken to a hostile audience and fascinated them by the power of her personality, the mesmeric power which is part of the endowment of an orator, and had so moved them that they rose at last and cheered her for her eloquence, whether they held her opinions or not.

Despite her "terror of an extraordinary achievement, a great success," Beth accepts what she sees as the responsibilities of her vocation unquestioningly (525). Moreover, Beth views her success as a duty to women and the women's movement, rather than as a personal or professional triumph.[88]

Beth's career as a speaker is foreshadowed throughout *The Beth Book*. From the title page Grand directs her audience to Beth's particular genius—her powers of speech. Wiser for her own arguments with editors and her experience of reviewers, Grand deliberately addresses the causes and consequences of women's silence by quoting a passage from *Othello:*

> IAGO: Come, hold your peace.
> EMILIA: 'Twill out, 'twill out:—I hold my peace,
>   Sir? no;
>   I'll be in speaking, liberal as the air:
>   Let heaven, and men, and devils, let
>   them all
>   All, all, cry shame against me, yet I'll
>   speak.

The significance of Iago's relation to Emilia echoes throughout relationships established in the novel. Not only does he force Emilia into complicity with himself, but he divides her from a woman she would serve and protect. Iago's various, fractious jealousies outrage every bond of affection and community before his wicked machinations culminate in Desdemona's murder and Othello's self-hatred. Emilia's story dramatizes not only the absolute necessity for women to "speak" but also the danger that threatens when they attempt to do so.

Given the radical implications of a woman publicly challenging the patriarchal hold on public discourse, Beth's evolution from artist to social critic to public lecturer has an important logic. In a far more immediate manner than the written text oratory depends upon collective, communal experience, an immediate responsibility to and engagement with an audience, and a desire to persuade, inspire, and motivate that audience to act. In the role of feminist orator Beth demonstrates the commitment the novel attributes to a feminist artist; unselfishly, she gives her talents to her community rather than to posterity. Her choice anticipates the decisions of suffrage artists ten years later. As both Lisa Ticknor and Janet Lyon have pointed out, members of the Women Artists' Suffrage League and the Actresses' Suffrage League devoted their talents to their community. The elaborate banners for suffrage processions were made by groups of women for public circulation and political ends; artists contributed posters, knowing that they would be mass-produced, sold to raise funds, and ignored as "art."[89] Similarly, Beth's oratory art circulates in the successes of the community she inspires rather than being static and fixed in a product she creates and possesses. Like the later suffrage art, its value is measured in its effect rather than in its uniqueness, inaccessibility, or fetishized quality as an object.

By presenting the development of Beth's character through childhood, marriage, and a writing career as necessary phases for the feminist artist, Grand works to expand and change definitions of art so that aesthetics can accommodate rather than avoid politics and political responsibility. Despite her own high-powered career as a journalist and novelist, Eliza Lynn Linton and other advocates of womanliness, like Phyllis Schaffley today, insisted that work, which gave women opportunities for economic independence and an impact on public life, would be the unsexing of women.[90] Grand recasts "work," of the most public kind, as an antidote to what she reconceptualizes as the self-interest and isolationism of femininity. Though Beth yearns to feel "no care beyond the cultivation of the arts, no service but devotion to them, no pleasure like the enjoyment of them—a selfish life made up of impersonal delights," as a feminist artist, she willingly sacrifices the Decadent's dream for the New Woman's life of action: "Beth could not have lived for herself had she tried. So that now, when the call had come, and the way in which she could best live for others was made plain to her, she had no thought but to pursue it" (524). Norma Clarke characterizes this scene and the events leading up to it as "a manual for women who have joined or may join the women's movement. It is an encouragement to them to do so, painting as it does an idealized and noble picture of the cause and the pleasures of dedication."[91] The narrator certainly encourages readers to identify with Beth's success by drawing the public into the novel at this point, for Beth receives innumerable telegrams and letters. Some voice anger, but most praise Beth's contribution warmly. But the most telling letter announces, "A great teacher has arisen among us, a woman of genius—." The novel itself could be characterized as Grand describes her female artist-activist in one of these letters as "one of the first swallows of a woman's summer" (527).

The closing scene of the novel troubles nearly all of Grand's critics. As the emblematic dawn and the empathetic messages arrive, Beth vacillates between the fullness of success and an indefinable sense of absence in a scene charged with romantic possibility. Across the fields Beth spies a "horseman" who reminds her of a knight and who evokes Tennyson's lines "A bowshot from her bower-eaves, / He rode between the barley sheaves" (527). The man is Arthur Brock, the American artist whom Beth had nursed through rheumatic fever during the previous winter, when she lived alone in a London attic. In some ways the ideal man (sensitive, gentle, communicative), he also falls short of perfection. For example, during the long winter, when Beth had offered to tell him about her divorce proceedings (which fail), he, like Lord Dawne in *Ideala,* "magnanimously" refused to hear the details because he assumed that of course she must be at fault, a presumption that insults Beth. Beth's early relationship with Arthur (during his illness) seems a regression to the very feminine characteristics Grand so often rails against; Beth sacrifices her money, her health, and her plans to write in order to keep Arthur alive until he can escape to the healthy life of the country with one of his artist friends. In many ways this part of the plot seems to be offered as proof that the New Woman retains the qualities of womanhood her critics feared she had lost, the abilities to nurture others and to sacrifice herself to others' needs. When Arthur leaves London, Beth never really expects to see him again. Moreover, it is Angelica rather than Arthur who comes to Beth's rescue. In a melodramatic scene Beth cheerfully waves good-bye to Arthur and swoons away from hunger. For months none of her friends have known Beth's whereabouts; however, just at this critical moment, Angelica drives by, catches sight of Beth, and whisks her away to her circle of London friends. This conclusion to Beth's London winter suggests that Arthur may appeal to Beth's affections, but he is no romantic hero.

Though it would be hard to avoid reading the conclusion as a romance, it is worth considering how that romance is qualified. First of all, Arthur's arrival is foreshadowed early in the novel in one of Beth's many semi-supernatural experiences. Throughout her childhood Beth has moments of inexplicable insight; she knows when both her father and Aunt Victoria will die, and she occasionally imagines a mysterious world peopled by her ancestors who encourage her early attempts to write and to create. While she is still living with her husband, Beth imagines a man like Arthur in a scene that has some of these supernatural qualities. Made desperate by Dan's affairs and his absurd suspicions of her, Beth has fits of jealous rage that she fears are a sign of madness. She only begins to recover after experiencing what may be a vision or simply a coincidence. As she looks out a window, she sees a horseman with "the face of a man from out of the long ago, virile, knightly, high-bred, refined; the face of one that lives for others, and lives openly." As they look at one another, he seems to recognize her, "and she felt herself as if she had seen him before but when or where, in what picture, in what dream, she could not tell" (432). Day after day the man rides by, and, though Beth makes no attempt to meet him, "the strange exalted sentiment which her knight had inspired . . . began, continued, and completed her cure." The narrator does not say that Beth falls in love with this mysterious stranger; instead, she "was full of love—a holy, impersonal love, such as we feel for some great genius, adored at a distance, for the grace of goodness he has imparted to us. And her heart being full of love, her brain teemed with ideas" (434). This unexpected romantic hero appears only for a short time and always at a distance so that he seems a kind of male muse rather than an object of romance. The emotions he inspires promote Beth's *career* by reawakening her desire to think and write. The narrator does not explicitly connect the mysterious stranger with Arthur; however, the description of the two horsemen and the lines from Tennyson Beth recalls when she sees each man urge a connection. For Grand, who never completely condemns heterosexual love or marriage (she only insists the institution of marriage must dramatically change), love promises one means to a feminist vocation rather than an end to a woman's growth or possibility for a career.

The close of the novel also resists the conventions of the romance plot because neither the character Beth nor Arthur would fit comfortably into the social order the marriage plot affirms. Arthur, like Beth, is characterized largely by his otherness: he is an American and an artist, hardly the hero of the traditional British marriage plot novel. We can only assume that Beth and Arthur are contemplating the adulterous, "free-love" relationship that Alfred proposed earlier. Though Grand's contemporary reviewers decried her treatment of venereal disease and her unsympathetic portrait of her husband, they were apparently so taken in by the conventions of romance in which this adulterous potential is conveyed that few took issue with this third conclusion. Even feminist critics like Norma Clarke, who lament the conclusion, seem oblivious to the subversive message that Beth is economically free not only to choose her career but also to arrange her romantic relationships. Chagrined that the last word of the novel is the lover's name, Clarke amusingly consoles us, "One can't help thinking it a pity, but then it is so thinly done, such an anaemic little rag for convention (and the man himself is so anaemic), that it almost (but not quite) doesn't matter."[92] Clarke also makes an important point about the sustained tension between the logics of the two plot movements: our anticipation of Beth's future career and the potential closure of this romance. Anticipating protests that "the feminist message is ultimately subverted by the conventions of popular fiction which demanded a romantic lover as the heroine's ultimate and truly significant destiny," Clarke replies: "But I don't think this is so . . . Rather than the feminism being subverted by the forms of the popular novel, I see the conventional popular novel subverted by an inspirational feminism, and a feminism which reached an enormously wide readership."[93] I would add to Clarke's assessment by arguing that even the romantic conclusion may be read as resistance to the closure of the novel, for, while Arthur Brock fulfills the promise of Beth's romantic desire, he invalidates the implicit marital contract of the romantic plot, a point not lost on one reviewer: "He is last seen stalking across the field toward her with redemption in his eye and, let us hope, divorce papers in his pocket; for to all seeming, she is still the wife of her very unpleasant first husband."[94] The promise of Beth's public, political career and private, personal affairs project our imaginations beyond the boundaries of the conventional novel. Even today it is hard to imagine where such a plot might lead.

Chapter 6

The Eugenic Plot:
From New Woman to Brave New World

After the publication of *The Beth Book* Sarah Grand's life once again changed course. The crowds and pace of London had never been to her liking, so in 1898 she moved to Tunbridge Wells, where she eventually shared a house with her stepson, Haldane, and his daughter, Felicitas, nicknamed Beth. In 1898 the death of her estranged husband from what she called "brain disease" freed her from her promise to avoid the public, political arena of the women's movement, and over the next two decades she organized and led several women's rights groups.[1] She was an active member of the Women Writers' Suffrage League (an auxiliary of the National Union of Women's Suffrage Societies), the Pioneer Club, and the Author's Club. In 1908 she spoke before the International Women's Suffrage Alliance in London. She organized the Tunbridge Wells branch of the Women's Citizens' Association and was elected vice president of the local Women's Suffrage Society, president of the local branch of the National Council of Women, and president and chief spokeswoman for the Tunbridge Wells branch of the National Union of Women's Suffrage Societies. During her presidency she enlisted an unprecedented number of members and supporters (especially for Tunbridge Wells), and in 1913 she and her Tunbridge Wells followers marched to London along with thousands of others in the famous Pilgrimage for women's suffrage.[2] Despite the citizens' of Tunbridge Wells initial suspicion of a radical suffragist among their midst, Grand recalled in letters and conversations that, when women finally won the vote, a crowd of neighbors appeared with flowers and banners to escort her to the polls.[3]

During these years of active political work Grand continued to publish short stories and essays in both British and American journals. She also wrote letters to the press, berating her critics, condemning the war against the Boers and advocating political and economic negotiation, instead, or defending the necessity for female suffrage.[4] These were the years, too, in which she supported herself as a female orator. Between 1900 and 1912 she traveled throughout England and the United States, delivering witty, humorous (according to her detractors, frivolous) analyses of the limits of "mere man." She claimed to have lectured seventy times in 1906 alone.[5] Letters, including several to her lecture agent, Mr. Christy, document her subjects ("The Art of Happiness," "Things We Forget to Remember," "Mere Man," "Her Infinite Variety"), her constant struggle to find new material,[6] a special invitation to The Hague in Amsterdam,[7] speaking to a crowd of two thousand at New Cross, her anxiety about fees and payment, and the recurrent attacks of "neurasthenia," which one of her doctors called the American writer's disease.[8] Writing to William Heinemann, her publisher, from Edinburgh, she says, "I have been having a most interesting progress through the country—large audiences everywhere, crowds in some places; and the most royal hospitality generally mingled with moments of positive neglect," and worrying, "I wonder if all this lecturing is making any difference in the demand for my books."[9] Her more serious speeches received less public attention. In a letter to a friend written in 1909 she asserts, "I am ready to appear on any platform and write for any paper that is for Women's Suffrage," and her public addresses at home in Tunbridge Wells not only inspired increased membership but also soothed the anxieties and anger of those fellow citizens who associated suffrage with the increasingly aggressive suffragettes.[10] She also published her last two novels, *Adnam's Orchard* (1912) and *The Winged Victory* (1916).

There are at least two very different ways to look at Sarah Grand's final novels. On one hand, her work after 1900 reflects feminism's greatest achievement and its Achilles' heel, the tendency to eschew single-minded support for one issue and, instead, to labor against innumerable forms of oppression by shouldering responsibility for a range of what sometimes seem to be contradictory causes. On the other hand, her novels demonstrate the breadth of her political commitments and her sophisticated, sweeping knowledge of a multitude of social problems and potential solutions. A reviewer for the *Literary Digest* calls *Adnam's Orchard* an "eloquent appeal for the 'back-to-the-soil' movement, and also an opportunity for the author to express her opinion on almost every modern movement, psychic, physical, or political,"[11] while the *Athenaeum* critic writes that *The Winged Victory* compares in its expansive embrace of "society" with the novels of William Makepeace Thackeray and George Meredith, prophesying that the novel's purpose will be accomplished in "widening the outlook of the average novel-reader."[12] The novel encompasses spiritualism, shifting class relationships, support for the arts and crafts and guild movements, the plight of landlords and tenants as a consequence of agricultural failures, the "Back to the Land" movement and socialist politics as expressed through that move-

Sarah Grand and "Mere Man"

One of Grand's public lectures, entitled "Mere Man," propelled
that phrase into common satiric usage. This cartoon appeared in
Harper's Weekly (2 November 1901) during Grand's American
tour. (Courtesy of Special Collections of the University of Iowa
Main Library.)

ment, the emigration of tenant farmers to the cities and even to foreign
countries, the cruel conditions of working-class women, and, for Grand
most important, the promises for social change offered by a group that
emerged in the 1890s, the eugenicists.

I conclude my study by considering where Grand's commitment to
women's rights and her battle against various forms of social oppression led
after she "became" a New Woman rather than a creator of fictional New
Women. "True" marriage had always been one object for Grand's charac-

ters, even though the novels focus on failed marriages. Marriage assumes an even more important task in these last novels; marriage between genetically superior partners promises not only individual happiness but a future "race" that will be too intelligent and sensible to permit oppression of any kind. Moreover, such marriages, based on moral, intellectual, and physical strength, rather than class, would end class conflict by abolishing class divisions.

In the wake of World War II and of German attempts to create a "super race," the eugenicists' ideas inspire only horror. Yet to many respectable Victorians and Edwardians eugenics was the darling child of Charles Darwin's theories of natural selection and evolution. The history of British eugenics and its relation to the woman's movement suggest why Grand and other feminists found eugenics so appealing and, specifically, why eugenics offers such hope yet culminates in such catastrophe in *Adnam's Orchard* and *The Winged Victory*.

The founding of the "science" of eugenics is a fascinating story in and of itself.[13] Drawing upon studies of evolution by Charles Darwin and Herbert Spencer and upon studies of heredity by Gregor Mendel and August Weisman, Sir Francis Galton began developing what he called the science of biometrics during the 1870s. In developing a working method, Galton and others established the groundwork for the field of statistics, but their real object was to determine and measure the statistical units of the laws that they believed governed heredity. Galton first used the term *eugenics* in 1883, in his book *Inquiries into Human Faculty and Its Development,* explaining:

> We greatly want a brief word to express the science of improving stock, which is by no means confined to questions of judicious mating, but which especially in the case of man, takes cognizance of the influences that tend in however remote a degree to give to the more suitable races or strains of blood a better chance of prevailing speedily over the less suitable than they otherwise would have had. The word *eugenics* would sufficiently express the idea.[14]

During the 1890s Galton had begun to work with Karl Pearson and W. F. R. Weldon in the statistics laboratory of the biometric school at University College London. Their research was reported in the journal *Biometrika,* which they founded in 1901, and in 1904 Galton himself provided funding and fellowships for a Eugenics Record Office.[15] In 1906 this office merged with Pearson's laboratory to become the Francis Galton Laboratory for the Study of National Eugenics, a statistical research organization that recorded every imaginable "empirical" detail that might demonstrate the role of heredity in intelligence, alcoholism, cancer, tuberculosis, albinism, "feeble-mindedness," criminology, and a host of other diseases or conditions apparent in what they called "biological populations."[16] William Greenslade points out that the work of Karl Pearson, in particular, was motivated by the fear that "the orders and types of undesirables were 'outbreeding' the middle and upper classes"; Greenslade also notes that Sidney Webb used Pearson's statistics to argue that excessive numbers of Irish and Jewish births threatened England with future degeneration.[17] The first chair of eugenics was established in 1911 (and occupied by Pearson from 1911 until 1933.)

For researchers in the newly emerging fields of sociology and psychology the statistical specificity and supposed objectivity of eugenics offered a longed-for authority and persuasiveness, and the flood of books and articles that appeared between 1890 and 1930 attests to the enthusiastic reception of eugenics by the scientific community and the general public as well.[18] To the dismay of many professional eugenicists, including Karl Pearson, in 1907 Francis Galton founded a second organization, the Eugenics Education Society, to consider how eugenics research might be implemented as social and political policy.[19] Galton's enthusiasm for eugenic social theory fired the imagination of the largely middle-class membership, many of whom were doctors and scientists but also women such as Lady Ottoline Morrell, Lady Isabel Somerset (a social purity feminist), and Lady Emily Lutyens.[20] While Pearson and other researchers hoped that their work would eventually provide the basis for state and medical intervention, most felt that the Education Society was premature and that its amateur status and its social and moral propositions might provoke ridicule (as often happened).

Despite the resistance of religious groups (particularly Catholics), of philanthropists, and of some feminists (like Dora Marsden, who wrote for the *Freewoman,* and writers for the *Vote*)[21] as well as of thinkers who looked to the environment to explain social problems, by 1909 the society had instituted its own journal, the *Eugenics Review.* During its peak year of activity, 1913, the society boasted a membership of more than a thousand. Eventually, the society claimed seventeen hundred members. The group principally consisted of upper-middle-class professionals and intellectuals—biologists, geneticists, sociologists, psychologists, doctors, teachers, writers, lawyers, even ministers—a membership Lyndsay Farrall describes as "middle class radicals."[22] To add to the group's respectability, in 1911 Major Leonard Darwin (Darwin's youngest son) became president, despite his father's doubt that his own research could be easily extended to human populations.

The group endorsed two different, sometimes contradictory strategies for improving future generations. "Negative eugenic methods" included either enforced or voluntary sterilization of "poor stock" and incarceration of "undesirables," such as the mentally deficient, criminals, and the victims of diseases like tuberculosis and cancer. "Positive eugenic methods" encouraged "good stock" to "breed." Some of the tamer suggestions included ways to incorporate eugenic education into educational curricula. The positive eugenicists also lobbied for tax breaks to encourage middle-class families to have more children. In addition, Galton proposed a program in which doctors would award eugenic certificates to those who voluntarily demonstrated their mental and physical health. One doctor, ironically named J. W. Slaughter, explained in the *Eugenics Review:*

> As courtship is a process of suggesting or displaying qualities and possessions, it may be that part of its regular routine will be the exhibition of the life insurance policy [the certificate]; fond mother should be at least as interested in this as in the young man's actual or perspective balance at the bank.[23]

A quick list of the topics discussed most often in the *Eugenics Review* reveals the disparate subjects the society linked to heredity: poverty, feeblemindedness, mental deficiency, criminals, venereal disease, epilepsy, alcoholism, sterilization, marriage, divorce, emigration and immigration, racial purity, sex ratios, fertility, birth control, and "race-motherhood."[24] Nevertheless, eugenics gained the support of a wide range of writers and intellectuals: Sidney Webb wrote articles in support of these ideas; H. G. Wells emplotted eugenics and "dysgenics" in many of his novels and advocated the cultivation of a "samurai" elite of natural aristocrats in his study, *Anticipations,* serialized in the *Fortnightly Review* in 1901; Harold Monro and Maurice Browne established the Samurai Press and advocated eugenics in their *Proposals for a Voluntary Nobility* (1907), which then prompted A. R. Orage's coverage of Wells and the Samurai concept of eugenic aristocracy in his periodical, the *New Age,* also in 1907.[25] Havelock Ellis wrote two books in support of eugenic solutions to social problems, *The Problem of Race-Regeneration* (1911) and *The Task of Social Hygiene* (1912). Also, in 1912 the suffragist and gynecologist Dr. Mary Scharlieb, a member of the Eugenics Society, published her *Womanhood and Race Regeneration.*[26]

Why would so many people, including many feminists, be drawn into the Eugenics Education Society? Perhaps the most important reasons take us back to Beth's literary antagonist, the aesthete, in *The Beth Book*. The fears of literary "decadence" and "degeneration" that I discussed in that chapter were merely the extension of a general fear that the English "race" was on a downhill course. Supporters of eugenics drew upon a wide, incoherent assortment of evidence to feed fears of Britain's imminent collapse.

The midcentury social problem novels of Elizabeth Gaskell and Charles Dickens as well as the sensation novels of Mary Elizabeth Braddon and Wilkie Collins had played to public fears that industrialization and urban sprawl opened a Pandora's box of crime and misery. By the 1890s many people were disappointed in the attempts of philanthropists, charitable organizations, and government committees to deal with the poverty, theft, prostitution, disease, and alcoholism that had come to be near media metonyms for the urban poor. Protesting the futility of external attempts to end these problems, a surprising number of middle- and upper-class people were prepared to endorse Karl Pearson's argument that *social* change alone was an exercise in futility. In *The Grammar of Science* Pearson writes:

> The bad man can by the influence of education and surroundings be made good, but the bad stock can never be converted into good stock—then we see how grave a responsibility is cast at the present day upon every citizen, who directly or indirectly has to consider problems relating to the state endowment of education, the revision of the administration of the Poor Law, and, above all, the conduct of public and private charities.[27]

Pearson's concerns were brought home to the general public in 1900 and after as a consequence of the Boer War (1900–1902). Not only did the press denounce military incompetence, but in a newspaper article in 1900 Arnold White stated that three of five men who attempted to enlist in the military had been rejected for physical reasons. Other studies of soldiers in the Boer War and World War I were used by military and medical authorities to argue that working-class soldiers were not only degenerating physically but actually shrinking in size. The government was alarmed enough by the early studies to appoint a committee to study the situation in 1902.[28]

The public's increasing anxiety about the harmful effects of industrialization and urbanization of England also contributed to the general conviction that those who inhabited the cities were in a state of decline. The eugenicists generally put the cart before the horse, insisting that genetic weakness spread in such "breeding populations," rather than accepting the socialists' view that such environments ruined the health and sanity of even the sturdiest inhabitants.

Two wars, combined with the imperialist fervor that dominated the Edwardian period, also sparked fears of despoiling "racial purity" and surrendering England's international stature. The word *race* had only the loosest meaning for the eugenicists. The term might be used to distinguish between skin colors, ethnic groups, nationalities, national origins (such as "the Anglo-Saxon race"), or even between classes within English society.[29] The Boer War and World War I raised questions about whether the English were purer, stronger, and more intelligent than other races, in particular the Germans. Most Britons smugly assumed their present superiority but feared the future; however, the British were alarmed by the influx of immigrants from colonized countries and by the emigration of dissatisfied laborers, especially farmers, to those colonies.

In addition, the British feared their loss of economic power as a consequence of the agricultural depression that began in the 1870s. By 1900 England depended heavily on Australia, the United States, and other European countries for cereals, dairy products, and meat. The Eugenics Society argued that this falling-off—of the power of the military, the potential workforce, and the agricultural economy—threatened to undermine the supposed superiority of the British race.

The eugenicists' most callous comments about the working-classes appear in discussions of another topic that contributed to enthusiasm for the cause, the declining birthrate. A number of studies demonstrated that although upper- and middle-class people were having fewer and fewer children, working-class families continued to have large families. While only a few eugenicists went so far as to advocate birth control publicly (as the Malthusian League did), all agreed that the upper classes must be convinced to reproduce more enthusiastically.

Sarah Grand was only one of many writers whose work was influenced by the promises of eugenics. George Bernard Shaw may have outraged the Eugenics Society in a 1910 lecture when he disingenuously advocated single motherhood, lethal chambers, and stud farms, but he gave the movement quite a boost in *Man and Superman*.[30] The master/slave relationship of the Eloi and the Morlocks in H. G. Wells's futuristic dystopia, *The Time Machine,* also demonstrates the influence of eugenic ideas on literature. In particular, eugenic ideas captivated the imagination of feminist writers and thinkers, including radical socialist-feminists Victoria Woodhull, Mona Caird, Jane Hume Clapperton, and Olive Schreiner, as we see when Schreiner invokes the rhetoric of race-motherhood in support of her own demand for women's work in *Woman and Labour:* "We demand this, not for our own sakes alone, but for the succour of the race."[31] Dale Bauer has documented similar sympathies in turn-of-the-century American women writers' work, in particular that of Edith Wharton and Charlotte Perkins Gilman. Gilman's *Herland* even explores the possible elimination of men from the reproductive process; her female characters experiment with parthenogenesis.[32]

These feminist writers' interest in eugenics reflected the appeal of the movement to a number of women both inside and outside the feminist movement. It is, of course, easy to react with condescension, shock, or outrage to those women's rights supporters who embraced eugenics. But the poor judgments of early feminists can teach us as much as their successes. The role of eugenics, in particular, demands our attention, considering that, while the terminology has changed and the issues have increased in complexity, when we take positions on reproductive issues such as birth control, artificial insemination (including the use of "genius" sperm banks), surrogate motherhood, genetic testing, birth selection, cloning, or abortion, we must navigate the same troubled waters. Therefore, rather than condemning them, we need to ask why writers like Grand, Schreiner, and Gilman, among others, took the eugenicists' proposals to their fictional drawing boards to see what a eugenic society would look like.

Here, again, the reasons that eugenics found female supporters are both complex and fascinating. First of all, from the beginning women played important roles both in the Eugenics Lab and the Eugenics Society. As Rosaleen Love points out in her essay "'Alice in Eugenics-Land': Feminism and Eugenics in the Scientific Careers of Alice Lee and Ethel Elderton," Ethel Elderton was the first assistant to the lab, where she remained for fourteen years, usually on an unpaid, volunteer basis. During the lab's most prosperous years five of the fourteen staff members were women.[33]

The Eugenics Education Society was founded by a group who left the Moral Education League after hearing Galton lecture in 1907. This group, half of whom were women, answered Galton's call for a eugenic science that would be a "new national religion."[34] The topics of lectures at the Eugenics Society—"Eugenics and Womanhood," "The New Woman and Race Progress," "Women and Eugenics"—positioned women centrally in the movement.[35] Predictably, though approximately half of the members were women throughout the organization's history, most of these women were "associate" rather than "full" members; this status required them to pay dues yet denied them voting rights. On the other hand, a quarter of the officers were women, and, as Richard Soloway shows, many of the female members were active in the moderate suffrage movement.[36] Lucy Bland also notes that many of these women served as "visiting lecturers" who spoke on behalf of the Eugenics Society and its policies to other organizations and to women's groups.[37]

Like many moderate suffragists, such women, including Sarah Grand, advocated marriage with intelligent, educated, "healthy" men as one acceptable, even desirable career for women. They would have approved of Grand's opinion in "The Modern Man and Maid" (1898) that "it is as if nature were fitting her to be the mother of men who will keep us in our proud place as the dominant race."[38] Moreover, several decades of working in social purity movements led many feminists, including Grand, to eugenics. Daniel Kevles points out that eugenics provided these women with scientific arguments for their earlier moral attacks upon the sexual double standard.[39] Penny Boumelha also argues that through the claims of eugenicists women found a means to rescript personal suffering as a social problem and then to call for state solutions to the problem (as Grand and other feminists had used the Contagious Diseases Acts decades earlier).[40] Also, as I have argued in earlier chapters, many women had developed increasing respect for doctors and medical researchers who promised deliverance from such terrors as venereal disease and alcoholism. Anna Davin's important essay, "Imperialism and Motherhood," focuses upon the most compelling reason for women to turn to eugenics: whatever a woman's politics, she could deploy her right to make unlimited claims as an actual or potential mother.[41]

From at least midcentury both women and men writers of advice books for women and of domestic novels had argued that women had the power and therefore the responsibility to improve the English race by choosing husbands with great care. Along with other late Victorians women's rights supporters increasingly looked from spiritual to scientific sources for solutions to worldly ills. Though a number of the Eugenic Society's leaders did believe that women should give up political demands in order to commit themselves to the birth and improvement of the British race, others, such as Karl Pearson, publicly sympathized with the women's demands for education, employment, and votes. As a respected colleague and friend of Olive Schreiner and a founding member of the Men and Women's Club, which organized in 1885, Pearson, and by extension his work, seemed worthy of these early feminists' trust. What could be more fitting for moderate, pro-family feminists than to assume leadership in a movement that offered incontestable, powerful social roles as mothers of a new race? Feminists used this power not only to validate motherhood but to justify other demands as well. As Rosaleen Love explains:

> Clearly the waste of human potential entailed in denying basic freedom to women was against the best interests of the race, and must be resisted. The future of the race lay with women, too, assisting in the evolutionary process, even if the need to fit women to their present environment for the sake of the future involved the indirect choice of a career over a direct response to the eugenic creed in marriage and child-bearing.[42]

The physicist W. C. D. Whetham and his wife bargained with women, proposing that only mothers should get the vote, while the early Eugenic Society leader Dr. Caleb William Saleeby, who was, like Grand, a participant in the Pioneer Club, demanded that all women be given the vote immediately because the suffrage campaigns distracted women from the responsibilities of racial motherhood, arguing that "the history of nations is determined not on the battle-field . . . but in the nursery."[43] At the same time, members of the moderate suffrage movement remained prominent in the society.

Grand's occasional use of quotations from Francis Galton's work as epithets in her earlier novels demonstrates her long-standing interest in eugenic ideas, and from the early 1890s Grand toyed with the eugenicists' plot. "Eugenia," a long short story published in *Our Manifold Nature,* draws attention to the eugenics debate both in its title and its theme. The female narrator sounds like one of Beth's disciples, if not Beth herself. She describes herself as "a humble artist, studying always in the life-school of the world, blinking at nothing that goes to the making or marring of life—more especially to the marring of it, for if we would make it lovely we must know exactly the nature of the diseases that disfigure it."[44] When the short story opens the narrator and her brother have gained access to the backstage of a trendy burlesque theater. Here she encounters a former childhood friend, Lord Brinkhampton, now dissolute and nearly destitute. He confides that he needs a wife, "something nice and young and fresh, with money," who is unsophisticated enough "to mistake the first man who proposes to her for an unsullied hero of romance." The narrator murmurs politely while silently critiquing his taste in life and literature: "there are women still who will introduce 'used up' brothers and so on to their girl friends as eligible husbands; but I belong to the party of progress myself" (110). Later they meet again, at the country house of the beautiful, unconventional, and just-of-age young orphan and heiress, Eugenia. The narrator judiciously watches Eugenia and Lord Brinkhampton get to know each other. As an artist, she tests their plot against the romance plot. In this case the plot is disrupted by the juxtaposition of "an *Ouidaesque* hero and a modern maiden":

> Here were the conventional elements of most romances—youth, beauty, rank, wealth, experienced man, inexperienced girl—but not a commonplace girl either. There was no knowing exactly how she would act under the circumstances, and the uncertainty was great enough to relieve the story from insipidity. (119)

The crisis of the romance plot precipitates a movement toward what becomes the eugenic plot in the late novels. In Emma Frances Brooke's 1894 novel, *A Superfluous Woman,* the protagonist, Jessamine Halliday, chooses a debauched Lord Heriot over the eugenically preferable Highland peasant farmer with whom she falls in love. Eugenia, however, shocks Lord Brinkhampton by not only rejecting his proposal but by proposing, Angelica fashion, to a "yeoman" farmer, ostentatiously named Saxon Wake. The language she uses to explain her decision to the narrator introduces eugenic fears that escalate in the late novels:

> Now, do you really think it is romantic to marry a man who has been sedulously deteriorating mentally, morally, and physically, in consequence of his weak-minded self-indulgence, from his earliest youth? . . . Your friend is a neuropath. He would probably bring insanity into the family, and so far we have kept clear of that. (119)

Whereas Brinkhampton's family and her own have slipped into familial decline, the yeomanry have progressed to what the characters call "moral strength" as well as physical strength. (In addition to valuing the natural and agricultural world, Saxon was also "wrangler" of his class and can play piano.) The narrator, early in the story, yearns for Eugenia to defy conventionalities:

> She was, in fact, essentially a modern maiden, richly endowed with all womanly attributes, whose value is further enhanced by the strength which comes of the liberty to think, and of the education out of which is made the material for thought. With such women for the mothers of men, the English-speaking races should rule the world. (139–40)

Therefore, in marrying Saxon, Eugenia makes the healthy rather than the socially astute choice of the true man and the purest British race, the Saxon. Grand's last two novels, *Adnam's Orchard* and *The Winged Victory,* turn once again to these questions, seeking an answer to social oppression in the biological promises of eugenics. Even as Grand worked for suffrage and other women's issues in the early 1900s, in fiction she turned from political or even social explanations to the new science, which promised controlled, dispassionate, long-term evolutionary, rather than legislative, reform.

Adnam's Orchard and *The Winged Victory* were to have been part of a trilogy. Apparently, the third novel would have yoked the protagonists of the first two works in a perfect eugenic marriage, as Grand attempted again to create a feminist plot within the constraints of the marriage plot. In retrospect we can see that Grand's depiction of the medical dangers threatening married women in her earlier novels *The Heavenly Twins* (1893) and *The Beth Book* (1897), especially venereal disease, might have prepared her readers for her eventual willingness to look to eugenic solutions to protect women from the horrors the law could not or would not. Eugenics, however, is not merely a topical or thematic issue in these two novels. Instead, a kind of eugenic logic governs the choice of protagonist, the structure of each novel—including the relationship between plots and subplots as well as among groups of characters—the balance of country and city settings, the social and political world of the novels, and the system of coincidences and oppositions that link the two novels. *Adnam's Orchard* also temporarily sets aside the character of the New Woman. Instead, from the eugenicists' data emerges the New Man, the spiritual, moral, intellectual, and physical equal of the New Woman.

Ella, the *Winged Victory* of the title, is first introduced in *Adnam's Orchard,* and the second novel is dominated by this protagonist. Ella is a very different character, however, from the New Women of Grand's earlier period. Neither a hoyden nor an unfulfilled genius, Ella has been raised among the working classes, and she is shrewd, ambitious, and industrious. In fact, we see her immersed in the world of work that Grand's former New Women longed for but seldom attained. In what proves to be a significantly untethered ending these eugenic wonders never meet in marriage.

By 1900 New Women novelists were beginning to suspect that the goals of the New Woman would be easier to accomplish if she had the right kind of masculine cohort, a prospect dimly implied by the appearance of the ambiguous lover at the end of *The Beth Book.* Many, like "Eugenia Newmarch," a writer for the *Englishwoman,* insisted that, if a eugenically desirable man appeared, the emancipated woman's advanced intellect and innate preference would direct her to him.[45] Olive Schreiner spoke even more to the point a year later in *Woman and Labour* (1911). She offers a sense of the New Woman's continuing fame (or infamy) when she writes that the New Woman "on every hand . . . is examined, praised, blamed, mistaken for her counterfeit, ridiculed or deified."[46] But Schreiner demands the eugenic partner who is a mere abstract possibility for Eugenia Newmarch—the New Man:

> Side by side with the "New Woman," corresponding to her, as the two sides of a coin cast in one mold, though differing from each other in superficial detail, are yet of one metal, one size, and one value; old in the sense in which she is old, being merely the reincarnation under the pressure of new conditions of the ancient forms of his race; new in the sense in which she is new, in that he is an adaptation to material and social conditions which have no exact counterpart in the past; more diverse from his immediate progenitors than even the woman is from hers, side by side with her to-day in every society and in every class in which she is found, stands—*the New Man!*[47]

Using the discourse of the eugenicists, Schreiner seeks a solution to what she calls woman's "parasitism" through a cross-cultural reconstruction of the history of gender and labor. Yet she assigns much of the blame to the limitations of male development and insists that the race cannot advance until the species creates or acknowledges a new kind of man. In *Adnam's Orchard* Grand delivers.

The setting of Grand's New Man fiction is an agricultural depression, and the novel reflects Grand's careful study of the British agricultural slump that is usually dated back to the 1870s as well as of proposed solutions. The novel also canvasses scientific solutions to the agricultural crisis that were being discussed in journals and newspapers during the early 1900s, such as the scientific development of better seed and dairy animals, increased market gardening, collective farming and the possible division of landed families' property, and improved working and living conditions for those who farmed but did not own the land.[48] Grand invokes the "back to the soil" arguments being launched by a number of individuals and groups who feared the degenerative effects of urban life: William Morris, the Fellowship of New Life (organized by many of the later founders of Fabianism), Henry Salt and the Humanitarian League, the government's "Three Acres and a Cow" campaign in 1885, the Home Colonisation Society (which urged the urban poor to form farm communities), and A. R. Orage (the editor of *New Age*).[49] The backdrop of the novel thus mirrors the nature of the New Man, for Adnam is the successful product of political and eugenic attempts at metaphoric and literal hybridization and innovation—with human stock.

Grand's New Man, Adnam, promises to meet all the eugenic New Woman's necessary requirements. His father, Emery Pratt, comes from ancient, respected English "yeoman stock," and Emery is a responsible, successful, down-to-earth farmer. Mrs. Pratt, Emery's second wife, left Germany and her aristocratic title behind to escape religious persecution. Though she and her husband get along beautifully, they are complete opposites, for she has a far-ranging intellect and a mystical second sense. Their child Adnam inherits the best of both worlds. He combines English and German blood (Germany was England's greatest military competitor), and his mixed heritage weds the two classes—the landed aristocracy and the farmers—who were socially and economically at odds, especially during the agricultural depression. He also has the potential to rescue the faltering agricultural economy because he combines a farmer's wisdom with a scientist's methods, in this case French "intensive culture" (now called greenhouses). Moreover, as a farmer who actually *owns* property, he can mediate between landowners and laborers. Adnam also meets a stiff requirement of one faction of women's movement, the social purity advocates, for he desires the perfect scientific farm establishment rather than farm maids; in fact, he scarcely notices any woman except his own mother. Thus, his own innate chastity guarantees that he is morally upstanding *and* free of degenerate diseases.

Adnam's perfections shine all the more brightly when thrown into relief against a "weedy specimen," his half-brother, Seraph.[50] Seraph's name bears ironic echoes, for this fallen angel is Adnam's chief antagonist as a consequence of Seraph's eugenic unsoundness. He is "a mongrel" (2), whose decadence is ultimately revealed through his "secret drinking" (354), one of the vices eugenicists believed to be hereditary. In keeping with the eugenic fantasy of creation, Grand invokes the biblical version of the first eugenic couple, destined to tend and people the earth, in her choice of Adnam's name. The conflict between the Pratt brothers, however, is also reminiscent of Joseph's story, for, while Ellery tries to be fair to his eldest son, Seraph, he clearly loves Adnam more, both for his own sake and his mother's. Moreover, Seraph's jealousy drives him to destroy Adnam's Edenic dreams by resurrecting the plot of Cain and Abel. In a drunken rage Seraph strikes out at Adnam by breaking the glass of the greenhouses and turning the taps on full so that in one night all of the plants perish. Despite Seraph's shame after he realizes what he has done, or perhaps as a consequence of it, Seraph plots a strategic marriage with a neighboring squire's daughter, which gives him an excuse to evict Adnam after their parents die unexpectedly. As the eldest son, Seraph inherits the Pratt land in accord with the eugenically unsound practice of primogeniture. The novel ends as Adnam is thrust out of his Eden and forced to go to London to seek his fortunes. To the surprise of the reader (who has just perused 623 pages) the conclusion reads, "Henceforth, Adnam's Orchard was the World. END OF PROLOGUE" (623). The mythic expansion of Adnam's scope suits the epic theme suggested by the biblical allusions to Eden. As the New Man, Adnam's responsibility will be to "go forth and multiply," once he finds the appropriate eugenic New Woman as his partner.

The comparison between Ellery Pratt's two sons also introduces another topic of great concern to the Eugenic Society, particularly female members. The novel suggests that one reason women needed rich, full, unhampered physical and intellectual lives was so that they could bear and raise strong, successful, wise children. Grand apparently shared this idea with other feminists who adapted the eugenic notion of race-motherhood to suit their own ends. Throughout the novel characters are judged, in part, according to the genetic and educational endowments offered by their mothers. Adnam benefits from his mother's commanding intellect and moral superiority, while Seraph must be partially excused for his selfishness, pettiness, and alcoholism because his mother was "a showy anaemic town girl, whose highest ideal of earthly bliss was to live the life of a parasite in luxurious idleness" (354). Even after Seraph cruelly dismisses Adnam, the townspeople blame his long-dead mother for his weaknesses, saying, "'I remember Seraph's mother,'" a judgmental remark that the narrator reinforces by adding, "The company understood that decent men could say no more, but Seraph was accounted for" (612–13).

The responsibilities of racial motherhood are addressed even more specifically when the duke, the chief landowner in the area, compares Ann, the daughter born to him and his duchess, with Ella Banks, who later emerges as the protagonist of *The Winged Victory*. Though *Adnam's Orchard* is scattered with hints that Ella is in reality the duke's illegitimate child, this suspicion is only confirmed in the melodramatic conclusion of *The Winged Victory*. One of the passages in *Adnam's Orchard* that rouses suspicion reveals the duke's belief in the mother's eugenic role:

> The mystery of heredity presented itself to his mind. Involuntarily he found himself comparing Ella to Ann: Ella so capable, self-reliant, self-possessed; Ann so deplorably the reverse. Ella's strength of character was a wise provision of nature, she would want it all. Ann would always be protected . . . Poor little delicate Ann. But what a contrast. The family certainly wanted new blood in it. The Brabant stock had lost its vigor. (351–52)

Though such praise or blame of the mother may seem equally insidious today, the novel attempts to give power to women, even in these negative examples, by insisting that their health and upbringing must be taken seriously since they pose such promise or such danger to the children they bear. In some respects Grand even presumes a more significant role for women than the founder of eugenics, Galton, would admit. He conducted endless studies of *male* lineage and insisted that fathers had a far more significant role than mothers in constituting the genetic makeup of children. (Even men's genes possessed patriarchal authority, it seems.) It remained for Havelock Ellis and female supporters within the eugenics movement to advance the racial motherhood theory. They gained little by doing so, for often the claim of the mother's hereditary role led to the argument that women should therefore devote all of their time and energy to childbearing.[51]

Though Adnam's struggles to rejuvenate agricultural life structure the plot for the most part, his experiments (which end in his personal failure but which do improve the lives of many other farmers) are entwined with several subplots that also advance the eugenic theme. Grand had learned the usefulness of the multiplot novel to emphasize and reinforce a particular idea in *The Heavenly Twins*. In that novel she intertwined the plots of three very different female protagonists to persuade readers that depriving women of education and work was dangerous to any type of woman. In this novel of the New Man she calls for a eugenic solution to the degeneration of both men and women through a series of subplots organized around members of different classes who live in the same community as the Pratts. Consumed with statistics, the eugenicists looked to *groups* rather than to individuals to find hereditary strengths and weaknesses, and these subplots reveal the hereditary inefficacy of marrying for reasons of class rather than eugenic fitness. In Grand's scheme we see characteristics of the "middle-class radicalism" described by Frank Parkin, for such fitness was as likely to be based on moral or spiritual compatibility as on good health or exceptional intelligence.[52] Just as venereal disease serves both as a physical danger and a metaphoric commentary for unjust gender power relations in *The Beth Book,* in Grand's last novels disease signals the very unscientific general moral decline that led to the formation of the Eugenics Education Society in the first place.

The most daring social critiques in the novel are leveled against the aristocratic classes, whose inherited property encourages laziness, irresponsibility, selfishness, drinking, and philandering, among a host of other ills. The duke and duchess of Castlefield Saye, their children Ninian, Eustace, and Ann, the duke's alcoholic cousin, Colonel Kedlock, and his madcap daughter, Lena, are the last of a great family that has lost its power to lead decisively and to act in the best interests of the somewhat feudal community over which they reign. The duke, though kindly, shirks his duties to the community, and in regard to his political duties he "was certain to be in his place to vote against any low Radical measure which might have for its avowed object to raise the standard of comfort among the lower orders"; otherwise, "the duke had never done anything particular with his own life but live it easily" (70). The duchess, who "went through life handicapped by incurable amiability" (75), adores her family but has no depth or intelligence. Though the sons are likable and attractive, neither has any purpose or direction. Eventually, Eustace marries Lena, to try and save her from herself. As the daughter of an alcoholic, she threatens to inherit her father's uncontrollable passions and love of drink. Ninian secretly falls in love with Ella, but Ella refuses to dally with him unless he offers marriage, and he is too cowardly to marry a commoner. The only really generous action on the family's part is the duke's kindly interest in Ella, and, as we eventually learn, this interest is motivated by his secret and guilty paternity. The novel presents the family not as evil but as a potential wealth of national leadership and benevolence squandered. Even the duke believes the family's decadence requires a eugenic curative. He repeatedly calls for new blood to improve the Brabant stock, little knowing that he thus encourages the unsuspecting Ninian to commit incest with his half-sister, Ella.

Other subplots involve lesser satellites of the duke's social circle. Squire Pointz's family group demonstrates even more than the duke's that the upper classes have lost their inherited "right" of command. By delegating his authority to an unscrupulous overseer, the squire ruins his property and condemns his tenants to squalor. His son runs off with a tenant's daughter, Emily Ryecote, and his wife steals his money to support his son's vices. The squire's one courageous act is to defy the laws that govern inheritance of property by leaving his farm to the only responsible member of his family, his daughter.

The novel also includes several subplots that provide a panorama of working-class life in the country. Though the workers are shown to have degenerated as well as their employers, the blame always returns to the upper classes. These subplots build readers' sympathy for the workers, but they also reinforce the authority and social status of the upper classes, since it is clear that the lives of the poor can *only* improve if the upper classes change their ways. Thus, Emily Ryecote's love of finery and power make her a *victim* of Algernon Pointz's lust, while radicals like Ella Banks's brother Luke are driven off the poorly managed land to seek work in the cities because of their landlords' ineptitude. Luke, whose political rhetoric is dismissed as mere lazy grumbling, represents the unhealthy, miserable condition of workers who lose their "natural" place in the rural setting because the once paternal landlords have evolved into money-hungry, irresponsible landowners, turning arable land into fallow pastures or hunting grounds for the rich.

This enormous cast of characters accomplishes two ends. By considering the groups that compose society, rather than focusing on the concerns of individuals, the novel creates a eugenic landscape in which to play out a drama of class as well as gender oppression. Having assumed an active role in the woman's movement herself, Grand turns her fictional attention to the problems of class struggles that remain at the margins of her earlier fiction. The solutions suggested by the novel are at once retrograde and radical. On one hand, the novel proposes that class conflict can be reconciled through biological engineering, mating the best stock of the various classes to create a super race that transcends the power struggles separating each class from the other. The unfair oppression of women would also end because women could assert their genetic equality through their equal participation in the eugenic solution as mothers of the race. While these biological solutions to class and gender conflicts may sound at best fantastic and at worst like a totalitarian nightmare, the future society the novel implicitly promises would be classless. The wealthy and titled would be required to compete for property and position in this eugenic meritocracy. In this respect, at least, the novel argues for a radical reworking of English society. Not incidentally, of course, selective breeding would eventually eliminate those who "won't" work, the ill, and the degenerate (in all the dangerous inclusiveness of the term). In other words, eugenics serves a middle-class fantasy that all but the most servile of the working classes could be eliminated over time.

Grand's final novel, *The Winged Victory,* thoroughly undermines the eugenic project mapped out in *Adnam's Orchard.* In the first novel Ella comes to live with her "father," one of Squire Pointz's tenants, after her grandmother dies. Her grandmother has taught Ella lace making, and after years of study and experimentation Ella succeeds in restoring a number of lost patterns. When she sells several beautiful pieces of lace that have taken years to make, Ella gains the duke's interest and sympathy, and in the duchess's name he establishes Ella in London to pursue a career in lace making. Just as Adnam promises to revitalize English agriculture (acting as a fictional representative of the arguments of groups like the back-to-the-land movement or the home colonization scheme), Ella dreams of restoring lace making to its proper place as a leading British art form (embodying the vision of reformist groups who promoted the arts and crafts movement and the reconstitution of guilds). She also determines to create a national lace-making industry so that lace makers can elevate their craft to an art and can sell their creations through her, thereby removing the middlemen who exploit female labor. Secretly, Ella also hopes that the duke's generous support of her project indicates his sympathy to the attraction between her and his eldest son, Ninian, particularly since she has heard him claim that the Brabant family needs new blood from more wholesome stock. Several hints in *Adnam's Orchard,* however, suggest that to complete the novel's eugenic project Adnam and Ella, who have long been friends, will meet in London and mingle their rich heredity—of the best of both classes, of superior intelligence and skill, of determination and hard work, and of strong character and physical beauty—in marriage. Instead, *The Winged Victory* ends in melodramatic disaster that lays waste to the promises and the threat of eugenics and at the same time finally frees Grand from the restraints of the marriage plot.

If *Adnam's Orchard* builds toward a new Jerusalem, *The Winged Victory* foreshadows Sodom and Gomorrah. Even the title, an epithet given to Ella by her one of her chief admirers (an aristocrat and a poet modeled on Oscar Wilde who publishes under the name "Joyday Flowers") anticipates Ella's inevitable downfall. The analogy is drawn based on Ella's beauty and grace; however, a minor character's pedantic disquisition on the statue foreshadows Ella's fate:

It would be interesting to know who was the model. It is probably a portrait, it may be of Arsinoe herself, the daughter of Ptolemy Soter, and doubtless a splendid figure. But the dates don't agree, for it was in 280 B.C. that she escaped from her second husband, Ptolemy Ceraunus, who threatened her with death, and found asylum in Samothrace until she was able to pass into Egypt, where, in 278, she married her brother, Ptolemy II, Philadelphus. (151)

In response to his listeners' disgust the speaker explains that such marriage "was customary at that time . . . but it is a question whether brother and sister are nearer in point of consanguinity than first cousins. Half-brother and half-sister probably are not."[53] Perhaps the physical disfigurement of the sculpture for which Ella is named condemns what the scholarly speaker denies. Regardless, the escalating, millennial character of the entire novel leaves Ella profoundly scarred though not ruined.

The darkness and futility of *The Winged Victory* are unprecedented in Grand's earlier work, and, if the texture and tone of the novel are Victorian, the ambience is Modernist. Perhaps the horrors of World War I had dashed her hopes for eugenic improvements. At any rate the setting shifts from the farmlands of *Adnam's Orchard* to London, and the city seethes with evil. By the end of the novel Ella seems heroic for merely surviving, rather than conquering, London society. To be a victim of human depravity rather than a perpetrator seems the most one can ask.

In *Adnam's Orchard* one of the New Man's ultimately sterile goals is to construct the utopian, agrarian world dreamed of by William Morris or socialists and advocates of the back-to-the-land movement in which landlords and tenants could coexist (and intermarry) in harmony. The novel depicts the duke and his family fairly sympathetically, particularly in an embarrassingly nostalgic passage in which the villagers' hearts are warmed when their "Lord" returns to Castlefield Saye (50–65). The narrator's ironic commentary hardly balances against the note of longing for a return to the good old days of patriarchal feudalism. Grand seems to share the problematic impulses of reformers like William Morris whose great human sympathies led to romanticized rescriptings of medieval communities in resistance to the complexities of late-Victorian and early-twentieth-century cities. The tension between the upper and lower classes that leads the duke to contemplate eugenic solutions to the Brabant family's decline escalates, however, into all-out class war in *The Winged Victory*. The novel's scathing portrayal of the upper classes suggests that, since writing *Adnam's Orchard,* Grand had lost faith in the eugenicists' claim that the upper classes were the best stock, representing the eugenic heights to which all should aspire.

The eugenicists' position on class, like their position on most topics, was contradictory and inconsistent. All agreed that the upper and middle classes produced too few children and the lower classes produced too many. But most eugenicists also believed that classes were determined biologically. Karl Pearson illustrates their rationale:

> The differentiation of men in physique and mentality has led to the slow but still imperfect development of occupational castes within all civilised communities . . . in a perfectly efficient society, there would always be castes suited to specialised careers—the engineer, the ploughman, the mathematician, the navvy, the statesman, the actor and the craftsman.[54]

Pearson concluded that it followed logically these people would then marry members of their own "castes." Galton had argued in *Hereditary Genius* both that the upper classes recruited marriage partners from the most desirable of the classes "below" and that superior laborers made their way upward through the class structure; consequently, the "lowest" classes—unskilled laborers, the unemployed, and the poor—must be some sort of eugenic fallout. Similarly, Edgar Schuster, who worked for the Eugenics Laboratory, concluded that the "chronic slum dweller" was a biological type, and, consequently, "we must be careful not to assume that the environment is thrust haphazard upon us for it is largely moulded by our own characters."[55] The most extremely class-biased eugenicists, such as W. C. D. and Catherine D. Whetham, adamantly supported the aristocracy's rights and privileges and only begged them to breed more fervently.[56]

Few of the eugenicists were quite so sycophantic. The largely middle-class membership generally doubted the usefulness of aristocratic privileges and practices such as the law of primogeniture and the effects of entail. Believing that competition and challenge weeded the eugenically unsound from the strong, most eugenicists ended up asserting that their own middle-class way of life was best for the race. A middle-class professional writer herself, Grand would probably have been sympathetic to these middle-class protectionists; however, before following the eugenic plot to its end *The Winged Victory* does explore an alternative plot that both offers an escape from the marriage plot and maps the class hostility that plays itself out in the eugenic marriage plot.

The complexity of middle- and upper-class reformers' relations to the working classes is inscribed in this significant subplot of *The Winged Victory*. Ella attempts to establish a lace cooperative in which she will serve the interests of working-class women by invigorating a dying cottage industry and eliminating exploitive middlemen. Yet this particular example of a potentially socialist project is probably based on an organization of upper-class women that set up a similar lace-making cooperative in the 1890s.[57] Fearful of rural immigrants to the city, won by nostalgic versions of an ordered, aesthetically pleasing past, these reformers reestablished lace schools, recruited workers, instituted a dazzling media campaign of pamphlets (complete with idealized photographs of lace makers who are framed by vine roses as they sit working in the window light of quaint cottages). The lace was sold in nonprofit showrooms in London, sponsored by the association.[58] The distance between the patronesses and their charges seems almost feudal, despite good intentions. Organizers set strict standards and imposed rigorous deadlines. A few scraps of notes and letters written by the workers (where Geoff Spenceley found them in the Lace Museum at Nottinghamshire) break through the mediating historical accounts of the upper-class philanthropists. One woman writes: "Please I set a wide lace, I done one down. But I could not see to set up, it is so close. I new I should not be asked to do it. I am sorry I could not do what you wanted, but you see I am over eighty years old, I can't help it." In the same vexed and anxious tone another protests: "I received your letter safe but was just going to see my sister as laid. Just at last we berid her yesterday. I will try and do the borders but i cannot do the lace for it is a long job to take as I am not fit to sit much now and my eyes are very midling. I cannot see to do it.[59] These liminal snippets cut relentlessly into the ostensibly seamless narratives of lace making written by the producers, the marketers, the consumers, the collectors, and the historians of lace. In part this is the story that Grand tries to tell in this last novel. The lace subplot potentially acts as an interruption to romance and marriage. It also admirably fulfills the demands for an ethical aesthetic called for in *The Beth Book*. As Ella argues, lace is "a life in cipher . . . a woman's life, an autobiography, I should say."[60]

What distinguishes Ella from the philanthropists is that she works *as* a lace maker *for* lace makers. Ella's sharp analyses of the upper-class patrons who use her lace venture to gain access to the duke and other celebrity patrons remind readers that the middlemen are not the only class the lace makers have to fear. The anonymous narrator explains:

> She had been brought up under the thumb of the governing class. Her earliest outlook upon life was from the peasant's cottage in which she was born, her earliest lessons in the ways of the world and in self-defence had been taught her there by her mother's mother, a lace-maker, with whom—her mother having died at her birth—she remained until the old woman's death. There she had lived in poverty during the first most impressionable years of her life. (44)

Nursed on venom and deprivation, Ella dreams of revenge: she schemes about the ways she will use the duke and his son to promote herself and other working women. On a material level she realizes all of her early dreams of a uniquely egalitarian business venture. The narrator tells us secondhand that Ella establishes lace schools that are clean, sanitary, and well-lit. She pays workers for their lace but also gives them a percentage of the cooperative's profits. Moreover, she herself takes the same wages as her lace makers. Financed by the duke, she travels to Europe, where she lays the groundwork for an international collective of women lace makers. And she uses her upper-class connections, with a knowing eye to their competitive drive to lead the fashion pack and to brush elbows with the duke and his aristocratic connections, to generate a market for the lace.

Ultimately, Ella becomes another author of sorts as well—making politics of art composed of women's labor. She realizes that the most powerful means of avenging and promoting her lace makers is the telling of stories not just of lace but of the lives of lace makers. Relentlessly, she and her supporters detail the conditions of the labor and its consequences: "Here is a marvellous piece of 'nun's work.' Sixty years it took to complete it. Only think! Two generations and more. When one worker went blind or died another was ready to take up the needle; ready to sacrifice her eyes, and it might be her life, to the task" (97). Later, Ella daringly implicates her growing clientele of philanthropic patronesses, inditing even herself, for their relations to the women workers as she imagines the history of a piece of antique lace:

> The brutal callousness of women appears in nothing more surely than in the cruelties they countenance in order to obtain material for their adornment . . . Doubtless this beautiful thing . . . has been steeped in tears, possibly it cost the worker her sight. And, oh, the thoughts! The torturing thoughts, the agony of despair and pain of which it might tell could it but speak? . . . This lace of mine is old, old; but the conditions under which such a piece could be produced in these enlightened times in the majority of cases would be as bad as ever. (294–95)

While Grand's novels never escape middle-class biases, this novel does, at least, represent lace-making cooperatives in such a way as to challenge middle-class readers to dissociate themselves from upper-class women and their cruel obliviousness to the lives of working women. Rather than defending her own class or lapsing into comfortable delusions of class unity to be accomplished either through the lower-class people's voluntary submission to their "superiors" or through the melding of classes by intermarriage, Grand dramatizes the irresponsibility and even viciousness of the upper classes and the rage of the lower classes. The potential alternative to the marriage plot—a socialist collective of women laborer-artists—seems lost, however, when the marriage plot itself implodes. The exploitative eugenic solution of using the lower classes to prop up the faltering aristocracy culminates in disaster, heightened by melodramatic actors and action.

In part the bleakness of *The Winged Victory* results from its focus on London's elite classes. Grand provides a few glimpses into the lives of slum dwellers, and the novel includes several moving descriptions of the sufferings of lace makers; however, the purpose of the novel is clearly to expose the privileged few who dominate the social and economic hierarchy of England because they are chiefly to blame for the misery of the poor, according to the novel. When Ella opens her showrooms of lace to the public, she innocently invites tragedy. Too late she learns that adulterous couples rendezvous in her library and unscrupulous gossips willfully misconstrue (and advertise) her intimacy with the duke and her bare acquaintanceships with other men. The decadent young men of the Land and Leisure Club, "a nursery for hereditary statesman" (141), wager against her virtue, and petulant women punish Ella for her beauty. Blinded by her single-mindedness of purpose and her naïveté, Ella falls victim to society's evils at last when she is tricked into visiting a man's rooms so that he can "prove" that her virtue is a mere pose. Terrified by his advances, she draws a pistol and shoots him. His last (redeeming) act is to take the gun and arrange his room so that it will appear his death is an accident or a suicide. The duke rescues Ella; however, she has been baptized in blood into the wicked ways of society.

Thereafter, Ella too becomes a prey of gossip, and, when a spiteful acquaintance hints that the duke's loving, fatherly gifts and visits are motivated by lust, Ella seeks revenge. Out of respect to the duke Ella has insisted that she can only marry his son Ninian if they receive the duke's blessing. Spurred by her suspicions of the duke's motivations, Ella secretly marries Ninian, and the Brabant family's doom is sealed. The novel ends with Ninian's disclosure to his parents, the horrifying revelation of incest, and Ninian's "heroic" suicide. Though Ella is finally reunited with the duke, her biological father, this novel suggests that heredity bequeaths doom rather than deliverance from human frailty.

As in *Adnam's Orchard,* Grand reinforces her theme through contrasting groups of characters. The Land and Leisure set is pitted against a "new breed" of Christians, a group of characters of various religions who advocate a kind of transcendental, supernatural spirituality. The drunken, profligate young and old members of the men's club demonstrate the extent to which the upper classes have degenerated. On the other hand, the morally

upstanding religious crew is equally incapable of resolving society's problems. Instead, they retreat into prayer and mournful contemplation of the
irreligious, like Ella. When the duke suggests that Ella may have the kind of
"Vision" that was the New Woman's special gift in *The Beth Book,* Ella vigorously denies this possibility. She believes she can trust only herself, and
her solitary, independent path leads to calamity. Thus, the novel resolutely
denies the usefulness of any system perpetuated by the upper classes to
resolve the problems of this world.

Somewhat ironically, the most likable character in this novel stands
high in the upper classes. For all of his vague, inarticulate, antiquated ways
the duke takes Ella's concerns about the working classes seriously. Under
her influence he shocks his friends and colleagues by consulting Labour
leaders and sponsoring Radical bills in the House of Lords. His admirable
efforts are undermined, however, by the secret of his past. He so fears the
loss of Ella's affection that he cannot find the courage to tell her that she is
his illegitimate daughter. When Ella finally learns that her mother was the
serving girl whom he seduced, she has already married her own half-
brother. Throughout the novel upper-class men and women alike lightly
dismiss the philandering of the wealthy men. Yet for a feminist like Grand
this aristocratic and masculinist exploitation of a woman, and a young, powerless working-class woman at that, may be the ultimate, unforgivable sin.
Despite the duke's desire to change, his early mistake destroys the Brabant
family and, in a sense, assassinates his own heir, for the only solution Ninian can fathom is suicide.

This leaves readers with the question: what is this novel's relation to
Grand's other, earlier New Woman novels? In a sense Ella is a New
Woman, but she inhabits a morbid, pestilent, morally corrupt fictional
world that could not even have been imagined by Grand's earlier female
protagonists. Ella has the strength and determination of her predecessors,
but her objectives and her method, particularly her willingness to exploit
upper-class characters for her ends, suggest a kind of cynicism that was not
a part of the earlier New Woman's character. Also, while Grand's other
New Woman characters worked principally for women's rights, Ella arrives
in London with two related objectives, both of which reveal her devotion
to working-class interests. Her first goal is to marry the duke's son, Ninian,
Lord Melton. The duke may argue that marrying "good stock" from the
lower classes will strengthen the decadent upper classes, but Ella has her
own agenda. She is attracted to Ninian, but she will marry him to revenge
the sufferings of her family and other tenant farmers at the hands of the
upper-class landlords. Her suspicion of the upper classes is inflamed by her
taste of society after she arrives in London, and not even the duke's kindness

softens the hard lessons experience teaches her. Her grandmother has instructed her that the only virtue of her stunning appearance is that beauty is a commodity desired by the rich, and the many proposals of marriage Ella receives prove this to be true:

> And Marchioness of Melton she would be, else beauty had lost its power and will was no determining factor in the lives of mankind—but not for vulgar pride of position, no! Her peasant blood in revolt, brought to the boil by the suffering and injustice she had witnessed, clamoured for retribution. Ella Banks aspired to rank and wealth only in order to have it in her power *"to make them pay"*—that greedy, selfish crew who withheld from the labouring classes all that made life worth living. (120)

Grand's other New Woman characters condemn the failure of marriage as a consequence of men's abuses of the extraordinary power society permits them. Here Ella views marriage as a means to her ends, and her view of her marriage sets what Grand must have imagined to be a version of working-class radicalism against the middle-class radicalism of most of the eugenicists. This juxtaposition presents an ironic picture of eugenic marriage, for it undermines the eugenic fantasies that romantic impulses could be manipulated to attract the eugenically superior to one another.

Ella also has a sophisticated sense of how international marketing works, and through marriage she wants to develop her own base of power. With the Brabant fortune she could create a profitable, secure market for her fellow lace makers from across Europe. After she learns of the duke's alleged plans to make her his mistress, Ella's ambition triumphs over any lingering affection she feels for the duke or the Brabant family:

> Ella had never admitted the power of love to redeem. She was fighting for the wronged, for punishing oppressors, for stamping them out. These rich and powerful people—she saw them now as scum on a stagnant pool, corrupting the air with poisonous exhalations. She hated them for the evil they did, for the good they did not do, for the suffering they caused, for the pain they never relieved. She had no conception of them as themselves victims of their age and of a system, nor of Society as a corporate mass bearing on the individual. She made no allowance for adverse circumstances, for custom, for the pressure of hereditary predisposition, for the unarmed state of those who have not been educated to do as they would be done by . . . High-handed by heredity, militant and vengeful by education, the habit of her mind prevailed. She had nothing to be grateful for, on the contrary, she had

everything to resent . . . But she did not forget her workers. They should not suffer. They should benefit! (603–4)

Ella's determination, a virtue in earlier New Women, leads to her doom because she lives in a world so morally complex that single-mindedness becomes blindness: this universe more malevolently destroys the potential for individual action than the gossiping community of George Eliot's *Middlemarch* suppresses Dorothea, but the social self-destructiveness is comparable. Ella has heroic aspirations, but her lonely, suspicious, angry vendetta against the upper classes chains her to them. On the other hand, the novel ends not with Ninian's death but with the duke's reconciliation with Ella and the duchess's acceptance of their relationship. Ella thus achieves *one* of her goals, for, as Ninian's "widow," she has the right to marshal the Brabant resources on behalf of her lace makers.

Perhaps Ella herself personifies the most vehement condemnation of the eugenicists' scheme. All unknown to her, the conflicting anger of the working classes and pride of the upper classes are her "hereditary" inheritance. Adnam's mixed heredity produced a heroic New Man; in Ella eugenic hybridization breeds disaster. *The Winged Victory* mutates into a late-Victorian Gothic, complete with seducers, murderesses, and incest, to convey the horrible underside of the eugenic indifference to and exploitation of the working classes and the poor, whom middle-class society label the "unfit."

The Winged Victory seems to be, finally, a condemnation not only of eugenics but of the marriage plot upon which the eugenic project depended. Intriguingly, Ann Heilmann discusses an even more literal rejection of eugenics in another, later New Woman novel by a woman writer. In Mona Caird's *Stones of Sacrifice* (1915) the protagonists join a socialist group that takes up the eugenic platform, leading the protagonists to start their own "Alternatives" group.[61] In a sense eugenics narrated the ultimate romance, the reconciliation of gender conflict, class conflict, political struggles, and social upheaval in the matchmaking of the perfect couple and the directing of all of women's energies into the perfection of the race. Grand never wrote the final novel of the trilogy, and, whatever the reason, its absence acts as a final refutation of the social roles envisioned for women in her lifetime. The family romance turns out to be a eugenic nightmare that the New Woman just barely survives.

Conclusion

That Sarah Grand is so little known, despite her status as a pioneer of New Woman fiction and her great popularity in her own day, invites the simple but crucial question, why? In part the fate of her work and that of Olive Schreiner, Mona Caird, Mary Cholmondeley, Emma Frances Brooke, George Egerton, and so many others has depended upon the ways in which "we"—book reviewers, literary critics, social historians, and classroom teachers—name, characterize, classify, represent, and juxtapose the works of these novelists. Even in the liberating milieu of cultural studies and even after investing years of work in reading and contextualizing the work of "marginal" or "liminal" or "excluded" or "lost" literature, many of "us" who study New Women literature (or comparable "women's" cultural productions) labor not only with the task of re-representing their significance to literary history and to women's history but with our own anxieties about their "value" or "worth" in the face of the traditional criteria for canonical fiction, that is, claims for a work's linguistic and stylistic complexity, its "universality," its unique, experimental "originality." My own doubts are laid to rest not by conventional academic accolades but by the enthusiasm, seriousness, and personal commitment with which my undergraduate classes respond to Grand's *The Heavenly Twins,* Elizabeth Robins's *The Convert,* and other New Women novels by women writers every time that I teach these novels.

To better understand how misrepresentation, whether malevolent or, as is more often the case, benevolent, acts quietly but insidiously to eclipse the work of unconventional and polemical writers, I want to conclude by tracing the path that Sarah Grand's novels followed into oblivion. My purpose is not to dismiss unfairly serious criticisms of Grand's work nor to urge a kind of reverse *in*discrimination but, rather, to document the powerful role reviewers and critics play, that "we" play, in creating cultural narratives about a writer's work or a literary movement that discourage any further investigation, often by damning with faint praise but in particular by oversimplifying, thoughtlessly classifying, or too easily dismissing. Grand offers a fascinating case study because she wrote with such insight about the very cultural forces that shaped her fate in literary history.

In *The Heavenly Twins* Grand self-consciously addresses the censoring, in particular, of female voices. Grand knew what she herself called "the silencing system" well, having fought throughout her lifetime both to defeat the system and to represent it in fiction so that other women might profit from her knowledge.[1] This system discredited feminist critiques of society in the 1890s by assuming that a truly womanly woman—obedient, loving, self-sacrificing, and innocent of the world outside the domestic sphere—would be *incapable* of asserting her individual will against the collective will of society. In her novels Grand defines this system as paternalistic men, parents, "good women," the church, social codes of marital and sex roles and marital behavior, the laws governing marriage, and the medical and psychological professions. It was in the interest of the system to suppress women's ideas when they threatened prevailing definitions of womanhood essential to the preservation of Victorian social order and to the marriage plot.

Despite Grand's impressive achievements as an activist and a writer, her literary work had been virtually ignored until Elaine Showalter discussed *The Heavenly Twins* and *The Beth Book* in *A Literature of Their Own* in 1977, and she herself was near-forgotten until Gillian Kersley's biography, *Darling Madame: Sarah Grand and Devoted Friend* appeared in 1983. The gradual dismissal of her work can be traced in reviews and reference works that demonstrate the vacillations of a largely middlebrow market, many of which I have discussed throughout this book. Like many New Woman novelists, Grand attempted to turn the desire of middlebrow consumers for culture, self-improvement, and identification with a collective of readers and writers to political ends. While her primary agenda followed liberal feminist demands for the vote, for easier access to education and professions, and for improved marriage and child custody laws, she also depended upon the power and pleasure of fiction to urge changes in class relations between women, agricultural improvements, and the creation of women's economic and labor collectives. In other words, Grand and many fellow New Woman writers saw an opportunity within middlebrow culture to create a community of largely middle-class women writers, journalists, playwrights, ac-tresses, orators, club women, educators, professionals, suffragists, and sympathetic male and female readers who would be moved by their reading to rewrite their lives and restructure their society. In response middlebrow as well as highbrow cultural guardians closed ranks against "literature with a purpose."

Soon after the publication of *The Heavenly Twins* a writer for the *Book-*

man, a publisher's trade journal written for a general audience, interviewed Sarah Grand. The unnamed writer appears sympathetic to Grand but repeatedly trivializes and even misrepresents her. The interviewer distorts both Grand's fiction and the New Woman figure by lifting a quotation out of the context of an earlier Grand novel, *Ideala* (1883), and investing it with an interpretation that has little to do with the novel. After quoting Ideala's statement "Love is the one thing worth living for," the reviewer adds, "not a selfish independence."[2] In fact, as we have seen, the speaker of these lines is separated from a vicious husband and abandons a lover to protect *his* reputation. Disillusioned with romance, Ideala struggles for an altruistic love that would permit her to devote the rest of her life to the cause of social justice. Love in this sense is revolutionary, since it impels Ideala to "radical chastity," to use a term from Kathleen Blake's *Love and the Woman Question in Victorian Literature.* Blake defines *radical chastity* as the deliberate choice to live a celibate life—as a recluse, a nun, or a single woman—which would permit a Victorian woman to live more or less autonomously within the Victorian social world. She suggests that radical chastity is the strategy of various New Women characters whom critics have misread as failing at love rather than triumphing over romance.[3] Ideala's distinction between altruistic love and romantic love, a distinction unacknowledged by the interviewer, equates love and independence (at least from men and wifehood) rather than polarizing the two.

After describing Grand's feminist approach and independent female characters, the *Bookman* reviewer hastily adds: "Yet with all their independences they are the most womanly of women. Sarah Grand has not the faintest sympathy with the bold and noisy female agitator."[4] (Several years later Grand became a member and local organizer of the National Union of Women's Suffrage Societies.) The reviewer continues, "She is never happier than when describing a peaceful home-life, such as . . . Angelica's at the close of 'The Heavenly Twins,'" an odd comment considering Angelica's tumults and tempests.[5] In the novel Angelica marries an elderly statesman who becomes her spokesman, presenting her speeches on women's rights and social reform. In a sense Angelica does accept the conventions of marriage. For instance, she sacrifices her desire to live independently and to form intimate platonic relationships with men, friendships based on unfettered comradeship and mutual interests rather than marriage and sexual commerce. Yet she also revises the conventions. She asks her husband for his hand and sets the terms of their relationship; also, she marries principally to gain the social liberties available to married women. Furthermore, the novel suggests that, if her home is peaceful, it is only because all in her household accommodate themselves to Angelica's feminist worldview.

Finally, the *Bookman* interviewer discredits Sarah Grand's insights by resorting to one of the oldest strategies used against women writers, the charge of inexperience: "She herself confesses that her knowledge of life has been confined to a somewhat narrow circle. She has no conception of the commonplace struggles which beset the lives of ordinary women."[6] Though male privilege apparently does not disqualify men writers from speaking for economically deprived characters, Grand's middle-class background prevents her from authentically articulating the concerns of "ordinary women." This criticism is particularly odd given that the writer concludes the review by saying, "Those who know her . . . are aware that the problem of the lives of poor women in London is at present engaging her deepest interest."[7]

A few years later, in 1901, a reviewer for the *Academy* rationalizes away the significance of Grand's work in yet another fashion. For this reviewer a true literary artist is a man and a man without a mission: "his large desire is, not to express in words any particular thing, but to express *himself,* the sum of his sensations." The reviewer pits this male aesthete against the writer of ideas, "burdened with a message prophetic, didactic, or reforming."[8] The reviewer then characterizes the writer of ideas:

> insofar as he is an artist, he is an artist by chance—simply because words, besides being the medium of an art, are also the best vehicle for the dissemination of ideas. The Word is his slave; and if, perchance, he treats it with a consideration that resembles love, he does so with a mercenary motive—in order to get the most out of it.
>
> Mrs. Grand belongs to this class.[9]

Superficially, the reviewer acknowledges the importance of Grand's message, yet, by condemning Grand as a materialist who has no real talent as a novelist, he casts doubt upon the novel's message and discredits the novelist as a reliable literary or social authority. The rest of the review alternates between lambasting *The Heavenly Twins* as a novel and exalting it as a "brilliant" indictment of female oppression and male privilege.

Even before Grand's death in 1943 her reputation began to decline. Until the past few years she seldom received more than a passing reference in chapters on the New Woman, usually in books written about male writers of the same period. Ironically, but predictably, in the few biographical sources that provide modern scholars with access to writers beyond the scope of the canon, she is uniformly misrepresented. The 1942 edition of *Twentieth Century Authors* describes *The Heavenly Twins,* her critique of the impostures of romance and restraints of marriage, as "a long romantic novel."[10] Misrepresentation, then, shifts to out-and-out condemnation.

Ignoring the many reviews of Grand's three best-known and most popular works, *Ideala, The Heavenly Twins,* and *The Beth Book,* the editor chooses two damning remarks about one of Grand's least-known works—powerful discouragement to potential readers unfamiliar with Grand's fiction. Speaking of *The Winged Victory,* published in 1916, the editor writes:

> The London *Times* called the latter novel a preposterous story preposterously related; the *Saturday Review* remarked that the novel was frankly impossible, viewed from the standpoint of art, but that one must pay a tribute to a personality which contrives to be entertaining "in spite of pleonastic excesses and creative failure."[11]

This editor unthinkingly repeats earlier criticism, even choosing the most exaggerated attack on her work as the phrase he will reprint. And so this biography perpetuates the "silencing system" and the erasure of Sarah Grand.

The 1955 edition of this reference work is somewhat kinder. Noting that *The Heavenly Twins* was "a tremendous success," the editor quotes an unnamed source (actually the *Times* obituary) that calls *The Heavenly Twins* "'the chief woman's rights novel of the period.'"[12] The editor also reports a comment from the London *Times* that Grand had "'widened the field of English fiction by freeing it from some of its former limitations as to subject and treatment.'"[13] The editor subverts these tributes to Grand, however, by then reprinting an indictment of her work from F. L. Mott's *Golden Multitudes: The Story of Best Sellers in the United States.* Thus, we are told that Grand's best work, *The Heavenly Twins,* is "ill-constructed, crammed with ideas and opinions and prejudices, and often over-written."[14] The brief biography tells us that Grand was a feminist, a leader, a thinker, and a pioneer. It also implies that we should not bother to read her. In this case the irony of Grand's literary exile is embedded in the very phrase used to demean her work. Here she is barred from the canon not because she is insane or sexually perverse, and not even exclusively because she is not a "good writer," whatever arbitrary definition that label encompasses. Instead, Mott condemns her work because "it is crammed with ideas and opinions and prejudices." It seems Sarah Grand is unacceptable in part because she is a woman capable of intellectual activity and discomfiting social analysis and because, implicit in the word *prejudices,* she is, in nineteenth-century terms, a feminist.

As the exciting work of the many more recent scholars I have discussed makes clear, the New Women novelists were writing in a contentious, unsettling, and in some ways liberating moment of experimentation. Reflecting upon an old century and facing a new one, men and women writers alike sampled existing genres while teasing the palate of literary tastes with exotic new possibilities. They built larger audiences, expansive networks and sometimes fragile communities of writers and publishers. These writers pursued some ineffable difference in their work that they obsessively refer to as "the new." The novels call for New Men, New Women, but also new forms and stories, new strategies for educating readers and inciting pleasure, anger, and activism. Appealing to a broad audience, from upper-class society women to working women, joined in a longing for self-directed education and pleasures of the text, these novelists traversed a new ideological, cultural, and economic terrain of middlebrow culture that emerged from the immense readership that no authors in Britain could have imagined before the educational initiatives of the nineteenth century. Many of the New Woman writers, like Sarah Grand, saw that nation of readers as recruits or potential converts. For her the middlebrow women's novel had militant potential. Writing, sharing work with other women writers, savoring audiences on the lecture circuit or in women's clubs and organizations, Grand struggled with a vision of a new world, of nearly unimaginable choices for her female characters, of an immediate, intimate, electrifying impact upon women readers.

Returning Grand's novels to literary history not only fills a gap in turn-of-the-century British literary studies, but her work also demands a rethinking of twentieth-century feminism. As so often happens in political as well as literary movements, the moderate position is ultimately more palatable to the general public than the radical. Ironically, however, acceptance can also be the cause of later critical dismissal. The ultimate irony would be an odd collaboration between, on one hand, conservative literary scholars who ignore New Women novels by women because they fail to meet aesthetic standards, and, on the other hand, progressive and/or radical feminists and other scholars who dismiss these novels as politically conservative.

Tracing the history of Sarah Grand and her fellow New Woman novelists teaches us about extremes, alternatives, compromises, collusions. Middle-class, middlebrow writers find the middle, of course. Fortunately, in seeking the middle, they push very hard, very often against conservative and radical outer limits. The moments of conservatism locate late Victorian anxieties and resistance to change. The moments of exchange across the social divides of class, education, gender, nation, along with the moments of dazzling, poignant, witty analysis of social institutions and of conventional relationships changed readers' lives forever.

Notes

Introduction

1. Emma Frances Brooke (d. 1926) published *A Superfluous Woman* (New York: Cassell, 1894). She also wrote other novels and a pamphlet entitled *Tabulation of the Factory Laws of European Countries in so Far as They Relate to the Hours of Labour, and to Special Legislation for Women, Young Persons, and Children* (1897). Mona Caird (1855–1932) was a prolific journalist and novelist, who wrote powerfully on vivisection as well as women's issues. Many of her essays are collected in *The Morality of Marriage and Other Essays on the Status of Woman* (London: George Redway, 1897). Her best-known New Woman novel is *The Daughters of Danaus* (1894; reprint, New York: The Feminist Press, 1989). Mary Cholmondeley's (1859–1925) *Red Pottage* (1899; reprint, New York: Penguin, 1985) deals self-reflexively with a woman writer's career. Jane Hume Clapperton infuses the New Woman novel with socialist politics in *Margaret Dunmore; or, A Socialist Home* (London: Swan Sonnenschein, Lowry and Co., 1888), while Lady Florence Dixie (1857–1905) imagines a feminist coup in the narrative *Gloriana: or, The Revolution of 1900* (London: Henry and Co., 1890). Menie Muriel Dowie (1867–1945) wrote *Gallia* (1895; reprint, London: Everyman, 1995). "George Egerton" is the pseudonym of Mary Chavelita Dunne (1859–1945). Egerton's *Keynotes* (1893) became so popular that her editor, John Lane of Bodley Head, published a fiction series under that title. She also published an important collection titled *Discords* (London: John Lane, 1894). Both books were reprinted under one cover by Virago in 1995. Socialist politics and urban tensions shape Isabella Ford's (1850?–1924) *On the Threshold* (London: Edward Arnold, 1895). Annie E. Holdsworth's (1857?–1910?) *Joanna Trail, Spinster* (London: W. Heinemann, 1894) deals with the problems faced by a prostitute attempting to reform. "Iota" is the pen name of Mrs. Mannington Caffyn (1855?–1926), author of *A Yellow Aster* (Leipzig: Bernard Tauchnitz, 1894). An early representation of a woman doctor figures in Arabella Kenealy's *Dr. Janet of Harley Street* (London: Digby, Long and Co., 1893), which also depicts an erotic sensibility that would now be called lesbian. Olive Schreiner (1855–1920) is best remembered for her novel *Story of an African Farm* (1883; reprint, New York: Oxford University Press, 1991), although she also wrote on politics and economics, as in *Woman and Labour* (1911; reprint, London: Virago, 1985), and she wrote experimental short stories. Frances McFall (1854–1943) changed her name to Sarah Grand; her novel *The Heavenly Twins* (1893; reprint, Ann Arbor: University of Michigan

Press, 1992) was a best-seller for ten years. These are only a few of the novelists who have been described as New Women writers.

Although I am focusing on the New Woman in fiction, the figure also had a lively life on the London stage. See Joel H. Kaplan and Sheila Stowell, *Theatre and Fashion: Oscar Wilde to the Suffragettes* (New York: Cambridge University Press, 1994), for accounts of theatrical versions of the figure. See also *New Woman Plays,* ed. Linda Fitzsimmons and Viv Gardner (London: Methuen, 1991); *The New Woman and Her Sisters: Feminism and Theatre, 1850–1914,* ed. Viv Gardner and Susan Rutherford (New York: Harvester Wheatsheaf, 1992); and Sheila Stowell, *A Stage of Their Own: Feminist Playwrights of the Suffrage Era* (Ann Arbor: University of Michigan Press, 1992), for women playwrights' representations of women.

2. The Married Women's Property Acts actually develop over several decades. An early version was introduced into Parliament in 1868 by J. G. Shaw-Lefevre. Outside Parliament a committee that included Josephine Butler and Elizabeth Wolstenholme tried to persuade the public to support the bill. It failed in 1868 and in 1869; a very diluted version was passed in 1870. A series of acts followed in 1873, 1882, and 1891 that gradually increased rights of women over property acquired after introduction of the acts. For details about each act, see Joan Perkin, *Women and Marriage in Nineteenth-Century England* (Chicago: Lyceum Books, 1989); and Mary Lyndon Shanley, *Feminism, Marriage and the Law in Victorian England, 1850–1895* (London: I. B. Tauris, 1989).

3. Excellent studies of women's history, particularly of improvements in education, of women's increasing presence in the workforce, and of the struggles for female suffrage, continue to appear. Several that focus on the 1890s are especially helpful in contextualizing New Woman fiction; in particular, see Joan Burstyn, *Victorian Education and the Ideal of Womanhood* (New Brunswick: Rutgers University Press, 1984); Pamela Fox, *Class Fictions: Shame and Resistance in the British Working-Class Novel, 1890–1945* (Durham: Duke University Press, 1994); Pat Jalland, *Women, Marrige, and Politics, 1860–1914* (New York: Oxford University Press, 1986); Philippa Levine, *Victorian Feminism, 1850–1900* (Tallahassee: Florida State University Press, 1987); Joan Perkin; Jane Rendall, ed., *Equal or Different: Women's Politics, 1800–1914* (Oxford: Basil Blackwell, 1987); David Rubinstein, *Before the Suffragettes: Women's Emancipation in the 1890s* (Brighton: Harvester Press, 1986); and Martha Vicinus, *Independent Women: Community and Work for Single Women, 1850–1920* (Chicago: University of Chicago Press, 1985). I still find Ray Strachey's eyewitness account, *The Cause* (1928; reprint, London: Virago, 1978), especially moving and informative.

4. See Penny Boumelha, *Thomas Hardy and Women: Sexual Ideology and Narrative Form* (Brighton: Harvester Press, 1982), 86.

5. For more detailed descriptions and analyses of "ideal womanhood," see Nancy Armstrong, *Desire and Domestic Fiction* (New York: Oxford University Press, 1987); Françoise Basch, *Relative Creatures: Victorian Women in Society and the Novel* (New York: Schocken Books, 1974); Joan Burstyn, *Victorian Education and the Ideal of Womanhood;* Mary Jean Corbett, *Representing Femininity: Middle-Class Subjectivities in Victorian and Edwardian Autobiographies* (New York: Oxford University Press, 1992); Leonore Davidoff and Catherine Hall, *Family Fortunes: Men and Women of the English Middle Class, 1780–1850* (Chicago: University of Chicago Press, 1987); Regenia Gagnier, *Subjectivities: A History of Self-Representation in Britain, 1832–1930* (New York: Oxford University Press,

1991); Elizabeth Langland, *Nobody's Angels: Middle-Class Women and Domestic Ideology in Victorian Culture* (Ithaca: Cornell University Press, 1995); Anita Levy, *Other Women: The Writing of Class, Race, and Gender, 1832–1898* (Princeton: Princeton University Press, 1991); and Mary Poovey, *Uneven Developments: The Ideological Work of Gender in Mid-Victorian England* (Chicago: University of Chicago Press, 1988).

6. See Grand's comments in Athol Forbes's interview, "My Impressions of Sarah Grand," *Lady's World* (June 1900): 883.

7. See Ellen Jordan, "The Christening of the New Woman: May 1894," *Victorian Newsletter* 48 (Spring 1983): 19. Though many studies of the New Woman cite this exchange as the source of the term *New Woman*, David Rubinstein in *Before the Suffragettes* (16–23), J. Ellen Gainor in *Shaw's Daughters: Dramatic and Narrative Constructions of Gender* (Ann Arbor: University of Michigan Press, 1991), and Ann Ardis in *New Women, New Novels: Feminism and Early Modernism* ([New Brunswick: Rutgers University Press, 1990], 10–11) note that the term had begun to circulate previously. This exchange does seem to have fixed the term in popular consciousness. Ann Heilman also examines the complicated implications of the label in "'The New Woman Fiction' and *Fin-de-Siècle* Feminism," *Women's Writing: The Elizabethan to the Victorian Period* 3 (1996): 197–216.

8. Two especially amusing examples are a poem in the *Idler* 6 (1895), entitled "To an 'Advanced Woman'" and attributed to Mabelle Pearse, and a cartoon of the Heavenly Twins in the *Idler* 14 (1899): 703. The "Mere Man" parody appeared in *Harper's Weekly*, 2 November 1901, during Grand's American tour. See also the parody by "A Mere Man," *The Domestic Blunders of Woman* (1899; reprint, Kent: Pryor Publications, 1994). The parody of *Leaves of Grass*, entitled "A Slight Adaptation," appears in *Punch*, 10 November 1894, 228.

9. Throughout my own book I rely, as anyone interested in Grand must, on the groundbreaking efforts of Gillian Kersley; see *Darling Madame: Sarah Grand and Devoted Friend* (London: Virago, 1983). Kersley found Gladys Singers-Bigger's journal and letters to and from Grand in the Bath Central Library and tracked down important biographical material that answers questions raised by the journal. I have now seen most of the primary sources Kersley discusses, and throughout this book I will note their location. In cases in which Kersley reprints the texts to which I refer, however, I also cite her study because readers can then easily gain access to the materials. I also wish to express my personal gratitude to Gillian Kersley, who has generously answered my questions, steered me toward resources, and encouraged my own attempts to understand and share Grand's life and work.

Carol Senf's introduction to the recent edition of *The Heavenly Twins* (1992) fills in a number of gaps in Grand's biography and cites hitherto overlooked reviews of the novel. Also, Marilyn Bonnell's "The Legacy of Sarah Grand's *The Heavenly Twins*: A Review Essay," *English Literature in Transition* 36 (1993): 466–79, drew my attention to William Blackwood's letters, and Marilyn Bonnell kindly shared sources and suggestions for which I am grateful.

10. In her letters Grand repeatedly corrects correspondents' use of her former name after she adopted her pseudonym. For example, on 1 August 1893, she writes: "I hope you will always call me 'Sarah Grand,' and address me so. I want to forget that I was ever known by any other name"; this letter is in the National Library of Wales.

11. See Gilbert and Gubar, "Ceremonies of the Alphabet: Female Grandmatologies and the Female Autograph," in *The Female Autograph,* ed. Domna Stanton (Chicago: University of Chicago Press, 1987), 29.

12. Grand also voices these sentiments in a letter to Henry Laboncere, dated 28 March 1894. The letter is held in the Special Collections of the University of California Library in Los Angeles (UCLA).

13. Grand discusses her husband with Frederick Henry Fisher in a letter dated 1 January 1907. The letter is now held in the Special Collections of UCLA.

14. Joan Huddleston provides the most comprehensive list of Grand's publications in *Sarah Grand: A Bibliography* (St. Lucia: University of Queensland Press, 1979), but I hesitate to make claims about an exact number of articles written by Grand, since she may very well have published anonymously in the United Kingdom and the United States.

15. Current feminist studies of the genre locate the appeal of these novels in the very characteristics Victorian reviewers and later literary scholars attacked. Elaine Showalter's pioneering *A Literature of Their Own: British Women Novelists from Brontë to Lessing* (Princeton: Princeton University Press, 1977) as well as her social and literary history of the 1890s, *Sexual Anarchy: Gender and Culture at the Fin de Siècle* (New York: Penguin, 1990); Penny Boumelha's historically contextualized analysis of New Women novels and women's sexuality in *Thomas Hardy and Women;* Martha Vicinus's rigorously researched study of single women's social circumstances and professional options in *Independent Women,* among other works that insist upon connections between women's social history and women's writing, thoughtfully and intricately delineate the complex social, financial, sexual, and imaginative tensions that produced the New Woman.

16. Crucial books for the study of the New Woman genre are Ann Ardis's *New Women, New Novels;* Gerd Bjørhovde's *Rebellious Structures: Women Writers and the Crisis of the Novel, 1880–1900* (Oslo: Norwegian Press, 1987); Rita S. Kranidis's *Subversive Discourse: The Cultural Production of Late Victorian Novels* (New York: St. Martin's Press, 1995); Lyn Pykett's *The "Improper" Feminine* (New York: Routledge, 1992); and Sally Ledger's *The New Woman: Fiction and Feminism at the Fin de Siècle* (Manchester: Manchester University Press, 1997). Ardis's dissertation, "'The Apple and the Ego of Woman': A Prehistory of English Modernism in the 'New Woman' Novels of the 1890's" (University of Virginia, 1988) though the foundation of her book, also includes additional information. Gail Cunningham's book, *The New Woman and the Victorian Novel* (London: Macmillan, 1978) offers a helpful descriptive chapter on a range of works, and Elaine Showalter's chapter on feminist writers in *A Literature of One's Own* is also an excellent introduction to the genre. In addition to Sally Ledger's own book, *The New Woman: Fiction and Feminism at the Fin de Siècle* (Manchester and New York: Manchester University Press, 1997), she also has edited a collection of articles on the New Woman for the journal *Women's Writing* titled *Women's Writing at the Fin de Siècle* (3, no. 3 [1996]). Just as Pamela Fox's *Class Fictions* and the essays in *Rediscovering Forgotten Radicals: British Women Writers, 1889–1939,* ed. Angela Ingram and Daphne Patai (Chapel Hill: University of North Carolina Press, 1993), are recovering connections between labor and feminist politics and political writing, important work is also beginning to appear on connections among imperialist policies, Victorian racial theory, and feminist writing: for example, see Laura Chrisman's essay, "Empire, 'Race' and Feminism at the *Fin de Siècle:* The Work of George Egerton and Olive Schreiner," in *Cultural Politics at*

the Fin de Siècle, ed. Sally Ledger and Scott McCracken (Cambridge: Cambridge University Press, 1995, 45–65); and Showalter, *Sexual Anarchy.*

The burgeoning studies of late-Victorian women travel writers also complicate current characterizations of New Women and New Women writers. These include Dea Birkett, *Spinsters Abroad: Victorian Lady Explorers* (New York: Oxford University Press, 1989); Helen Callaway, *Gender, Culture and Empire: European Women in Colonial Nigeria* (Urbana: University of Illinois Press, 1987); Mary Louise Pratt, *Imperial Eyes: Travel Writing and Transculturation* (New York: Routledge, 1992); Susan Morgan, *Place Matters: Gendered Geography in Victorian Women's Travel Books about Southeast Asia* (New Brunswick: Rutgers University Press, 1996); Antoinette Burton, *Burdens of History: British Feminists, Indian Women, and Imperial Culture, 1865–1915* (Chapel Hill: University of North Carolina Press, 1994); Catherine Barnes Stevenson, *Victorian Women Travel Writers in Africa* (Boston: Twayne, 1982); Sara Mills, *Discourses of Difference: An Analysis of Women's Travel Writing and Colonialism* (New York: Routledge, 1991); Billie Melman, *Women's Orients: English Women and the Middle East, 1718–1918: Sexuality, Religion and Work* (Ann Arbor: University of Michigan Press, 1995); Anne McClintock, *Imperial Leather: Race, Gender, and Sexuality in the Colonial Conquest* (New York: Routledge, 1995). Also see Terry Lovell, *Consuming Fiction* (London: Verso, 1987); Kate Flint, *The Woman Reader, 1837–1914* (New York: Oxford University Press, 1993); Margaret Diane Stetz, "Life's 'Half-Profits': Writers and Their Readers in Fiction of the 1890s," in *Nineteenth-Century Lives: Essays Presented to Jerome Hamilton Buckley,* ed. Laurence S. Lockridge, John Maynard, and Donald Stone (Cambridge: Cambridge University Press, 1989, 169–87); "The New Grub Street and the Woman Writer of the 1890s," *Transforming Genres* (New York: St. Martin's Press, 1994, 21–45); Margaret Beetham, *A Magazine of Her Own: Domesticity and Desire in the Woman's Magazine, 1800–1914* (New York: Routledge, 1996).

17. Several studies of individual writers have been very important in laying the groundwork for discussions of New Woman fiction, especially Nancy Fix Anderson, *Woman against Women in Victorian England: The Life of Eliza Lynn Linton* (Bloomington: Indiana University Press, 1987); Ruth First and Ann Scott, *Olive Schreiner* (London: Andre Deutsch, 1980); and Kersley, *Darling Madame.*

18. Judith Butler, *Gender Trouble: Feminism and the Subversion of Identity* (New York: Routledge, 1990).

Chapter 1

1. George Eliot, *Middlemarch,* ed. Bert G. Hornback (New York: W. W. Norton, 1977), 818.

2. For example, see Showalter, *A Literature of Their Own;* Boumelha, *Thomas Hardy and Women;* DuPlessis, *Writing beyond the Ending;* and, for a specific discussion of Grand's work, Norma Clarke's essay, "Feminism and the Popular Novel of the 1890's: A Brief Reconsideration of a Forgotten Novelist," *Feminist Review* 20 (1985): 91–104.

3. Cunningham, *New Woman in Victorian Fiction,* 17.

4. See *Ideala: A Study from Life* (privately printed, 1888; reprint, London: Heinemann, 1893), 209. Future references cited in the text.

5. Tanner, *Adultery and the Novel: Contract and Transgression* (Baltimore: Johns Hopkins University Press), 16.

6. Tanner, *Adultery and the Novel,* 15.

7. Hinz, "Hierogamy versus Wedlock: Types of Marriage Plots and Their Relationship to Genres of Prose Fiction," *PMLA* 91 (1976): 900.

8. Hinz, "Hierogamy versus Wedlock," 903.

9. Boone, "Wedlock as Deadlock and Beyond: Closure and the Victorian Ideal," *Mosaic* 17 (1984): 71. Boone elaborates his broader argument far more fully in a crucial recent study of the marriage plot, *Tradition Counter Tradition: Love and the Form of Fiction* (Chicago: University of Chicago Press, 1987).

10. See Leslie Rabine, *Reading the Romantic Heroine* (Ann Arbor: University of Michigan Press, 1985).

11. For a history of the legal evolution of marriage in the nineteenth century, see Shanley, *Feminism, Marriage, and the Law.* For a thorough account of the Jackson v. Jackson case, see Rubinstein, *Before the Suffragettes,* 54–58. Grand refers to this case in "The Woman's Question: An Interview with Sarah Grand," conducted by Sarah Tooley, in the *Humanitarian* 8 (1896); and in "Women in the Queen's Reign," *Ludgate* (1898): 216.

12. See Shanley on the reform bills. Philippa Levine also discusses the several reform bills and suffrage debates and outlines the members' double-handed dealings with women in the suffrage parties, who depended on Liberal members to represent their interests, in *Victorian Feminists.*

13. See Tooley, *Humanitarian* 8 (1896): 163–64.

14. Bernstein traces the language of primitivism in reviewers' attacks on sensation fiction in her wittily titled "Dirty Reading: Sensation Fiction, Women, and Primitivism," *Criticism* 36 (Spring 1994): 213–41. In that essay she draws attention to the failure of other studies of middlebrow literature to consider the "primitivist overtones" of the "browing" hierarchy (241). Also, see Janice Radway's two recent essays on middlebrow culture, "Mail Order Culture and Its Critics: The Book-of-the-Month Club," *Cultural Studies,* 512–27; and "On the Gender of the Middlebrow Consumer and the Threat of the Culturally Fraudulent Female," *South Atlantic Quarterly* 93 (Fall 1994): 871–93, which culminated in *A Feeling for Books: The Book-of-the-Month Club, Literary Taste, and Middle-Class Desire* (Chapel Hill: University of North Carolina Press, 1997).

15. Tad Friend, *New Republic,* 2 March 1992, 25.

16. See Joan Shelley Rubin's *The Making of Middlebrow Culture* (Chapel Hill: University of North Carolina Press, 1992). Lawrence Levine's *Highbrow/Lowbrow: The Emergence of Cultural Hierarchy in America* (Cambridge: Harvard University Press, 1988) locates the emergence of "highbrow" in the 1880s and of "lowbrow" after 1900 (221); he doesn't discuss the middle.

17. Jane Tompkins, *Sensational Designs; The Cultural Work of American Fiction, 1790–1860* (Oxford: Oxford University Press, 1985), 200.

18. Cross's account of J. C. Collins's battle with Oxford, where he was a mere occasional lecturer, treats Collins as a hero. Cross also provides an astute account of the politics and changing conceptions of language as well as literature as constituents of nationalism shaping these debates, in *The Common Writer: Life in Nineteenth-Century Grub Street* (Cambridge: Cambridge University Press, 1985), 62–75.

19. Cross, *The Common Writer,* 216.

20. Cross, *The Common Writer*, 216–17.

21. Linda Hughes's unpublished essay, "My Sister, My Self: Networking and Self-Promotion Among Fin-de-Siècle Women Poets" also offers a fascinating account of women writers' networks.

22. Walter Besant, "Literature as a Career,"*Forum* 13 (August 1892): 694.

23. Edmund Gosse, "The Decay of Literary Taste," *North American Review* 161 (1895): 110.

24. Gosse, "Decay of Literary Taste," 110, 118.

25. James Hepburn, *The Author's Empty Purse and the Rise of the Literary Agent* (London: Oxford University Press, 1968), 55–57.

26. Hepburn, *Author's Empty Purse*, 18–31.

27. See Margaret Stetz, "Sex, Lies, and Printed Cloth: Bookselling at the Bodley Head in the Eighteen-Nineties," *Victorian Studies* 35 (1991): 71–86, on this literary star system.

28. In addition to Kranidis, *Subversive Discourse*, and Lovell, *Consuming Fictions*, see Gaye Tuchman and Nina Fortin, *Edging Women Out* (New Haven: Yale University Press, 1989).

29. Rubin, "Chapter One," 1–33.

30. George Moore, *Literature at Nurse, or Circulating Morals* (London: Vizetelly, 1885).

31. Lyn Pykett, *Engendering Fiction* (New York: Edward Arnold, 1995), 33–38.

32. Flint's argument that the sensation writers and the New Women writers both engaged actively with the readers is as persuasive as her readings of these paintings (*The Woman Reader, 1837–1914*, 15).

33. Flint, *The Woman Reader, 1837–1914*, 43.

34. Thomas Hardy, "Candour in English Fiction," *New Review* 2 (1890): 17.

35. Tooley, "Woman's Question," 168–69.

36. Grand uses this term in the 1923 foreword to *The Heavenly Twins*, and it reappears in an essay, partly based on an interview, written about her by L. A. M. Priestley McCracken, "Madame Sarah Grand and Women's Emancipation," *Vote* 34, 25 August 1933, n.p.

37. This unpublished letter to William Blackwood, of 18 June 1892, is held in the Special Collections of the National Library of Scotland.

38. Grand, "The New Woman and the Old," *Lady's Realm* 4 (August 1898): 466.

39. Untitled review, *Vanity Fair*, 18 October 1894, 265.

40. Review of Eliza Linton, *In Haste and Leisure, Athenaeum*, 30 March 1895, 405.

41. Bridgett Elliott discusses the visual iconography associated with the New Woman and its influence on Aubrey Beardsley's drawings of actresses in "New and Not So 'New Women' on the London Stage" in *Victorian Studies* 31 (1987): 33–57. Her sources include cartoons, book covers, posters, and playbills.

42. Ann Ardis, *New Women, New Novels*, 212.

43. Millicent Garrett Fawcett, review of *The Woman Who Did, Contemporary Review* 67 (1895): 630.

44. Fawcett, review of *The Woman Who Did*, 631.

45. Elizabeth Chapman, *Marriage Questions in Modern Fiction* (London: John Lane, 1894), xiii.

46. Lovell, *Consuming Fictions,* 33.

47. Hogarth, "Literary Degenerates," *Fortnightly Review* 63 (1895): 587.

48. Hogarth, "Literary Degenerates," 591.

49. Hogarth, "Literary Degenerates," 591.

50. Stutfield, "The Psychology of Feminism," *Blackwood's Magazine* 161 (1897): 105.

51. I am using Joanna Russ's terminology from her still important book *How to Suppress Women's Writing* (Austin: University of Texas Press, 1983) to describe rhetorical devices that define and control literary culture (39).

52. Russ, *How to Suppress Women's Writing,* 25.

53. Stutfield, "Psychology of Feminism," 111.

54. Stutfield, "Psychology of Feminism," 116.

55. Stutfield, "Psychology of Feminism," 116. Complaints against her male characters were among Grand's pet peeves. In 1895 she protested to Frederick Henry Fisher, editor of *Literary World,* against a reviewer in *Great Thoughts:* "He declares that I only paint one type of man. As a matter of fact, I have only described three specimens of the gentle kind of being whom he accuses me of traducing, and those three were anything but monsters. That he can call such men as my Tenor, Dr. Galbraith, Lord Dawne [in addition to these characters from *The Heavenly Twins,* she goes on to list male characters from short stories] I could not have much stood if I had not seen Mr. Reverend's portrait, and they call that paper *Great Thoughts!*" The letter is dated 16 May 1895 and is in the Special Collections Library of UCLA.

56. The works I discuss here represent only a fraction of the book reviews, occasional essays, and editorials on the "degenerative" effects of introducing sexuality into fiction and the fearful consequences for the individual reader and ultimately for society. Interestingly, one group of critics feared the passions of women readers would enslave women once they were aroused, while another group feared that women who read of sexual exploitation, venereal disease, and male promiscuity would forswear sex all together and threaten humanity with extinction. Even a few titles suggest the number and scope of such articles: "The Strike of a Sex" (which attacks Grand); Amelia Barr, "Discontented Women"; John Paul MacCorrie, "The War of the Sexes"; Charles Whibley, "The Encroachment of Women"; and Ronald McNeil, "Another Chelsea Manuscript." These essays cover a five-year period from 1894 to 1899.

57. James Ashcroft Noble, "The Fiction of Sexuality," *Contemporary Review* 67 (1895): 494.

58. Noble, "Fiction of Sexuality," 493.

59. Noble, "Fiction of Sexuality," 493.

60. The extent of the belief in female frigidity continues to be a debated topic. See Edward Carpenter's discussions of sexuality (and his intriguing footnotes) in *Love's Coming of Age: A Series of Papers on the Relations of the Sexes* (Manchester: Labour Press, 1896). Nancy Cott's article "Passionlessness: An Interpretation of Victorian Sexual Ideology: 1790–1850" (*SIGNS* 4 [1979]: 219–36) suggests that historians have overemphasized women's frigidity, while Sheila Jeffreys, in *The Spinster and Her Enemies: Feminism and Sexuality, 1830–1930* (London: Pandora, 1985), discusses the feminists who led purity crusades.

Chapter 2

1. Grand's comments appear in the foreword to a 1923 edition of *The Heavenly Twins* (xiii). Joan Huddleston has compiled an extremely helpful bibliography of Grand's work, *Sarah Grand: A Bibliography*. I rely on this bibliography throughout this study for my information about the publishing and reprinting of Grand's work. *A Domestic Experiment* was published by Blackwood and Sons in 1891. *Singularly Deluded* appeared in *Blackwood's* 152 (August–December 1892) and was published in one volume by D. Appleton of New York in 1893. Subsequent references to these editions appear in the text. Grand also published something between fiction and a lecture about the dangers of Chinese foot binding, called *Two Dear Little Feet*, in 1880. She and other New Women writers sometimes used the image of foot binding in their novels to characterize the condition of women in England. In 1884 Grand also collaborated on *Constance of Calais: A Dramatic Cantata*, for which she wrote the libretto. It is now held in the Special Collections department of the University of Michigan.

2. For example, see Showalter, *A Literature of Their Own*; and Clarke, "Feminism and the Popular Novel," 91–104.

3. The letter to William Blackwood is dated 28 June 1892 and is in the Special Collections of the National Library of Scotland.

4. *Athenaeum*, 18 February 1893, 215.

5. *Spectator*, 16 May 1891, 700.

6. See the 28 June 1892 letter to William Blackwood, which details her attempts to publish her early works.

7. In the 1930s Grand's friend Gladys Singers-Bigger attempted to publish excerpts from Grand's work as a book called *The Sarah Grand Miscellany*. The dowager duchess of Beaufort wrote a foreword, and a local philosopher and writer, Charles Whitby, M.D., B.A. Cantab., wrote a fairly extensive biographical introduction. The book was never published, but the manuscript, with Grand's emendations, including these comments, is in the Bath Public Libary. For a more detailed account of the early years of Grand's marriage and of her travels, see Kersley, *Darling Madame*, esp. 3–63.

8. Grand also wrote another early novel, *Babs the Impossible* (London: Hutchinson, 1901), perhaps during these years. The novel takes up many of the same themes as her other works, so I have omitted discussion of it to avoid repetition. The phallic tower that houses one of the key male characters is, however, a fairly amazing structure.

9. This letter to Frederick Henry Fisher is dated 22 March 1894 and is in the Special Collections at the UCLA Library.

10. *Spectator*, 18 March 1893, 373.

11. Kersley attributes the squib *Battleton Rectory* to Q. Murray. Her citation in *Darling Madame* notes it was published in 1885 by John Heywood (341 n. 18).

12. See Kersley, *Darling Madame*, 50–51.

13. Asa Briggs, *Victorian Things* (London: Batsford, 1988); and Thomas Richards, *The Commodity Culture of Victorian England: Advertising and Spectacle, 1851–1914* (Stanford: Stanford University Press, 1990). Also see Philippa Tristram, *Living Space in Fact and Fiction* (New York: Routledge, 1989).

14. By the 1890s suicide had began to be considered as a psychological disorder rather than a sin. The most famous instance of the New Woman's choice of suicide in

preference to a loveless marriage is probably Kate Chopin's American novel *The Awakening* (1899). Changing conceptions of suicide in the nineteenth century are discussed in Barbara Gates, *Victorian Suicide: Mad Crimes and Sad Histories* (New York: Princeton University Press, 1988); and Olive Anderson, *Suicide in Victorian and Edwardian England* (New York: Oxford University Press, 1987).

15. Philippe Perrot, *Fashioning the Bourgeoisie: A History of Clothing in the Nineteenth Century,* trans. Richard Bienvenu (1981; reprint, Princeton: Princeton University Press, 1994), 7.

16. Valerie Steele, *Fashion and Eroticism: Ideals of Feminine Beauty from the Victorian Era to the Jazz Age* (New York: Oxford University Press, 1985, 132); quoting from [Mary Eliza] Mrs. Hugh Reginald Haweis, *The Art of Beauty* (1879; reprint, New York: Garland Publishing Co., 1978), 11, 17.

17. Steele, *Fashion and Eroticism,* 143; quoting from Hawcis, *Art of Beauty,* 18.

18. Joel H. Kaplan and Sheila Stowell, *Theatre and Fashion,* 60–69. The plays are Sydney Grundy, *The New Woman* (London: Chiswick, 1894); and Arthur Wing Pinero, *The Notorious Mrs. Ebbsmith* (London: Heinemann, 1895).

19. Steele, *Fashion and Eroticism,* 150–52.

20. Steele, *Fashion and Eroticism,* 130–31.

21. Steele, *Fashion and Eroticism,* 134.

22. Lady Harburton founded the Rational Dress Society in 1881 to warn women of the dangers of tight lacing and other constrictive clothing. The society also advocated split skirts, bloomers, and physical exercise. Grand was invited to join the society while she was still living in Warrington. After her arrival in London she wrote and spoke regularly in her capacity as a committee member, and her participation in the group quickly acquainted her with prominent feminists in London (see Kersley, *Darling Madame,* 67). The movement is described in Stella Mary Newton's *Health, Art, and Reason: Dress Reformers of the Nineteenth Century* (London: John Murray, 1974).

23. Steele, *Fashion and Eroticism,* 139; quoting C. T., *How to Dress Well: A Manual of the Toilet for the Use of Both Sexes* (London: George Routledge and Sons, 1868), 43.

24. Steele, *Fashion and Eroticism,* 139; quoting from the anonymous *Etiquette of Good Society* (London, Paris, and New York: Cassell, Peter Galpin and Co, 1880), 77–79.

25. Steele, *Fashion and Eroticism,* 152–56.

26. This was the title story of the collection *Emotional Moments* (London: Hurst and Blackett, 1908).

27. Virginia Woolf, *A Room of One's Own* (1929; reprint, New York: Harcourt Brace, 1981), 85–86.

28. See Martha Vicinus's essay " 'One Life to Stand beside Me': Emotional Conflicts in First Generation College Women in England," *Feminist Studies* 8 (1982): 603–28. Vicinus writes: "During the last thirty years of the nineteenth century, women's friendships became more intense and all-encompassing; love absorbed the burdens of pioneering work" (603). In another article " 'They Wonder to Which Sex I Belong': The Historical Roots of the Modern Lesbian Identity," *Feminist Studies* 18 (Fall 1992): 467–97; reprinted in *Lesbian Subjects: A Feminist Studies Reader,* ed. Martha Vicinus (Bloomington: Indiana University Press, 233–59), Vicinus points out that romantic friendships are just one expression of the woman-identified woman during the period. She provides examples of the transvestite, the female (cross-dressed) soldier, the mannish lesbian, and

the "occasional lover of women" (475). For the late nineteenth century several studies of women's intimate friendships are especially helpful: Carroll Smith-Rosenberg, "The Female World of Love and Ritual: Relations between Women in Nineteenth Century America," *SIGNS* 1 (1975): 11–29, which also appears in a revised version in *Disorderly Conduct: Visions of Gender in Victorian America* (New York: Alfred A. Knopf, 1985); Vicinus, *Independent Women;* essays from *Hidden from History: Reclaiming the Gay and Lesbian Past,* ed. Martin Duberman, Martha Vicinus, and George Chauncey (New York: NAL Books, 1989), including Smith-Rosenberg, "Discourses of Sexuality and Subjectivity: The New Woman, 1870–1936," 264–80; Lillian Faderman, *Surpassing the Love of Men: Romantic Friendships and Love between Women from the Renaissance to the Present* (1981; reprint, London: Women's Press, 1991); and Ledger's chapter "The New Woman and Emergent Lesbian Identity," in *New Woman,* 122–49. Ledger also recommends Joseph Bristow, ed., *Sexual Sameness: Textual Differences in Gay and Lesbian Writing* (London and New York: Routledge, 1992); Lesbian History Group, *Not a Passing Phase: Reclaiming Lesbians in History, 1840–1985* (London: Women's Press, 1989); Neil Miller, *Out of the Past: Gay and Lesbian History from 1869 to the Present* (New York: Vintage, 1995); and George Chauncey, "From Sexual Inversion to Homosexuality: Medicine and the Changing Conceptualization of Female Deviance," *Salmagundi* (1982): 114–46. Though I have not yet seen it, Laurel Meredith Erickson's dissertation, "Odd Women: Late Victorian Fiction and the Work of Female Desire (Sexual Identity)" (University of Michigan, 1997) should be an important contribution too.

29. Faderman's *Chloe Plus Olivia: An Annotated Anthology of Lesbian Literature from the Seventeenth Century to the Present* (New York: Viking, 1994) is a gold mine not only of primary texts but also of detailed biographical and historical introductions to periods and writers.

30. The overt description of affairs and lovemaking in Anne Lister's diary, *I Know My Own Heart: The Diaries of Anne Lister,* ed. Helena Whitbread (London: Virago, 1988), is evidence that some women did have active sexual lives with other women as well as romantic feelings for them. Ledger makes the important point, however, that in fiction men were more likely than women to represent "lesbian" relationships, which they generally treated (as in the French novels I mention) as ominous. See Ledger's intriguing discussions in *New Woman* of George Meredith's *Diana of Crossways* (1885), 133–38, and of George Moore's *A Drama in Muslin* (1886), 38–41.

31. Ardis, *New Women, New Novels,* 138. Tess Cosslett disagrees; she argues that in most New Woman novels "the sources of her power are individualistic, they do not come from a bond with other women," *Woman to Woman: Female Friendship in Victorian Fiction* (Brighton: Harvester Press, 1988).

32. Adrienne Rich, "Compulsory Heterosexuality," in *Powers of Desire: The Politics of Sexuality,* ed. Ann Snitow, Christine Stansell, and Sharon Thompson (New York: Monthly Review Press, 1983), 177–205.

33. I refined my ideas about Leslie Sommers's role in the novel in conversations with Karen Ford, and I wish to thank her for her rigorous questions and helpful suggestions.

34. Martin Burgess Green, *Dreams of Adventure, Deeds of Empire* (New York: Basic Books, 1979), 23. Also see his recent book *Seven Types of Adventure Tale: An Etiology of a Major Genre* (University Park: Pennsylvania State University Press, 1995).

35. John G. Cawelti *Adventure, Mystery, and Romance* (Chicago: University of Chicago Press, 1976), 40.

36. See Paul Zweig, *The Adventurer,* chap. 5, "The Flight from Women" (New York: Basic Books, 1974), 61–80.

37. Green, *Dreams of Adventure,* 57.

38. Lyn Pykett, *Engendering Fictions,* 66–74. Also see Elaine Showalter's chapter "King Romance," in *Sexual Anarchy.*

39. Before any of the novels appeared in print, Grand published several short stories in children's magazines. Three appeared in *Aunt Judy's Magazine:* "Mama's Music Lessons" (December 1878), "School Revisited" (June 1880), and "The Great Typhoon" (April 1881).

40. Marjorie Garber, *Vested Interests: Cross-Dressing and Cultural Anxiety* (New York: Routledge, 1992), 186.

41. Andrew Forrest, *The Female Detective* (London: War and Lock, 1864); Wilkie Collins, *The Law and the Lady* (first published in *Graphic,* 1874; reprint, London: Oxford University Press, 1992); Milton Danvers, *The Doctor's Crime; or, Simply Horrible* (London: Diprose and Bateman, 1891); *A Desperate Dilemma; or, An Unheard of Crime* (London: Diprose and Bateman, 1892); *The Detective's Honeymoon; or, The Doctor of the "Pinjarrah"* (London: Dipose and Bateman, 1894); George R. Sims, *Dorcas Dene, Detective,* 2d ser. (London: F. V. White, 1898).

For histories of the female detective, see Patricia Craig and Mary Cadogan, *The Lady Investigates: Women Detectives and Spies in Fiction* (New York: St. Martin's Press, 1981); Maureen Reddy, *Women and Crime: Feminism and the Crime Novel* (New York: Continuum, 1988); Kathleen Gregory Klein, *The Woman Detective: Gender and Genre* (Urbana: University of Illinois Press, 1994); Fay Blake, "Lady Sleuths and Women Detectives," *Turn of the Century Women* 3 (1986), 29–42; and Heidi Johnson's forthcoming dissertation from the University of Iowa, "Circumstantiality: A Cultural Theory of the Female Sleuth in Victorian Fiction."

42. *Critic* 23, 9 December 1893, 375.

43. See Eliza Lynn Linton, "The Wild Women as Politicians," *Nineteenth Century* 30 (1891): 79. For a survey of *Punch* sallies against women who defied feminine conventions in dress, see Susan C. Shapiro, "The Mannish New Woman: *Punch* and Its Precursors," *Review of English Studies* 42 (November 1991): 510–22.

44. *Spectator,* 18 March 1893, 373.

45. The problem of how to represent Victorian middle-class female characters as women "in the street" in any category other than a prostitute—for example, as detective, as flaneuse, or as a shopper—is taken up in several recent studies. See Ann Friedberg, Window Shopping: Cinema and the Postmodern (Berkeley: University of California Press, 1993); Janet Wolff, *Feminine Sentences: Essays on Women and Culture* (Berkeley: University of California Press, 1990); and Deborah Epstein Nord, *Walking the Victorian Streets: Women, Representation, and the City* (Ithaca: Cornell University Press, 1995). Sally Ledger's chapter "The New Woman in the Modern City" (in *New Woman*) provides an excellent overview of discussions of the female flaneuse; she argues, contrary to earlier claims that women had no place in the streets, that in fact the New Woman and real Victorian women were crucial figures in the organization of turn-of-the-century modern, urban life. She notes as examples the urban careers of many New Women

characters, women's clubs, women's appearances at museums, exhibitions, and department stores, and the emergence of cafes and tea shops for female customers (150–76).

46. I discuss the problem for the Victorian female detective of being criminalized by rather than in control of either public spaces or unsavory knowledge, in "Wilkie Collins, Detection, and Deformity," *Dickens Studies Annual* 26 (1998): 285–310.

47. For discussions of the ways in which feminine behavior was interpreted as madness in the nineteenth century, see Sandra Gilbert and Susan Gubar, *Madwoman in the Attic: The Woman Writer and the Nineteenth-Century Literary Imagination* (New Haven: Yale University Press, 1979); Elaine Showalter, *The Female Malady* (New York: Pantheon, 1985); and Janet Oppenheim, *"Shattered Nerves": Doctors, Patients, and Depression in Victorian England* (New York: Oxford University Press, 1991), esp. the chapters "Manly Nerves" and "Neurotic Women." This possibility is explored in fiction as well, for example, in Wilkie Collins's, *A Woman in White* (1860).

48. *Spectator,* 18 March 1893, 373.

49. Many studies of female Gothic attempt to account for the treatment of the heroine of Gothic romance and for women readers' responses to physical and/or psychological imprisonment in enclosures like the castle, the rural retreat, even the ancestral home. See Ellen Moers, *Literary Women* (Garden City, N.Y.: Doubleday, 1976); Gilbert and Gubar, *Madwoman in the Attic;* Tania Modleski, *Loving with a Vengeance: Mass-Produced Fantasies for Women* (New York: Methuen, 1982); Kate Ellis, *The Contested Castle: Gothic Novels and the Subversion of Domestic Ideology* (Urbana: University of Illinois Press, 1989); Eugenia DeLamotte, *Perils of the Night: A Feminist Study of Nineteenth-Century Gothic* (New York: Oxford University Press, 1990); Michelle A. Masse, *In the Name of Love: Women, Masochism, and the Gothic* (Ithaca: Cornell University Press, 1992); Alison Milbank, *Daughters of the House: Modes of the Gothic in Victorian Fiction* (New York: St. Martin's Press, 1992); Susan Wolstenholme, *Gothic (Re)Visions: Writing Women as Readers* (Albany: State University of New York, 1993); Jacqueline Howard, *Reading Gothic Fiction: A Bakhtinian Approach* (New York: Oxford University Press, 1994); and Anne Williams, *Art of Darkness: A Poetics of Gothic* (Chicago: University of Chicago Press, 1995). DeLaMotte and Williams offer helpful summaries of the history of feminist work on the position of the female character in Gothic fantasy. See esp. Williams's chapters on "The Female Plot of Gothic Fiction" and "The Male as 'Other.'"

50. Gillian Beer, *Darwin's Plots: Evolutionary Narrative in Darwin, George Eliot and Nineteenth-Century Fiction* (1983; reprint, London: Ark Paperbacks, 1985), suggests how thoroughly popularizations of Darwin infused Victorian literary culture, while Cynthia Eagle Russett investigates the impact of Darwinism on definitions of femininity in *Sexual Science: The Victorian Construction of Womanhood* (Cambridge: Harvard University Press, 1989).

Chapter 3

1. Anonymous, *Saturday Review,* 2 September 1888, 277.

2. "Sarah Grand and Mr. Ruskin," *Woman's Signal,* 25 January 1894, 57. The 8 March 1894 issue includes part of a serial, "Between the Lights," subtitled "In the

Rapids," by "Aurora," in which characters from many New Woman and anti–New Woman novels converse, including Ideala.

3. "Sarah Grand and Mr. Ruskin," 57.

4. These comments form part of Charles Whitby's introduction to the unpublished *Sarah Grand Miscellany* (for details, see chap. 2 n. 4). Grand describes this period again in her interview with Athol Forbes (883).

5. From a letter to Frederick Henry Fisher, dated 10 May 1898, in Special Collections at UCLA.

6. Carol Senf provides details of the sales in the introduction to *The Heavenly Twins* (1993 ed.).

7. According to Huddleston, the novel went through three more editions: Appleton published it in New York in 1893; Optimus of New York published it in 1894; and Donohue, Henneberry of Chicago published it in 1899. All future references will be to the Appleton edition and will appear in the text.

8. This letter of 9 April 1890 is held by Pennsylvania State University's Pattee Library.

9. Grand discusses the setting of the trilogy in a letter to Walter Powell, written 7 December 1923, and held by the Central Library of Birmingham.

10. *Saturday Review,* 2 September 1888, 277.

11. M. M. Bakhtin, *The Dialogic Imagination: Four Essays,* ed. Michael Holquist, trans. Caryl Emerson and Michael Holquist (Austin: University of Texas Press, 1981), 313–14. To see how feminist scholars have adapted the work of Bakhtin, see Dale M. Bauer and S. Jaret McKinstry, eds., *Feminism, Bakhtin, and the Dialogic* (Albany: State University of New York Press, 1991).

12. Bakhtin, *Dialogic Imagination,* 315.

13. Bakhtin, *Dialogic Imagination,* 326.

14. Rabine, *Reading the Romantic Heroine,* 18.

15. Boumelha, *Thomas Hardy and Women,* 66–67. For further discussion of women writers' direct address to readers, see Robin Warhol, *Gendered Interventions: Narrative Discourse in the Victorian Novel* (New Brunswick: Rutgers University Press 1989).

16. Rabine, *Reading the Romantic Heroine,* 19.

17. Susan Sniader Lanser, *Fictions of Authority* (Ithaca: Cornell University Press, 1992), 6. A key argument about New Woman fiction in Lyn Pykett's *Engendering Fictions* is that such disruptions and interruptions in New Woman writing suggest the modernist sensibility of these novels, contrary to the usual tendency to categorize them as Victorian (57).

18. Kranidis, *Subversive Discourse,* 53; quoting Alice Kahler-Marshall, *Pen Names of Women Writers from 1600 to the Present* (Camp Hill: n.p., 1985), xi.

19. This is the central thesis of Sylvia Strauss's historical study, *"Traitors to the Masculine Cause": The Men's Campaign for Women's Rights* (Westport, Conn.: Greenwood Press, 1982).

20. See Grand's interview with Sarah Tooley, "The Woman Question," *Humanitarian* 8 (March 1896): 162.

21. Grand discusses this point in the foreword to the 1923 edition of *The Heavenly Twins,* xi.

22. The problem of "speaking for" has become a crucial concern within feminist

circles in recent years, and the dynamics protested by this novel are very similar. In current debates the proclivity of white Western middle-class feminists, and even more particularly heterosexual women, to speak for groups of women who share only the characteristic of gender has been protested by lesbians, women of color, and women from developing nations. Thus, "benevolence" and "good intentions" become the bane of the person or collective spoken for and the obstacle rather than the avenue to collaboration and change. I'm fascinated that the argument repeatedly advanced in women's nineteenth-century fiction (the need for learning new strategies of reading) seems related to the insistence today that feminists privileged by race and class must learn alternative listening.

23. *Critic*, 21 October 1893, 255.

24. Elsie Michie, *Outside the Pale: Cultural Exclusion, Gender Difference, and the Victorian Woman Writer* (Ithaca: Cornell University Press, 1993), 92.

25. See esp. Joseph Boone, *Tradition Counter Tradition*; Boumelha, *Thomas Hardy and Women*; and Jane Eldridge Miller, *Rebel Women: Feminism, Modernism, and the Edwardian Novel* (London: Virago, 1994).

26. The nature of female desire and its inscription in fiction continues to inspire feminist critics' and theorists' speculation and analysis. In relation to New Woman fiction Boumelha's discussion of laws and theories governing sexual expression and self-definition is an important complement to more abstract (but less historically informed) theorizing.

27. See Anna Clark, "Humanity or Justice? Wifebeating and the Law in the Eighteenth and Nineteenth Centuries," in *Regulating Womanhood: Historical Essays on Marriage, Motherhood, and Sexuality,* ed. Carol Smart (New York: Routledge, 1992), 187–206; and Clark's *Women's Silence, Men's Violence: Sexual Assault in England, 1770–1845* (London and New York: Pandora Press, 1987).

28. Discussing George Egerton's short stories in *Keynotes*, Penny Boumelha provides an important insight into the relationship between motherhood and nineteenth-century definitions of womanhood. She argues that, despite New Women writers' protests against being treated unfairly on the basis of their sex, they eventually fell back on the same kind of biological essentialism, for example, by demanding rights on the basis of female moral superiority. Boumelha sees this contradiction most dramatically expressed in Egerton's recuperation of "desire into instinct," particularly maternal instinct: "The unresolved contradiction between 'instinct' and the transcendence of 'animalism' mars the spiritualising of the woman's sexuality through reproduction; motherhood is made not merely an anatomical potentiality to most women, but, to take up Egerton's own word, the 'keynote' of womanhood" (*Thomas Hardy and Women,* 89). Sally Ledger also discusses the New Woman's attachment to maternity in *New Women,* especially in her opening chapter, "Who Was the New Woman?"

Grand herself argued the limits of the woman's sphere in a letter in which she chastizes her more conservative friend Gladys Singers-Bigger for a lack of sympathy for the argument in Virginia Woolf's *A Room of One's Own:* "Will you be able to imagine, I wonder, what the one thing necessary was, which was denied her [Rachel Tindall, a mutual friend]. You have been singularly fortunate if you cannot—or, to me, singularly content with the lot that was mapped out for you—I mean too content ever to be aware of how some were being cramped and suffering by being forcibly kept in places in which they had no room to expand. I am all with you in regard to the Woman's Sphere, only I don't see it as contained in the walls of a house. The whole world is the Woman's Sphere. And, in my experience, the best home-makers are the women who know well the world outside of the customary and conventional limits." Her comments appear in a letter dated 26 January 1930. (This was one of many insensitive comments made to the adoring if conservative Singers-Bigger, who lived in straightened circumstances and later died in utter poverty.) The letter is held by the Bath Central Library and is also quoted by Kersley in *Darling Madame* (199).

29. Grand, "Does Marriage Hinder a Woman's Development: A Discussion," *Lady's Realm* 5 (March 1899): 576.

30. Elaine Baruch, "The Feminine *Bildungsroman:* Education through Marriage," *Massachusetts Review* 22 (1981): 344.

31. Baruch, "Feminine *Bildungsroman,"* 352.

32. Amanda Anderson demonstrates how flexible and encompassing the term *fallen* was throughout the century, showing that any attempt to discuss categories like "seduced," "fallen," or "prostitute" is deeply complicated by class prejudices (then and now) in *Tainted Souls and Painted Faces: The Rhetoric of Fallenness in Victorian Culture* (Ithaca: Cornell University Press, 1993). Also see Judith Walkowitz, *Prostitution and Victorian Society: Women, Class, and the State* (New York: Cambridge University Press, 1980) and *City of Dreadful Delight: Narratives of Sexual Danger in Late-Victorian London* (London: Virago, 1992); Ledger, *New Woman;* and Nord, *Walking the Victorian Streets,* for discussions of the class dynamics at work in characterizations of women's sexual life outside of marriage.

33. I came up with this list of terms by randomly sampling twenty 1890s articles describing femininity, womanliness, or ideal womanhood. These are the words that most often appear. For a far less cavalier analysis of constructions of femininity in the nineteenth century, see Armstrong, *Desire and Domestic Fiction;* and Judith Lowder Newton, *Women, Power, and Subversion: Social Strategies in British Fiction, 1778–1860* (Athens: University of Georgia Press, 1981). Both studies analyze the function (and revelations) of courtesy books and educational tracts designed for women. These texts present female "influence" as a viable form of power for women, an idea that first emerges in the late eighteenth century. Grand's own desire to cling to the feminine even as she asserted feminist arguments is evident in her frequent use of quotations from Ruskin.

34. See Eve Kosofsky Sedgwick, *Between Men: English Literature and Male Homosocial Desire* (New York: Columbia University Press, 1985), 1–17.

35. See Anderson, *Rhetoric of Fallenness.* Also see Carol Smart's anthology, *Regulating Womanhood: Historical Essays on Marriage, Motherhood, and Sexuality* (London and New York: Routledge, 1992).

36. Sedgwick's account of such triangulated relations in *Between Men* helps to account both for the two male lovers' obliviousness to Ideala's desires and their fascination with each other.

37. As Gail Cunningham points out in *The New Woman and the Victorian Novel,* "uncensored reading" was often considered the cause of the New Woman's discontent. In *Ideala* and *The Beth Book* female characters' readings of the men who control their lives become their most significant means of identifying the effects of patriarchy. I discuss the

role of the feminist reader and her relation to the reading of novels and other texts in the next two chapters. Judith Fetterley's study was one of the early explorations of the female reader: *The Resisting Reader: A Feminist Approach to American Fiction* (Bloomington: Indiana University Press, 1978).

38. "Sarah Grand and Mr. Ruskin," 57.

39. *Saturday Review,* 2 September 1888, 277.

40. Lyn Pykett, "The Cause of Women and the Course of Fiction: The Case of Mona Caird," in *Gender Roles and Sexuality in Victorian Literature,* ed. Christopher Parker (Aldershot: Scolar Press, 1995), 137; quoting from Mona Caird, "A Defence of the So-Called Wild Women," *Nineteenth Century* 31 (1892): 818.

41. See Bakhtin, *The Dialogic Imagination* for an extended discussion of the competing perspectives that disrupt the prevailing, hegemonic ideological thrust of a novel and the culture that produces it. Peter Garrett's *The Victorian Multiplot Novel: Studies in Dialogic Form* (New Haven: Yale University Press, 1980) demonstrates the usefulness of reading Victorian novels, in particular, through this critical lens.

42. Lovell's book *Consuming Fictions* is a significant contribution to the study of the economic and political forces driving the publishing industry and of the reading communities, in particular, women's reading communities and the writers who addressed them, as shaped by the ideological and financial constraints that determined literary culture (85; see also 83 and 107, on the address of literature to women).

43. Lovell, *Consuming Fictions,* 89.

44. Lovell, *Consuming Fictions,* 132.

45. Joseph Boone's groundbreaking work on the marriage plot began with two articles, "Wedlock as Deadlock and Beyond" and "Modernist Maneuverings in the Marriage Plot: Breaking Ideologies of Gender and Genre in James's *The Golden Bowl,*" *PMLA* 101 (1986), and culminated in his book, *Tradition Counter Tradition.*

46. Boone, "Wedlock as Deadlock," 376.

47. Rabine, *Reading the Romantic Heroine,* 17.

48. Susan Winnett, "Coming Unstrung: Women, Men, Narrative and Principles of Pleasure," *PMLA* 105 (May 1990): 507.

Chapter 4

1. This "poem" was reprinted from the *Westminister Gazette* (n.d.) in both *Critic,* 28 July 1894, 56; and in *Outlook* 50, 4 August 1894, 191.

2. "The Author of 'The Heavenly Twins,'" *Critic,* 2 December 1893, 361.

3. Grand tells this story without citing Meredith in the foreword to the 1923 edition of *The Heavenly Twins.* She identifies Meredith and quotes the report in a first-edition presentation copy she gave to her stepson, Chambers Haldane McFall. This book is now in the Lilly Library's Michael Sadlier Nineteenth-Century Fiction Collection at Indiana University. An ink inscription on the flyleaf of volume 1, in Sarah Grand's writing, reads: "To dear old Chambers. In grateful and affectionate acknowledgment of all I owe to his help and patience, and in memory of the long, long weary hours he devoted to reducing the amorphous mass of manuscript, and carving the story out of the redundant rubbish in which it was encrusted." It is dated "7th February 1893." On the back

flyleaf of volume 1 Grand neatly wrote out Meredith's comments that I include in the text, citing S. M. Ellis's *George Meredith: His Life and Friends in Relation to His Work* (London: Grant Richards, 1920), even noting the page number (247). She goes on:

> Meredith, as a reader for Chapman & Hall, rejected *The Heavenly Twins* for the above reason. He probably saw the book before it was revised, and it may have been revised on his advice, transmitted to me when the manuscript was returned, but I cannot remember. When I was staying at the Burford Bridge Hotel, Sept. 1896, writing The Beth Book, I asked him one day, as we walked together on Box Hill, why he rejected *The Twins*. He sighed deeply, at the same time drawling: "It was such a very long book, Sarah."

She concludes with her account of their friendship. After her initials, S. G., she dates this later entry 27 March 1919, Tunbridge Wells.

One other amusing detail: in a very small way she may have taken revenge. In her short story "Eugenia" the female ancestor of the title character has brought a curse on the family by marrying a cowardly nobleman, Lord Willoughby, perhaps a tongue-in-cheek reference to the pompous main character of Meredith's own novel, *The Egoist* (1879).

4. Elaine Hadley, *Melodramatic Tactics: Theatricalized Dissent in the English Marketplace, 1800–1885* (Stanford: Stanford University Press, 1995), 191.

5. See the 1923 foreword to *The Heavenly Twins*, xiii.

6. Grand described the reading in an unpublished letter to William Blackwood, dated 28 June 1892 and held by the National Library of Scotland: "Mrs. Manningberd suggested that I should invite a number of the Pioneer Club and read portions aloud. The first reading, with the outline I gave of the whole story, produced quite an extraordinary sensation, and I have been begged to repeat it to a much larger audience. All these people are unanimously of the opinion that the book will be an even greater success than *Ideala*. They strongly advise me to publish it." The minutes of the Pioneer Club were published in *Shafts* and regularly list Grand as a speaker at the club's Thursday night debates.

7. Margaret Shurmer Sibthorp, *Shafts,* 25 February 1893, 268.

8. This same letter identifies William Blackwood as the writer of the "thunderclap letter" quoted anonymously in the foreword. Her first reference to his criticism is her answering letter of 23 September 1891, also unpublished, held by the National Library of Scotland.

9. Foreword to *The Heavenly Twins* (1923 ed.), xiv.

10. Foreword, to *The Heavenly Twins* (1923 ed.), xiv.

11. Letter to William Blackwood, 23 September 1891, held by the National Library of Scotland.

12. Letter to William Blackwood, 23 September 1891.

13. John St. John, *William Heinemann: A Century of Publishing, 1890–1990* (London: Heinemann, 1990), 10.

14. St. John, *William Heinemann,* 10.

15. According to Huddleston, the novel went through seven British editions and two American editions; it was also translated into Dutch and German. The most recent

edition is the 1992 edition from the University of Michigan Press. All future references to *The Heavenly Twins* will be taken from the 1992 edition and cited in the text.

16. Twain read *The Heavenly Twins* soon after it was published. He praised the twins but berated Grand's syntax and plot improbabilities. He began his novel *Pudd'nhead Wilson and Those Extraordinary Twins* in 1892, the year before Grand's novel was published. Robert Rowlette discusses the connection between the two writers in "Mark Twain, Sarah Grand, and *The Heavenly Twins*," *Mark Twain Journal* 16 (1972): 17–18.

17. Hardy made this comment to Florence Henniker in a letter written 16 September 1893. The letter is reprinted in *One Rare Fair Woman: Thomas Hardy's Letters to Florence Henniker, 1893–1922*, ed. Evelyn Hardy and F. B. Pinion (London: Macmillan, 1972), 26. Grand met Meredith while she was staying in the Surrey Hills, where he had a house. She recalled their friendship in letters to various friends. The most accessible account is that of Gladys Singers-Bigger, who recalls Grand's memories of Meredith in a journal entry of March 1930: "She used to sit on the floor and talk to him and he would get her little bottles of Champagne which he could not share, and would say, 'Ah! Sarah! If only we had met 10 years ago!' meaning that then he would have been able to join her in the refreshment" (reprinted in Kersley, *Darling Madame,* 90).

18. See *Our Theatres in the Nineties* (London: Constable, 1932), 2:170.

19. Stanley Weintraub describes Grand's influence on Shaw and his play in "G. B. S. Borrows from Sarah Grand: *The Heavenly Twins* and *You Never Can Tell*," *Modern Drama* 14 (1971): 288–97. The article is a fascinating study of a literary relationship, but Weintraub's tone toward Grand and her work is dismissive. Shaw obviously did not share Weintraub's perspective. In a letter to literary critic Golding Bright, Shaw classifies Grand with Ibsen, Whistler, and Wagner as one who has "a touch of genius," in *Collected Letters, 1874–1897*, ed. Dan H. Laurence (London: Max Reinhardt, 1965), 461. Shaw also remembered the reception of *The Heavenly Twins* in a *Saturday Review* essay that is reprinted in volume 2 of *Our Theatres in the Nineties:* "We all remember the frantic fury of the men, their savage denunciations of Madame Sarah Grand, and the instant and huge success of her book. There was only one possible defense against it; and that was to deny boldly that there was anything unwholesome in the incontinences of men—nay, to appeal to the popular instinct in defense of the virility, the good-heartedness, and the loveable humanity of Tom Jones. Alas for male hypocrisy!" (qtd. in Weintraub, "G. B. S. Borrows from Sarah Grand," 290).

20. In the 1923 foreword Grand names many of her friends. She also writes that "a deaf ear was turned to pleas for reform made by women. The right of free speech was denied them. The newspapers boycotted reports of their meetings. The efforts men ventured to make on their behalf might be mentioned, but only to be ridiculed. It did not pay to bother about women's grievances; they had not votes" (xi). Also see L. A. M. Priestley McCracken, "Madame Sarah Grand and Women's Emancipation," *Vote,* 25 August 1933, n.p.

21. In *The Power of Lies: Transgression in Victorian Fiction* (Ithaca: Cornell University Press, 1994) John Kucich describes the novel as organized along two plot lines, that of the twins and another "structured around the opposition of two competing models of 'angelic' womanhood," the competing plots of Evadne and Angelica (248–49). Though I admire Kucich's study, my approach positions Edith's as a crucial third plot against which to read the other two plots.

22. See Flint, *The Woman Reader, 1837–1914;* and the section on New Woman fiction (305, 294–316). Also see Margaret Beetham, *A Magazine of Her Own,* esp. 115–30.

23. In *Rebellious Structures,* which includes the best structural study of *The Heavenly Twins* that I have read, Gerd Bjørhovde discusses the multiplicity and plurality of forms that frustrated reviewers because they could not easily classify what to all appearances possessed the most conventional fictional form, that of the three-volume novel. Calling *The Heavenly Twins* "a kind of three-volume Trojan horse" that "entered a conventional literary form and undermined it from within" (92), Bjørhovde surveys the forms with which Grand interrupts the conventional novel, including romance, prose comedy, the problem-novel, and "a psychological study of the effects of heredity, environment and repression on character." In addition, as she demonstrates, critics also found the style and tone of the novel difficult to pinpoint, for it slips "from satirical analysis of society to tremendous verbal wit and slapstick comedy; it is sentimental as well as scientifically objective, lyrical as well as analytical" (90). As Bjørhovde points out, Grand's contemporaries objected to what they saw as inconsistencies; a reviewer for the *Spectator* admired Grand's "intellectual and ethical interest" as well as her characters but faults the novel for being "hap-hazard," "an exaggeration," and too weighted with "her polemics" (*Spectator,* 25 March 1893, 395). Later, in 1925, Harold Williams complains that the "narrative wanders by devious ways, and the whole leaves upon the mind a sense of utter formlessness," in *Modern English Writers: Being a Study of Imaginative Literature, 1890–1914* (London: Sedgewick and Jackson, 1919), 91. Bjørhovde defends the "vacillation" that characterizes the form and narration of *The Heavenly Twins,* arguing that the repeated shifts in form and perspective successfully prevent readers' impulse to sympathize so deeply with characters that they miss the political commentary about the lives of female characters. She also suggests that the chime of the Morningquest cathedral, heard in the opening and at several points in the novel, may function like the chime of Big Ben in *Mrs. Dalloway* to create structural unity (95). Bjørhovde's study of the potential subversiveness of multiple generic forms in *The Heavenly Twins* is a helpful counterpart to my approach to the novel, for I find this same multiplicity at work in the Grand's splitting of the female bildungsroman into female *bildungsromane,* as a means of revising and invigorating the marriage plot with a female story and feminist politics.

24. This quotation appears in an unpublished letter to Frederick Henry Fisher. The letter is dated 22 March 1894 and is in the Special Collections at UCLA.

25. Penny Boumelha argues that in the New Woman novels melodrama acts to "punctuate" realism in order to emphasize the difficulties that follow when an unconventional heroine marries: "The melodrama is intensified by the desire to make representative the experiences of the female character, and the shift away from a single focal heroine to a number of female characters sometimes lends a note of extravagance to the marital abuses evoked" (*Thomas Hardy and Women,* 82). Her argument supports my claim that the writers used melodrama in part to dramatize connections of women from different classes.

26. Hadley, *Melodramatic Tactics,* 3, 183.

27. Peter Brooks, *The Melodramatic Imagination: Balzac, Henry James, Melodrama, and the Mode of Excess* (New Haven: Yale University Press, 1976), 11–12.

28. Martha Vicinus, "'Helpless and Unfriended': Nineteenth Century Domestic Melodrama," *New Literary History* 13 (1981): 128.

29. Vicinus, "'Helpless and Unfriended,'" 128, 137.

30. Vicinus, "'Helpless and Unfriended,'" 134.

31. E. Ann Kaplan, "Theories of Melodrama: A Feminist Perspective," *Women and Performance: A Journal of Feminist Theory* 1 (1983): 46.

32. Kaplan, "Theories of Melodrama," 47.

33. Hadley, *Melodramatic Tactics,* 3.

34. Clarke, "Feminism and the Popular Novel," 99.

35. Like many of her feminist contemporaries, Grand supported the social purity campaigns that captured the public's attention during the 1890s and thereafter. Sheila Jeffreys attributes the movement to two inimical sources: the activism to end the Contagious Diseases Acts and an evangelical reawakening. The movement drew its impetus from eugenics, demands for equality in the form of male chastity (rather than female sexual liberation), women's anger at the sexual abuse of children and at child prostitution, and temperance groups, among other seemingly incompatible influences. Jeffreys's book *Spinster and Her Enemies* is one of the first attempts to study the radical implications of a movement usually dismissed as naive and ultraconservative. While her study is provocative, the class politics and the intersections with eugenics are still hard to accept. Ledger discusses Grand's novel in relation to the social purity movement in *New Woman* (111–18). For further information about the social purity movement, see also Lucy Bland, *Banishing the Beast: English Feminism and Sexual Morality, 1885–1914* (Harmondsworth: Penguin, 1995); Joseph Bristow, *Vice and Vigilance: Purity Movements in Britain since 1700* (Dublin: Gill and Macmillan, 1977); and Jeffrey Weeks, *Sex, Politics, and Society: The Regulation of Sexuality since 1800* (New York: Longman, 1981).

36. See Elaine Showalter's 1986 essay "Syphilis, Sexuality, and the Fiction of the Fin de Siècle," in *Sex, Politics, and Science in the Nineteenth Century Novel,* ed. Ruth Yeazell (Baltimore: Johns Hopkins University Press, 1986), 95–108.

37. Showalter argues that when photographers chose the women in asylums to be photographed (in the interest of science), they tended to choose more attractive women and to encourage the women to assume poses that conformed to popular images of "fey" females—in particular Ophelia. Though these photographs were supposedly used for research, Showalter assumes a more general public awareness of them that translated into fictional portraits of madwomen and, even more strikingly, into actresses' interpretations of madness. See *Female Malady,* 13–17, 90–92.

38. In addition to Judith R. Walkowitz's two books that deal with prostitution, *Prostitution and Victorian Society* and *City of Dreadful Delight,* also see Lucy Bland, *Banishing the Beast;* Elsie Michie's two excellent chapters on literary representations of the prostitute in *Outside the Pale: Cultural Exclusion, Gender Difference, and the Victorian Woman Writer;* Amanda Anderson, *Tainted Souls and Painted Faces: The Rhetoric of Fallenness in Victorian Culture;* Lynda Nead, *Myths of Sexuality: Representations of Women in Victorian Britain* (Oxford: Basil Blackwell, 1988); and Paul McHugh, *Prostitution and Victorian Social Reform* (London: Croom Helm, 1980).

39. Showalter, "Syphilis, Sexuality and the Fiction of the Fin de Siècle," 95, 108.

40. In *The Power of Lies* John Kucich makes the important point that, while Grand sometimes shows sympathy for working and poor women, she does not hesitate to invoke xenophobic stereotypes against the Irish and the French (271). (In addition, in

several of her short stories she "orientalizes" a number of characters from countries in the Far East.)

41. Boumelha, *Thomas Hardy and Women*, 64.

42. Both Kersley and Carol Senf note Grand's childhood idealization of Butler.

43. Foreword, *The Heavenly Twins* (1923), xii. Grand's admiration for Josephine Butler dated back to her childhood. An interviewer for the *Bath Daily Chronicle* wrote that at fifteen she had "formed a club to perpetuate the principles of Josephine Butler, the social reformer. School authorities objected to her action, and 'representations' were made by the headmistress to the effect that another school would be more suitable for so bright a child." Gillian Kersley quotes from the article, dated 19 June 1928 (Kersley, *Darling Madame*, 28).

44. Hadley, *Melodramatic Tactics*, 185–214.

45. Janet Lyon, "Militant Discourse, Strange Bedfellows: Suffragettes and Vorticists before the War," *differences* 4, no. 2 (1992): 116.

46. Grand's fiction takes up the subject of "good women" and the dangers they posed to daughters, young women, and one another throughout her career. One of the most poignant yet trenchant characterizations of the good woman and her policing power is the short story "The Yellow Leaf," in *Our Manifold Nature*. Here the good women are introduced by the hoyden heroine, Adalesa Shutt, who vigorously warns a friend to avoid her aunt, Lady *Marsh:* "heaven help me from having to encounter a feather-bed woman!" (7). Grand's ongoing frustration with Mrs. Humphrey Ward provided frustrating personal evidence of the power of good women to suppress the voices of radical women writers. In both fiction and in her essays Grand argued against the elevation of ignorance to innocence, a view she believed to be circulated most widely by middle-class mothers and their surrogates. See, for example, her contribution to "The Tree of Knowledge" (a roundtable discussion) in the *New Review* (June 1894), in which she goes so far as to say: "I do not think parents are, as a rule, the best people to enlighten their children. At present they are not often properly educated themselves" (680). She also addresses the subject in "The New Woman and the Old," in the *Lady's Realm* 4 (1898): 466–70. In terms of politics she criticized the resistance of good women to women's suffrage, for example in "The New Woman and the Old"; in her interview with Sarah Tooley, "The Woman Question," and in the 1923 foreword *The Heavenly Twins,* to name but a few of many references. In later discussions with her friend Gladys Singers-Bigger she also complained about the women who fought against the vote and then immediately took advantage of it. Singers-Bigger notes the conversation in her journal.

47. Sarah Tooley, in "Some Women Novelists," *The Woman at Home,* (1896), explains how, according to Grand, she chose the name Evadne: "When Sarah Grand was writing the story she was at a loss for a name for one of her heroines, and asked Mr. Arthur Clementi Smith, then a schoolboy, the son of a friend of hers, if he would find a name out of the common. Schoolboy-like, he went to his Greek classics, and wrote out from them a list of nice-sounding names. From among these Sarah Grand selected Evadne, "well-pleasing one" (177). Grand recalls this story in the 1923 foreword to the novel.

48. See Lati Mani, "Contentious Traditions: The Debate on *Sati* in Colonial India,"

in *The Nature and Context of Minority Discourse,* ed. Abdul R. JanMohamed and David Lloyd (New York: Oxford University Press, 1990), 319–56, on British responses to sati.

49. Linda Petersen, *The Determined Reader: Gender and Culture in the Novel from Napoleon to Victoria* (New Brunswock: Rutgers University Press, 1986), 28.

50. Petersen, *Determined Reader,* 29.

51. Petersen, *Determined Reader,* 28.

52. See Kucich, *The Power of Lies,* chap. 6.

53. Jerome H. Buckley's study *Season of Youth: The Bildungsroman from Dickens to Golding* (Cambridge: Harvard University Press, 1974) outlines the phases of the male bildungsroman. Because most scholars interested in the bildungsroman form begin with Buckley's analyses of male development, female *bildungsromane* have suffered the dismissal and/or misinterpretation that often follows when critics assume male plots and male experience are "universal."

54. Flint, *The Woman Reader, 1837–1914,* 253–55. The paintings are reproduced on 254.

55. Annette Kolodny's article "A Map for Misreading: or, Gender and the Interpretation of Literary Texts," *New Literary History* 11 (1980): 451–67, suggests reading strategies for women similar to Evadne's approach to male texts. Evadne also shares characteristics with the female reader Fetterley characterizes in *Resisting Reader.* As Patricino Schweickart warns women readers in "Reading Ourselves," in *Gender and Reading: Essays on Readers, Texts, and Contexts,* ed. Elizabeth Flynn and Patricino Schweickart (Baltimore: Johns Hopkins University Press, 1986), the appearance of universality often blinds readers, particularly women, to misogynist subtexts or false generalizations about "human" experience that are not true to female experience. The essays in Schweickart and Flynn's anthology *Gender and Reading* provide a helpful historical and sociological context for the study of women's reading experiences.

56. Jane Miller, *Women Writing about Men* (New York: Pantheon Books, 1986), 11.

57. In *The Beth Book* these solitary rooms become almost a motif. As a young girl, Beth converts an attic room into a mock classroom, an adventurer's den, and a young poet's hideaway. After she marries Beth discovers a room so improbable that Elaine Showalter calls it "a housewife's daydream," in *A Literature of Their Own* (209). At the top of her house, behind a curtain, and through a low crawl space, Beth finds a beautifully decorated sitting room complete with a fireplace and a window that overlooks the garden but is hidden by ivy. She constructs her own separate home here, decorating the room with mementos of her childhood, and, even though she disappears for hours at a time while she sews, reads, and writes in her secret nook, no one ever suspects the existence of the room. Kate Flint notes that at least one periodical writer advised that all older girls should have their own room. See "What Shall We Read?" *Young Woman* 1 (1892): 26; quoted in Flint, *The Woman Reader, 1837–1914,* 104–5.

58. Nearly all feminist studies of the female *bildungsromane* emphasize the impasse to female development when the female character marries or deliberately resists acting on the knowledge she has gained as part of her experience; two of the earliest feminist critics to make this point were Bonnie Hoover Braedlin, "Alther, Atwood, Ballantyne, and Gray: Secular Salvation in the Contemporary Feminist *Bildungsroman,*" *Frontiers* 4 (1979): 18–22; and Annis Pratt, *Archetypal Patterns in Women's Fiction* (Brighton: Harvester Press, 1982). More recently, Rachel Blau DuPlessis, in *Writing beyond the Ending: Narrative*

Strategies of Twentieth-Century Women Writers (Bloomington: Indiana University Press, 1985), has argued that the most striking difference between nineteenth- and twentieth-century women writers is that recently writers like Doris Lessing are finding alternative relationships—for instance, triangles rather than dyads—that overcome this limitation (91).

59. Kucich, "Curious Dualities: *The Heavenly Twins* (1893) and Sarah Grand's Belated Modernist Aesthetics," *The New Nineteenth Century: Feminist Readings of Underread Victorian Fiction* (New York: Garland, 1996), 195–204.

60. Joanna Russ, *How To Suppress Women's Writing*, 25.

61. Russ, *How To Suppress Women's Writing*, 40.

62. For details about the "Battleton Rectory" parody, see chap. 2 n. 9. Grand describes her unhappiness in several letters and most fully in notes she made to the projected publication of *The Sarah Grand Miscellany*. Though the book was not published, the manuscript with her notes is held by the Bath Central Library.

63. In *Women of the Regiment: Marriage and the Victorian Army* (New York: Cambridge University Press, 1984) Mina Trustram describes the lives of a variety of "military women" from wives to prostitutes. Her book challenges general conceptions of the culture of the military as primarily male.

64. William Barry published "The Strike of a Sex," in *Quarterly Review* 179 (1894): 299, anonymously.

65. [Barry], "Strike of a Sex," 300–301.

66. [Barry], "Strike of a Sex," 302.

67. See especially unpublished letters to Frederick Henry Fisher dated 11 November 1894 and 23 November 1894. The letters are in the Special Collections of the UCLA Library. This quotation appears in the 23 November letter.

68. Showalter, *A Literature of Their Own*, 207.

69. Clarke, "Feminism and the Popular Novel," 98.

70. See Janet Oppenheim's, *"Shattered Nerves."*

71. In order to prove that Evadne is capable of sexual response and that the tension between her desires and her principles wears upon her as well as upon her husband, Grand includes several incidents that suggest there is a sexual side to Evadne's character. As the Colonel and his friends hang decorations for a party, Evadne is struck by how handsome her husband looks in his short-sleeved shirt, and after a brief flutter of attraction she regrets all the more that his past makes a physical relationship impossible for her. Grand may have been following current medical theory: as Janet Oppenheim points out, one of the most influential psychologists of the day, John Conolly, argued that "'the mortifications of celibacy'" could cause hysterical symptoms (qtd. in Oppenheim, *"Shattered Nerves,"* 203).

72. Lucy Bland discusses one group that did support free love, the Legitimation League, which was established in 1893. The league published the journal *Adult*. She also discusses responses to free love among feminists and from different classes of women. See *Banishing the Beast*, 156–61.

73. In *The Modern Man and Maid* (London: Horace Marshall, 1898; and New York: Crowell, 1898) Grand laments about men: "They do not understand that it [marriage] is an institution for the perfecting of life. To them it is but a superior kind of prostitution, and they marry for the most frivolous of all reasons, because they are in love—that is to

say, are suffering from a temporary illusion of the senses." She also protests men's perspective that is a "private affair which concerns them alone" rather than an institution that has "its effect for good upon the organization of the community at large" (62–63). Surely, these same claims could be made about women's views of marriage, since romance depends so heavily on the fantasy that a private life in a private sphere could exist. Her argument for marriage as a community-based institution underlies her ultimate vision of reform—that is, that marriage should be a legal institution guaranteed to protect women's rights and interests. Grand's interview with Sarah Tooley in the *Humanitarian* (1896) also elaborates her criticisms of marriage practices and argues for marital reform rather than free love outside marriage or other alternatives.

74. The topic of hysteria crops up throughout Galbraith's section. Early in chapter 4 Dr. Galbraith describes a woman who suffered from hysteria to his dinner guests; the tale produces one of the first sparks of interest he sees in Evadne (who is numb with the misery of her own marriage at this point). Later, Galbraith learns the details of Evadne's marriage from an acquaintance and confides his horror at her mental suffering to the reader, suggesting that hysteria could result. He also discusses another young woman's case of hysteria with Evadne, describing the "transference" stage and recalling that the woman used symptoms of illness to engage his attention. The subject clearly fascinates Evadne, at least until she finds her own defense in no longer listening to stories of human suffering of any kind. This quotation appears in Bjørhovde, *Rebellious Structures*, 115–25.

75. Kucich interprets Evadne's actions as wearing a series of social "masks" that both allow her to survive and prevent her from overcoming her circumstances; he ties her masks to his larger argument about feminist writers' inability to reconcile their desire for social truth with their fears of fictional pretense. See *Power of Lies* (256–57), and his article "Curious Dualities."

76. This is the subject of a chapter in Barbara Ehrenreich and Deidre English's study, *Complaints and Disorders: The Sexual Politics of Sickness* (Old Westbury, N.Y.: The Feminist Press, 1973). See also Lorna Duffin's essay "The Conspicuous Consumptive: Woman as an Invalid," in *The Nineteenth Century Woman: Her Cultural and Physical World,* ed. Sarah Delamont and Lorna Duffin (London: Croom Helm, 1978), 26–56. She emphasizes the role of doctors in shaping middle-class women's attitudes toward illness, noting that "women were ill because they were women" or "women became ill if they tried to do anything outside the female role clearly defined for them" (31). Ultimately, both of these studies show how illness becomes a confirmation of a woman's womanliness; in other words, women were defined as inherently ill due to their biological and social natures.

77. Though Evadne uses needlework to numb her intellect, sewing functions quite differently in *The Beth Book,* for in the later novel this activity binds Beth to other women. She learns to sew from her beloved Aunt Victoria Bench, and she tries to repay the money her husband more or less steals from her mother by selling embroidery on commission. Still later, in Adnam's Orchard and *A Winged Victory,* Ella, the female protagonist, revives an ancient lace-making technique. Her needlework provides her with an excellent income, but she is also depicted as an accomplished artist rather than as a domestic worker or even an artisan.

78. Pykett, *The "Improper" Feminine,* 174.

79. Bjørhovde, *Rebellious Structures,* 120.

80. Kucich, "Curious Dualities," 195.

81. Bjørhovde, *Rebellious Structures,* 120.

82. Susan Kingsley Kent, *Sex and Suffrage in Britain, 1860–1914* (Princeton: Princeton University Press, 1987), 119.

83. In addition to Janet Oppenheim, see Flint's chapter in *The Woman Reader, 1837–1914,* "Medical, Physiological and Psychoanalytic Theory"; Delamont and Duffin, *Nineteenth Century Woman;* Bland, *Banishing the Beast;* Carol Dyhouse, *Girls Growing up in Late Victorian and Edwardian England* (London: Blackwell, 1989); Thomas Laqueur, *Making Sex: Body and Gender from the Greeks to Freud* (Cambridge: Harvard University Press, 1990); Frank Mort, *Dangerous Sexualities: Medico-Moral Politics in England since 1830* (London: Routledge and Kegan Paul, 1987); Ornella Moscucci, *The Science of Woman: Gynaecology and Gender in England, 1800–1929* (Cambridge: Cambridge University Press, 1990); and Cynthia Eagle Russett *Sexual Science.*

84. Grand mentions her desire to write such an article to her literary agent, William Morris Colles, in an unpublished letter of 4 October 1894. The letter is now held in the Harry Ransom Collection of the University of Texas at Austin.

85. See Lyon, "Militant Discourse, Strange Bedfellows," 118.

86. Grand denied that she was indebted to Ibsen. As I note in an earlier chapter, in an unpublished letter of 22 March 1894 to Frederick Henry Fisher she says Fisher has guessed right that Ibsen is not a great influence: "I had not read a line of Ibsen that I know of when I wrote *The Heavenly Twins,* and I have not even yet read *Ghosts.* Ibsen, in fact, was a name of no significance to me until I saw myself mentioned as a follower of his. All my little knowledge of the social questions I feel so strongly about I have collected from observation and medical books."

87. See Ehrenreich and English, *Complaints and Disorders,* esp. the chapter entitled "The Cult of Invalidism."

88. Bjørhovde, *Rebellious Structures,* 119.

89. Kucich, *Power of Lies,* 256.

90. See Carroll Smith-Rosenberg's essay, "The Hysterical Woman: Sex Roles and Role Conflict in Nineteenth-Century America," *Social Research* 39 (1972): 678.

91. Wendy Langford, "'Snuglet Puglet Loves to Snuggle with Snuglet Puglet': Alternative Personalities in Heterosexual Love Relationships," in *Romance Revisited,* ed. Lynne Pearce and Jackie Stacey (New York: New York University Press, 1995), 259.

92. Bjørhovde, *Rebellious Structures,* 116.

93. Lyn Pykett develops a comparison between the strategies and reception of the 1860s sensation fiction and the 1890s New Woman literature in *The "Improper" Feminine.*

94. Grand offers a detailed reception history of the novel in the 1923 foreword.

95. This review appears in *Athenaeum,* 18 March 1893, 342.

96. [William Barry], "The Strike of a Sex," *Quarterly Review* 179 (1894): 294.

97. *Punch* 106 (24 February 1894): 93.

98. Frederick Whyte, *William Heinemann: A Memoir* (Garland: Garden City, N.Y.: Doubleday, 1929), 105–6.

99. Kersley, *Darling Madame,* 91. The untitled, undated newspaper clipping recounting this story is held by the Bath Central Library.

100. T. E. Donnison, "Famous Book Covers as They Might Have Been," *Idler* 14 (1899): 703.

101. Amy Cruse, *After the Victorians* (London: Allen and Unwin, 1938), 130.

102. See Carolyn Heilbrun, *Toward a Recognition of Androgyny* (New York: Alfred A. Knopf, 1973), 34–35.

103. See Charlotte Goodman, "The Lost Brother, the Twin: Women Novelists and the Male-Female *Bildungsroman*," *Novel* 17 (1983): 30–31, 42.

104. The "performative" has now attained the status of its own area of theory. Butler's *Gender Trouble* is generally considered the first book, however, to circulate widely the argument that gender could be a culturally learned set of behaviors that could then be performed, as opposed to being biologically inherent.

105. In the short story "The Yellow Leaf," in *Our Manifold Nature* (London: Heinemann, 1894), clothes are also treated as the beginning of the end of pleasure and freedom for a young woman. When her conventional aunt protests her short skirts, Adalesa protests, "Long dresses! . . . no thank you! I know what is expected of long dresses" (11).

106. Clarke, "Feminism and the Popular Novel," 100.

107. Clarke, "Feminism and the Popular Novel," 100.

108. Bjørhovde, *Rebellious Structures,* 103.

109. See Kucich, *Power of Lies,* 263; and Linda Dowling, "The Decadent and the New Woman in the 1890's," *Nineteenth-Century Fiction* 33 (1979): 450.

110. The Bath Central Library owns a copy of the 1899 edition. As part of Heinemann's Popular Novels series, it sold for one shilling and sixpence. In *Notable Women Authors of the Day* (London: Maclaren and Co., 1906) Helen Black recalls reading "a volume entitled 'The Tenor and the Boy,' which had originally formed part of the famous 'Heavenly Twins,' but was just published as a separate work by itself" (318).

111. Gladys Singers-Bigger's journal discusses the play in an entry dated 8 August 1931. In the same entry she says that Grand claimed "some Americans" had also created a play from *Babs the Impossible,* but, when the authors submitted it for Grand's approval, "they had so vulgarised it that she would not consent to its production. Later she heard that they had produced it under another name and had made a million dollars with it." In a letter dated 15 September 1924 and addressed to Mr. Pinker, a literary agent, Grand discusses her disagreement with Heinemann over who owned the film rights to *The Heavenly Twins.* Annoyed with Heinemann, she was considering asking the Society of Authors to take up her claim to the performance and film rights in court, but she didn't carry through. The letter is housed in the Berg Collection of the New York Public Library (and I thank Anne Stapleton, who tracked it down for me).

112. Though Laura Mulvey herself has raised questions about the cross-gendered process of interpolation that she traces first in an essay and then the book *Visual and Other Pleasures* (Bloomington: Indiana University Press, 1989), the model still richly complicates our understanding of why women seem to cooperate in constituting themselves as objects.

113. I have already noted Hugh Stutfield's attack on Grand's men. In "Strike of a Sex," *Quarterly Review* 179 (1894): 833–45, Barry discusses six of her male characters, briefly indicting the characterization of each. (He also calls Grand a woman dressed up in a beard.) Many recent critics, including Showalter, Cunningham, and Clarke, also find her men flat and unconvincing. Grand clearly felt puzzled (as well as annoyed) that readers found her male characters unbelievable or even hostile projections. In an unpublished letter of 16 May 1895 to Frederick Fisher she protests a review in *Great Thoughts*

that calls her male characters "monsters," and years later, in a letter to Fisher dated 1 January 1907, she again bemoans a "Personal Sketch" Fisher has sent, asking: "But why, I wonder, do you accuse me of bitterness against the male sex . . . nobody gets along better with men than I do—as well with men as with women." These letters are held by Special Collections of UCLA.

114. For information on Barry, see Isobel Rae, *The Strange Life of Dr. James Barry* (London: Longmans, Green, 1958); Jessica Grove and Olga Racster, *Dr. James Barry—Her Secret Story* (London: G. Howe, 1932); June Rose, *The Perfect Gentleman* (London: Hutchinson, 1977). Marjorie Garber discusses Barry in *Vested Interests*, pointing out that Mark Twain wrote a "postscript" to his travel book *Following the Equator* (1897) about Barry and that an "E. Rogers, Lieutenant Colonel" wrote a novel about Barry called *The Modern Sphinx* (1881). See Garber, *Vested Interests*, 288–89, 204. For a more general historical study of cross-dressing, see Vern L. Bullough and Bonnie Bullough, *Cross Dressing, Sex, and Gender* (Philadelphia: University of Pennsylvania Press, 1993).

115. Tooley, "Woman's Question," 168.

116. This unsigned newspaper article, dated 3 May 1901, is held at the Bath Central Library and is also reprinted in Kersley, *Darling Madame*, 49.

117. Bailey T. Saunders, "Sarah Grand's Ethics," *Open Court: A Weekly Journal Devoted to the Religion of Science*, 4 April 1895, 4449.

118. Frederick Bird, "A Three-Volume Tract," *Lippincott's Monthly Magazine* 52 (July–December 1893): 638.

119. Walter Besant, review of *Babs the Impossible*, *Academy*, 20 April 1901, 347–48.

120. Margaret Sibthorp, review of *The Heavenly Twins*, *Shafts*, 25 February 1893, 268.

Chapter 5

1. The letter to Frederick Henry Fisher, dated 4 December 1897, is held at the Special Collections of UCLA's library.

2. In Gladys Singers-Bigger's journal entry of 27 August 1933 she comments that Grand said "she had put nothing but what was historical in that book as she wanted to make it sound sincere." Grand was probably referring as much to details of daily life as to her personal life. This passage is reprinted in Kersley, *Darling Madame*, 250.

3. See Ann Ardis, " 'Retreat with Honour': Mary Cholmondeley's Presentation of the New Woman Artist in *Red Pottage*," in *Writing the Woman Artist: Essays on Poetics, Politics, and Portraiture*, ed. Suzanne W. Jones (Philadelphia: University of Pennsylvania Press, 1991), 333–50; and her discussion of *Red Pottage* in *New Women, New Novels*, 128–33.

4. Arthur Waugh, "Reticence in Literature," *Yellow Book* 1 (1894): 210.

5. In *Engendering Fictions* Pykett argues that these same criteria "stated or implied a preference for what was to become the dominant high modernist aesthetic" (64).

6. Grace Stewart, *A New Mythos: The Novel of the Artist as Heroine, 1877–1977* (St. Albans: Eden Press Women's Publications, 1979), 12.

7. Grand was writing *The Beth Book* at the same time that the conception of "adolescence," as we now know it, was being being established as a separate life stage, following the increasing attention to childhood as a distinct stage through the nineteenth

century. Psychologist Granville Stanley Hall's book *Adolescence: Its Psychology and Its Relations to Physiology, Anthropology, Society, Sex, Crime, Religion, and Education,* which crystallized the definition of this life phase, was published in 1904 and based on his work with children in the 1880s and 1890s. In *The Woman Reader* Flint notes that women's autobiographies, in particular, tend to focus on childhood, as did their autobiographical fiction. She uses a term from Richard Coe's *When the Grass Was Taller: Autobiography and the Experience of Childhood* (New York: Yale University Press, 1984) to describe this form: *Jugenderinnerungen* (190).

8. Recent studies of the Decadents and/or Aesthetes have richly complicated attempts to define or name members of the group and have offered challenging alternative readings of the cultural work performed by writers and artists such as Wilde, Beardsley, Whistler, Symonds, Dowson, and others. The parodic stereotype of the Aesthete that Grand deploys for her particular purposes is a far cry from the fascinating, multifaceted, challenging version of the Aesthetes examined in such works as Richard Dellamora, *Masculine Desire: The Sexual Politics of Victorian Aestheticism* (Chapel Hill: University of North Carolina Press, 1990); James Eli Adams, *Dandies and Desert Saints: Styles of Victorian Masculinity* (Ithaca: Cornell University Press, 1995); Elaine Showalter, *Sexual Anarchy;* and Regenia Gagnier, *Idylls of the Marketplace: Oscar Wilde and the Victorian Public* (Stanford: Stanford University Press, 1986), to name but a few recent studies. Interestingly, although *The Beth Book* poses the Decadent as a particular character, the novel uses the word *Stylists* as a category to name those characters, thereby treating such characters as well as their writing as a linguistic and aesthetic effect. Two recent studies share this view: Linda Dowling, *Language and Decadence in the Victorian Fin de Siècle* (Princeton: Princeton University Press, 1986); and John Reed, *Decadent Style* (Athens: Ohio University Press, 1985).

9. Studies of the female artist include the collection of articles edited by Suzanne W. Jones, *Writing the Woman Artist: Essays on Poetics, Politics, and Portraiture;* Susan Gubar "The Birth of the Artist as Heroine: (Re)production, the *Kunstlerroman* Tradition, and the Fiction of Katherine Mansfield," in *The Representation of Women in Fiction,* ed. Carolyn G. Heilbrun and Margaret R. Higgonet (Baltimore: Johns Hopkins University Press, 1983); Josephine Donovan, "Toward a Women's Poetics," in *Feminist Issues in Literary Scholarship,* ed. Shari Benstock (Bloomington: Indiana University Press, 1987); and Rita Felski, *Beyond Feminist Aesthetics: Feminist Literature and Social Change* (Cambridge: Harvard University Press, 1989).

10. See Jane Marcus, "Still Practice, A/Wrested Alphabet: Toward a Feminist Aesthetics," *Art and Anger: Reading like a Woman* (Athens: Ohio University Press, 1988), 222.

11. DuPlessis, *Writing beyond the Ending,* 103.

12. Though differently, Ardis in *New Women, New Novels;* Pykett in *The "Improper" Feminine;* Kranidis, *Subversive Discourse;* and Ledger in *New Woman* discuss the phenomenon in New Woman fiction of wrestling with conventions of the novel, in light of the late-Victorian debates over realism and naturalism. For the purposes of this study I am focussing chiefly on the particular boundaries and conventions delimited by the marriage plot because, as a plot, marriage offers such a strong example of the power of multiple discourses and material practices to coalesce as fictional probabilities in this period.

13. This is from an undated letter to William Heinemann, which he stamped as hav-

ing been received on 17 August 1896. This letter is now in the Mortimer Rare Book Room of Smith College.

14. DuPlessis says that the "woman of genius" was a figure created by bourgeois women as a compromise between "conventional notions of womanhood" and "conventional romantic notions of the genius":

> Genius theory is a particular exaggeration of bourgeois individualism, and its evocation increases the tension between middle-class women as a special group and the dominant assumptions of their class. Because it is precisely expression and the desire to refuse silence that are at issue in artistic creation, the contradiction between dominant and muted areas can also be played out in the motif of the imbedded artwork, another narrative marker of these *Kunstlerromane*. (85)

She offers *The Beth Book* as an example of a work in which the woman of genius "observe[s] the pieties" by choosing love over art (87). Though Terry Lovell agrees that the "woman-as-genius" is the creation of middle-class women writers, she argues that female genius figures are distinguished by their "masculine" features. To avoid encouraging readers to label these female characters as working-class, writers portrayed the characters as *intellectually* equal rather than depicting them working in jobs that men might have (*Consuming Fictions*, 122–23).

15. Christine Battersby provides an overiew of genius theory and its changes over time, demonstrating the ways in which the definitions specifically exclude the possibility that women could possess genius in *Gender and Genius: Towards a Feminist Aesthetic* (London: Women's Press, 1989).

16. *Oxford English Dictionary*, 2d ed., 44–45.

17. Neetens, *Writing and Democracy: Literature, Politics and Culture in Transition* (New York: Harvester Wheatsheaf, 1991), 110.

18. All future references to *The Beth Book* will refer to the Virago edition and will be cited in the text. This extract is from p. 233 of that edition.

19. This review appears in *Athenaeum*, 18 March 1893, 743.

20. Neetens traces Grand's notions of genius to "Rousseau, the English Romantics and the American Transcendentalists" (as I do), describing it as "conceived as a presocial, religiously tinted 'further faculty', associated with nature, spontaneity and ecstasy, which seeks an outlet in artistic expression" (*Writing and Democracy*, 110). Battersby would warn that attempting to emulate the aesthetics of male Romantic writers would lead Grand to a dead end. After discussing the ways in which theories of Romanticism attach the "feminine" to the male artists and then dispense with females, she further argues that, unlike the male artist or genius figure, women artists often express the need for community as opposed to solitude as a condition for work: "A lot of the metaphoric language of collectivity and the denial of creation as a solitary act that we find in texts and works by women artists is an expression of their need to find a group to which they feel they can belong. There are alternative traditions of women's art that, picked out, would promote a better understanding and appreciation of female creativity. But Romanticism does not bring these continuities into focus" (46).

21. Grand was clearly taken with this quotation (whether because of the emphasis on childhood or the threat of Jesuit education). She repeats this same phrase in *Adnam's Orchard* years later.

22. This complaint from a 13 November 1897 issue of the *Spectator* (691) is echoed by a reviewer for the *Bookman* (December 1897), who grumbles that *The Beth Book* was "a lengthy, wearisome, awkward book" (106), and later in 1936 by Robert Palfrey Utter and Gwendolyn Bridges Needham, *Pamela's Daughters* (New York: Macmillan, 1936), who claim that Grand "delivers a tirade which increases in vehemence and diffuseness till the reader feels sure the condition is pathological androphobia" (431). Penny Brown praises Grand's insights into a child's psychology in *The Captured World: The Child and Childhood in Nineteenth-Century Women's Writing in England* (New York: St. Martin's Press, 1993), 170–80.

23. *Spectator*, 13 November 1897, 691–92.

24. *Academy*, 10 April 1901, 393.

25. *Woman's Signal*, 2 December 1897, 354–55.

26. Susan Casteras, "Excluding Women: The Cult of the Male Genius in Victorian Painting," in *Rewriting the Victorians: Theory, History, and the Politics of Gender,* ed. Linda Shires (New York: Routledge, 1992), 129.

27. Pykett, *The "Improper" Feminine*, 6.

28. Several other significant feminist studies of women's writing have, like Pykett's work, characterized detail as both a stylistic and thematic form of resistance to dominant literary forms. In addition to Naomi Schor's seminal study *Reading in Detail: Aesthetics and the Feminine* (New York: Methuen, 1987), see Karen Ford's *Gender and the Poetics of Excess: Moments of Brocade* (Hattiesburg: University Press of Mississippi, 1997). Ford argues that, in the works of Emily Dickinson, Sylvia Plath, and other women poets, we see women writers protesting the values of patriarchal critics with excessive, exaggerated uses of language, rather than with strategies of "subversion." Her work suggested to me that Grand's detailed description of Beth's development may have a similar function, especially since her earlier work had so often been attacked.

29. Pykett, *The "Improper" Feminine*, 27.

30. Pykett offers an intriguing image of the child Beth's "subjectivity" as "partly that of the Wordsworthian infant, trailing clouds of glory, and partly a late-nineteenth-century version of the Kristevan semiotic—that domain of instinctual, psychosexual drives that, according to Kristeva, precedes language and is repressed as the child enters the realm of the symbolic and of social communication" (178). *The "Improper" Feminine* considers Beth's transformation, registered in a series of Beth's womblike fantasies of another world, in light of Kristeva's semiotic as a movement form "a pre-conscious, pre-linguistic race-memory to a mysterious ancestry and a world of dream and the irrational" from which she is separated by the acquisition of language (179). This particular theoretical perspective on Beth's memories of the prelinguistic order offers a persuading way of describing and valorizing her status as genius or artist. Rather than a Wordsworthian lapse into the oblivion and care of adulthood, however, I read Beth's career changes as a progression toward an increasingly social and politicized aesthetic that her visionary powers permit her not only to understand but to articulate. To become a social activist Beth must reject the interiority the novel ascribes both to femininity and to a romantic version of the artist.

31. Penny Brown, *The Captured World*, 173.

32. Lovell, *Consuming Fictions*, 122–23, 127–28.

33. See Adrienne Rich, *Of Woman Born: Motherhood as Experience and Institution* (New York: Norton, 1976), 236.

34. Carroll Smith-Rosenberg discusses the powerful, comfortable bonds between nineteenth-century American mothers and daughters who have the same goals—marriage, family, and continued closeness within an extended family—in *Disorderly Conduct* (see esp. 30–35).

35. See Rich, *Of Woman Born*, 24.

36. Rich, *Of Woman Born*, 246. From her earliest novels Grand puzzles over the ways in which women force other women to suppress their unconventional desires and, instead, to conform to social expectations. In this novel, for example, Ideala angrily chastises a roomful of women who treat Beth coldly because of their objection to her husband's career: "How you treat each other, you women! And you are as wanting in discernment, too, as you are in kindness and sympathy. She has had to put on that mask of coldness to hide what you make her suffer, and it will take long loving to melt it now, and make her look human again" (390).

37. B[lanche] A[lthea] Crankanthorpe, "The Revolt of the Daughters (No. 1): A Last Word on 'The Revolt,'" *Nineteenth Century* 35 (1894): 427; quoted and discussed in Flint, *The Woman Reader, 1837–1914*, 84.

38. Flint, *The Woman Reader*; Pykett, *The "Improper" Feminine;* and (focusing on the 1860s) Jenny Bourne Taylor, *In the Secret Theatre of Home: Wilkie Collins, Sensation Narrative, and Nineteenth-Century Psychology* (London: Routledge, 1988), all discuss the imagined danger of "inappropriate" reading material to girls and women readers as that danger is expressed in novels, advice books, periodical essays, and medical and psychological literature.

39. Kucich, *Power of Lies*, 271.

40. This is Pykett's key thesis in *The "Improper" Feminine*.

41. Grand offers insights into the contradictory relationships between mistresses and servants in her characterization of Mrs. Caldwell's and Harriet's occasional alliances. Partly because she is lonely, Mrs. Caldwell frequently consults Harriet about dreams, signs, and portents. The narrator offers an ironic explanation: "Superstition is a subject on which the most class-proud will consult with the lowest and the wickedest; it is a mighty leveler downwards" (124). But the two women also discuss the details of their days and the small world in which they live: "Little things naturally become of great importance in such a life, and Harriet kept up the supply; she being the connecting link between Mrs. Caldwell and the outer world" (125).

42. In his analysis of the New Woman's difficulty in negotiating between political "truth" and the imaginative inventions (or lies) of the artist, John Kucich suggests that genius may be a stage Beth has to pass through; her "progress involves a gradual renunciation of the 'servant's tricks' of her childhood," adding that servants are shown to be far more comfortable with tales of horror. See *Power of Lies*, 264–65.

43. Vineta Colby offers a stark portrayal of the lives of elderly spinsters in her study, *The Singular Anomaly: Women Novelists of the Nineteenth Century* (New York: New York University Press, 1970). For a far more encouraging picture of single women, see Vicinus, *Independent Women*. Dorothy Yost Deegan, in *The Stereotype of the Single Woman in the American Novel: A Social Study with Implications for the Education of Women* (New York:

Octagon Books, 1969), examines representations of older women in America during the same period.

44. In the *Spectator* (13 November 1897) the reviewer denounces Grand's "detailed recital of the squalid sufferings of the heroine," protesting that "the author's arguments have all been set forth in one of her previous novels. All that she has done is to give them a cruder and more lurid setting" (691–92). Writing for the *Saturday Review* (20 November 1897) under the name Frank Danby, Julia Frankau thoroughly praises the novel but condemns her "strange and hideous obsession" and "iconoclastic fervour" about the controversies "that raged twenty years ago around the dead C. D. Acts" (323). The *Academy* (13 November 1897) reviewer writes, "The characters cannot get away from the uninviting round of views about marital relations, sexual problems, and the Contagious Diseases Acts," and concludes: "Books like this are not wanted. They do not amuse; they do not instruct; they do not edify" (393). The writer for *Bookman* (6 [December 1897]) seems to contradict the other critics; rather than arguing that the Contagious Disease Acts are old news, he insists that this information should be suppressed, and he follows his own advice by referring to the issue so euphemistically that he nearly obscures his point:

> Madame Grand makes an unjustifiable showing of uncleanness with scarcely a suggestion of remedy or so much as a claim to be giving information. No thinking man or woman need be told anything that *The Beth Book* tells. The loftiest soul aiming at the stars cannot go far along life's journey without gathering knowledge of these terrible things hidden by the way. A few are fortunate to see them at a distance; many, less lucky, come close to them through bitter experience; the happiest may not hope to escape wholly, and the fuller the saddening acquaintance, the greater the shrinking from meeting in fiction horrors too well known in life. (363)

Finally, the reviewer in the *Nation* (66 [9 June 1898]) protests the "unwholesome ingredients" and declares, "The implied confidence in public interest in this enormous mess of largely repulsive details almost reaches the sublime—yes, goes even a step further" (446).

45. This passage is quoted in Constance Rover, *Love, Morals, and the Feminists* (London: Routledge, Kegan, Paul, 1970), 75.

46. See Walkowitz, *Prostitution and Victorian Society*.

47. Elizabeth C. Wolstenholme Elmy, *Shafts* 5 (May 1897): 153.

48. Elmy, *Shafts* 5 (March 1897): 85.

49. *Shafts* 5 (March 1897): 87. Substantiating Elmy's fears, an article in the *Dial* (1 February 1898, 77–79) lodges this complaint against Grand's novel: "It might be described as a tract directed against a certain class of hospitals for women, although even on this point the writer's logic is painfully to seek. To assume that the sex is degraded by the provision of such hospitals is an utterly impossible thesis, yet it seems to be maintained in all seriousness by this writer."

50. Elmy, *Shafts* 5 (May 1897): 154.

51. See Lyon, "Militant Allies, Strange Bedfellows." Ledger also characterizes New Woman fiction in terms of "reverse discourse," in *New Woman*, 20–24.

52. See Kersley, *Darling Madame*, 46.

53. Kersley found military records that seem to corroborate this claim; see Kersley, *Darling Madame,* 47.

54. George Eliot's portrait of Dr. Lydgate in *Middlemarch* also focuses on the impact a particular kind of medical career could have on a doctor *and* his wife. To satisfy his wife's social ambitions Lydgate sacrifices his plans to pursue medical research and, instead, makes a fortune pandering to the real and imagined illnesses of middle- and upper-class women.

55. See Duffin, "Conspicuous Consumptive," 29. Also see Oppenheim, *"Shattered Nerves,"* who points out, in all fairness, that women doctors like Arabella Kenealy and Mary Scharlieb also supported discriminatory policies (197–98).

56. Duffin, "Conspicuous Consumptive," 27–28. Also see the sources listed in chap. 4 n. 83.

57. I was deeply grateful to encounter the sentence "Decadence is a notoriously difficult term to define" in Elaine Showalter's *Sexual Anarchy* (169). The term *Decadent* is usually associated with French writers such as Baudelaire and Huysmann and, in England, with their followers. As Showalter explains, however, the term was used pejoratively by the middle classes to denote anything that seemed "unnatural, artificial, and perverse, from Art Nouveau to homosexuality, a sickness with symptoms associated with cultural degeneration and decay" (169). Most famously, of course, the Decadents and/or Aesthetes are credited with the phrase *art for art's sake,* lifted from Walter Pater's *The Renaissance* (1873) and a red rag to an activist like Grand. For a fuller discussion of the term and its problematic uses, see Dowling, *Language and Decadence;* Reed, *Decadent Style;* R. K. R. Thornton, *The Decadent Dilemma* (London: Edward Arnold, 1983), chap. 3; and, for a study of the Aestheticism movement, see Dellamora, *Masculine Desire.*

58. Wendell Harris discusses the thirteen novels published in the series, focusing on their relation to the Decadent movement, in his study "John Lane's Keynotes Series and the Fiction of the 1890s," *PMLA* 83 (1968): 1407–13.

59. Dowling, "Decadent and the New Woman," 440–41.

60. Many nineteenth-century reviewers and critics made no distinction between the work written by the Decadents and the New Women. See, for example, B. A. Crackanthorpe, "Sex in Modern Literature"; Hogarth, "Literary Degenerates"; Quilter, "Gospel of Intensity"; *Contemporary Review* 67 (June 1894): 762–82; or either of Hugh Stutfield's attacks on the New Women writers.

61. In addition to Dowling's "Decadent and the New Woman" most of the 1990s studies of New Woman fiction discuss the issue of class in what has been described as largely a middle-class form of the novel. For example, while John Kucich and Nim Weetens assume Grand never escapes very conventional class biases, Kranidis, *Subversive Discourse;* Ledger, *New Woman;* and Ardis, *New Women, New Novels* and in essays, argue that Grand and other New Women writers had fairly progressive class politics, as part of a feminist agenda, for the 1890s. Also, other New Woman writers explicitly took up socialist politics. Angela Ingram and Daphne Patai's collection of essays, *Forgotten Radicals: British Women Writers, 1889–1939,* is a fine resource. See especially Chris Waters, "New Women and Socialist-Feminist Fiction: The Novels of Isabella Ford and Katharine Bruce Glasier"; and Ann Ardis, "'The Journey from Fantasy to Politics': The Representation of Socialism and Feminism in Gloriana and *The Image-Breakers.*"

62. Dowling, "Decadent and the New Woman," 442–44.

63. Dowling, "Decadent and the New Woman," 437.

64. Bridget Elliott describes parodic cartoon versions of the New Woman in two 1894 issues of the *Pall Mall Budget* and compares these drawings of the New Woman with Aubrey Beardsley's sexualized illustrations of George Egerton's *Keynotes* in "New and Not So 'New Women' on the London Stage. Rosie Miles's discussion of the illustrations and parodies of George Egerton and her work is also illuminating in "George Egerton, Bitextuality and Cultural (Re)production in the 1890s," *Women's Writing: The Elizabethan to the Victorian Period* 3 (1996): 243–59. See also Kaplan and Stowell, *Theatre and Fashion.*

65. This passage is quoted in Sandra Siegel's essay "Literature and Degeneration: The Representation of 'Decadence,'" in *Degeneration: The Dark Side of Progress,* ed. J. Edwards Chamberlin and Sander Gilman (New York: Columbia University Press, 1985), 209.

66. Siegel, "Literature and Degeneration," 209.

67. See *The Trials of Oscar Wilde* and the introduction by Montgomery Hyde (London: W. Hodge, 1948); and Richard Ellman's *Oscar Wilde* (New York: Alfred Knopf, 1988). Elaine Showalter points out that the term *homosexual,* which she attributes to an 1869 usage by the Hungarian writer Karoly Benkert, began to circulate in England after the translation of Krafft-Ebing's *Psychopathia Sexualis* in the 1890s and that it therefore emerges at about the same moment as the term *New Woman* (*Sexual Anarchy,* 171).

68. *Punch,* 21 December 1895, 297; quoted in Ledger, "New Woman and the Crisis of Victorianism," 24.

69. *Speaker,* 13 April 1895, 403; quoted by John Stokes in *In the Nineties* (New York: Harvester Wheatsheaf, 1989), 14. I am indebted to Sally Ledger for this reference.

70. See *New Women, New Novels,* 187 n. 33. Ardis notes this advertisement in the midst of raising another important issue. She suggests that, in separating themselves from Wilde and other Decadent writers, publishers like William Heinemann and John Lane may have also backed away from women writers who had shared the "erotomaniac" label, further evidence that the New Woman's self-protective maneuverings may have been futile (45).

71. See essays by Chris Waters and Ann Ardis in *Forgotten Radicals: British Women Writers, 1889–1939.* Kathy Psomiades and Talia Shire are editing a forthcoming collection of essays on female Decadent writers that will challenge most of our current conceptions of this literary category.

72. Arthur Symons, "The Decadent Movement in Literature," *Harper's New Monthly Magazine* 87 (1893): 858–59.

73. Ann Ardis examines the critical history of realism to show how New Woman fiction came to be positioned "in opposition to both classic English realism and French naturalism" (30), in chapter 2 of *New Women, New Novels,* "The Controversy over Realism in Fiction, 1885–1895" (29–58), and Rita Kranidis discusses the distinctions between realist fiction that dealt with women's issues and New Woman fiction in chapter 5, "Defining the Political: The 'Realistic' Appropriation" (107–28). Though their studies focus on the early twentieth century, two additional books are especially helpful on realism and the New Woman writing: Miller, *Rebel Women;* and Pykett, *Engendering Fictions.*

74. Flint, *The Woman Reader, 1837–1914,* 38.

75. Dowling, *Language and Decadence,* 104.

76. See Dowling, "Decadent and the New Woman," 449; and Kucich, *Power of Lies*, 263.

77. Symons, "Decadent Movement in Literature," 858.

78. Ironically, while Maurice Beebe's study *Ivory Towers and Sacred Founts: The Artist as Hero in Fiction from Goethe to Joyce* (New York: New York University Press, 1964) provides an excellent introduction to the traditions of the male artist, his exclusion of female artists leads to the same oversights in critical studies dependent upon his work that we see in studies of the bildungsroman that begin with the field mapped out by Jerome H. Buckley, *Season of Youth*.

79. Beebe, *Ivory Towers and Sacred Founts*, 6.

80. Beebe also describes the artist of the "Ivory Tower" tradition, a detached, solitary figure who can only create by removing himself from the world.

81. See Ellen Moers, *The Dandy: Brummell to Beerbohm* (New York: Viking Press, 1960); also see Adams, *Dandies and Desert Saints*.

82. See William T. Stead, "The Novel of the Modern Woman," *Review of Reviews* 10 (1894): 73.

83. Rachel Blau DuPlessis argues that ultimately *The Beth Book* is a failed artist plot:

> The sentiment about impropriety, the loss of a sense of feminine coherence, and a tremendous ambivalence toward a profession appear in another turn-of-the-century work, Sarah Grand's *The Beth Book* . . . ambivalence toward the female artist is again present, and the norms of femininity are carefully elaborated. Allocation of narrative force points in one direction; the ideological priorities set in the resolution point in another. The description of genius offers a vocabulary of passionate and frustrated striving; the events of the plot offer the conciliations and closures demanded by the femaleness of the artist. (89)

84. This passage is quoted in Kersley, *Darling Madame*, 108.

85. Ledger, *New Woman*, 157; quoting from Margaret Lonsdale, "Platform Women," *Nineteenth Century* 15 (1884): 414.

86. See Neetens, *Writing and Democracy: Literature, Politics and Culture in Transition* (Brighton: Harvester Wheatsheaf, 1991), chap. 5: "Feminist Positions: Sarah Grand and Elizabeth Robins." He describes the community Beth forms at the end of the novel as "a group of advanced Ruskinian intellectuals and artists" committed to the women's movement and to character versus social position (112–13). He notes that this community, presented as being a "bohemia *avant la lettre*" is congenial to genius and compares it to the "new life movement" described in a quotation he takes from Sheila Rowbotham: "'people in a progressive cultural circle, who were concerned in a purely personal way with what they sometimes described as 'the new life.' This meant vague aesthetic rejection of the ugliness and commercialism of nineteenth-century captalism. It could mean sandals, Buddhism, cottages, market gardening, communal living, cooperative villages, acute bouts of self-consciousness, and the occasional free union. It could also mean the 'New Woman' and 'Ibsenism'" (qtd. from Sheila Rowbotham, *Women, Resistance and Revolution* [Harmondsworth: Penguin Books, 1974], 70).

87. Grand probably takes her phrases from Eliza Lynn Linton's essays, although Linton's more colorful phrases were quickly taken up by other antifeminist writers. See Linton "The Girl of the Period," *Saturday Review*, 14 March 1868, 339–40; "Modern Man-

Haters," *Saturday Review,* 29 April 1871, 528–29; "The Wild Women as Politicians," *Nineteenth Century* 30 (1891): 79–88; "The Wild Women as Social Insurgents," *Nineteenth Century* 30 (1891): 596–605, among others.

88. Among actual women speakers who received a great deal of notice, Ledger mentions Annie Besant and Florence Fenwick Miller. She also notes that speaking women were additionally upsetting because of the locations in which they spoke such as lecture halls but also music halls. As Ledger astutely observes, in Henry James's novel *The Bostonians,* Basil Ransom is horrified that Verena Tarrant is about to speak at the Boston Music Hall (*New Woman,* 157–63).

89. Lyon, "Militant Allies, Strange Bedfellows," 111. Also see Lisa Tickner's beautifully illustrated book *The Spectacle of Women: Imagery of the Suffrage Campaign, 1907–14* (London: Chatto and Windus, 1987).

90. For a fascinating literary biography of the contradictory life and work of Linton, see Nancy Fix Anderson, *Woman against Women in Victorian England: A Life of Eliza Lynn Linton.*

91. Clarke, "Feminism and the Popular Novel," 104.

92. Clarke, "Feminism and the Popular Novel," 103.

93. Clarke, "Feminism and the Popular Novel," 104.

94. *Nation* 66, 9 June 1898, 417.

Chapter 6

1. Grand described her relation to her husband in a letter to William Heinemann, dated 18 September 1903, which is now in the Mortimer Rare Book Room at Smith College.

2. Gillian Kersley's biographical study of Grand, *Darling Madame,* offers a vivid picture of these Grand years. In addition, the letters, especially those written to William Heinemann and to William Blackwood, ring with the yearning, excitement, and determination that inspired Grand.

3. One version of the story appears in *Vote* 34, 25 August 1933, n.p.

4. The Bath Central Library has a copy of the letter in which Grand strongly protests the Boer War.

5. See her letter to Frederick Henry Fisher, dated 1 January 1907 and held by the Special Collections Library of UCLA.

6. See especially the letters to Grand's lecture agent Mr. Christy dated 1 May 1907; 13 March 1904; and 15 March 1904, also in Special Collections of the UCLA Library.

7. Grand refers to the invitation in the letter to Fisher dated 1 January 1907.

8. In a 23 September 1903 letter to Mr. Christy, Grand's attempt at humor contrasts painfully with her description of her condition: "At present I am a most miserable invalid, a case of *neurasthenia* (is not that the way to spell it?) 'American writer' the doctors call it facetiously. The consequence of over-strain and influenza. And I am just raging—when I am not weeping . . . and now the doctors say, that I must go in for two months of the Weir Mitchell treatment (the rest cure) as my only chance of recovering my strength for the writing work." The letter is held by the Special Collections Library of UCLA.

9. The letter to William Heinemann, dated 6 December 1900, is held by the Mortimer Rare Book Room at Smith College.

10. Grand recalled making this vow in a letter written to Bertha Newcombe in January of 1909. (The letter is held by the Fawcett Collection.)

11. Anonymous review, *Literary Digest,* 1 March 1913, 228.

12. Anonymous review, *Athenaeum* (September 1916): 420.

13. The early chapters of Richard A. Soloway's *Demography and Degeneration: Eugenics and the Declining Birthrate in Twentieth-Century Britain* (Chapel Hill: University of Chapel Hill Press, 1990) provide not only extensive historical background but astute social and political analyses of the popularization of eugenics as a response to fears of infertility and later to debates over contraception. Lyndsay Farrall provides an excellent bare-bones overview of the British eugenics movement, *The Origins and Growth of the English Eugenics Movement, 1865–1925* (New York: Garland, 1985). His book includes an essential bibliography of primary sources and a helpful analysis of the eugenicists' goal of asserting their study as a science. Geoffrey R. Searle's *Eugenics and Politics in Britain, 1900–1914* (Leyden: Noordhoff International Publishing, 1976), a social history of eugenics as a movement rather than a science, maps out the complex cultural context that contributed to the popularity of eugenics. His treatment of British attitudes toward race, imperialism, class, and political parties is introductory but very useful. Although Daniel J. Kevles's *In the Name of Eugenics: Genetics and the Uses of Human Heredity* (1985; reprint, Harmondsworth: Penguin, 1986) gives equal attention to the American and the British eugenic movements, he offers the most rigorous analysis of the conflicts among the founders of eugenics and includes a chapter on the opponents to the movement. This book also explores eugenic issues that arose after 1920 and the scientific fields such as human genetics and biochemistry that were influenced by eugenics. Moreover, Kevles provides a detailed essay on sources for the study of eugenics and a variety of related topics. See also Frank Mort, *Dangerous Sexualities;* Daniel Pick, *Faces of Degeneration: A European Disorder, c. 1848–c. 1918* (New York: Cambridge University Press, 1989); and Marouf A. Hasian, *The Rhetoric of Eugenics in Anglo-American Thought* (Athens: University of Georgia Press, 1996). William Greenslade's *Degeneration, Culture, and the Novel, 1880–1940* (New York: Cambridge University Press, 1994) ties arguments about degeneration and eugenic responses specifically to the turn-of-the-century novel.

14. See Francis Galton, *Inquiries into Human Faculty and Its Developments* (London: Macmillan, 1883), 24–25. See also D. W. Forrest, *Francis Galton: The Life and Work of a Victorian Genius* (London: Elek, 1974).

15. Farrall, in *Origins and Growth,* explains the importance of biometrics and the development of statistics in reshaping the sciences, especially the late-nineteenth-century divisions of biology into anatomy and physiology. He also surveys the research published in the journal and discusses the people and politics that shaped the journal. See esp. 88–102, 103–79.

16. In the early years the editors of *Biometrika* devoted much of their time to challenging Gregor Mendel's theory of heredity after Mendel's papers were discussed and reissued in 1900, and these refutations were usually based on studies of animals. After Pearson became the sole editor in 1906, however, most of the articles in the journal were devoted to measurements that sought to describe and predict human evolution (Farrall, *Origins and Growth,* 88–102).

17. Greenslade, *Degeneration,* 199.

18. As early as the 1870s, but certainly by the 1890s, articles about eugenics and related issues began to appear in periodicals with a general readership, such as *Fraser's Magazine, Spectator, Contemporary Review,* and *Fortnightly Review,* among others. Farrall lists a number of these essays in his bibliography. Perhaps more telling is a story Kevles recalls in *In the Name of Eugenics.* In 1913 (a year after the publication of *Adnam's Orchard*) a London woman who was pregnant attended plays and concerts and solicited conversations with several well-known writers to improve the eugenic prospects of her unborn child, whom she named Eugenette Boyce. Kevles found a newspaper article from the London *Daily Sketch* (3 October 1914) and various other press clippings among the papers of the Eugenics Education Society that heralded the event as the birth of England's first eugenic baby. This interpretation of eugenics and the kind of publicity it invited explains why many of the eugenic scientists lamented the activities of the Eugenic Education Society.

19. For a brief history of this organization, see Farrall, *Origins and Growth,* 206–50. Searle devotes most of his study, *Eugenics and Politics in Britain, 1910–1914,* to the Eugenic Society's activities. Also see Pauline M. H. Mazumdar, *Eugenics, Human Genetics and Human Failings: The Eugenics Society, its Sources and Its Critics in Britain* (London: Routledge, 1992).

20. Bland, *Banishing the Beast,* 228.

21. Bland, *Banishing the Beast,* 242.

22. Farrall uses Frank Parkin's term from Parkin's 1968 study, *Middle Class Radicalism: The Social Basis of the British Campaign for Nuclear Disarmament* (Manchester: Manchester University Press, 1968). He agrees with Parkin's thesis, which characterizes both working and middle-class reformers rather condescendingly,

> that whereas working class radicalism could be said to be geared largely to reforms of an economic or material kind, the radicalism of the middle class is directed mainly to social reforms which are basically moral in content . . . It is argued in fact that the main pay-off for middle class radicals is that of a psychological or emotional kind—in satisfaction derived from expressing personal values in action. (2)

I think Parkin's analysis also suggests why middle-class feminists would have been attracted to eugenic ideas. Like professionals, largely detached from both the upper classes and the working classes, these women could translate eugenic solutions into moral precepts because they themselves (and their descendants) could only benefit from the social upheaval that would follow a shift to eugenic "values." Searle also discusses the role that class played in the organization in a separate essay, "Eugenics and Class," in *Biology, Medicine and Society,* ed. Charles Webster (New York: Cambridge University Press, 1981, 217–42). In addition, see Donald MacKenzie's essay "Eugenics in Britain," *Social Studies of Science* 6 (1976): 499–532.

23. Searle includes a chapter on each of these eugenic positions in *Eugenics and Politics in Britain.* He quotes this passage from Slaughter's essay, "Selection in Marriage" (Searle, *Eugenics and Politics,* 150–62).

24. The *Eugenics Review* still exists today. Farrall provides a breakdown of the types of articles published in the first twelve volumes, categorizing them according to type and style (230–38). Richard Soloway notes Galton's use of the term *race-motherhood* in a

speech Galton gave to the Anthropological Institute. The speech is recorded in Pearson, *Life, Letters, and Labours of Francis Galton,* 226. This example comes from Soloway, "Feminism, Fertility, and Eugenics in Victorian and Edwardian England," in *Political Symbolism in Modern Europe: Essays in Honor of George L. Mosse,* ed. Seymour Drescher, David Sabean, and Allen Sharlin (London: Transaction Books, 1982), 131. Other nineteenth- and twentieth-century eugenicists use the term unselfconsciously as though it had entered common usage.

25. Greenslade, *Degeneration,* 194–95.

26. For details about Scharlieb's work, see Oppenheim, *"Shattered Nerves,"* 280. Lucy Bland also discusses Scharlieb's role and that of other medical writers and women's rights supporters in *Banishing the Beast,* 232.

27. See Karl Pearson, *The Grammar of Science* (1892; reprint, London: W. Scott, 1951), 29.

28. Searle quotes from White's article, which originally appeared in the *Weekly Sun* on 28 July 1900. White also published a book advocating eugenic ideas, *Efficiency and Empire* (London: Methuen, 1901). These military statistics were later used as evidence that British workers were dangerous to the empire, in articles like "Where to Get Men," in the *Contemporary Review* 82 (January 1902): 78–86, published anonymously but written by General Frederick ("Miles") Maurice.

29. Farrall points out that in Pearson's work the term *race* was used as though it were a synonym for *heredity,* which may help to explain the nonacademic eugenicists' confusion.

30. Kevles gives the most thorough (and amusing) account of Shaw's lecture. Shaw delivered his speech at Caxton Hall in March of 1910, and it was reported in the *Daily Express.* Among other things Shaw suggested that murderers should be executed for killing potentially desirable "eugenes."

31. Woodhull, as always, was extremely controversial. Most of her conclusions antagonized more conventional eugenicists. In *The Rapid Multiplication of the Unfit* (London: n.p., 1891), for example, she uses the language of the eugenicists, but her point is that the race is degenerating because of women's *exhaustion,* so she is really writing social analysis. Mona Caird's essays are collected in *The Morality of Marriage.* Clapperton is especially interesting because, like Schreiner, she wrote both fiction and nonfiction. Her utopian novel is entitled *Margaret Dunmore; or, a Socialist Home* (1888). She was also more radical than most eugenicists, for she publicly supported birth control. This quotation appears in Schreiner, *Woman and Labour,* 27.

32. See Dale Bauer, *Edith Wharton's Brave New Politics* (Madison: University of Wisconsin Press, 1994).

33. In her essay "'Alice in Eugenics-land,'" in *Annals of Science* 36 (1979), Love recalls a story about Alice Lee that has a special significance for those who are writing or have written dissertations. Lee was one of the first women to receive a degree at London University. After teaching math at Bedford College, she began to work for Pearson. She conducted a research project to see whether there really were correlations between skull size and intelligence, using the measurements of the skulls of thirty-five male anatomists who had agreed to have their heads measured at a conference in 1898. Lee used her own formula to interpret the estimated correlations then ranked the skulls in order of decreasing size. To turn the story over to Love:

in so doing (the nightmare of any doctoral student) she placed one of her future examiners, Sir William Turner, eighth from the bottom. Judging from the fuss which attended the examination of the thesis, Sir William Turner was not amused, though of course the point of Alice Lee's argument was that skull capacity was quite unrelated to the intellectual distinction of the men, and by corollary of women too. (150)

Love cites Lee's research focus to show how important it was for the eugenic movement to include a female perspective, since theories of female inferiority had long been based on the belief that women's skull size doomed them to a dwarfed mental life. She also notes that, when Elderton conducted a study of the birthrates in communities of working-class women in the North, she took the unprecedented step of *asking* the women for their point of view and was shocked to learn of the numbers of illegal abortions, many of which left women scarred for life even if they survived the procedure.

34. Galton's speech is reprinted in his *Essays in Eugenics* published by the Eugenics Society in 1909 and reprinted by University Microfilms International in 1979 (37–38).

35. See Daniel J. Kevles, *In the Name of Eugenics,* 317; and Greenslade, *Degeneration,* 207.

36. See Richard Soloway, "Feminism, Fertility, and Eugenics in Victorian and Edwardian England," 141.

37. Bland, *Banishing the Beast,* 229.

38. See Sarah Grand, *The Modern Man and Maid* (London: Horace Marshall, 1898), 9.

39. Kevles, *In the Name of Eugenics,* 65. Also see Lucy Bland, "The Married Woman, the 'New Woman,' and the Feminist: Sexual Politics of the 1890s," in *Equal or Different: Women's Politics, 1800–1914,* 124–26.

40. Boumelha, *Thomas Hardy and Women,* 21.

41. Anna Davin, "Imperialism and Motherhood," *History Workshop Journal* 5 (1978): 9–65. In his study of the rhetoric of eugenics Marouf Arif Hasian argues that British women used three rhetorical strategies to promote their right to make claims in the context of eugenics: they offered vocal support for programs that "many hard-line eugenicists considered to be 'dysgenic'" such as insisting the government pay for benefits for all British citizens, not just the for the fit; they attacked antifeminist claims as interfering with "voluntary motherhood," which allowed them to argue that no woman should have to suffer unwanted pregnancies and which allowed for the inclusion of "New Women"; and they appropriated conservatives' terms to justify their own agendas, for example, by arguing that fears of bacterial infection justified the demand for male purity and self-control (*Rhetoric of Eugenics in Anglo-American Thought,* 78–80).

42. See Rosaleen Love, "'Alice in Eugenics-Land,'" 103.

43. See Soloway, "Feminism, Fertility, and Eugenics,"142–45. This quotation appears in Greenslade (*Degeneration,* 206) and is taken from *Parenthood and Race Culture: An Outline of Eugenics* (London: Cassell and Co., 1909), 285.

44. Grand, "Eugenia," in *Our Manifold Nature* (London: Heinemann, 1894), 103. Future references are cited in the text.

45. The essay appeared in *Englishwoman* 28 (1910): 36–38.

46. See Schreiner, *Woman and Labour,* 266.

47. Schreiner, *Woman and Labour,* 253–54.

48. Two useful introductions to the complex origins and consequences of the agricultural depression are P. J. Perry, *British Agriculture, 1875–1914* (London: Methuen, 1973); and Roy Douglas, *Land, People and Politics: A History of the Land Question in the United Kingdom, 1878–1952* (London: Allison and Busby, 1976).

49. For discussions of socialists and environmentalist responses to the agricultural depression, see Peter Gould, *Early Green Politics: Back to Nature, Back to the Land, and Socialism in Britain, 1880–1900* (New York: St. Martin's Press, 1988); and Wallace Martin, *The "New Age" under Orage* (Manchester: Manchester University Press, 1967).

50. I am using the 1912 Heinemann edition. All future references will be noted in the text.

51. Galton considers the hereditary role of the father in *Hereditary Genius: An Inquiry into Its Laws and Consequences* (1869, reprint, London: Macmillan, 1914). Soloway discusses Galton's belief in his essay "Feminism, Fertility, and Eugenics" (126–27). He points out that Galton did suspect that women had hereditary influence on clergymen and judges. Galton suspected that the reason women had little influence could either be hereditary inferiority or the tendency of exceptional women not to marry. To refute his claims, in 1890 Eleanor Mildred Sidgwick, the principal of Newnham College, conducted a study of Newnham graduates, demonstrating that, while educated women married somewhat later, they tended to marry in the same numbers and to produce nearly the same numbers of children as uneducated women of their class (Soloway, "Feminism, Fertility, and Eugenics," 131). Within the eugenic camp Galton's studies of women's hereditary insignificance were countered by Havelock Ellis. See "Eugenics and St. Valentine," *Nineteenth Century* 59 (1906): 784. For a detailed discussion of Galton's theoretical bias, see Soloway, *Demography and Degeneration*.

52. See Frank Parkin, *Middle-Class Radicalism,* for his social history of and definition of middle-class radicalism.

53. Grand seems to be quite daring here, but it is also true that Ethel Elderton conducted research to determine how offspring of first cousins were affected genetically. This detail and innumerable others indicate either Grand's fascination with the activities of the eugenicists *or* the extent to which eugenics had permeated the public consciousness.

54. I quote this passage from Searle (*Eugenics and Politics,* 51). It comes from an editorial in *Annals of Eugenics* 1 (1915–26): 3.

55. Searle (*Eugenics and Politics,* 48) quotes this passage from "The Scope of the Science of Eugenics," *British Medical Journal,* 1 August 1913, 225.

56. Searle dryly notes that the Whethams's views, which appeared in *Family and the Nation,* were published in 1907, the year of the People's Budget, adding, "the political significance of this hardly needs underlining" (*Eugenics and Politics,* 56).

57. Ann Ardis explores the connections between New Woman fiction and socialist politics in *New Woman, New Novels.* See also the essays in *Rediscovering Forgotten Radicals: British Women Writers, 1889–1939.*

58. Geoff Spenceley, in "The Lace Associations: Philanthropic Movements to Preserve the Production of Hand-Made Lace in Late Victorian and Edwardian England," *Victorian Studies* 16 (1973): 433–52, provides a fascinating account of the project Grand fictionalizes. The story of the transition of lace making from homes to textile factories and of attempts to preserve lace making as an art are numerous. For example, see

William Felkin, *Felkin's History of the Machine Wrought Hosiery and Lace* (1867; reprint, London: David and Charles, 1967); Mrs. F. Nevill Jackson, *A History of Hand-Made Lace* (London: n.p., 1900); Mrs. Bury Palliser, *History of Lace,* revised by Mr. Jourdain and Alice Dryden (London: Sampson Low, Marston and Co., 1902); and an especially enlightening recent work, Santina Levey, *Lace: A History* (London: Victoria and Albert Museum, 1983).

59. Quoted in Spenceley, "Lace Associations," 448.

60. I am using the 1916 Heinemann edition of *The Winged Victory,* 305. All future references will appear in the text.

61. Ann Heilmann, "The 'New Woman' Fiction and Fin-de-Siècle Feminism," special issue: "Women's Writing at the Fin de Siècle," ed. Sally Ledger, *Women's Writing* 3 (1996): 207–8.

Conclusion

1. Grand discusses "the silencing system" in the 1923 foreword to *The Heavenly Twins.*

2. *Bookman* 3–4 (1892–93): 108.

3. See the introduction to Kathleen Blake's *Love and the Woman Question in Victorian Literature: The Art of Self-Postponement* (Brighton: Harvester Press, 1983) for her analysis of chastity as a woman writer's strategic way of creating time and space to pursue her career as a poet or novelist.

4. *Bookman,* 107.

5. *Bookman,* 107.

6. *Bookman,* 107.

7. *Bookman,* 107–8.

8. *Academy,* 10 April 1901, 347.

9. *Academy,* 10 April 1990, 347.

10. *Twentieth Century Authors,* ed. Stanley Kunitz and Howard Haycraft (New York: H. W. Wilson Co., 1942), 563.

11. *Twentieth Century Authors* (1942 ed.), 563.

12. *Twentieth Century Authors,* ed. Stanley Kunitz and Howard Haycraft (New York: H. W. Wilson Co., 1955), 381.

13. *Twentieth Century Authors* (1955 ed.), 381.

14. *Twentieth Century Authors* (1955 ed.), 381.

Works Cited

Abel, Elizabeth, Marianne Hirsch, and Elizabeth Langland, eds. *The Voyage In: Fictions of Female Development*. Hanover, N.H.: University Press of New England, 1983.

Adams, James Eli. *Dandies and Desert Saints: Styles of Victorian Masculinity*. Ithaca: Cornell University Press, 1995.

Adburgham, Alison. *A Punch History of Manners and Modes, 1841–1940*. London: Hutchinson, 1961.

Adnam's Orchard, Review of. *Bookman* (January 1913): 228.

Adnam's Orchard, Review of. *Literary Digest,* 1 March 1913, 478.

Adnam's Orchard, Review of. *Times Literary Supplement,* 24 October 1912, 464.

Alaya, Flavia. "Victorian Science and the 'Genius' of Woman." *Journal of the History of Ideas* 34 (1977): 261–80.

Alcott, Louisa May. *Alternative Alcott*. Edited by Elaine Showalter. New Brunswick: Rutgers University Press, 1988.

Alexander, Sally. *Becoming a Woman and Other Essays in 19th and 20th Century Feminist History*. London: Virago, 1994.

Allen, Grant. *The Woman Who Did*. 1895. Reprint. New York: Oxford University Press, 1995.

Altick, Richard. *The English Common Reader: A Social History of the Mass Reading Public, 1800–1900*. Chicago: University of Chicago Press, 1957.

Anderson, Amanda. *Tainted Souls and Painted Faces: The Rhetoric of Fallenness in Victorian Culture*. Ithaca: Cornell University Press, 1993.

Anderson, Nancy Fix. *Woman against Women in Victorian England: A Life of Eliza Lynn Linton*. Bloomington: Indiana University Press, 1987.

Anderson, Olive. *Suicide in Victorian and Edwardian England*. New York: Oxford University Press, 1987.

"Apple and Ego of Woman, The." *Westminister Review* 131 (1889): 374–82.

Ardis, Ann. "'The Apple and the Ego of Woman': A Prehistory of English Modernism in the 'New Woman' Novels of the 1890's." Ph.D. diss., University of Virginia, 1988.

———. "'The Journey from Fantasy to Politics': The Representation of Socialism and Feminism in *Gloriana* and *The Image-Breakers*." In *Rediscovering Forgotten Radicals: British Women Writers, 1889–1939*. Edited by Angela Ingram and Daphne Patai, 43–56. Chapel Hill: University of North Carolina Press, 1993.

———. *New Women, New Novels: Feminism and Early Modernism*. New Brunswick: Rutgers University Press, 1990.

———. "'Retreat with Honour': Mary Cholmondeley's Presentation of the New Woman Artist in *Red Pottage*. In *Writing the Woman Artist: Essays on Poetics, Politics and Portraiture.* Edited by Suzanne W. Jones, 333–50. Philadelphia: University of Pennsylvania Press, 1991.

Arling, Nat. "What Is the Role of the 'New Woman'?" *Westminister Review* 150 (November 1898): 576–87.

Armstrong, Nancy. *Desire and Domestic Fiction: A Political History of the Novel.* New York: Oxford University Press, 1987.

Arnold, Bennett. *Fame and Fiction: An Inquiry into Certain Popularities.* London: Grant Richards, 1901.

Aurora [pseud.]. "Between the Lights: In the Rapids." *Woman's Signal,* 8 March 1894, 160.

———. "Between the Lights: The Tree of Knowledge." *Woman's Signal,* 14 June 1894, 412.

"Author of *Babs the Impossible, The.*" *Academy* 60 (April 1901): 347–48.

"Author of *The Heavenly Twins, The.*" *Critic* 23 (5 August 1893): 92.

"Author of *The Heavenly Twins, The.*" *Critic* 23 (2 December 1893): 361.

Babs the Impossible, Review of. *Athenaeum* 20 (April 1901): 494–95.

Babs the Impossible, Review of. *Book Buyer* n.s. 22 (April 1901): 240.

Babs the Impossible, Review of. *Bookman* (London) 20 (May 1901): 55.

Babs the Impossible, Review of. *Bookman* (New York) 13 (1901): 185–86.

Babs the Impossible, Review of. *Independent,* 28 March 1900, 733–34.

Bakhtin, Mikhail. *The Dialogic Imagination: Four Essays.* Edited by Michael Holquist. Translated by Carly Emerson and Michael Holquist. Austin: University of Texas Press, 1981.

Barr, Amelia E. "Discontented Women." *North American Review* 162 (1896): 201–9.

[Barry, William]. "The Strike of a Sex." *Quarterly Review* 179 (1894): 289–318.

Baruch, Elaine. "The Feminine *Bildungsroman*: Education through Marriage." *Massachusetts Review* 22 (1981): 335–57.

Basch, Françoise. *Relative Creatures: Victorian Women in Society and the Novel.* New York: Schocken Books, 1974.

Battersby, Christine. *Gender and Genius: Towards a Feminist Aesthetics.* London: Women's Press, 1989.

Bauer, Dale M. *Edith Wharton's Brave New Politics.* Madison: University of Wisconsin Press, 1994.

Bauer, Dale M., and S. Jaret McKinstry, eds. *Feminism, Bakhtin, and the Dialogic.* Albany: State University of New York, 1991.

Beebe, Maurice. *Ivory Towers and Sacred Founts: The Artist as Hero in Fiction from Goethe to Joyce.* New York: New York University Press, 1964.

Beer, Gillian. *Darwin's Plots: Evolutionary Narrative in Darwin, George Eliot and Nineteenth-Century Fiction.* 1983. Reprint. London: Ark Paperbacks, 1985.

Beetham, Margaret. *A Magazine of Her Own? Domesticity and Desire in the Woman's Magazine, 1800–1914.* New York: Routledge, 1996.

Bernstein, Susan David. "Dirty Reading: Sensation Fiction, Women and Primitivism." *Criticism* 86 (Spring 1994): 213–41.

Besant, Walter. "Literature as a Career." *Forum* 13 (August 1892): 693–708.

Besant, Walter, Eliza Lynn Linton, and Thomas Hardy. "Candour in English Fiction."
    New Review 2 (1890): 6–21.
Besant, Walter, Sarah Grand, Thomas Hardy, Max Nordau, Elizabeth Linton, et al.
    "The Tree of Knowledge." *New Review* 10 (1894): 675–90.
The Beth Book, Review of. *Academy,* 13 November 1897, 393.
The Beth Book, Review of. *Athenaeum,* 27 November 1897, 743–44.
The Beth Book, Review of. *Bookman* (December 1897): 363–64.
The Beth Book, Review of. *Catholic World* 66 (January 1898): 560–62.
The Beth Book, Review of. *Nation,* 9 June 1898, 446–47.
The Beth Book, Review of. *New York Times,* 4 December 1897, 11.
The Beth Book, Review of. *Saturday Review,* 20 November 1897, 557–58.
The Beth Book, Review of. *Spectator,* 13 November 1897, 691–92.
The Beth Book, Review of. *Woman's Signal,* 2 December 1897, 354–57.
Bird, Frederic M. "A Three-Volume Tract." Review of *The Heavenly Twins. Lippincott's*
    Magazine 52 (July–December 1893): 637–40.
Birkett, Dea. *Spinsters Abroad: Victorian Lady Explorers.* Oxford: Basil Blackwell, 1989.
Bjørhovde, Gerd. *Rebellious Structures: Women Writers and the Crisis of the Novel,*
    1880–1900. Oslo: Norwegian Press, 1987.
[Black, Clementina]. *Illustrated London News* 102, 3 June 1893, 670.
Black, Helen. *Pen, Pencil, Baton, and Mask: Biographical Sketches.* London: Spottiswoode
    and Company, 1896.
———. "Sarah Grand." *Notable Women Authors of the Day,* 320–28. London: Maclaren
    and Company, 1906.
Blake, Fay. "Lady Sleuths and Women Detectives," *Turn of the Century Women* 3 (1986):
    29–42.
Blake, Kathleen. *Love and the Woman Question in Victorian Literature: The Art of Self-Post-*
    ponement. Brighton: Harvester Press, 1983.
Bland, Lucy. *Banishing the Beast: English Feminism and Sexual Morality, 1885–1914.* Lon-
    don: Penguin, 1995.
———. "Feminist Vigilantes in Late-Victorian England." In *Regulating Womanhood:*
    Historical Essays on Marriage, Motherhood and Sexuality. Edited by Carol Smart, 33–52.
    London: Routledge, 1992.
———. "Marriage Laid Bare: Middle-Class Women and Marital Sex, 1880–1914." In
    Labour and Love: Women's Experience of Home and Family. Edited by Jane Lewis,
    123–46. Oxford: Blackwell, 1986.
———. "The Married Woman, the 'New Woman' and the Feminist: Sexual Politics of
    the 1890s." In *Equal or Different: Women's Politics, 1800–1914.* Edited by Jane Rendall,
    141–64. Oxford: Basil Blackwell, 1987.
Bonnell, Marilyn. "The Legacy of Sarah Grand's *The Heavenly Twins:* A Review Essay."
    English Literature in Transition 36 (1993): 466–79.
———. "Sarah Grand and the Critical Establishment: Art for [Wo]man's Sake." *Tulsa*
    Studies in Women's Literature 14 (Spring 1995): 123–48.
———. "Sarah Grand: The New Woman and Feminist Aesthetics." Ph.D. diss., Penn-
    sylvania State University, 1992.
Boone, Joseph Allen. "Modernist Manueverings in the Marriage Plot: Breaking Ideolo-
    gies of Gender in James' *The Golden Bowl.*" *PMLA* 101 (1986): 374–88.

————. *Tradition Counter Tradition: Love and the Form of Fiction.* Chicago: University of Chicago Press, 1987.

————. "Wedlock as Deadlock and Beyond: Closure and the Victorian Marriage Ideal." *Mosaic* 17 (1984): 65–81.

Boumelha, Penny. *Thomas Hardy and Women: Sexual Ideology and Narrative Form.* Brighton: Harvester Press, 1982.

Braddon, Mary Elizabeth. *Lady Audley's Secret.* 1887. Reprint. New York: Dover Publications, 1974.

Bradfield, Thomas. "A Dominant Note of Some Recent Fiction." *Westminister Review* 142 (November 1894): 537–45.

Braendlin, Bonnie Hoover. "Alther, Atwood, Ballantyne, and Gray: Secular Salvation in the Contemporary Feminist *Bildungsroman.*" *Frontiers* 4 (1979): 18–22.

Brantlinger, Patrick. "What Is 'Sensational' about the 'Sensation Novel'?" *Nineteenth Century Fiction* 37 (1982–83): 1–28.

Briggs, Asa. *Victorian Things.* London: Batsford, 1988.

Bristow, Joseph. *Vice and Vigilance: Purity Movements in Britain since 1700.* Dublin: Gill and Macmillan, 1977.

————, ed. *Sexual Sameness: Textual Differences in Gay and Lesbian Writing.* New York: Routledge, 1992.

[Brooke, Emma Frances]. "Each Sex Its Own Moralist: A Collectivist's Reply." *New Review* 13 (1895): 629–39.

————. *A Superfluous Woman.* London: W. Heinemann, 1894.

————. *Tabulation of the Factory Laws of European Countries in So Far as They Relate to the Hours of Labour, and to Special Legislation for Women, Young Persons, and Children.* London: Grant Richards, 1892.

Brooks, Peter. *The Melodramatic Imagination: Balzac, Henry James, Melodrama, and the Mode of Excess.* New Haven: Yale University Press, 1976.

Brown, Penny. *The Captured World: The Child and Childhood in Nineteenth-Century Women's Writing in England.* New York: St. Martin's Press, 1993.

Buckley, Jerome H. *Season of Youth: The Bildungsroman from Dickens to Golding.* Cambridge: Harvard University Press, 1974.

Bullough, Vern L., and Bonnie Bullough. *Cross-Dressing, Sex, and Gender.* Philadelphia: University of Pennsylvania Press, 1993.

Burstyn, Joan N. *Victorian Education and the Ideal of Victorian Womanhood.* New Brunswick: Rutgers University Press, 1984.

Burton, Antoinette. *Burdens of History: British Feminists, Indian Women, and Imperial Culture, 1865–1983.* Chapel Hill: University of North Carolina Press, 1994.

Butler, Josephine. *An Autobiographical Memoir.* London: Arrowsmith, 1909.

————. *Personal Reminiscences of a Great Crusade.* London: Horace Marshall and Son, 1896.

Butler, Judith. *Gender Trouble: Feminism and the Subversion of Identity.* New York: Routledge, 1990.

Caine, Barbara. *Destined to Be Wives: The Sisters of Beatrice Webb.* Oxford: Oxford University Press, 1986.

————. *Victorian Feminists.* New York: Oxford University Press, 1992.

Caird, Mona. "A Defence of the So-Called Wild Women." *Nineteenth Century* 31 (1892): 811–29.

———. "Marriage." *Westminister Review* 130 (August 1888): 186–201.

———. *The Morality of Marriage and Other Essays on the Status and Destiny of Woman.* London: George Redway, 1897.

———. *The Daughters of Danaus.* 1894. Reprint. New York: The Feminist Press, 1989.

Callaway, Helen. *Gender, Culture and Empire: European Women in Colonial Nigeria.* Oxford: Macmillan, 1987.

Carpenter, Edward. *Love's Coming-of-Age: A Series of Papers on the Relations of the Sexes.* Manchester: Labour Press, 1896.

Casteras, Susan P. "Excluding Women: The Cult of the Male Genius in Victorian Painting." In *Rewriting the Victorians: Theory, History, and the Politics of Gender.* Edited by Linda M. Shires, 116–46. New York: Routledge, 1992.

Cawelti, John G. *Adventure, Mystery, and Romance.* Chicago: University of Chicago Press, 1976.

Chapman, Elizabeth. *Marriage Questions in Modern Fiction, and Other Essays on Kindred Subjects.* London: John Lane, 1897.

"Character Note: The New Woman." *Cornhill Magazine* 23 (1894): 365–68.

"Chat with Sarah Grand, A." *Hub,* 17 October 1896, 419–20.

Chaudhuri, Nupur, and Margaret Strobel, eds. *Western Women and Imperialism: Complicity and Resistance.* Bloomington: Indiana University Press, 1992.

Chauncey, George. "From Sexual Inversion to Homosexuality: Medicine and the Changing Conceptualization of Female Deviance." *Salmagundi* (1982): 114–46.

Cholmondeley, Mary. *Red Pottage.* 1897. Reprint. London: Virago Press, 1985.

Chrisman, Laura. "Empire, 'Race' and Feminism at the *Fin de Siècle:* The Work of George Egerton and Olive Schreiner." In *Cultural Politics at the Fin de Siècle.* Edited by Sally Ledger and Scott McCracken, 45–65. Cambridge: Cambridge University Press, 1995.

Clapperton, Jane Hume. *Margaret Dunmore, or a Socialist Home: A Vision of the Future.* London: Swan Sonnenschein, Lowrey and Company, 1888.

———. *Scientific Meliorism and the Evolution of Happiness.* London: K. Paul Trench and Company, 1885.

Clark, Anna. "Humanity or Justice? Wifebeating or the Law in the Eighteenth and Nineteenth Centuries." In *Regulating Womanhood: Historical Essays on Marriage, Motherhood, and Sexuality.* Edited by Carol Smart, 187–206. New York: Routledge, 1992.

———. *Women's Silence, Men's Violence: Sexual Assault in England, 1770–1845.* New York: Pandora Press, 1987.

Clarke, Norma. "Feminism and the Popular Novel of the 1890s: A Brief Consideration of a Forgotten Novelist." *Feminist Review* 20 (1985): 91–104.

Coe, Richard. *When the Grass Was Taller: Autobiography and the Experience of Childhood.* New York: Yale University Press, 1984.

Cohen, Ed. *Talk on the Wilde Side: Toward a Genealogy of a Discourse on Male Sexualities.* New York: Routledge, 1993.

Colby, Vineta. *The Singular Anomaly: Women Novelists of the Nineteenth Century.* New York: New York University Press, 1970.

Collins, Philip. "'Agglomerating Dollars with Prodigious Rapidity': British Pioneers on the American Lecture Circuit." In *Victorian Literature and Society: Essays Presented to Richard D. Altick.* Edited by James R. Kincaid and Albert J. Kuhn, 3–29. Athens: Ohio State University Press, 1984.

Collins, Wilkie. *The Law and the Lady.* 1874. Reprint. London: Oxford University Press, 1992.

———. *The Woman in White.* 1860. Reprint. New York: Oxford University Press, 1996.

Corbett, Mary Jean. *Representing Femininity: Middle-Class Subjectivity in Victorian and Edwardian Women's Autobiographies.* New York: Oxford University Press, 1992.

Coslett, Tess. *Woman to Woman Friendship: Female Friendship in Victorian Fiction.* Brighton: Harvester Press 1988.

Cott, Nancy. "Passionlessness: An Interpretation of Victorian Sexual Ideology, 1790–1850." *SIGNS* 4 (1979): 219–36.

Cotterell, George. Review of *The Heavenly Twins. Academy,* 29 April 1893, 368–69.

———. Review of *Our Manifold Nature. Academy,* 26 May 1894, 434.

Courtney, W. L. *The Feminine Note in Fiction.* London: Chapman and Hall, 1904.

Crackanthorpe, B[lanche] A[lthea]. "The Revolt of the Daughters (No. 1): A Last Word on 'The Revolt.'" *Nineteenth Century* 35 (1894): 424–29.

———. "Sex in Modern Literature." *Nineteenth Century* 37 (April 1895): 607–16.

Crackanthorpe, Hubert. "Reticence in Literature: Some Roundabout Remarks." *Yellow Book* 2 (1894): 259–69.

Craig, Patricia, and Mary Cadogan. *The Lady Investigates: Women Detectives and Spies in Fiction.* New York: St. Martin's Press, 1981.

Cross, Nigel. *The Common Writer: Life in Nineteenth-Century Grub Street.* Cambridge: Cambridge University Press, 1985.

Cruse, Amy. *After the Victorians.* London: Allen and Unwin, 1938.

Cunningham, A. R. "The 'New Woman Fiction' of the 1890's." *Victorian Studies* 17 (1973): 177–86.

Cunningham, Gail. *The New Woman in Victorian Fiction.* London: Macmillan, 1978.

Cvetkovich, Ann. *Mixed Feelings: Feminism, Mass Culture and Victorian Sensationalism.* New Brunswick: Rutgers University Press, 1992.

Daims, Diva, and Janet Grimes, eds. Asst. ed. Doris Robinson. *Toward a Feminist Tradition: An Annotated Bibliography of Novels in English by Women, 1891–1920.* New York: Garland, 1982.

Danby, Frank [Julia Frankau]. Review of *The Beth Book. Saturday Review* 24, 20 November 1897, 557–58.

Danvers, Milton. *A Desperate Dilemma; or, An Unheard of Crime.* London: Diprose and Bateman, 1892.

———. *The Detective's Honeymoon; or, The Doctor of "Pinjarrah."* London: Dipose and Bateman, 1894.

———. *The Doctor's Crime; or, Simply Horrible.* London: Diprose and Bateman, 1891.

Davidoff, Leonore, and Catherine Hall. *Family Fortunes: Men and Women of the Middle Class, 1780–1850.* Chicago: University of Chicago Press, 1987.

Davin, Anna. "Imperialism and Motherhood." *History Workshop Journal* 5 (1978): 9–65.

Deegan, Dorothy Yost. *The Stereotype of the Single Woman in the American Novel: A Social Study with Implications for the Education of Women.* New York: Octagon Books, 1969.

Degler, Carl. "What Ought to Be and What Was: Women's Sexuality in the Nineteenth Century." *American Historical Review* 79 (1974): 1469–90.

Delamont, Sarah, and Lorna Duffin, eds. *The Nineteenth Century Woman: Her Cultural and Physical World*. London: Croom Helm, 1978.

Delamotte, Eugenia. *Perils of the Night: A Feminist Study of Nineteenth-Century Gothic*. New York: Oxford University Press, 1990.

Dellamora, Richard. *Masculine Desire: The Sexual Politics of Victorian Aestheticism*. Chapel Hill: University of North Carolina Press, 1990.

Devereux, Mrs. Roy. *The Ascent of Woman*. London: John Lane, 1896.

Dix, Gertrude. *The Image Breakers*. London: Heinemann, 1900.

Dixie, Lady Florence. *Gloriana; or, The Revolution of 1900*. London: Henry and Company, 1890.

Dixon, Ella Hepworth. *The Story of a Modern Woman*. 1894. Reprint. London: Merlin, 1990.

Doggett, Maeve. *Marriage, Wife-Beating, and the Law in Victorian England*. London: Weidenfeld, 1992.

Dolman, Frederick. "Ladies Clubs." *Ludgate* n.s. 3 (November 1898): 14–18.

A Domestic Experiment, Review of. *Athenaeum,* 28 February 1891, 278.

A Domestic Experiment, Review of. *Spectator,* 16 May 1891, 700.

"Donna Quixote." Illustration. *Punch* 106 (April 1894): 194.

[Donnison, T. E., illus.]. "Famous Book-Covers as They Might Have Been." *Idler* 14 (1899): 703.

Donovan, Josephine. "Toward a Women's Poetics." In *Feminist Issues in Literary Scholarship*. Edited by Shari Benstock, 98–109. Bloomington: Indiana University Press, 1987.

Doughty, Terri. "Sarah Grand's *The Beth Book:* The New Woman and the Ideology of the Romantic Ending." In *Anxious Power: Reading, Writing, and Ambivalence in Narratives by Women*. Edited by Carol J. Singley and Susan Elizabeth Sweeney, 185–96. Albany: State University of New York, 1993.

Douglas, Roy. *Land, People, and Politics: A History of the Land Question in the UK, 1878–1952*. London: Allison and Busby, 1976.

Dowie, Menie Muriel [Mrs. Henry Norman]. *Gallia*. 1895. Reprint. Edited by Helen Small. London: Everyman, 1995.

Dowling, Linda. "The Decadent and the New Woman in the 1890s." *Nineteenth Century Fiction* 33 (1979): 434–53.

———. *Language and Decadence in the Victorian Fin de Siècle*. Princeton: Princeton University Press, 1986.

Duberman, Martin Baum, Martha Vicinus, and George Chauncey, eds. *Hidden from History: Reclaiming the Gay and Lesbian Past*. London: Penguin, 1990.

Duffin, Lorna. "The Conspicuous Consumptive: Woman as an Invalid." In *The Nineteenth Century Woman: Her Cultural and Physical World*. Edited by Sarah Delamont and Lorna Duffin, 26–56. London: Croom Helm, 1978.

DuPlessis, Rachel Blau. *Writing beyond the Ending: Narrative Strategies of Twentieth-Century Women Writers*. Bloomington: Indiana University Press, 1985.

Dyhouse, Carol. *Feminism and the Family in England, 1880–1939*. Oxford: Blackwell, 1989.

———. *Girls Growing Up in Late Victorian and Edwardian England.* London: Routledge and Kegan Paul, 1981.

Eastwood, Mrs. "The New Woman in Fiction and in Fact." *Humanitarian* 5 (November 1894): 375–79.

Egerton, George [Mary Chavelita Dunne]. *Keynotes and Discords.* 1893 and 1894. Reprint. London: Virago, 1983.

Ehrenreich, Barbara, and Deidre English. *Complaints and Disorders: The Sexual Politics of Sickness.* Old Westbury, N.Y.: The Feminist Press, 1973.

Eliot, George. *Middlemarch, An Authoritative Text: Background, Reviews, Criticism.* Edited by Bert G. Hornback. New York: W. W. Norton, 1977.

Elliott, Bridget. "New and Not So 'New Women' on the London Stage: Aubrey Beardsley's *Yellow Book* Images of Mrs. Patrick Campbell and Rejane." *Victorian Studies* 31 (1987): 33–57.

Ellis, Havelock. "Eugenics and St. Valentine." *Nineteenth Century* 59 (1906): 784.

Ellis, S. M. *George Meredith: His Friends in Relation to His Work.* London: Grant Richards, 1920.

Ellman, Richard. *Oscar Wilde.* New York: Alfred A. Knopf, 1988.

Elmy, Elizabeth C. Wolstenholme. "Protest of the Ladies' National Association for the Repeal of the Contagious Diseases Acts." *Shafts* 5 (May 1897): 153–55.

———. [Report on Contagious Diseases Acts]. *Shafts* 5 (March 1897): 85–88.

———. [Report on Contagious Diseases Acts.] *Shafts* 5 (July–August 1897): 220–22.

"Ethelmer, Ellis." [Elizabeth Wolstenholme Elmy]. *The Phases of Love.* Congleton, U.K.: Women's Emancipation Union, 1897.

———. *Woman and the Law.* Congleton, U.K.: Women's Emancipation Union, 1894.

Etiquette of Good Society. London: Cassell, Peter Galpin and Company, 1880.

Faderman, Lillian. *Chloe Plus Olivia: An Anthology of Lesbian Literature from the Seventeenth Century to the Present.* New York: Viking, 1994.

———. *Surpassing the Love of Men: Friendship and Love between Women from the Renaissance to the Present.* 1981. Reprint. London: Women's Press, 1991.

"Famous Women Novelists." *Luddington Magazine* (April 1893): 572.

Farrell, Lyndsay. *The Origins and Growth of the English Eugenics Movement, 1865–1925.* New York: Garland, 1985.

Fawcett, Millicent Garrett. Review of *The Woman Who Did,* by Grant Allen. *Contemporary Review* 67 (1895): 625–31.

Felkin, William. *Felkin's History of the Machine Wrought Hosiery and Lace.* Introduction and index by Stanley Chapman and Sheila M. Uppadine. London: David and Charles, 1967.

Felski, Rita. *Beyond Feminist Aesthetics: Feminist Literature and Social Change.* London: Hutchinson Radius, 1989.

———. *The Gender of Modernity.* Cambridge: Harvard University Press, 1995.

Fenwick-Miller, Mrs. "The Ladies Column." *Illustrated London News* 103, 5 August 1893, 167.

Fernando, Lloyd. *"New Women" in the Late Victorian Novel.* University Park: Pennsylvania State University Press, 1977.

Fetterley, Judith. *The Resisting Reader: A Feminist Approach to American Fiction.* Bloomington: Indiana University Press, 1978.

First, Ruth, and Ann Scott. *Olive Schreiner*. London: Andre Deutsch, 1980.

Fitzsimmons, Linda, and Viv Gardner, eds. *New Woman Plays*. London: Methuen, 1991.

Flint, Kate. *The Woman Reader, 1837–1914*. Oxford: Clarendon Press, 1993.

Forbes, Athol. "My Impressions of Sarah Grand." *Lady's World* 11 (June 1900): 880–83.

Ford, Karen. *Gender and the Poetics of Excess: Moments of Brocade*. Oxford: University Press of Mississippi, 1997.

Ford, Isabella. *On the Threshold*. London: Edward Arnold, 1895.

Forrest, Andrew. *The Female Detective*. London: War and Lock, 1864.

Forrest, D. W. *Francis Galton: The Life and Work of a Victorian Genius*. London: Elek, 1974.

Foster, Shirley. *Victorian Women's Fiction: Marriage, Freedom, and the Individual*. London: Croom Helm, 1985.

"Four Good One-Volume Novels." Review of *Singularly Deluded*. *Spectator*, 18 March 1893, 393–94.

Fox, Pamela. *Class Fictions: Shame and Resistance in the British Working-Class Novel, 1890–1945*. Durham: Duke University Press, 1995.

Fraiman, Susan. *Unbecoming Women: British Women Writers and the Novel of Development*. New York: Columbia University Press, 1993.

Friedberg, Ann. *Window Shopping: Cinema and the Postmodern*. Berkeley: University of California Press, 1993.

Gagnier, Regina. *Idylls of the Marketplace: Oscar Wilde and the Victorian Public*. Stanford: Stanford University Press, 1986.

———. *Subjectivities: A History of Self-Representation in Britain, 1832–1920*. New York: Oxford University Press, 1991.

Gainor, Janet Ellen. *Shaw's Daughters: Dramatic and Narrative Constructions of Gender*. Ann Arbor: University of Michigan Press, 1991.

Gallia, Review of. *Saturday Review*, 23 March 1895, 383–84.

Galton, Francis. *Essays in Eugenics*. London: Eugenics Education Society Press, 1909.

———. *Hereditary Genius: An Inquiry into Its Laws and Consequences*. 1869. Reprint. London: Macmillan, 1914.

———. *Inquiries into Human Faculty and Its Development*. 1883. Reprint. London: J. M. Dent and Sons, 1973.

Garber, Marjorie. *Vested Interests: Cross-Dressing and Cultural Anxiety*. New York: Routledge, 1992.

Gardiner, Juliet. *The New Woman: Women's Voices, 1880–1918*. London: Collins and Brown, 1993.

Gardner, Viv, and Susan Rutherford, eds. *The New Woman and Her Sisters: Feminism and Theatre, 1850–1914*. New York: Harvester, 1991.

Garrett, Peter K. *The Victorian Multiplot Novel: Studies in Dialogical Form*. New Haven: Yale University Press, 1980.

Gates, Barbara. *Victorian Suicide: Mad Crimes and Sad Histories*. Princeton: Princeton University Press, 1988.

Gilbert, Sandra, and Susan Gubar. "Ceremonies of the Alphabet: Female Grandmatologies and the Female Autograph." In *The Female Autograph*. Edited by Domna Stanton, 21–48. Chicago: University of Chicago Press, 1987.

————. *The Madwoman in the Attic: The Woman Writer and the Nineteenth Century Literary Imagination*. New Haven: Yale University Press, 1979.

————. *No Man's Land: The Place of the Woman Writer in the Twentieth Century*, vol. 2: *Sexchanges*. New Haven: Yale University Press, 1989.

————. *No Man's Land: The Place of the Woman Writer in the Twentieth Century*, vol. 1: *The War of the Words*. New Haven: Yale University Press, 1988.

Goodman, Charlotte. "The Lost Brother, the Twin: Women Novelists and the Male-Female *Bildungsroman*." *Novel* 17 (1983): 28–43.

Gorsky. Susan R. "The Art of Politics: The Feminist Fiction of Sarah Grand." *Journal of Women's Studies in Literature* 1 (1979): 286–300.

Gosse, Edmund. "The Decay of Literary Taste." *North American Review* 161 (1895): 109–18.

————. *Questions at Issue*. London: Heinemann, 1893.

Gould, Peter C. *Early Green Politics: Back to Nature, Back to the Land, and Socialism in Britain, 1880–1900*. New York: St. Martin's Press, 1988.

Grand, Sarah [Frances Bellenden-Clarke McFall]. *Adnam's Orchard*. London: Heinemann, 1912.

————. "At What Age Should Girls Marry?" *Young Woman* 7 (February 1899): 161–64.

————. *Babs the Impossible*. London: Hutchinson, 1901.

————. *The Beth Book*. New York: Appleton, 1897.

————. "Case of the Modern Married Woman." *Pall Mall Gazette* 51 (February 1913): 203–10.

————. "Case of the Modern Spinsters." *Pall Mall Gazette* 51 (1913): 55.

————. *Constance of Calais: A Dramatic Cantata*. Music by Francis Edward Gladstone. Libretto by Mrs. D. Chambers McFall. London: Weekes, 1884.

————. "Does Marriage Hinder a Woman's Self-Development? A Discussion." *Lady's Realm* 5 (March 1899): 576–77.

————. *A Domestic Experiment*. Edinburgh: Blackwood, 1891.

————. "The Duty of Looking Nice." *Review of Reviews* (August 1893).

————. *Emotional Moments*. London: Hurst and Blackett, 1908.

————. Foreword to *The Heavenly Twins*. London: Heinemann, 1923: v–xvi.

————. "The Great Typhoon." *Aunt Judy's Magazine* 19 (April 1881): 358–70.

————. *The Heavenly Twins*. Privately printed, 1892. 3 vols. Introduction by Carol Senf. Reprint. Ann Arbor: University of Michigan Press, 1992.

————. *The Human Quest: Some Thoughts in Contribution to the Subject of the Art of Human Happiness*. London: Heinemann, 1900.

————. *Ideala: A Study from Life*. Privately printed, 1888. Reprint. London: Heinemann, 1893.

————. "Introduction." *Mid-Victorian Memories,* i–lxvi. London: John Murray, 1919.

————. "Is It Ever Justified to Break Off an Engagement?" *Home Magazine and the Ladies Field* (1896–97): 1016–19.

————. "Mama's Music Lessons." *Aunt Judy's Magazine* 14 (June–July 1878): 489–95, 527–36.

————. "The Man of the Moment." *North American Review* 158 (May 1894): 620–27.

————. "Marriage Questions in Fiction: The Standpoint of a Typical Modern Woman." *Fortnightly Review* 375 (March 1898): 378–89.

———. "Mere Man." *Saturday Review,* 8 January 1901, 733–45.

———. "The Modern English Girl." *Canadian Magazine* 10 (1898): 300.

———. "The Modern Girl." *North American Review* 158 (June 1894): 706–14.

———. "The Modern Girl." *Temple Magazine* 2 (February 1898): 323.

———. *The Modern Man and Maid.* London: Horace Marshall, 1898.

———. "The Modern Young Man." *Temple Magazine* 2 (September 1898): 883–86.

———. "A Momentary Indiscretion." *Cosmopolitan* 20 (December 1895): 169–76.

———. "The Morals and Manners of Appearance." *Humanitarian* 3 (August 1893): 87–94.

———. "The New Aspect of the Woman Question." *North American Review* 158 (March 1894): 270–76.

———. "The New Woman and the Old." *Lady's Realm* 4 (August 1898): 466–70.

———. "The 'New Woman' in Her Relation to the 'New Man.'" *Westminister Review* 147 (March 1897): 335–37.

———. "On Clubs and the Question of Intelligence." *Woman at Home* 9 (June 1900): 839–42.

———. "On the Choice of a Husband." *Young Woman* 7 (October 1898): 1–3.

———. *Our Manifold Nature.* London: Heinemann, 1894.

———. "A Page of Confessions." *Woman at Home* 3 (October 1894): 65.

———. "Preface." *As They Are.* By "Bartholomew," vii–xii. London: H. J. Drane, 1908.

———. "Sarah Grand on the Old and New Woman." *Woman's Signal,* 1 September 1898, 140.

———. "School Revisited." *Aunt Judy's Magazine* 18 (June–July 1880): 473–81, 537–46.

———. "Should Married Women Follow Professions?" *Young Woman* 7 (April 1899): 257–59.

———. *Singularly Deluded.* 1892. Reprint. Edinburgh: Blackwoods, 1893.

———. "Some Recollections of My School Days." *Lady's Magazine* (January 1901): 42–43.

———. *The Tenor and the Boy.* London: Heinemann, 1899.

———. *Two Dear Little Feet.* London: Jarrods, 1873.

———. *Variety.* London: Heinemann, 1922.

———. "What to Aim At." *The New Party.* Edited by Andrew Reid, 355–61. London: Hodder, 1894.

———. *The Winged Victory.* London: Heinemann, 1916.

Grand, Sarah, contributor. *The Wit and Wisdom of Modern Women Writers.* Edited by Frances Tyrell-Gill. London: Grand Richards, 1902.

Green, Martin Burgess. *Dreams of Adventure, Deeds of Empire.* New York: Basic Books, 1979.

———. *Seven Types of Adventure Tale: An Etiology of a Major Genre.* University Park: Pennsylvania State University Press, 1991.

Greenslade, William. *Degeneration, Culture and the Novel, 1880–1940.* Cambridge: Cambridge University Press, 1994.

Grove, Jessica, and Olga Racster. *Dr. James Barry: Her Secret Story.* London: G. Howe, 1932.

Grundy, Sydney. *The New Woman.* London: Chiswick, 1894.

Gubar, Susan. "The Birth of the Artist as Heroine: (Re)production, the *Kunstlerroman* Tradition, and the Fiction of Katherine Mansfield." In *The Representation of Women in Fiction*. Edited by Carolyn Heilbrun and Margaret Higonnet, 19–59. Baltimore: Johns Hopkins University Press, 1983.

Hadley, Elaine. *Melodramatic Tactics: Theatricalized Dissent in the English Marketplace, 1800–1885*. Stanford: Stanford University Press, 1991.

Haggard, H. Rider. "About Fiction." *Contemporary Review* 52 (1887): 172–80.

Hannigan, D. F. "Sex in Fiction." *Westminister Review* 143 (1895): 616–25.

———. "The Tyranny of the Modern Novel." *Westminister Review* 143 (March 1895): 303–6.

Hardy, Thomas. "Candour in Fiction." *New Review* 2 (1890): 15–21.

———. *One Rare Fair Woman: Thomas Hardy's Letters to Florence Henniker, 1893–1922*. Edited by Evelyn Hardy and F. B. Pinion. London: Macmillan, 1972.

Harkness, Margaret [John Law, pseud.]. *A City Girl*. 1887. Reprint, New York: Garland, 1984.

———. *In Darkest London*. London: William Reeves, 1891.

Harris, Wendell. "John Lane's Keynotes Series and the Fiction of the 1890s." *PMLA* 83 (1968): 1407–13.

Hasian, Marouf A. *The Rhetoric of Eugenics in Anglo-American Thought*. Athens: University of Georgia Press, 1996.

Haweis, [Mary Eliza] Mrs. Hugh Reginald. *The Art of Beauty*. 1879. Reprint. New York: Garland, 1978.

"Heavenly Twins Again, The." *Critic* 24, 5 August 1894, 308.

The Heavenly Twins, Review of. *Athenaeum*, 18 March 1893, 342.

The Heavenly Twins, Review of. *Black and White* 5, 11 March 1893, 298.

The Heavenly Twins, Review of. *Book News* 11 (August 1893): 515–16.

The Heavenly Twins, Review of. *Bookman* 3–4 (1892–93): 107–8.

The Heavenly Twins, Review of. *Critic* 23, 7 October 1893, 219–20.

The Heavenly Twins, Review of. *Englishwoman's Review*, 18 July 1893, 197–98.

The Heavenly Twins, Review of. *Nation* 57, 16 November 1893, 374–75.

The Heavenly Twins, Review of. *New Outlook* 48, 18 November 1893, 905.

The Heavenly Twins, Review of. *Pall Mall Gazette*, 3 April 1893, 3.

The Heavenly Twins, Review of. *Punch* 106, 24 February 1894, 93.

The Heavenly Twins, Review of. *Shafts*, 25 February 1893, 268.

The Heavenly Twins, Review of. *Spectator*, 25 March 1893, 395–96.

The Heavenly Twins, Review of. *Westminister Review* 139 (April 1893): 460.

Heilbrun, Carolyn. *Toward a Recognition of Androgyny*. New York: Alfred A. Knopf, 1973.

Heilmann, Ann. "The 'New Woman' Fiction and Fin-de-Siècle Feminism." Special issue: "Women's Writing at the Fin de Siècle." Edited by Sally Ledger. *Women's Writing* 3 (1996): 197–216.

Hepburn, James. *The Author's Empty Purse and the Rise of the Literary Agent*. London: Oxford University Press, 1968.

Hewitt, Emma Churchman. "The 'New Woman' in Her Relation to the New Man." *Westminister Review* 147 (1897): 335–37.

"'Hill-Top Novels' and the Morality of Art." *Spectator* 23 (November 1895): 722–24.

Hinz, Evelyn. "Hierogamy versus Wedlock: Types of Marriage Plots and Their Relationship to Prose Fiction." *PMLA* 91 (1976): 900–913.

Hogarth, Janet E. "Literary Degenerates." *Fortnightly Review* 63 (1895): 586–92.

———. "The Monstrous Regiment of Women," *Fortnightly Review* 68 (1897): 926–36.

[Holly, F. M.]. Review of *Babs the Impossible*. *Bookman* 13 (April 1900): 733–34.

"How Novelists Work: An Interview with Sarah Grand." *Review of Reviews* 11 (January 1895): 91.

Howard, Jacqueline. *Reading Gothic Fiction: A Bakhtinian Approach*. Chicago: University of Chicago Press, 1995.

Holdsworth, Annie E. *Joanna Trail: Spinster*. London: Heinemann, 1894.

Huddleston, Joan, comp. *Sarah Grand: A Bibliography*. St. Lucia: University of Queensland Press, 1979.

Hughes, Linda. "My Sister, My Self: Networking and Self-Promotion among Fin-de-Siècle Women Poets." MS.

Hughes, Winifred. *The Maniac in the Cellar: Sensation Novels of the 1860s*. Princeton: Princeton University Press, 1980.

Hulme, Leslie Parker. *The National Union of Women's Suffrage Societies, 1897–1914*. New York: Garland, 1982.

Hurley, Kelly. *The Gothic Body: Sexuality, Materialism, and Degeneration at the Fin de Siècle*. Cambridge: Cambridge University Press, 1996.

Hyde, Montgomery. *The Three Trials of Oscar Wilde*. New York: Dover, 1962.

Ideala, Review of. *Critic*, 21 October 1893, 255.

Ideala, Review of. *Saturday Review*, 1 September 1888, 277.

Ideala, Review of. *Nation*, 16 November 1893, 374–75.

Ideala, Review of. *Spectator*, 12 January 1889, 55–56.

Ignota [pseud.]. "The Awakening of Woman." *Westminister Review* 152 (July 1899): 69–72.

Ingram, Angela, and Daphne Patai, eds. *Rediscovering Forgotten Radicals: British Women Writers, 1889–1939*. Chapel Hill: University of North Carolina Press, 1993.

Iota [Kathleen Mannington Caffyn]. *A Yellow Aster*. Leipzig: Bernard Tauchnitz, 1894.

Jackson, Mrs. Emily Nevill. *A History of Hand-Made Lace*. London: L. U. Gill, 1900.

Jalland, Pat. *Women, Marriage and Politics, 1860–1914*. Oxford: Clarendon Press, 1986.

James, Henry. *The Bostonians*. 1886. Reprint. New York: Penguin, 1987.

Jeune, Lady Mary. "The New Woman and the Old: A Reply to Sarah Grand." *Lady's Realm* 4 (September 1898): 600–604.

Jeffreys, Sheila. *The Spinster and Her Enemies: Feminism and Sexuality, 1830–1930*. London: Pandora Press, 1985.

"Jim's Wife's Husband: A Chat with Mme. Sarah Grand." *Woman* (literary supplement), 2 May 1894, i–ii.

Jones, Suzanne W., ed. *Writing the Woman Artist: Essays on Poetics, Politics and Portraiture*. Philadelphia: University of Pennsylvania Press, 1991.

Johnstone, Edith. *A Sunless Heart*. London: Ward, Lock and Bowden, 1894.

Jordan, Ellen. "The Christening of the New Woman, May 1894." *Victorian Newletter* 48 (1983): 19–21.

Jordan, John O., and Patten, Robert L., eds. *Literature in the Marketplace: Nineteenth-Century Publishing and Reading Practices*. Cambridge: Cambridge University Press, 1995.

Kaplan, E. Ann. "Theories of Melodrama: A Feminist Perspective." *Women and Performance: A Journal of Feminist Theory* 1 (1983): 40–48.

Kaplan, Joel H., and Sheila Stowell. *Theatre and Fashion: Oscar Wilde to the Suffragettes.* Cambridge: Cambridge University Press, 1994.

Kenealy, Arabella. *Dr. Janet of Harley Street.* London: Digby, Long and Company, 1893.

Kent, Susan Kingsley. *Sex and Suffrage in Britain, 1860–1914.* 1987. Reprint. London: Routledge, 1990.

Kenton, Edna. "A Study of the Old 'New Woman': Part I" *Bookman* 37 (April–May 1913): 154–58.

———. "A Study of the Old 'New Woman': Part II." *Bookman* (1913): 261–64.

Kersley, Gillian. *Darling Madame: Sarah Grand and Devoted Friend.* London: Virago, 1983.

Kevles, Daniel J. *In the Name of Eugenics: Genetics and the Uses of Human Heredity.* New York: Alfred A. Knopf, 1985.

Klein, Kathleen Gregory. *The Woman Detective: Gender and Genre.* Urbana: University of Illinois Press, 1994.

Kolodny, Annette. "A Map for Misreading: Or, Gender and the Interpretation of Literary Texts." *New Literary History* 11 (1980): 451–67.

Kranidis, Rita S. *Subversive Discourse: The Cultural Production of Late Victorian Feminist Novels.* New York: St. Martin's Press, 1995.

Kucich, John. *The Power of Lies: Transgression in Victorian Fiction.* Ithaca: Cornell University Press, 1994.

———. "Curious Dualities: *The Heavenly Twins* (1893) and Sarah Grand's Belated Modernist Aesthetics." In *The New Nineteenth Century: Feminist Readings of Underread Victorian Fiction.* Edited by Barbara Leah Harman and Susan Meyer, 195–204. New York: Garland, 1996.

Kunitz, Stanley, and Howard Haycraft, eds. *Twentieth Century Authors.* New York: H. W. Wilson Company, 1942 and 1955.

Lacquer, Thomas. *Making Sex: Body and Gender from the Greeks to Freud.* Cambridge: Harvard University Press, 1990.

Lang, Andrew. "From Realism to Romance." *Contemporary Review* 52 (1887): 683–93.

Langford, Wendy. "'Snuglet Puglet Loves to Snuggle with Snuglet Puglet': Alternative Personalities in Heterosexual Love Relationships." In *Romance Revisited.* Edited by Lynne Pearce and Jackie Stacey, 251–64. New York: New York University Press, 1995.

Langland, Elizabeth. *Nobody's Angels: Middle-Class Women and Domestic Ideology in Victorian Culture.* Ithaca: Cornell University Press, 1995.

Lanser, Susan Sniader. *Fictions of Authority: Women Writers and Narrative Voice.* Ithaca: Cornell University Press, 1992.

Ledger, Sally. "Gissing, the Shopgirl, and the New Woman." *Women: A Cultural Review* 6 (Winter 1995): 263–74.

———. "The New Woman and the Crisis of Victorianism." *Cultural Politics at the Fin de Siècle.* Edited by Sally Ledger and Scott McCracken, 22–44. Cambridge: Cambridge University Press, 1995.

———. "The New Woman, *The Bostonians* and the Gender of Modernity." *Barcelona English Language and Literature Studies* 7 (1996): 55–62.

————. *The New Woman: Fiction and Feminism at the Fin de Siècle.* Manchester: Manchester University Press, 1997.

Ledger, Sally, ed. *Women's Writing at the Fin de Siècle.* Special edition of *Women's Writing* 3 (1996).

Ledger, Sally, and Scott McCracken, eds. *Cultural Politics at the in Fin de Siècle.* Cambridge: Cambridge University Press, 1995.

Leppington, Blanche. "The Brutalisation of Man." *Contemporary Review* (June 1895): 725–43.

Lesbian History Group. *Not a Passing Phase: Reclaiming Lesbians in History, 1840–1985.* London: Women's Press, 1989.

Levey, Santina. *Lace: A History.* London: Victoria and Albert Museum, 1983.

Levine, Lawrence. *Highbrow/Lowbrow: The Emergence of Cultural Hierarchy in America.* Cambridge: Harvard University Press, 1988.

Levine, Philippa. "'So Few Prizes and So Many Blanks': Marriage and Feminism in Later Nineteenth-Century England." *Journal of British Studies* 28 (April 1989): 150–74.

————. "Venereal Disease, Prostitution and the Politics of the Empire: the Case of British India." *Journal of the History of Sexuality* 4 (April 1994): 579–602.

————. *Victorian Feminism, 1850–1900.* Tallahassee: Florida State University Press, 1987.

Levy, Amy. "Women and Club Life." 1888. Reprinted in *The Complete and Selected Works of Amy Levy, 1861–1889.* Edited by Melvyn New, 533–38. Gainesville: University of Florida Press, 1993.

Levy, Anita. *Other Women: The Writing of Class, Race, and Gender, 1832–1898.* Princeton University Press, 1991.

"The Life of Sarah Grand." *Review of Reviews* 16 (1897): 595.

Linton, Eliza Lynn. "Candour in English Fiction." *New Review* 2 (1890): 10–14.

————. "The Girl of the Period." *Saturday Review,* 14 March 1868, 339–40.

————. "Modern Man-Haters." *Saturday Review,* 29 April 1871, 528–29.

————. "The Wild Women as Politicians." *Nineteenth Century* 30 (1891): 79–88.

————. "The Wild Women as Social Insurgents." *Nineteenth Century* 30 (1891): 596–605.

Lister, Anne. *I Know My Own Heart: The Diaries of Anne Lister, 1791–1840.* Edited by Helena Whitbread. London: Virago, 1981.

Lister, Sandra P. "Sarah Grand and the Late Victorian Feminist Novel." Master's thesis, Manchester Polytechnic, 1977.

Lonsdale, Margaret. "Platform Women." *Nineteenth Century* 15 (1884): 409–15.

Love, Rosaleen. "'Alice in Eugenics-Land': Feminism and Eugenics in the Scientific Careers of Alice Lee and Ethel Elderton." *Annals of Science* 36 (1979): 145–58.

Lovell, Terry. *Consuming Fictions.* London: Verso, 1987.

Lyon, Janet. "Militant Discourse, Strange Bedfellows: Suffragettes and Vorticists before the War." *differences* 4, no. 2 (Summer 1992): 100–133.

M., D. B. "The New Woman." (Poem) *Shafts* 2 (March 1895): n.p.

MacCorrie, John Paul. "'The War of the Sexes.'" *Catholic World* 63 (August 1896): 605–18.

Mackay, Jane, and Pat Thane. "The Englishwoman." In *Englishness: Politics and Culture, 1880–1920.* Edited by Robert Colls and Philip Dodd, 191–229. London: Croom Helm, 1986.

MacKenzie, Donald. "Eugenics in Britain." *Social Studies of Science* 6 (1976): 499–532.

Mangum, Teresa. "Wilkie Collins, Detection, and Deformity." *The Dickens Studies Annual* 26 (1998): 285–310.

Mani, Lati. "Contentious Traditions: The Debate on *Sati*." In *The Nature and Context of Minority Discourse*. Edited by Abdul R. JanMohamed and David Lloyd, 319–56. New York: Oxford University Press, 1990.

Marcus, Jane. "Still Practice, A/Wrested Alphabet: Toward a Feminist Aesthetics." *Art and Anger: Reading like a Woman*, 215–49. Athens: Ohio University Press, 1988.

Marshall, Alice Kahler. *Pen Names of Women Writers: From 1600 to the Present*. Camp Hill, Penn.: privately printed, 1985.

Marshall, Wallace. *The "New Age" under Orage*. Manchester: Manchester University Press, 1967.

Masse, Michelle A. *In the Name of Love: Women, Masochism, and the Gothic*. Ithaca: Cornell University Press, 1992.

Matheson, E. "The New Woman." Poem. *Shafts* 3 (August 1895): 69.

Maurice, Frederick. "Where to Get Men." *Contemporary Review* 81 (January 1902): 78–86.

Mazumdar, Pauline M. H. *Eugenics, Human Genetics and Human Failings: The Eugenics Society, Its Sources and Its Critics in Britain*. London: Routledge, 1992.

McClintock, Anne. *Imperial Leather: Race, Gender and Sexuality in the Colonial Context*. New York and London: Routledge, 1995.

McCracken, L. A. M. Priestly. "Sarah Grand and Women's Emancipation." *Vote* 34, 25 August 1933, n.p.

McHugh, Paul. *Prostitution and Victorian Social Reform*. New York: St. Martin's Press, 1980.

McNeil, Ronald. "Another Chelsea Manuscript." *Macmillan Magazine* 80 (1899): 425–31.

Melman, Billie. *Women's Orients: English Women and the Middle East, 1718–1918, Sexuality, Religion and Work*. Ann Arbor: University of Michigan Press, 1995.

"A Mere Man." *The Domestic Blunders of Women*. 1899. Reprint. London: Kent, Pryor Publications, 1994.

Michie, Elsie. *Outside the Pale: Cultural Exclusion, Gender Difference, and the Victorian Woman Writer*. Ithaca: Cornell University Press, 1993.

Milbank, Alison. *Daughters of the House: Modes of the Gothic in Victorian Fiction*. New York: St. Martin's Press, 1992.

Miles, Rosie. "George Egerton, Bitextuality and Cultural (Re)Production in the 1890s." *Women's Writing* 3, no. 3 (1996): 243–59.

Miller, Jane. *Women Writing about Men*. New York: Pantheon Books, 1986.

Miller, Jane Eldridge. *Rebel Women: Feminism, Modernism and the Edwardian Novel*. London: Virago, 1994.

Miller, Neil. *Out of the Past: Gay and Lesbian History from 1869 to the Present*. New York: Vintage, 1995.

Mills, Sara. *Discourses of Difference: An Analysis of Women's Travel Writing and Colonialism*. New York: Routledge, 1991.

Modleski, Tania. *Loving with a Vengeance: Mass-Produced Fantasies for Women*. New York: Methuen, 1982.

Moers, Ellen. *The Dandy: Brummell to Beerbohm*. New York: Viking Press, 1960.

———. *Literary Women*. London: Women's Press, 1978.

Morgan, Susan. *Place Matters: Gendered Geography in Victorian Women's Travel Books about Southeast Asia*. New Brunswick: Rutgers University Press, 1996.

Morgan-Dockrell, Mrs. C. "Is the New Woman a Myth?" *Humanitarian* 8 (1896): 339–50.

Mort, Frank. *Dangerous Sexualities: Medico-Moral Politics in England since 1830*. London: Routledge and Kegan Paul, 1987.

Moscucci, Ornella. *The Science of Woman: Gynaecology and Gender in England, 1800–1929*. Cambridge: Cambridge University Press, 1990.

Moore, George. *Literature at Nurse, or Circulating Morals: A Polemic on Victorian Censorship*. 1884. Edited by Pierre Coustillas. Reprint. Brighton: Harvester, 1976.

Mott, F[rank] L[uther]. *Golden Multitudes: The Story of Best Sellers in the United States*. New York: Macmillan, 1947.

Mulvey, Laura. *Visual and Other Pleasures*. Bloomington: Indiana University Press, 1989.

Murray, Q. *Battleton Rectory*. London: John Heywood, 1885.

Navarette, Susan. "As You Like It: A Source for Sarah Grand's *The Heavenly Twins*." *Turn-of-the-Century Women* 4 (1987): 42–47.

Nead, Lynda. *Myths of Sexuality: Representations of Women in Victorian Britain*. Oxford: Basil Blackwell, 1988.

Neetens, Wim. *Writing and Democracy: Literature, Politics and Culture in Transition*. Brighton: Harvester Wheatsheaf, 1991.

"New Novels." *Spectator* 79 (1897): 691–92.

"New Writers: Sarah Grand." *Bookman* 3–4 (July 1893): 107–8.

"Newmarch, Eugenia" [pseud.]. Editorial. *Englishwoman* 28 (1910): 36–38.

Newton, Judith Lowder. *Women, Power, and Subversion: Social Strategies in British Fiction, 1778–1860*. Athens: University of Georgia Press, 1981.

Newton, Stella Mary. *Health, Art, and Reason: Dress Reformers of the Nineteenth Century*. London: John Murray, 1974.

Noble, James Ashcroft. "The Fiction of Sexuality." *Contemporary Review* 67 (April 1895): 490–98.

Nord, Deborah Epstein. *Walking the Victorian Streets: Women, Representation, and the City*. Ithaca: Cornell University Press, 1995.

Nordau, Max. *Degeneration*. 1895. Reprint, Lincoln: University of Nebraska Press, 1993.

Oppenheim, Janet. *"Shattered Nerves": Doctors, Patients, and Depression in Victorian England*. New York: Oxford University Press, 1991.

Our Manifold Nature, Review of. *Athenaeum*, 5 May 1894, 575–76.

Our Manifold Nature, Review of. *Bookman* 6 (May 1894): 56–57.

Our Manifold Nature, Review of. *Critic* 24, 7 April 1894, 231–32.

Our Manifold Nature, Review of. *Saturday Review*, 15 September 1894, 301.

Our Manifold Nature, Review of. *Spectator*, 7 April 1894, 474–75.

Ouida [Marie Louise De La Ramee]. "The New Woman." *North American Review* 158 (May 1894): 610–19.

Palliser, Mrs. Bury. *History of Lace*. Revised by Mr. Jourdain and Alice Dryden. London: Sampson Low, Marston and Company, 1902.

Parkin, Frank. *Middle-Class Radicalism: The Social Basis of the British Campaign for Nuclear Disarmament.* Manchester: Manchester University Press, 1968.

Pateman, Carole. *The Sexual Contract.* Stanford: Stanford University Press, 1988.

Patmore, Coventry. *The Angel in the House: The Betrothal.* Boston: Tichnor and Field, 1856.

Payne, William Morton. "Recent Fiction." Review of *The Beth Book. Dial,* 1 February 1898, 77–79.

Pearse, Mabella. "To an Advanced Woman." *Idler* 6 (August 1894): 140–41.

Pearson, Karl. Editorial. *Annals of Eugenics* 1 (1915–26): 3.

———. *The Grammar of Science.* 1892. Reprint. London: W. Scott, 1951.

———. *The Life, Letters, and Labours of Francis Galton.* 3 vols. London: Cambridge University Press, 1914–30.

Perkin, Joan. *Women and Marriage in Nineteenth-Century England.* Chicago: Lyceum Books, 1989.

Perrot, Philippe. *Fashioning the Bourgeoisie: A History of Clothing in the Nineteenth Century.* Princeton: Princeton University Press, 1994.

Perry, P. J. *British Agriculture, 1875–1914.* London: Methuen, 1973.

Petersen, Linda. *The Determined Reader: Gender and Culture in the Novel from Napoleon to Victoria.* New Brunswick: Rutgers University Press, 1986.

Petrie, Glen. *A Singular Iniquity: The Campaigns of Josephine Butler.* New York: Viking Press, 1971.

Pick, Daniel. *Faces of Degeneration: A European Disorder, 1848–1918.* Cambridge: Cambridge University Press, 1989.

Pinero, Arthur Wing. *The Notorious Mrs. Ebbsmith.* London: Heinemann, 1895.

Poovey, Mary. *The Proper Lady and the Woman Writer: Ideology as Style in the Works of Mary Wollstonecraft, Mary Shelley, and Jane Austen.* Chicago: University of Chicago Press, 1984.

———. *Uneven Developments: The Ideological Work of Gender in Mid-Victorian England.* Chicago: University of Chicago Press, 1988.

Pratt, Mary Louise. *Imperial Eyes: Travel Writing and Transculturation.* New York and London: Routledge, 1992.

Pykett, Lyn. "The Cause of Women and the Course of Fiction: The Case of Mona Caird." In *Gender Roles and Sexuality in Victorian Literature.* Edited by Christopher Parker, 128–41. Aldershot: Scolar Press, 1995.

———. *Engendering Fictions: The English Novel in the Early Twentieth Century.* New York: Edward Arnold, 1995.

———. *The "Improper" Feminine: The Women's Sensation Novel and the New Woman Writing.* New York: Routledge, 1992.

———. *The Sensation Novel: From* The Woman in White *to* The Moonstone. Plymouth: Northcote House, 1994.

Quilter, Harry. "The Gospel of Intensity." *Contemporary Review* 67 (June 1894): 762–82.

Rabine, Leslie. *Reading the Romantic Heroine: Text, History, Ideology.* Ann Arbor: University of Michigan Press, 1985.

Radway, Janice A. *A Feeling for Books: The Book-of-the-Month Club, Literary Taste, and Middle-Class Desire.* University of North Carolina Press, 1997.

———. "The Scandal of the Middlebrow: The Book-of-the-Month Club, Class Fracture, and Cultural Authority." *South Atlantic Quarterly* 89 (Fall 1990): 703–36.

——. "On the Gender of the Middlebrow Consumer and the Threat of the Culturally Fraudulent Female." *South Atlantic Quarterly* 93 (Fall 1994): 871–93.

Rae, Isobel. *The Strange Life of Dr. James Barry.* London: Longmans, Green, 1958.

Reddy, Maureen. *Women and Crime: Feminism and the Crime Novel.* New York: Continuum, 1988.

Reed, John. *Decadent Style.* Athens: Ohio University Press, 1985.

Rendall, Jane, ed. *Equal or Different: Women's Politics, 1800–1914.* Oxford: Blackwell, 1987.

Rich, Adrienne. "Compulsory Heterosexuality." In *Powers of Desire: The Politics of Sexuality.* Edited by Ann Snitow, Christine Stansell, and Sharon Thompson, 177–205. New York: Monthly Review Press, 1983.

——. *Of Woman Born: Motherhood as Experience and Institution.* New York: W. W. Norton, 1976.

Richards, Grant. *Author Hunting: Memories of Years Spent Mainly in Publishing.* 1934. Reprint, London: Unicorn Press, 1960.

——. "Women Writers in '93." *Woman's Signal,* 11 January 1894, 20.

Richards, Thomas. *The Commodity Culture of Victorian England: Advertising and Spectacle, 1851–1914.* Stanford: Stanford University Press, 1990.

Robins, Elizabeth. *The Convert.* 1907. Reprint. New York: Women's Press, 1980.

Rose, Jonathan. "Rereading the English Common Reader: A Preface to a History of Audiences." *Journal of the History of Ideas* 53, no. 1 (January–March 1992): 47–70.

Rose, June. *The Perfect Gentleman.* London: Hutchinson, 1977.

Rover, Constance. *Love, Morals, and the Feminists.* London: Routledge and Kegan Paul, 1970.

——. *The Punch Book of Women's Rights.* South Brunswick: A. S. Barnes, 1970.

Rowlette, Robert. "Mark Twain, Sarah Grand, and *The Heavenly Twins.*" *Mark Twain Journal* 16 (1972): 17–18.

Rubin, Joan. *The Making of Middlebrow Culture.* Chapel Hill: University of North Carolina Press, 1992.

Rubinstein, David. *Before the Suffragettes: Women's Emancipation in the 1890s.* Brighton: Harvester, 1986.

Russ, Joanna. *How to Suppress Women's Writing.* Austin: University of Texas Press, 1983.

Russett, Cynthia Eagle. *Sexual Science: The Victorian Construction of Womanhood.* Cambridge: Harvard University Press, 1989.

Ryan, Mary P. *Women in Public: Between Banners and Ballots, 1825–1880.* Baltimore: Johns Hopkins University Press, 1990.

Saintsbury, George. "The Present State of the Novel." *Fortnightly Review* 42 (1887): 410–17.

"Sarah Grand and Mr. Ruskin." *Woman's Signal,* 25 January 1894, 57.

Saunders, T. Bailey. "Sarah Grand's Ethics." *The Open Court: A Weekly Journal Devoted to the Religion of Science* 9, 4 April 1895, 4447–50.

Schor, Naomi. *Reading in Detail: Aesthetics and the Feminine.* New York: Methuen, 1987.

Schreiner, Olive. *Story of an African Farm.* 1883. Reprint. London: Oxford University Press, 1992.

——. *Woman and Labour.* 1911. Reprint. London: Virago, 1985.

Schuster, Edgar. "The Scope of the Science of Eugenics." *British Medical Journal*, 2 August 1913, 223–25.

Schweickart, Patricino. "Reading Ourselves." In *Gender and Reading: Essays on Readers, Texts, and Contexts*. Edited by Elizabeth Flynn and Patricino Schweickart, 17–44. Baltimore: Johns Hopkins University Press, 1986.

Searle, G[eoffrey] R[ussell]. "Eugenics and Class." In *Biology, Medicine, and Society*. Edited by Charles Webster, 217–42. London: Cambridge University Press, 1981.

———. *Eugenics and Politics in Britain, 1900–1914*. Leyden: Noordhoff International Press, 1976.

Sedgwick, Eve Kosofsky. *Between Men: English Literature and Male Homosocial Desire*. New York: Columbia University Press, 1985.

Senf, Carol. "Introduction." *The Heavenly Twins*. Ann Arbor: University of Michigan Press, 1992.

Shanley, Mary Lyndon. *Feminism, Marriage, and the Law in Victorian England*. Princeton: Princeton University Press, 1989.

Shapiro, Susan. "The Mannish New Woman: *Punch* and Its Precursors." *Review of English Studies* 42 (November 1991): 168, 510–22.

Shaw, George Bernard. *Collected Letters, 1874–1897*. Edited by Dan H. Laurence. London: Max Reinhardt, 1965.

———. *Our Theatres in the Nineties*. Vol. 2. 3 vols. London: Constable, 1932.

Showalter, Elaine. *The Female Malady: Women, Madness, and English Culture, 1830–1980*. New York: Pantheon Press, 1985.

———. *A Literature of Their Own: British Women Novelists from Brontë to Lessing*. Princeton: Princeton University Press, 1977.

———. *Sexual Anarchy: Gender and Culture at the Fin de Siècle*. New York: Penguin, 1991.

———. "Syphilis, Sexuality, and the Fiction of the Fin de Siècle." In *Sex, Politics, and Science in the Nineteenth Century Novel*. Edited by Ruth Yeazell, 95–108. Baltimore: Johns Hopkins University Press, 1986.

Showalter, Elaine, ed. *Daughters of Decadence: Women Writers of the Fin de Siècle*. London: Virago, 1993.

———, ed. *The New Feminist Criticism: Essays on Women, Literature and Theory*. New York: Pantheon Press, 1985.

[Sibthorp, Margaret Shurmer]. Review of *The Heavenly Twins*. *Shafts* 1 (February 1893): 268.

———. "Is the Present Increase in Women Authors a Gain to Literature?" *Shafts* 2 (April 1895): 239–40.

Siegel, Sandra. "Literature and Degeneration: The Representation of 'Decadence.'" In *Degeneration: The Dark Side of Progress*. Edited by J. Edward Chamberlin and Sander Gilman, 199–219. New York: Columbia University Press, 1985.

Sims, George R. *Dorcas Dene, Detective*. Ser. 2. London: F. V. White, 1898.

Singularly Deluded, Review of. *Athenaeum*, 18 February 1893, 215.

Singularly Deluded, Review of. *Critic* 23, 9 December 1893, 375.

Singularly Deluded, Review of. *Spectator*, 18 March 1893, 363–64.

Slaughter, J. W. "Selection in Marriage." *Eugenics Review* 1 (1908–10): 150–62.

"Slight Adaptation, A." Parody of *Leaves of Grass*. *Punch*, 10 November 1894, 228.

Smart, Carol, ed. *Regulating Womanhood: Historical Essays on Marriage, Motherhood, and Sexuality*. New York: Routledge, 1992.

Smith-Rosenberg, Carroll. "Discourses of Sexuality and Subjectivity: The New Woman, 1870–1936." In *Hidden from History: Reclaiming the Gay and Lesbian Past*. Edited by Martin Duberman, Martha Vicinus, and George Chauncey, 264–80. London: Penguin, 1990.

———. *Disorderly Conduct: Visions of Gender in Victorian America*. New York: Alfred A. Knopf, 1985.

———. "The Female World of Love and Ritual: Relations between Women in Nineteenth-Century America." *SIGNS* 1 (1975): 1–29.

———. "The Hysterical Woman: Sex Roles and Role Conflict in Nineteenth-Century America." *Social Research* 39 (1972): 652–78.

Soloway, Richard. *Demography and Degeneration: Eugenics and the Declining Birthrate in Twentieth-Century Britain*. Chapel Hill: University of North Carolina Press, 1990.

———. "Feminism, Fertility, and Eugenics in Victorian and Edwardian England." In *Political Symbolism in Modern Europe: Essays in Honor of George L. Mosse*. Edited by Seymour Drescher, David Sabean, and Allen Sharlin, 121–45. London: Transaction Books, 1982.

"Some Famous Lady Cyclists." *Lady's Realm* 2 (September 1894): 537–45.

Somerset, Lady. Review of *Our Manifold Nature*. *Woman's Signal*, 19 April 1894, 261–62.

Spenceley, Geoff. "The Lace Associations: Philanthropic Movements to Preserve the Production of Hand-Made Lace in Late Victorian and Edwardian England." *Victorian Studies* 16 (June 1973): 433–52.

Spender, Dale. *Women of Ideas and What Men Have Done to Them*. London: Routledge and Kegan Paul, 1982.

Spender, Dale, and Lynne Spender, eds. *Gatekeeping*. Special issue of *Women's Studies International Forum* 6 (1983).

[Stead, William T.]. "The Book of the Month: The Novel of the Modern Woman." *Review of Reviews* 10 (1894): 64–74.

Steele, Valerie. *Fashion and Eroticism: Ideals of Feminine Beauty from the Victorian Era to the Jazz Age*. New York: Oxford University Press, 1985.

Stein, Joseph. "The New Woman and the Decadent Dandy." *Dalhousie Reivew* 55 (1975): 54–62.

Stetson, Dorothy M. *A Woman's Issue: The Politics of Family Law Reform*. Westport, Conn.: Greenwood Press, 1982.

Stetz, Margaret Diane. "Life's 'Half-Profits': Writers and Their Readers in Fiction of the 1890s." In *Nineteenth-Century Lives: Essays Presented to Jerome Hamilton Buckley*. Edited by Laurence S. Lockridge, John Maynard, and Donald Stone, 169–87. Cambridge: Cambridge University Press, 1989.

———. "The New Grub Street and the Woman Writer of the 1890s." *Transforming Genres: New Approaches to British Fiction of the 1890s*, 21–45. New York: St. Martin's Press, 1994.

———. "Sex, Lies, and Printed Cloth: Bookselling at the Bodley Head in the Eighteen-Nineties." *Victorian Studies* 35 (1991): 71–86.

Stevenson, Catherine Barnes. *Victorian Women Travel Writers in Africa*. Boston: Twayne, 1982.

Stewart, Grace. *A New Mythos: The Novel of the Artist as Heroine, 1877–1977.* St. Albans, Vt.: Eden Press Women's Publications, 1979.

St. John, John. *William Heinemann: A Century of Publishing, 1890–1990.* London: Heinemann, 1990.

Stoddart, Jane T. "Sarah Grand: Illustrated Interview." *Woman at Home* 3 (1895): 247–52.

Stokes, John. *In the Nineties.* Brighton: Harvester Wheatsheaf, 1989.

Stone, Lawrence. *The Family, Sex, and Marriage in England, 1500–1800.* New York: Harper and Row, 1977.

Stowell, Sheila. *A State of Their Own: Feminist Playwrights of the Suffrage Era.* Ann Arbor: University of Michigan Press, 1992.

Strachey, Ray. *The Cause: A Short History of the Women's Movement in Great Britain.* 1928. Reprint. London: Virago, 1988.

Strauss, Sylvia. *"Traitors to the Masculine Cause": The Men's Campaign for Women's Rights.* Westport: Greenwood Press, 1982.

Stutfield, Hugh. "The Psychology of Feminism." *Blackwood's Magazine* 161 (1897): 104–17.

———. "'Tommyrotics.'" *Blackwood's Magazine* 157 (1895): 833–45.

Symons, Arthur. "The Decadent Movement in Literature." *Harper's New Monthly Magazine* 87 (November 1893): 858–67.

Sypher, Eileen. *Wisps of Violence: Producing Public and Private Politics in the Turn-of-the-Century British Novel.* London and New York: Verso 1993.

T., C. *How to Dress Well: A Manual of the Toilet for the Use of Both Sexes.* London: George Routledge and Sons, 1868.

Tanner, Tony. *Adultery and the Novel: Contract and Transgression.* Baltimore: Johns Hopkins University Press, 1979.

Taylor, Jenny Bourne. *In the Secret Theatre of Home: Wilkie Collins, Sensation Narrative, and Nineteenth-Century Psychology.* London: Routledge, 1988.

"Tedious and Unpleasant." Review of *The Beth Book. Academy,* 13 November 1897, 393.

"Tell Me, Mrs. Grand." *Critic* 25, 28 July 1894, 56.

Thane, Pat. "Late-Victorian Women." In *Later Victorian Britain, 1867–1900.* Edited by T. R. Gourvish and Alan Day, 175–208. Basingstoke: Macmillan, 1988.

Thornton, R. K. R. *The Decadent Dilemma.* London: Edward Arnold, 1983.

Tickner, Lisa. *The Spectacle of Women: Imagery of the Suffrage Campaign, 1907–1914.* London: Chatto and Windus, 1987.

Tomes, Nancy. "A 'Torrent of Abuse': Crimes of Violence between Working-Class Men and Women in London, 1840–1875." *Journal of Social History* 2 (Spring 1978): 328–45.

Tompkins, Jane. *Sensational Designs: The Cultural Work of American Fiction, 1790–1860.* New York: Oxford University Press, 1985.

Tooley, Sarah. "Some Women Novelists." *Woman at Home* (1896): 176–78.

———. "The Woman's Question: An Interview with Sarah Grand." *Humanitarian* 8 (March 1896): 160–69.

Tristrum, Philippa. *Living Spaces in Fact and Fiction.* New York: Routledge, 1989.

Trotter, David. *The English Novel in History, 1895–1920.* New York: Routledge, 1993.

Trustram, Myna. *Women of the Regiment: Marriage and the Victorian Army*. New York: Cambridge University Press, 1984.

Tuchman, Gaye, with Nina Fortin. *Edging Women Out: Victorian Novelists, Publishers, and Social Change*. New Haven: Yale University Press, 1989.

Tynan, Katherine. *The Middle Years*. London: Constable and Company, 1916.

Utter, Robert Palfrey, and Gwendolyn Bridges Needham. *Pamela's Daughters*. New York: Macmillan, 1936.

Vicinus, Martha. "'Helpless and Unfriended': Nineteenth-Century Domestic Melodrama." *New Literary History* 13 (1981): 127–43.

———. *Independent Women: Work and Community for Single Women, 1850–1920*. Chicago: University of Chicago Press, 1985.

———. "'One Life to Stand beside Me': Emotional Conflicts in First Generation College Women in England." *Feminist Studies* 8 (1982): 603–28.

———. "Rediscovering the New Woman of the 1890s: The Stories of 'George Egerton.'" In *Feminist Re-Visions: What Has Been and Might Be*. Edited by Vivien Patraka and Louise Tilly, 12–25. Ann Arbor: University of Michigan Women's Studies Program, 1983.

———. "They Wonder to Which Sex I Belong: The Historical Roots of the Modern Lesbian Identity." 1992. Reprinted in *Subjects: A Feminist Studies Reader*. Edited by Martha Vicinus, 233–59. Bloomington: Indiana Univerity Press, 1996.

Walkowitz, Judith R. *City of Dreadful Delight: Narratives of Sexual Danger in Late-Victorian London*. London: Virago, 1992.

———. "Male Vice and Female Virtue: Feminism and the Politics of Prostitution in Nineteenth-Century Britain." *History Workshop Journal* 13 (1982): 77–93.

———. *Prostitution and Victorian Society: Women, Class, and the State*. New York: Cambridge University Press, 1980.

Ware, Vron. *Beyond the Pale: White Women, Racism, and History*. London and New York: Verso, 1992.

Warhol, Robin. *Gendered Interventions: Narrative Discourse in the Victorian Novel*. New Brunswick: Rutgers University Press, 1989.

Waters, Chris. "New Women and Socialist-Feminist Fiction: The Novels of Isabella Ford and Katharine Glasier." In *Rediscovering Forgotten Radicals: British Women Writers, 1889–1939*. Edited by Angela Ingram and Daphne Patai, 25–42. Chapel Hill: University of North Carolina Press, 1993.

Watt, Ian. *The Rise of the Novel: Studies in Defoe, Richardson, and Fielding*. Berkeley: University of California Press, 1957.

Waugh, Arthur. "London Letter." Review of *The Heavenly Twins*. *Critic* 22, 8 April 1893, 223–24.

———. "London Letter." *Critic* 24, 16 June 1894, 414–15.

———. "London Letter." *Critic* 23, 19 August 1893, 128.

———. "Reticence in Literature." *Yellow Book* 1 (1894): 201–19.

Weeks, Jeffrey. *Sex, Politics, and Society: The Regulation of Sexuality since 1800*. New York: Longman, 1981.

Weintraub, Stanley. "George Bernard Shaw Borrows from Sarah Grand: *The Heavenly Twins* and *You Never Can Tell*." *Modern Drama* 14 (1971): 288–97.

Whetham, W[illiam] C[ecil] D[ampier], and C[atherine] D. Whetham. *The Family and the Nation: A Study in Natural Inheritance and Social Responsibility.* London: Longmans and Company, 1909.

Whibley, Charles. "The Encroachment of Women." *Nineteenth Century* 41 (1897): 531–37.

[Whitbread, Catherine M.]. "The 'Sarah Grand' Sex Theory." *Modern Review* 2 (July 1893): 286–91.

White, Arnold. *Efficiency and Empire.* London: Methuen, 1901.

———. *Weekly Sun,* 28 July 1900, n.p.

Whyte, Frederick. *William Heinemann: A Memoir.* Garland City, N.J.: Doubleday, 1929.

Williams, Anne. *Art of Darkness: A Poetics of Gothic.* Chicago: University of Chicago Press, 1995.

Williams, Harold. *Modern English Writers: Being a Study of Imaginative Literature, 1890–1914.* London: Sedgewick and Jackson, 1919.

Wilson, Elizabeth. *The Sphinx in the City: Urban Life, the Control of Disorder, and Women.* London: Virago, 1991.

Winchester, Boyd. "The Eternal Feminine." *Arena* 27 (1902): 367–73.

The Winged Victory, Review of. *Athenaeum* (September 1916): 420–21.

The Winged Victory, Review of. *Publisher's Weekly* 90, 14 October 1916, 1281.

The Winged Victory, Review of. *Times Literary Supplement,* 24 August 1916, 404.

Winnett, Susan. "Coming Unstrung: Women, Men, Narrative and Principles of Pleasure." *PMLA* 105 (May 1990): 505–18.

Wolff, Janet. *Feminine Sentences: Essays on Women and Culture.* Berkeley: University of California Press, 1990.

Wolstenholme, Susan. *Gothic (Re)Visions: Writing Women as Readers.* Albany: State University of New York Press, 1993.

"Women in the Queen's Reign." *Ludgate* n.s. 4 (1898): 216–17.

"Women of Note in the Cycling World." *Hub* 1, 17 October 1896, 419–20.

Woodhull Martin, Victoria Claflin. *The Rapid Multiplication of the Unfit.* London: n.p., 1891.

Woolf, Virginia. *A Room of One's Own.* 1929. Reprint. New York: Harcourt Brace, 1981.

W. O. W. O. [Margaret Oliphant]. "The Anti-Marriage League." *Blackwood's Magazine* 159 (1896): 135–49.

Zangwill, I. Review of *The Beth Book. Cosmopolitan* 24 (February 1898): 454–56.

Zweig, Paul. *The Adventurer.* New York: Basic Books, 1974.

Index